THE SHIFT SERIES BOX SET ONE

—·—

BECA LEWIS

PERCEPTION PUBLISHING

CONTENTS

LIVING IN GRACE

What Others Are Saying About Living In Grace

"*Beca Lewis' new book will more than 'shift' you—it will send a bloody tsunami your way! Read and open your heart. Read and prepare for abundance!*"—Joline Godfrey, CEO, Independent Means, Inc.

"*A Refreshing and powerful new look at the results of shifting perceptions to your true spiritual nature.*"—Alan Cohen, author of 24 books including The Dragon Doesn't Live Here Anymore

"*Beca's book reminds us to adjust the view of life and naturally, shift will happen - in all the very best ways. A wonderful and practical guide to living life in amazing grace!*"—Susan Gilbert, New Media Strategy Consultant, Best Selling Author and Entrepreneur

"*Shift to Spiritual Perception and you will change your life! Perception does rule, and in the everyday and spiritual use of this truth as so succinctly and clearly revealed in this book, you will fulfill your promise and achieve your destiny. Wow!*"—James Wanless, PhD, author of Voyager Tarot and Intuition@Work

"*I could say the book is terrific and it is. But better than terrific, the book is important. It is important in that everyone should read it.*

The message of the book presented with conviction is that thoughts are things and we need to watch what we think for the good of ourselves and mankind. Ms. Lewis gets down to what is probably real, what is core, and that therefore makes an important book...better than merely a terrific book." —Warren Gruenig, CEO

— · —

DEDICATION

To my children, Charles, Christin, and Laurie, and grandchildren, Madison, Montana, Cassidy, Logan, and Maxton and Del's children, Del, Jessie, John, Mesa, and Michael, who teach me so much about true love.

To my sister, Jamie, and my sister-friends, who have supported and believed in The Shift System, and in me, as we have grown and developed through the years.

To my husband, Del, who, by sharing his special knowledge and awareness, fills in the gaps of The Shift System and my life. Del reveals balance, harmony and the knowledge of true substance to all who know him. This book was completed and sustained through Del's wisdom.

To Dorothy Hardy, my mentor and best friend, who believed, long before I did, that I could and would help to make spirituality practical for others, but first demanded that I make it practical in my own life.

Thank you Dorothy, wherever you may be—this is for you and for all the years you believed in me, and for your demonstration of Living in Grace.

1

— · —

THE SEVEN STEPS TO SHIFT

Step One—Be Willing
Step Two—Become Aware
Step Three—Understand Signs and Symbols
Step Four—Learn Perception Rules
Step Five—Shift To Spiritual Perception
Step Six—Walk As One
Step Seven—Celebrate With Gratitude

2

—·—

PREFACE

This book is about perception and how to shift our perception to Living in Grace. This Shift of Perception will demonstrate the truth that we are all living as and in Grace now. There has never been a single moment that we have not or will not be Living in Grace.

However, in this place I will call the "Earth state of mind" there appear to be paths that we must walk to remember this fact. On these paths, we search for meaning, power, and reasons for our existence. Most people in the Earth state of mind walk the "material path."

On this path, the Earth, the universe, and everything we are and do is material. In the material world, perception, physical power reigns.

Some of us have "upgraded" to the "mental path" of believing it is a mental world, and everything is within and of our own thinking. We use mind-power to accomplish our goals and live a better life. In this point of view, the mind-body connection comes into play. We begin to say, "I can do it! All I have to do is visualize enough, and get my mind and thinking straight."

Mind-power employs methods such as visualization and hypnotism to accomplish its goals. This mental path will sometimes diverge into another path, the path of mysticism.

The world today is fascinated by this mental or mystical power and is calling it the "Spiritual revolution". Talk of God is accepted and is now found in all walks of life.

It is an improved point of view over the physical standpoint, but it is not the path where this book will take you.

There is one more path—and it is the path of One Mind, that path of non-power, the true Spiritual path. This is The Shift to being completely conscious that all that we are, know, and see, is in truth Spiritual. This is Living in Grace.

It is hard to write a book about spirituality and make it practical at the same time. I have to use physical words and mental exercises to make a point. Sometimes I talk about "getting things" or "improving your life."

However, getting things and improving one's life is a result of the consciousness that this is a Spiritual universe, not my reason for writing this book. Getting things and improving life is not the point. An improved life is the fruit of the awareness of, and the living out of, the Truth that there is only One—of everything—and that One is Spirit. It is the choice to Shift to Spiritual Perception.

The Shift to Spiritual Perception explains the power of perception. It is our point of view, our perception that determines our world and the life we lead. This book presents The 7 Steps To Shift and an eight step-by-step system based on the word GRACIOUS, which makes the necessary process of perception-shifting easy to remember and simple to use.

The book is an attempt to bridge the belief system of living in a physical world to the actuality that everything is actually spiritual. It is the best I know as of this moment. I know it to be true that it is a Spiritual Universe and that Heaven is here and now, because it is part of my experience.

How to remain in that consciousness, and how to communicate this understanding, is the path that I appear to be traveling.

There is no place on any path to stop and say, "I know it now, there is no more to learn." Even as I write this book I am yielding, or dying, to the old "point of view" and improving my consciousness of the Spiritual One.

Follow the guidance in this book only as it appears as Truth to you. Use this book to guide you, but it is not Truth itself. As you use the tools in this book to change your point of view and your state of mind, you will find this out for yourself, and we will reunite together in the awareness of Grace.

3

SECTION ONE

SPIRITUAL PERCEPTION

4

— • —

ONE

If the doors of perception were cleansed, everything would appear to man as it is, infinite.—William Blake

Have you ever wondered what your life would be like if everything you ever thought came true? You could think of true love and within moments the doorbell would ring and your personal true love would be standing on the doorstep, ready and able to begin to live a life full of love just with you. Perhaps you would think of having more money than you could ever spend, and once again the doorbell would ring and on the doorstep would be a box full of money.

The truth is, we do have our thoughts come true. So why don't we have all we've ever wanted? Why are so many of our lives filled with "quiet desperation"? Why don't we live with constant unlimited abundance?

Perception produces reality and what is perceived to be reality magnifies.

The answer is powerful and simple. We receive in our lives exactly what we believe to be true and what we believe we deserve. In order to live the life we were meant to live we must change our point of view and focus on the Truth of our Being.

All shifts are a decision to change a point of view. The Spiritual Shift is the continuous moment-by-moment personal, conscious, choosing of Spiritual Reality over the cramped, limited belief in many personal realities.

It is the decision not to believe or act out of duality or separation.

As we are willing to choose to become conscious of, and remain in the awareness of Grace, our ego-based small-i thoughts disappear and are replaced by Divine Mind's Thoughts. As a result, we recognize the material universe, as it really is —Spiritual Reality—and who we really are, the reflection of the One.

Isn't it a perfect time to follow your irresistible movement toward the Divine and yield to the State of Grace?

What will happen as you read this book? There is no guarantee that your life will be better. There is no guarantee that money will flow in the door and everybody will love you. This is not "no-work" solution to the problems in your life. Choosing spiritual consciousness makes great demands upon us.

What will happen is that you will find a focus that will make world success both meaningless and a natural event. Your life will change. Not because you want it to, not because you are trying to prove something, fix something, or get better at something.

It will change because you have chosen to take the time to do the only important thing in life. You have chosen to take the time to change your focus and build your own personal inner conviction of the existence of the State of Grace.

Possibilities are an outgrowth of a Shift of Perception to what is beautiful, good, and true. Life is abundant when we celebrate it from the Source and not from the outcome.

You must be the change you wish to see in the world.—Mahatma Gandhi

The world is now too dangerous for anything less than Utopia—R. Buckminster Fuller

On this planet there are something like five billion human beings, so there are five billion perceptions of reality. Everyone can be looking at the same object, but seeing it very differently.... One's perspectives, one's view of things determines...how one experiences change, life, and the purpose of life. —Dalai Lama, Gathering Sparks

SMALL R REALITY OR BIG R REALITY?

Belief systems are now being defined in the language of physics and other sciences. But science is not saying anything new. It is simply restating those views that were understood in different words and symbols thousands of years ago. —Bob Tober, Space Time and Beyond

Your assumptions are your windows on the world. Scrub them off every once in a while, or the light won't come in. —Alan Alda

I remember when I first became really interested in what I call big R Reality. When I was about seven years old, I was in the neighbors' yard playing ball with their dog. The ball was a large white softball and the grass had just been mowed. It was early evening, and I knew that I had to be home before the streetlights went on, but I pushed the time limit by throwing the ball up one more time.

Neither the dog nor I saw it come down. I was worried, because being late was not an option. The dog and I ran all over the yard looking for the ball. If I had been a dog, I would have been barking as frantically as he was.

Finally, I stopped in the middle of the yard, put my hands on my hips stomped my foot and said, "OK God, I know you know where this ball is, so I want to see it right now!" I looked down and the ball was at my foot.

I had no time to be surprised. Instead, I snatched up the ball and ran home. Later, when I had a chance to think about it, I asked myself..."Hummm, did that ball come out of a Twilight Zone episode?" You know, where each scene of our life is constructed "back stage." Perhaps someone had forgotten to put the ball back into that scene, and added it when I asked to see it. Or...was that ball always there and I just couldn't see it because of my state of mind?" My seven-year-old brain did not phrase it quite that way, but that was the essence of the question.

I have come to see that the ball was already there. My state of mind kept me from seeing it just as our state of mind and a belief system sees through the hole of our point of view rather than seeing the whole of what is already ours, already present.

MY POINT OF VIEW SHIFTED!

Without being fully aware of it, I had started a lifelong search to understand how the ball "just" appeared. What I discovered for myself, as many have before me, is that everything has already been created. We already have everything we could ever need or want. What we receive from this infinite supply is what we perceive to be reality. The most limiting thought of all is that we receive only what we believe we deserve to receive.

How did it get this way? In this state of mind, we call "living on Earth," we have accepted a substitute version of Reality. This can be called the small r reality. We use this personal paradigm as the guide, or pattern, for our standard of living. It is how we define ourselves.

There is only one Truth. We are unlimited Spiritual beings. However, in this Earth state of mind, instead of living in Truth, we live a dream story about limits and evolution. We call this world material. We say things about this world, like "this is how it is." Or:

"If God had wanted us to (fill in your favorite saying)..., He would have given us..."

We are living in an age where we can hook up to a computer generated program and live an event as if it were real. Our thoughts, emotions and sensations react to what the computer is giving to us. This is called virtual reality.

Now imagine for a moment that the life we live is just us hooked up to a program that we believe through and through.

Like virtual reality, it feels, tastes, smells and acts upon us as if it were real. But it is not. As we shift our viewpoint, we can shift our virtual reality to Reality. Just as disconnecting from the computer program releases us to "reality," disconnecting from the program of our training and culture releases us to Reality.

Isn't it exhilarating and freeing to know that the only thing that needs to change is our point of view, our belief? Let's begin together to leave behind the old and take up the Truth, using the Seven Steps to Shift as our guides.

5

—·—

Two

- The First Step To Shift—Be Willing.

He who would may reach the utmost height, but he must be eager to learn.—Buddha

Are you willing to be aware of the abundance, in all its forms, that already is present? Are you willing to let go of the beliefs that hold you and bind you to a sense of lack? Are you willing to become what you are meant to be? Are you willing to be worthy?

The single most important key to The Shift to Spiritual Perception is the first step of *Being Willing.* There is no way around this first step. Being Willing cannot be forced on anyone or faked.

Being Willing involves every moment and every thought. It includes being willing to let go, willing to do what is asked, willing to be open, willing to set boundaries, willing to have no desires, willing to have everything, willing to follow inspiration, willing to wake up, willing to stop hurting, willing to be happy, willing to not be liked, willing to be loved, willing to let Truth be the one and only guide—all these are examples of willing.

We must be willing for anything to happen. If we are not willing, nothing will ever be accomplished. We will either not start, or we will sabotage the effort. To be willing we must yield and let go of our own ego and our thoughts of how it ought to be. If we are going to move to an unlimited Reality, we must desire to see the Truth, no matter what the cost to our cherished beliefs.

This willingness is not about applying human will. Any time we force an issue by using the human ego and will, we are heading down a path that will eventually bring trouble. Although it may accomplish the immediate purpose, we have lost the larger goal of moving towards unlimited abundance and Truth.

It is our human perception of ourselves that has limited us in the first place. Human will carries us only so far before letting us down. Human will blinds us to what is true. Our desire is to be willing, not willful.

The process of Shifting is the preparing of the human mind to consent. Our task is to teach our mind with logic and love to let go. We are not attempting to make our small minds better. We are in the process of asking our human mind our—self-perception, our personality, the voice inside who says "this is me" — to step aside and yield to the larger unlimited Mind.

We do not change our minds; we release them. We learn to yield to a full and loving picture. This picture benefits all it touches. Our own small picture will usually benefit only us. Being willing also applies to how we deal with others. We cannot force other people into anything unless they are willing.

Think of all the heartache we would save ourselves and those we love by simply noticing whether they are willing to do whatever we are asking them to do, and if they're not, by letting them work it out in their own way. All we can do for those we love is to provide a place where they feel it is safe to be willing.

CROSS THE COW GATE.

Our willingness lies in our ability to step past our fears. In the movie "Camilla," Jessica Tandy plays the role of a woman who has a chance to step forward into a life that she has dreamed of for years. Since she had originally come from the country, she describes a cow gate as an obstacle that keeps the cows from wandering out of the pasture.

It is not really a gate and there is no fence, just boards laid into the road. The cows, not liking the feel of the boards, will not cross this gate even though there is nothing really keeping them in. By the end of the film, she does step through her personal cow gate into her new life.

What keeps us in our unfenced pasture and not moving on to our dreams are things we think we do not like to "step over," or things we do not want to do. It could be as simple as not wanting to make a phone call. It is not the large things or actions that keep us from our dreams; it is the small things that we are not willing to do that impede our progress.

Once we are willing to move to unlimited reality, either these little things melt away or we gain the courage to cross over the willingness threshold into an unlimited life that has always been awaiting our return.

There is neither an end nor a beginning to Being Willing. It is the constant conscious yielding to Truth, which is Heaven here and now.

Even if you are on the right track, you will get run over if you just sit there. —Will Rogers

• The Second Step To Shift—Become Aware.

Awareness is an art. In its purest form it is the ever- expanding constant consciousness of the State of Grace. In small r reality, awareness first brings to light the belief in two opposite points of view called "good" and "bad." These opposites appear in every area of life. If one group of people says something is good, another group believes just the opposite. In small r reality our minds create both good and evil states. We plan, scheme and try to make things happen. In Reality, what we perceive as our minds are avenues for awareness, through which divine ideas flow.

Our lack of awareness keeps us at one end of a point of view in a distorted, conditioned mind, which is out of balance and at odds with the other end. Awareness of Reality brings the understanding that one is no better than the other, and that the belief in opposites or separation is a product of human conditioning. To release our small minds it is often necessary to become aware of our current physical, emotional, and mental states to uncover hidden thoughts and habits, which keep us from experiencing the State of Grace.

Change your life question or statement.

Each of us has a "life question or statement" that we continually say to and about ourselves. That question or statement colors everything else that we see and think. Although it is called a "life question or statement", it usually keeps us in a state of "death" or the inability to see and live Life as we were meant to live it. It is a belief about how the world works.

This belief is an outgrowth of the life we think we are supposed to live, which was created by our conditioned worldview. To experience a totally abundance-filled life, our current life question must be uncovered and replaced with one that serves and expands our perception instead of limiting our life.

The question or statement we say or ask is usually not evident to us, but it is certainly evident to our friends and family. To find the belief that is determining your point of view, ask someone who loves you what it is you keep on saying.

Here are some examples of common life questions that many people continually ask. The wording may be different but the meaning is the same.

- Why is life so unfair?
- Why is life so hard for me?
- Why do other people have all the luck?
- Why doesn't anybody love me?
- Why don't I know what to do?

No matter what the question is, it is framing the outcome of our life, because what we believe to be reality magnifies. Every time the question is asked, the reality it is manufacturing becomes more entrenched.

A few years ago, I decided consciously to choose my own life question(s). The object was to stop unconsciously listening to an old limited life question and switch to one that would help me to consciously experience the presence of Grace.

I made up a few questions to ask myself that would remind me to move away from the limited point of view of myself, to who I really am and the life I was meant to live.

The changes I found myself making without a forceful effort were astonishing. I still ask myself the following questions consciously a few times a day—especially when I am making any kind of decision.

- Am I running?
- Am I hiding?
- Am I lying?
- Am I waiting?

There is no right or wrong to the answers. What they provide is awareness. Once aware, we can choose to rise above this limited point of view, and Become Aware of the place of the One—or the still place—the State of Grace.

- THE THIRD STEP TO SHIFT—UNDERSTAND SIGNS AND

SYMBOLS.

Matter is matter only to the material state of consciousness, but once we rise to a mental state of consciousness, matter is not matter, but mind. —Joel S. Goldsmith, *The Thunder of Silence*

The outside, visible world is the projection of the internal and non-visible world of our point of view. The signs and symbols of the universe are not the Truth but messages that can be interpreted to discover either the essence of the Truth they are revealing or the lie they are telling.

Signs and symbols make up every part of life—from traffic to nature. Being Aware of the difference between signs and symbols of what is True and the reversal of what is True is critical to understand. Signs and symbols are not anchors but guideposts on our path. If we believe them to be real and Truth rather than signs and symbols, we will be locked into the accumulation of things rather than be free to be the full expressions of boundless Life.

In the Chapter Unkink The Hose, we will further discuss how to observe and use signs and symbols to become more aware of belief systems that govern our perception of reality.

LIGHT—AS SYMBOL.

Whenever I look into a mirror now, I think of the light. I know that I am seeing only a small fragment of my own totality. The figure staring back at me is the barest representation of what is there and what I may actually be. —Joe McMoneagle, *Mind Trek*

Quantum physicist Arthur Zajonc says, "Understanding the true nature of light requires looking not only with the eyes, but with the soul." He and a friend designed an exhibit as part of a science project he called "Eureka." It consisted of a box with a projector whose light shown directly into the box without touching any part of the box.

Obviously within the box was pure light. However, when they looked through a view port into the box there was only blackness. When they inserted a wand, it revealed the light by reflecting it back. Without an object on which light can fall, there is only darkness.

We take light for granted. We think it is part of our world. But it is not. It is part of an invisible world, like the wind. Both are only visible in their interaction with an object.

God, like the light and wind, is invisible. God is always invisible. Without us—God's reflection—God would not be apparent. Everything we see is a result of God, the abundance of God, the supply of God, but not God Itself.

QUANTUM PHYSICS—AS SYMBOL.

What quantum mechanics says is that nothing is real and that we cannot say anything about what things are doing when we are not looking at them. Nothing is real unless it is observed...and we have to accept that the very act of observing a thing changed it. —John Gribbon, *In Search of Schrodinger's Cat: Quantum Physics and Reality*

The chair on which you are sitting is constructed out of fundamental laws, rather than out of such material objects as atomic particles—an almost theological concept. —Allen D. Allen, *Does Matter Exist? The Foundations of Physics*

Physics describes the behavior and idea of energy, which is still a material element.

However, the essence of physics can take us further into an understanding that this is in Reality a Spiritual world.

Those of us who are not physicists can take the easy way out by considering physics in a way that it will be helpful to Shift out of our point of view. Quantum physics informs us that everything is a wave until it is observed. Then it turns into a particle. What does that mean? First of all the word "observed" in this context means "think about."

Quantum physics is saying that there is nothing "real" until we think about it; then it becomes solid (real) to us. Therefore, every moment is new if we choose to live it in Reality.

This idea explodes ruts! It means that the moment we change what we're thinking, or what we believe to be true, our world changes accordingly. Why don't we see this? We will discuss the answers to that question later—but for now just a hint. Could it be we have a habit of holding on to our point of view so that we can hold on to who we think we are? Quantum physics reminds us that we cannot separate the observed from the observer. The dream and the dreamer are one.

THE COMPUTER—AS SYMBOL.

The discovery of how our DNA is put together rocked the world. The implications of this breakthrough are interesting and bring to mind the thought of "how we are like a computer," or how the computer is a symbol of Truth.

Now that we know the order of the DNA sequence, scientists are able to understand which part of the DNA strand to "fix" or "change" to produce the results they might want—like perfect health, or intelligence.

Looking at it simplistically, it means they will fix the bugs in our computer programming, and perhaps continually upgrade our software. By plugging into their system, we will hopefully become better in all ways.

Instead of reacting either way to this idea, look at it as a symbol of what is true spiritually.

What if we understood that what appears to be a material DNA is really a spiritual idea? What if we understood that the main computer is really Divine Intelligence—or One Mind—and that our personal computer system is part of the One Computer System called God? This One Computer is always expressing perfection. As we become aware of this perfection our world, appears "upgraded."

Our "free will" has given us the choice to believe that we are separate from Mind, God, or the One Computer. But believing it does not make it so. The moment we remember— wake up to, experience, think through, and know—that we are not separate, our DNA bugs disappear; because it was our sense of being separate that produced the illusion of "bugs" in the first place. As we wake up to the Truth of our connection we experience an upgraded, newer and better understanding of who we really are.

THE INTERNET—AS SYMBOL.

Connecting to the Internet is a wonderful symbol of connecting to the Kingdom of Heaven. How?

First—look at how we get on-line to the Internet. We use a connection service. Which one do we use? There are many choices. Does it matter which one we use? Not really. We determine the parameters that we are comfortable with to get on-line. But we will eventually all get there if that is where we are choosing to go.

Should I judge how you make your connection? Should it be important to me, which one you use?

Should I punish you if you use the wrong one, or assume that you will be punished because you use one that is different from mine? No. Neither should we be judging the way or the method that others choose to reach the Kingdom of Heaven. It is their choice. Each one of us walks a different path, but if the intention is clear, we will all eventually connect. Of course, for me, I want the fastest, clearest, simplest, and most service-oriented way possible.

Once we get to the Internet, how is it like the Kingdom of Heaven? Check this out—we are all there and it is each person's unique contribution that makes it actually exist. We get more and more out of the Internet as more of us contribute and participate. It is our unique expression of an idea that brings it to life—whether it is the Internet or the Kingdom of Heaven.

Like the Internet, the Kingdom of Heaven is impartial. It does not know whether we are male, female, beautiful, or ugly. It exists because we exist. It is our point of view that creates what we see of either one.

What else is the same? Some of us say we can't "do" the Internet. Some of us say we can't "find" the Kingdom of Heaven. Again, it is a matter of simply looking and seeing that both are here now.

To see and use both, we need to clear out and let go of habits and thoughts that keep us in the rut of our current thinking of how it is and then we can choose the Kingdom of Heaven.

We may argue that the Internet has serious problems. There are some really terrible sites (sights) and many people who find pleasure in trying to destroy our joy in it. And so—what is different here? Who is doing this? People and their choices are producing this result.

The Internet as an idea is not doing any of this. It can't. A negative, and sometimes evil, point of view attempts to use this impartial idea to express what is not good, but the idea of the Internet itself remains impartial.

What can we do about the negative side? Start by choosing not to participate or give power to the negative symbol of the Internet. Stop being interested (either because we are curious or disgusted) at those things that appear to be bad or evil. Set boundaries. Protect yourself. Don't believe the point of view that says things are not good now.

Dial up. Get in. Participate. Share. Express yourself. The result? We all experience an improved version of a symbol of the Oneness and expression of the Kingdom of Heaven.

- ### The Fourth Step To Shift—Learn Perception Rules.

There is one "law" in the physical universe that can never be overturned or negated. The law that *Perception produces reality and what is perceived to be reality magnifies.* And its corollary:

An error in the premise must appear in the conclusion.—Mary Baker Eddy, *Science And Health With Key To The Scriptures.*

Our point of view produces the visible. We verify what we believe through our senses and then agree that what we have verified is reality. With this agreement our personal reality reproduces itself again and again. Every reproduction creates a stronger belief.

Belief produces emotion. Emotion strengthens our belief and the cycle continues.

Nothing we experience is how it "really" is. Everything we experience is the out-picturing of our highest understanding of Truth. We are seeing our "point of view" and calling it reality.

The reality rut.

Something that keeps us from stepping over our personal cow gate are the ruts we live in. What is a rut? A rut is something that happens over and over and over again in much the same way. The more we do and live in the rut, the deeper it gets. We live in ruts because we are so busy taking care of our daily lives we think we don't have the time or energy even to examine the ruts—let alone step out of them.

We get into ruts because we have forgotten that what we believe to be reality magnifies. We look at the reality we have created by our own thinking, and think again that it is real. Our belief strengthens. After all, we can see, feel, taste, and touch it, and get emotional about it. With each confirmation we receive from the outside world saying that lack and limitation are true, our rut gets deeper.

A newly sighted person, blind from birth, does not immediately see the people and things around him. He first sees light. From there he "learns" to see by listening and touching what is already familiar. In time, he sees the form. We know that after being given their sight, some people decide it is easier to stay blind, and revert to sightlessness.

Isn't this decision just like most of us sometimes? We perceive a new truth and begin to move towards it. But, it involves work, and what before seemed so difficult and limiting now becomes the easier path to take. We retreat to the familiar of what we already know.

However, we deserve more. Rut living is not what we were designed to do. It is not our purpose. Our purpose is to express our personal talents and gifts as an unlimited Spiritual being, not to be bound to the sense of lack inherent in rut living. We can Shift our thoughts into high gear, an expanded view, and accelerate into abundance.

To get out of any rut we have to Shift our beliefs about what is real. This is a Shift in thinking. Whatever we shift our thinking to becomes our reality. When you Shift your point of view, the world Shifts with you. Why is this true? Because the world we call "real" exists only in our own perception.

WELCOME TO SPACESHIP EARTH.

Paradigm: Pattern: an outstandingly clear or typical example. A philosophical and theoretical framework of a discipline within which theories, laws, generalizations, and the experiments performed in support of them are formulated.

POINT OF VIEW = PARADIGM = RUT:

Ruts (paradigms) are dug inch by inch, even before we are born. Those eagerly—or not—awaiting our arrival are preparing both the mental and physical ground for our life. They begin by projecting whom we will look like. They attach hereditary beliefs to us. They envision our future. They already either like or don't like the impact we are having and will have on their own lives.

Once we are born, it is almost as if we have crash-landed in alien territory. We are totally new to the life system in which we find ourselves. No matter what our family or culture, the lifestyle is already set up and we must learn to adjust and fit in. We began to understand what works and what doesn't. We adapt in order to survive and hopefully to thrive.

We hear what people say about us and about how the world works, and we believe it. We decide to agree with what we are learning about being here at this time, in this state of consciousness we call Earth, because we want to fit in. In time we forget what we knew before we "landed": that we are Spiritual—not material—beings. We start believing the current system of reality, whatever it may be. We have accepted the worldview. The master hypnotist—our culture—has us hypnotized.

We must change the way we see the world. We are in a crisis of perception. What we need is a new vision of the world.—Fritjof Capra, *The Turning Point*

The eye refuses to see what the mind does not know.—Deepak Chopra

27

How ruts work.

Ruts, a.k.a. paradigms, filter information. They provide evidence to us that tell us this is how life is, so don't bother asking for more. Or they prove to us that we were always right, so therefore we have nothing more to learn. When we say, "This is who I am," we are stating our paradigm.

A paradigm operates in much the same way as a computer file. The computer will feed back anything that has been put into it. It cannot receive, let alone understand, any information that does not fit exactly within parameters. When we go to the memory banks and pull up the file called "father," for example, we will see on the screen everything we have told the computer about father, nothing more.

The most important function of a paradigm is to act as a filter. Every bit of information that comes to us is filtered through our paradigm. Only the information that fits into what is defined by the paradigm (such as home, country, spouse, parent) comes through. We never know about most information available to us because the paradigm says "no."

Most of the time, our paradigm does not allow us the chance to make a decision about what we think we want to know. However, if the paradigm called "me" is broad enough to let the information reach a decision level, we will still "consciously" filter according to our idea of who and what we are and who we are capable of being.

We will say "no" to anything that does not fit our belief system. If there is any other reality available to us, we are effectively kept from knowing it.

At this point, we are the paradigm.

Sometimes we demand more. We attempt to change our mind, or change the paradigm. To change we agree to enlarge or Shift our point of view. How do we do that?

Going back to the example of the computer file "father:" If we want a larger picture of "father" we must supply the computer with more information. We cannot go to the computer to get that information, as it can only tell us what we already know. Once we gather additional information from other sources and add it to the database, the file (paradigm) is expanded.

For example, most of us have experienced the expanding or shifting of a paradigm when we decide to buy a car. Have you ever noticed that as soon as you begin to think about a certain kind of car you see them everywhere? What happened? Did the company begin to manufacture more of these cars and somehow they magically arrived on the streets just for us to see? Obviously they were already there. We just expanded our paradigm—our point of view—enough to see them. This was a Shift in thought.

THE LIES OUR SENSES TELL.

You will see it when you believe it.—Wayne Dyer

How does a person learn to sing if he's never heard a song, doesn't know about words, melody and pitch; worse, if he doesn't know he has a voice?—Robert Monroe

Awareness is the source of the seeing.—Deepak Chopra

What gives us the information regarding our perception of what we call reality? Our senses. What they report back to us we take as literal truth. If we can see, hear, taste, feel, or smell it—it must be true.

But let's step back. Since everything starts in thought and then becomes what we believe to be reality, then it follows that all our senses are doing is reporting back what we have thought to be real, not what is real. What we call reality is a phenomenon resulting from the way our thought focuses to create an incomplete awareness.

This idea often shows up symbolically in the world. For example, while reading this page we think that we are reading the black letters. In reality, we are seeing or reading the white light. Black is the absence of light. To read we focus on the negative or the absence of light as if it were real.

This is what we do in life. We focus on what appears as the absence of a good quality such as "love" and see "hate" and believe that it is real. When we learn to focus on what is real, what is unreal vanishes, because it never existed in the first place.

Fight or flight is another example of learned behavior that must be unlearned if we are to become conscious of Reality. In our human past, it was necessary to react to a negative event by either fighting or fleeing. We had to remember the negative to survive. The cave dweller absolutely needed to link the sound of a snapped twig with the possibility of a bear approaching because he had to either fight the bear or flee from it. We have carried that focus with us throughout human history, even when we don't need it. We continue to focus primarily on the negative. It is that focus that maintains its existence—nothing else.

Our Earth state of mind, or paradigm, is a negative one. It constantly suggests to us that there is lack. It continually brings to our attention the negative quality of not enough of anything. Every form of communication suggests that there is a lack of everything: time, money, love, companionship, health—the list is endless. To Shift from the negative world rut, we first must Shift our personal one. We must constantly Shift our focus from lack to the focus of the Truth of omnipresent supply.

We cannot listen to what the outside senses tell us because they are only "telling us" what they "think" we want to see. They lie to us to support our beliefs. There are many examples of how the senses lie to us as they report back our current viewpoint. We cannot see things that we are not currently aware of because we see what we believe.

An example of this is the story of the landing of the Spaniards in Mexico. When the Indians saw white men standing on their shores, they thought the men were gods. The Indians had not seen them arrive, so they concluded that they must be all-powerful.

Although the Spaniards' longboats were moored within sight, the Indians had no context for such contraptions and thus did not see them. Eventually the Spaniards took the Indians out in a canoe and showed them the wake of the longboats. The Indians saw the wake, and accepted that there was something causing it that they were not seeing. After accepting the possibility that something existed that they could not see, eventually the ships became visible to them.

EMOTION AS MAGNIFIER.

There is a wonderful Star Trek episode where Captain Kirk and Spock and other members of the crew are trapped in what appears to be a force field. They are subjected to watching the horror of other crew members being tortured in front of them, but they are not able stop it. They cannot get out of the force field that holds them. They try every possible method to release themselves. Finally, Spock conjectures that the field is magnifying their emotions. He asks them all to stop, clear their minds, and release their emotions. Instantly they are free.

I had a memorable example of this experience. I was in the process of preparing to teach the detachment part of The Shift seminar, when my husband (at that time) and I were invited to a party. When I attend a party, I usually find myself talking to whoever finds me sitting in a corner. My ex-husband, on the other hand goes to parties and within minutes he is surrounded by a crowd.

After talking to a friend for an hour or so, I went to get something to eat, and walked past him and the usual crowd of people surrounding him.

He called me over to introduce me to the group and asked me to tell them what I did. I was immediately tongue-tied and couldn't think of how to describe it, so I explained the Star Trek story to them.

While we were talking, a large dog had been jumping up on the group with its big paws, licking everyone. The group was understandably annoyed and kept pushing him away, but he kept coming back for more.

I suggested to the group that the dog was enjoying the attention being paid to him, even if to us it was negative attention, and that this was very much like the Star Trek episode.

The emotion of annoyance was keeping the dog around. Just for fun, I asked them to stop thinking about the dog at the count of three. They agreed.

I counted, and immediately, within a split second, the dog's head flew up and he literally ran from the group. We watched him go, in awe. Even I did not expect such an immediate and dramatic result.

How does this apply to our lives? Emotion magnifies whatever we perceive as reality. Keep emotion only on what we want to reproduce—good—and we will find we are already in Heaven.

HOW TO LEAVE A RUT.

Sit down before fact like a little child, and be prepared to give up every preconceived notion, follow humbly wherever and to whatever abyss Nature leads, or you shall learn nothing.—T.H. Huxley

The first problem for all of us, men and women, is not to learn, but to unlearn.—Gloria Steinem

The first step in leaving a rut is Being Willing to accept that there is more to life than the life we are living.

The second step in leaving a rut is to Become Aware of the rut. We all are in some kind of rut. Some ruts are deeper than others, but until we are all living limitless lives in every area of life, we are still in a rut somewhere.

The third step out of the rut is to understand that no matter how good life is now, it is not as good as it gets.

To Shift a point of view, return to a childlike mind. Watch young children who have been surrounded by love. These children are free of ruts. They are not thinking, "This is how it is." To them all things are new and open to possibility. They are not worried about changing their point of view because they would lose too much or appear too foolish. They don't think, "I am not supposed to do this." All they are doing is living in the moment and gaining understanding. Children do not filter information—they entertain possibilities.

WHAT WE PERCEIVE TO BE REALITY MAGNIFIES.

Before we can go anywhere, we need to know our starting point. Self-truth is the first truth. Since we are the dreamers dreaming the dream, or the mapmakers making the map, it is wise to know who we think we are. If we can't tell the truth to ourselves, how can we know Truth?

Take a moment and write down who you believe yourself to be. What are you thinking? What are you feeling? Who and what is in your life now? How do you feel about each of these people, places, and things? Tell the truth—it is the first step to freedom—but please don't attach any significance to these things. They are simply a set of beliefs.

- Who am I today?

- What am I thinking?

- What am I feeling?

- Who is in my life now?

- How do I feel about each of these people?

- What work am I doing?

- How do I feel about this work?

OK. Now that you have told the truth, as you know it today, you can begin to know and understand yourself and what appear to be your problems. However, first let's take a look at what makes up a problem. How many times have you faced a problem with effort? We think, "If I work harder at the job, relationship, business—things will get better."

We throw our entire being into fixing the problem. And what happens? It gets worse. There is a simple reason for this. Let's go back to the beginning. What you think about and believe becomes your reality. *What you perceive to be reality magnifies.*

The problem has become real because each time you think of the problem, you focus on it as a problem.

Add to that the fact that the problem is never actually the problem—it is a symptom of a choice you don't remember making that is now dictating "reality." Focusing on the problem with effort magnifies it. This is because all emotion acts just like a magnifying glass. It makes bigger or more "real" whatever it is focusing on. The mind only goes along for the ride.

Some people spend years trying to remember their choices. Once they uncover them, they spend more time trying to figure out how they made them. Then they have to figure out why they made each choice. Finally, they must learn how to forgive themselves and others for the reasons for the choice. This method will work, in time.

However, there is a simpler way. It starts with knowing the Truth of who we are, and acting out of that Truth now. When we study what is Real, what is unreal becomes apparent and can be easily confronted and resolved. When we focus on what is Real, what is unreal becomes obvious.

When we focus on the unreal, what is Real remains hidden.

For example: When a bank is training its tellers to distinguish between a real or counterfeit bill it first shows them what a real one looks like. Fake bills are then obvious to them. Of course, the bank might also teach them what tricks can be used to make the bills appear real.

But first, tellers must know what real money looks like. This works in our lives too. The Bible tells us to think only on what is good, beautiful, and pure, for a good reason. We will then know what is not good, beautiful, and pure when we see it. What is not good becomes totally obvious. However, most of us have been taught to look at what doesn't work and then try to fix it! Have you noticed how hard this is?

This is not a denial of our choices, but an uncovering of them in order to choose consciously. We begin to notice the tricks that have been played on us to make something appear real when it is not. It is a process of bringing all the pieces of ourselves together. We begin to retrieve parts of our emotional self that we left behind at different levels of growth because of the choices we made.

As we begin to uncover our choices and then release any pain that they prompted, our vision clears. If we are burdened with pain from our unconscious choices, we spend much of our lives surviving.

35

As we gather and heal our internal awareness, we are free to release the energy that was being used merely to survive, and instead we can focus that energy towards higher realms. This transforms our consciousness.

THE STAR TREK POINT OF VIEW.

Let me give you an easy way to start seeing the world differently. Pretend that you're going watch an episode of Star Trek. This is a show about a group of people who know that they are traveling on the same spaceship. They also know their mission. Their mission is to "go where no one has gone before." They even know how they are going. They are going boldly. A few minutes into the show an "it" appears. This is something that seems to be a threat, or at least a dangerous mystery.

Here's what the crew does not do. No one says, "Wow, what did we (or I) do to cause this to happen? Must be my (or your) karma catching up with me." No one blames anyone, including themselves. No one says, "Why me?" No one says, "I have such bad luck." No one judges the "it."

What they do is rally around someone on the crew who seems to have an insight into this "it." As a team, they take on the challenge. They are always willing to look for and listen to creative and insightful solutions from anyone.

What happens next? Deeper into the show the captain is faced with a decision. In some way, he must decide whether to live up to his highest understanding of what is right, or take the easier way and save the crew and/or himself. Of course, he chooses the high moral ground and that turns out to be the right answer and the "it" disappears.

Wait, there's more. What else they don't do is sit around rehashing the "it" story. What they do is play, talk, and love. Basically they have relationships.

There is one last step. It's a week later and it's time for Star Trek.

You flip on the show and what you don't see is anyone saying, "Whoa, we better not boldly go where no one has gone before, because remember what happened last time!"

If we simply choose this Star Trek point of view, the unlimited life can begin to be ours.

WE'RE THE LID ON OUR LIVES—LET'S TAKE OFF THE LID!

Our real self is not the captive of space and time.—W.R. Inge, Mysticism in Religion

For a number of years I taught dance classes. One of my favorite classes was for children around three years old. I never met a child at that age that didn't have rhythm. If they started class later, say after first grade, the only ones who had retained their rhythm were those who believed that it was innate to them or who never questioned their ability. If they were adults, many of the beginner dancers had totally accepted the notion that they lacked rhythm. That point of view absolutely buried the truth that their rhythm was still within. They had allowed their personal worldview to wall off, or "lid off," a basic ability.

However, even the three-year-olds would often say to me, "I can't." To counteract this I would put an empty cardboard box outside the door. I requested that they deposit any bad feelings or thoughts and the words "I can't" inside the box before they came in.

They totally understood this request and made quite an event out of dropping thoughts and words into the box. They knew that they could pick them up and have them again after class, but they never did.

I still have a memory of one little girl happily swinging her waist-long hair as she skipped out of the room saying, "Mommy, I can do anything I want!"

Why should we put the lid on when the joy is streaming out? Saying "I can't" causes what is called a scotoma, a blind spot, which literally tells our brain not to see anything that would prove that we could.

We are all born originals—why is it so many of us die copies?—Edward Young

LILACS AND THE TRAIN.

Years ago, I experienced spring in the Eastern United States for the first time in thirty-three years. I grew up in Pennsylvania and my favorite part of spring was the lilacs blooming. I loved them for their abundance, their fragrance, their color, and the fact that they always seemed to bloom for my birthday, which is in mid-May. It had been so long since I lived in the East I was not sure what lilac bushes looked like before they had leaves. During the month of April I looked everywhere for lilac bushes. I worried because I did not see any buds on any bush that looked like a lilac to me. How would they be ready to bloom by mid-May?

The first week in May, as I sat on my front porch wondering about lilac bushes, it occurred to me that perhaps they might bloom earlier than I thought.

In less than a fraction of a second—that change of perception, that shift in point of view, that tiny thought that perhaps things were not just as I remembered, or wanted it to be—produced a huge blooming lilac bush less than fifty feet away from me.

In shock, I looked around and saw another one about 100 feet away.

What happened? Did they materialize out of thin air—or were they there all along, and it was my state of mind, my point of view, my perception of reality that totally and completely blocked the fully blooming lilac bush from my sight? You know the answer.

Here is another example. Once we lived a block from a railroad track. When the trains came through it felt and sounded like they were going directly through the house. Two trains passed through our town at night. One arrived about 12:30 a.m. and another one at 4:30 a.m. For about a month, we thought that the trains were not coming through anymore because we didn't hear them. One night, I was awake at both those times and there they were—right on time, so loud the house shook.

The trains never stopped coming through. We were what was different, not the trains. What were we? Asleep.

Seeing what is present is as simple as both of these examples. The lilacs were right in front of me and the train was still coming through. In one case, I had a point of view or paradigm—which filtered out any information about seeing blooming lilacs until mid-May. And in the other, I had a point of view that I was not awake.

Perception shifting is easy. Wake up and/or open your thought to even the smallest possibility that what you want, wish for, look for, desire, has already been provided for you, and the possibility that how you thought it was going to be might be different, and you too will look up and see what you want blooming right there—in front of you. Once you see one new idea, more will appear.

I guarantee this—I promise you this—but you must be the one who says wholeheartedly, "There is more than meets the eye, and I am willing to perceive it, now."

The only permanent solution to experiencing a different reality is to Shift and let the law of perception work on our behalf.

Things do not change; we change.—Henry David Thoreau

No army can withstand the strength of an idea whose time has come.—Victor Hugo

As soon as man does not take his existence for granted, but beholds it as something unfathomably mysterious, thought begins.—Albert Schweitzer

Most people are about as happy as they make up their minds to be.—Abraham Lincoln

6

SECTION TWO

THE SHIFT TO GRACIOUS

7

_— · —_

THREE

_W_ _hen you come to a fork in the road, take it._—Yogi Berra

When you face a fork in the road, step on the exhilarator!—Pat Riley

READY—SET—SHIFT.

Why not change our point of view? After all, who really wants
to live in a rut? We have seen that perceiving magnifies, so why not
perceive something that would be more enjoyable. Here is a tool that
can be used to get that "lid called you" out of the way.

The lid called you, or who you think you are, doesn't really want
to change. If I am trying to accomplish something that a part of Beca
is afraid of, or not ready for, or doesn't want, I have to struggle with
myself.

Sometimes I am unaware that conditioned culture-impacted Beca
is not in on what I want. I only find out later, when she has sabotaged
me. Of course, I am now referring to myself as two people. First, there
is the person called Beca who has grown up adapting and fitting into
her culture or worldview. Then there is the other person to whom
I have given a separate name, who is my inner core and who already
knows the Truth.

42

I know that we all have this inner core. To help uncover it, I suggest you too give yourself another name.

As you read this, perhaps a name popped into your head. If one did, don't deny it. You can change it later if you want to, but use it for now even if you didn't like it. If one didn't come to you, just grab any name, and use it for now; again, you can change it later.

Often you will find that name you didn't like at all will turn out to represent a strength or quality you will be proud of expressing. Write a brief history of this new name. Have fun with it. You don't have to be a human, or from this planet. What you do want is a new, broader, happier point of view for your new name.

Now that you have a new name and new history, you have a different standing point from which to view any situation. You have a vehicle that helps you to say "what if" and not be attached. You can now have a discussion with the culture-impacted you and the true you, and not attach yourself to your problem.

The people who have graduated from my Shift Class know how to have a discussion with another Shift Mate using the Shift name to access another point of view—with themselves and with each other. Once you find someone who enjoys this idea, exchange names, and remind each other of who you really are.

One woman reminds herself who she really is by putting her Shift name on the backside of her nameplate on her desk. Those facing her see her regular name, but she sees the name that reminds her of her true self. She uses this knowledge to expand her point of view in her day-to-day business dealings, which has resulted in a huge increase in her business and greater peace of mind.

Another woman took the name that popped into her mind, and instantly didn't like, but lived with it anyway.

One day it dawned on her that this was truly how she wanted to live her life, and now she uses it as a logo for her new business. Both of these women have pulled strength and insight from within, just by reminding themselves that they are much more than what appears on the surface.

My new name is:

My new back-story is:

Which path?

Before we can go any farther, there is a choice to be made. We have reached a crossroads with three paths. The first is the physical path. All that we have discussed up to now can be used simply to improve your physical life. The second path is the mental path. Using perception rules on this path will also improve your physical life, but will do so by improving the way that you think. The final path is the spiritual path.

Choosing this path is not a choice to improve anything but a choice to yield to the divine State of Grace and become aware of the Kingdom of Heaven within. Before you choose, consider this.

Is it possible that "this" is all a game? And if it is a game:

- Do you know the rules?

- Do you know the purpose?

- Do you have any idea how you are doing?

Will you pretend with me for a moment? Let's call the universe, as we know it, a state of mind. The universe state of mind has a series of rules and constructs upon which we have all agreed.

The Earth is also a state of mind with its own specific rules and parameters that we have all agreed upon. This Earth state of mind is where most of us reside ninety-nine percent of the time, without knowing it is only an agreed-upon game.

The game called "Earth state of mind" is very different from all other games we play, because in other games we know we are playing a game. In this game, we have forgotten it is a game, and so we take it as a solid, for-real, this-is-the-way-it-is place.

What this Earth state of mind game has in common with all other games is that like every other game it has something to overcome, something to achieve in order to win, and rules.

In the Earth game, we must overcome the belief of lack. We must stop believing any statement that says there is not enough—of anything.

Check it out. Every one of our precepts about Earth starts with the concept "there is not enough." We all agree at least some of the time that there is not enough time, patience, resources, expertise, love, kindness, money, patience etc., don't we?

In the Earth game, there are two things we need to do in order to win—and move on—first: We must overcome the belief of lack.

Second: At the same time all (all not some) of our relationships must be harmonious and balanced. Yes it is easy to say and hard to do. But in order to "win" we must overcome the belief of lack in everything and be conscious of the abundance that is always and forever present.

This overcoming and consciousness would perfect every relationship we have. We would begin within ourselves and then branch out to family, friends, our home, our town, mankind, our world and everything in it—from our shoes to the icebergs in Antarctica.

The most difficult part of this game is that when we start with the belief that there is lack, it is hard to have perfect relationships with anything at all. Obviously, to truly win the game, we have to first know:

- That it is a game.

- That there is no lack.

Why is there really no lack? **Because the One Mind is not playing this game**. It—as Principle—continues to exist only as a state of continuous supply and Love. It knows nothing of the Earth game of lack we have all agreed to play. It is our perception of the game that makes the game what it is in every moment. And it is our change of perception about the game that changes the results of the game. Ah—the tangled web we weave.

Since we are in the middle of pretending that there is a game called Earth state of mind, we need to know the rules of the Earth game:

- Unlike the show Survivor, in this game there is no final winner. In fact, if you are the only one left, you lose. In this game of survival, all must survive in order for you to win.

- You must participate. Sitting on the sidelines saying, "I don't want to play" won't get you anywhere—it just delays the inevitable.

- The only way out of the game is to play.

- You can win only when you play as yourself—not pretending to be what you are not, or hiding what you are. Therefore, part of the game is discovering your unique expression and living it.

- In order to win, you have to assist as many people as possible to win with you.

There can be no desire to be or create a loser. However, some

- people will make a choice to be a loser until the next round.

- You cannot change another person's choice to lose.

- You must keep an open door in case the person wants to play again to win.

- You can't play for anyone; you can't take anyone's place.

- You can never drag people to the finish line, but you can encourage them to keep going.

- You must be able to recognize and walk away from those whose only goal is to keep anyone—even the person you like the least—from winning.

- You must learn to protect yourself and those you love in a way that does not harm others.

- You must always take the "good of the whole" into account, but at the same time, be true to yourself.

- All alliances are to be made for the good of all, not for the alliance.

- No action can ever be made in retaliation or revenge. Wars do not work—any kind, any size—ever. To win, you must find a better way.

- Accumulating anything and then not being willing to let go does not win points. It only slows you down.

The best players:
- Know the rules.

- Play by the rules.

- Spend time becoming aware of who they (and everyone else) really are, and use that perception to Shift the game.

- Trust that the more they play well the more they will remember who they are outside the game.

- Understand that sometimes what looks like losing is in reality winning.

- Know that when they understand that there is no lack, the rules are obvious and easy to follow.

- Walk their talk.

In the Earth game, the good do finish first and the bad...well sometimes we—and they—think they have won. However, look at their relationships, which is the whole point of the Earth game. You know—game over, you lose—now do it again. Or game over—you win—you can move up and on. You choose.

What do you get "here" if you win? This is the good part. Here in this Earth game you will always be wealthy, to your taste, just as you want it to be. Not because that is what you have chosen to be, but because your perception will have shifted to see that you are. You will always be at peace with your decisions and you will always feel loved.

But best of all: You will know it is a game, and you will have experienced, even if for only a moment, the door opening to an abundant Truth that no one can ever take away from you.

In addition, you may find you never have to play a state-of-mind game again.

However, if you do, it will be even more fun than the one you are playing now.

I know we were just pretending, but consider this, what if it is true? Which path will you take? I am hoping you will choose the road less traveled—the Spiritual path of Grace.

TAKE THE LONELIER PATH.

Two roads diverged in a wood, and I—I took the one less traveled by, And that has made all the difference.—Robert Frost, *The Road Not Taken*

What is the road less traveled? Perhaps Robert Frost was referring to the path that most of us think is the lonelier path. It would appear lonelier because the majority of the people are not on this path. Very few choose the Spiritual path of Grace. On this path what used to be important drops away. At first, this may indeed seem a lonely place. Stay on the path long enough and countless abundance appears; and what dropped away will be replaced ten-fold.

In order to stay on the Spiritual path of Grace we must choose to live our highest understanding of what is moral and right. As we become more aware of Spiritual Truth our understanding of what is moral and right evolves.

However, it's easy to continue doing something even after we know it to be wrong, because we haven't gotten around to realizing that it no longer meets our standards. The less-traveled path asks us to answer to the call of Spirit and not the siren call of small r reality.

Habits can, and will, keep us doing something that no longer serves our well-being. We must be ever-vigilant and alert as our understanding unfolds.

For those of us who have based our entire life on a certain point of view it can be even harder to relinquish it. In fact, the more successful we are at promoting our point of view, the larger our following, the more humbleness on our part is necessary to leave what we now know to be a limited point of view and Shift to Living in Grace. Our entire lives as we know them may drop away from us. It takes faith, a choice of willingness, to make this step. The path of Grace is not the easy path. It requires a great deal of us. Nevertheless, eventually we will all have to choose this one. Why not now?

To believe in the things you see and touch is no belief at all; but to believe in the unseen is a triumph and a blessing.—Abraham Lincoln

HEAVEN—HARMONY—BALANCE—BORING? NOT.

Mark Twain once said that he wasn't interested in going to Heaven. After all, how could it be Heaven if he couldn't do the things that were fun to him here on Earth? Exactly. The same sentiment is found in all of us whether we are aware of it or not.

In my mid-twenties, I started telling anyone who was within two feet of me about God and Heaven. I was a "new convert" to the principles of One Mind and perfection. I talked and talked and people balked and balked. What didn't they like? The idea of perfection. Yuck. Perfection is boring. Where is the fun? Where is the drama? Where is the excitement?

I was stunned into silence and thought, "How could perfection be boring?" Two words that often describe Heaven are balance and harmony. Are these two states boring?

Harmony is the fullness of many notes blended in infinite ways to produce unlimited variations of sound. One note alone is not harmony. Harmony takes many different forms, but it is not boring.

Balance is not static. Anyone who has ever tried to balance knows that hundreds of little muscles in the body move constantly to produce what looks like a still point. Balance is not boring.

Webster's dictionary defines heaven as "A state or place of complete happiness or perfect rest attained by the good after death; the state or place of perfect union with God; any place of great beauty and pleasure; a state of great happiness..."

Does this mean we have to die to reach Heaven? Yes and no. And this may be the reason for our resistance to Heaven here and now. It is not that we think it is boring, we think we will have to change to "get there." Absolutely—we have to change.

It is easier to resist Heaven because we think it is boring than to resist Heaven because it is demanding. To be in Eden, paradise, nirvana, heaven, the Promised Land, Shangri-la—any place of complete bliss and delight and peace—we have to give up preconceived notions about what is harmony or bliss. We have to yield to the Divine Ego. We must grow.

I planted morning glories outside my porch and watched as the tendrils searched for places to twine. I was constantly untwisting the branches as they twined in onto themselves because I had neglected to make enough places for them grow. As I untwisted, I reflected that it is the morning glories' nature to twine. Nothing will stop the irresistible movement of that drive.

Our nature is to twine too, to grow outward, express ourselves, and bloom. But, we often neglect to provide a place to grow; or where we are growing is too weak to hold our weight. We will then twine back into ourselves, and call it anger, boredom, depression, rebellion. To bloom and grow as intended we must provide the structure of Truth.

Just as our understanding of musical harmony improves with study—so does our understanding of spiritual harmony. As we become more aware of God, what we consider to be fun changes. We will have to change. We will have to die to what we used to think was harmony and is now discord.

In balance, what is still is the mind. Once I visited my parents' gym and tried out a piece of equipment that required balance. As I stepped onto the equipment my mom said, "Keep your mind still."

If we keep our mind still in what we know as Heaven—the awareness of our beingness in One Mind—we always have balance.

It is easy to be in Heaven. We are already here. "The Kingdom of Heaven is within." What can feel hard is being conscious of it, acknowledging, and living it. It can seem hard to give up what we already know not to be harmony. But it is only hard if we hold onto a limited boring sense of perfection. This perfection is the one that we think we have to produce, be responsible for, and keep in place.

This perfection is really personal ego and the limited sense of self; hanging on hoping it doesn't have to die.

Supreme happiness is different for each of us at different times of our lives. Like balance, Heaven is not static. What Heaven demands of us is the willingness to die. Not die as the physical death of the body, but the death of a point of view—actually many points of view—all of them limited and ego-driven. The word perfection implies movement and all that would be necessary for us to consider something perfect. Nothing about perfection is boring.

Give up personal ego for the One Ego, become conscious of only Love and in less than a moment Heaven appears. Bliss is defined in Buddhism or Hinduism as a "state of blissful peace and harmony beyond the suffering and passions of individual existence; a state of oneness with eternal Spirit." Since the eternal Spirit is God, and God is All and the only creator, power, movement, growth, joy, fun, activity—and we are that expression of all that God is—then can Heaven be boring? No!

ALL ARE CALLED, FEW HAVE CHOSEN.

I know I have misquoted the Bible. It really says, "For many are called, but few are chosen." (Matthew 22:14) I never could get behind that statement. To me a God operating as a Principle of Infinite Love cannot help but leave the door open to everyone. Love will always pour out Love. The sun is a wonderful example of this kind of Love. When the sun shines, it shines on us all without exception. Even when it is hidden from us it is still shining.

There is no judgment as to who we are or where we live. It doesn't change the quality of its sunshine either.

If you have chosen other paths in the past, as we all have, there is no need to fear choosing the path of Grace now. God as Principle knows nothing about any other path or state other than Grace. It is only our perception that we once walked the "wrong" path that keeps us from Grace. Grace is now, always has been, and always will be—waiting for us to become conscious that we have always lived in the State of Grace.

For now, in our limited perception, it looks as if we must walk a path to get to it. Like plants that bend to the sun, we yearn to choose Grace. It is up to us to answer "yes." It is totally up to you.

This is your moment of exercising your free will. You can take any path you wish. It is your choice. Just one reminder; sooner or later you and I will yield to the Divine Mind. Sooner or later we will have to choose the State of Grace. May I ask again? Why not now?

8

— · —

FOUR

- THE FIFTH STEP TO SHIFT—SHIFT TO SPIRITUAL PERCEPTION.

When we chose the path of Spirituality, our point of view from that point forward must be that of Reality. There is no room for standing on both sides of the issue. Let's be clear about what we mean by Reality. Reality is Heaven here and now.

Reality is the Truth that what appears to be material is really Spiritual. Reality is One—of everything. There is no separation or duality. Reality is the reflection, the thought, and the creation of One Mind. The Reality is, there was never a separate material creation.

Much of the time we have to argue attorney-style with our small-i (ego) so that it will step aside and yield to Truth. Here is the premise we are going to ask our small-i to agree to in order to walk the Spiritual path of Grace.

The Shift premise.
- There is a Higher Power.

- That Higher Power is Mind.

- There is only One Mind.

- That Mind is Infinite Intelligence.

- That Mind is Perfect Love.

- That Mind is the ONLY Cause and Creator.

- That Mind is God and Its idea = I AM.

If you read the above and thought "religion," stop! It doesn't matter if you resisted this premise because it reminded you of religion, or if you loved it because it reminded you of religion. This is not a religious premise. Please don't place unlimited abundance within the codes and rules of religious belief. All religions have this premise at their core, but they have mostly strayed from it in order to maintain their reason for being.

If you resist knowing and accepting that there is a Higher Power, God, then perhaps you are not yet ready to live from an unlimited viewpoint, and it's still more comfortable for you to stay with your current life than to let go of limiting ideas. If so, wait to read this book when you are ready and willing. If you are willing at least to just look at the possibility, read on.

The most important part of this Shift is to desire to know and act from the understanding of what is True—and what is True is all is God. We could also use the word Good since Good and God were originally the same word. Substitute the word Good for God if it helps you to avoid any preconceived notions about God. However, when I am using the word Good instead of God, it is not the good that is the opposite of evil, which is a limited and dualistic approach. Good in this context means Perfect One.

If you are ready for an unlimited viewpoint, you know and accept that there is a Higher Power, or at least you are willing to look at the possibility. You can call this Higher Power any name you wish as long as it contains the understanding that there is only One, an Infinite Loving Intelligence. To make this point clear, I will discuss it from the standpoint that God, Higher Power, is Mind.

You can call God the One Taste, One Engineer, Love, Good, whatever registers within as True for you.

Is there a God? As a teenager, I briefly questioned this. My first taste of religion had been one where questioning was not allowed. This presented me with ideas from which I could draw no logical conclusions. It suggested that we could never understand God and were not allowed to try. It told me that I could never be good, that guilt was part of my being. I could not accept these teachings, so in tossing out the religion I also tossed out my understanding that there is a Higher Power.

This didn't last long. Simple things told me there was Something much more, in day-to-day life, guiding others and me.

It was an internal knowing. It was the blast of joy that came from seeing the clouds one day as I started down the stairs at my dorm. I glanced up and saw the sky through a skylight. It was awareness of the simple beauty of what I was looking at, and of the incredible Intelligence of what must have created it. It was the awareness that even though I thought I was painting a picture, or choreographing a dance, something higher than my human self was guiding me. I knew without question, as you do, that there is a Higher Power. There was something greater than my human self. I just didn't know how to make use of that knowledge. I wanted to know more about this Higher Power. After much reading, thinking and listening, I understood that One Mind is the only answer.

Only an Infinite Intelligent Mind could hold the world and the infinity of being in Its thought. Could there be two minds running the world? No. Even two human minds can never agree totally on everything.

It has to be One Mind, an Infinite Intelligence.

The next step in this premise is that there is only One Cause and Creator. Since there is only One Mind, there can be just one Cause, one Creator. Since there is only One power, there is no other power to create something other than perfection. This means there is nothing that we did or didn't do that could remove us from of the State of Grace, or from being the reflection of One Loving Mind. We can breathe a sigh of relief! All we need do to is yield to the State of Grace to become conscious of the Truth of One.

The radical view that we'll soon begin to live from is that there is only One Mind, One Cause, One Creator, and It is Intelligent Infinite Love. This means that perfection, joy, and good are the Truth about who we are. The Truth is not some goal to achieve or someplace to go. When we make this kingdom of God—One Mind, Love—the starting point, all other needs are met. Heaven is here, at hand, and ours now, because it is Truth. We can live on Main Street and still be living in Heaven, because there is only One Creation, God's, and that One is Spiritual. This is our Spiritual point of view.

LOVE'S PROMISE—THE SPIRITUAL LAWS OF GRACE.

1. *But, seek ye first the kingdom of God, and his righteousness; and all these things shall be added unto thee.* —Matthew 6:33, *Bible*

2. *Ask, and it shall be given you; seek, and ye shall find; knock, and it shall be opened unto you.*—Matthew 7:7, *Bible*

3. *And it shall come to pass, that before they call, I will answer.*—Isaiah 65:24, *Bible*

Let's look at the Laws that must proceed from the fact that there is only One Mind, One Infinite Loving Intelligence.

Although many have taught us how to step on the road to freedom, and many books guide us there, the Bible is one book that has stated clearly the universal Laws. And it was Christ Jesus who fully interpreted these laws for us and demonstrated that they come from the One Mind, which is Love. Following these laws, we can understand how and why Shifting works.

These are real Laws. These are not laws as we often think of laws, which can be negotiated, or side-stepped by a spin on the circumstances. These Laws cannot be put aside even for a moment. These are the Laws that set the ground of our being and cannot be anything but true in every moment.

Let's start with the **First Spiritual Law**. "Seek ye first the kingdom of God, and his righteousness; and all these things shall be added unto thee." This is the most important Law of all because it is the underlying Truth supporting the rest of the Laws.

Seek—what does that mean? It is an active statement. Seek means go after, strive, learn about, test, try on, use, get, know. Don't just wait, hope, or dream—seek. Who seeks? We do. We cannot ask someone else to seek (see) for us. We must find the awareness and understanding within. Our salvation, awareness, does not rest on another's work, but on our own. Of course, we use others' wisdom to guide us but we must live Truth ourselves. In the end, seeking becomes seeing what is True and resting in that knowledge. We are not seeking to find God. After all, we have never been separated from It. We are seeking to be conscious of God.

How do we seek? First. Not after we take care of everything else. Not after we have tried every other method to accomplish something. No. First we seek. What do we seek? Ah, the kingdom of God. What is the kingdom of God? It is the complete awareness and consciousness of One God. It is Truth. It is Heaven. We are seeking the absolute reign and habitation of God, the kingdom of Love. We are seeking the place where there are no limitations or filters from any paradigm.

Libraries are filled with sages' attempts at answering the question, "What is the kingdom of God?" But let us gather all that knowledge together for ourselves, follow the guidance of the Christ consciousness, and call the kingdom of God that which is all-loving, truthful, available, complete, perfect, continuous, absolute, omnipotent, omniscient, omnipresent, omniaction—One.

We seek this state of being, the Divine state of Being—and what happens? In the state of consciousness we call "life on Earth," what we need becomes visible to us. The action we take in the world is to seek first what is Truth and the rest will follow. Just as surely as a wake follows a boat, what we desire to see follows our understanding God First.

The Second Spiritual Law says—"Ask, and it shall be given you; seek, and ye shall find; knock, and it shall be opened unto you." This is again an active state. However, it is primarily a promise. If we ask, it will be given. If we seek, we will find. It is the motive that counts. Our motive must be to seek Truth. Our motive is to integrate what we know about Truth into our daily active lives, not to get things. We must live the Truth. We cannot just keep the knowledge behind a wall, using it only as a periodic catharsis to feel close to God.

We must keep God within all our actions. If we do this, when we knock, we will see the already open door.

The Third Spiritual Law is perhaps the most comforting. "Before they call, I will answer." Wow! This means before I even know I need something; it is already prepared for me. It's like being hungry and thinking, "When I get home I'll have to make some food," and when you arrive, someone has already prepared a wonderful meal, ready for you just to sit down and partake. This is the continuous blessing being given to us.

BECA LEWIS

EXPECT EASE AND SIMPLICITY.

Early in life, we begin to believe that if things are hard to do, that is good. We are told to value hard work, so if it came to us easily its value was less. Is this what we wish for our children? As we hold them in our arms the first year of their lives do we look upon them with love and think, "I wish for you hard work and labor?"

Could an Infinite Loving One, the essence of Father-Mother Love, even think this thought? No. A Principle of Love does not know an opposite of Itself. Love would wish for us more than we can ever wish for ourselves, or for those we love. It goes even farther than that. Love does not "wish" for anything because Love is infinite supply, and Its individual expressions (you and me) are expressions of that supply.

As we express the activity of Love (One Mind), we will find that all is easy and simple, but probably not comfortable. In our human minds, we believe that uncomfortable is hard. But it doesn't have to be.

Since we are still appearing to live in the rut of thinking we're separate from God, we may experience discomfort as we step out of that rut. This discomfort is not Mind imposed or Mind wished; it's our holding on to old points of view. The faster we relinquish our belief that we are separate from God the less discomfort we'll feel. Simple does not mean that we don't have actions to take and things to learn. However, we'll be able to measure our understanding of alignment and harmony with the One Mind (Love) by the ease and simplicity that greets us as we live our lives. Remember, "Before you call, I will answer" is a Law of Life. All we are doing is shifting our point of view to the One Loving Mind, and as we do, that which has already been created will appear. Once again, we are choosing the path of Spirituality. We choose to live from the point of view of Reality and the State of Grace.

WE ARE NOT CREATORS OR CO-CREATORS.

Since there is only Mind, there is only one Creator. However, in this New Age world we are often spoken of as co-creators and creators. Can this be true? Are we actually co-creators? No! God knows nothing of a life that is less than perfection, so It could not co-create an imperfect life. In that sense, we are not co-creators. We are also not co-creators in the Reality of One Perfect Love. We are reflection, thinking, and expression, of the One Mind, not co-creators.

Are we creators? Have we created the situations that we find ourselves in, the life we live? The answer is yes—in the sense that we do experience a life that is based on our point of view.

It is our perception that determines our reality, so in that way we are creators; but again not co-creators since God does not know of imperfection. Our thoughts and words manifest into what appears as something outside. This is the mental world. As we awaken to our true heritage, that this is a Spiritual world, then what appears outside becomes more as God knows it to be.

Guilt and fear only serve to make any problems we experience more real. Emotion does magnify what we perceive to be reality. Emotions such as guilt and fear keep the problem real and personal. We do not attach a reason or purpose to the "its" that appear in our lives. Some "its" appear because the worldview has such a strong belief in the reality of the "its."

As in the Star Trek point of view, we must confront and dissolve any "its" that appear. We do this by knowing the Truth, not by feeling and living in guilt and fear. It helps to remember that if what we are seeing is not perfect, then it is only a belief, an illusion, and it can and will dissolve immediately when we step into Truth, just as the darkness dissolves when we turn on the light.

It is important to remember that nothing will ever harm our True being. No matter what the external picture may be, we are always safe in Love. It is how we approach the "its" in our thoughts that give them power. Relax. Know that all we have to do is Shift to Living in Grace.

GRACIOUS PERCEPTION RULES.

But how do we stay in the Spiritual point of view all the time? We know now that what we perceive as reality magnifies to produce more of the same.

We know that we become conscious of the unlimited Reality by Shifting our point of view. But, how do we Shift our thinking? In the middle of a belief of problem or lack, how do we get back to Grace? Sometimes we are aware of Grace without any effort on our part, as Love takes over. Other times we have to "talk ourselves into it." The GRACIOUS steps are designed for just those times.

For the next eight chapters we'll look at eight steps we can use to remain aware and awake, to uncover and dissolve the beliefs that are creating a limited reality, and to stay conscious of the State of Grace.

Follow the path of the unsafe, independent thinker. Expose your ideas to the dangers of controversy. Speak your mind and fear less the label of 'crackpot' than the stigma of conformity. And on issues that seem important to you, stand up and be counted at any cost.—Thomas J. Watson

What we think determines what we are and do, and conversely, what we are and do determines what we think.—Aldous Huxley

All that we are is the result of what we have thought: it is founded on our thoughts, it is made up of our thoughts.—Dhammapada

After years of probing the spectacular mysteries of the Universe, I have been led to a firm belief in the existence of God. The grandeur of the cosmos serves only to confirm my beliefs in the certainty of a creator. I just cannot envision this whole Universe coming into being without something like divine will. The natural laws of the Universe are so precise that we have no difficulty building a space ship to fly to the moon and can time the flight with the precision of a fraction of a second. —Werner Von Braun

9

FIVE

OUR GOAL IS PURITY.

Hold thought steadfastly to the enduring, the good, and the true, and you will bring these into your experience proportionally to their occupancy of your thoughts.—Mary Baker Eddy, *Science and Health with Key to the Scriptures*

Finally, brethren, whatsoever things are true, whatsoever things are honest, whatsoever things are just, whatsoever things are pure, whatsoever things are lovely, whatsoever things are of good report, if there be any virtue, and if there be any praise, think on these things.—Philippians 4:8, *Bible*

Be pure. What a concept; one I was sure I could never live up to. But when I learned that the original meaning of the word pure was "freedom from improper views" I began to believe it was something I might accomplish. I found I could change my improper views as soon as I was clear on what was meant by "improper."

The most basic improper view is that we are separate, that Spirit or God has to come to us—rather than that we are an inseparable part of Spirit. Eliminate this view and we can begin to live our lives knowing that Heaven is normal and that we are already there.

GOOD, TRUE, BEAUTIFUL, AND PURE.

How do we put God First? To begin, we must see and live with only God, in action. This means that we must focus our thought only on what is good, true, beautiful, and pure. This may feel impossible because our habit is to focus on the negative.

Dr. Albert Ellis, an early advocate of cognitive therapy, said that we walk around with about 5,000 distorted ideas about ourselves. This means we may have about 50,000 negative thoughts a day! Remember the Earth game (or small r reality) claims there is not enough. We have the habit of seeing what does not work, which is the absence of Truth.

With this habit of seeing the negative first, it may appear difficult to change our focus. However, it will be easy if we just remember who we are. Shifting is not a process of becoming someone else who can focus on the good, the true, and the beautiful; it's remembering that we are the expression of God. In other words, all we ever have been in Reality is the expression of good, true, beautiful, and pure. We must stop identifying with what we are not, and start knowing and living from the Truth of who we are.

Putting God First means consistently asking ourselves: "How does God 'see' this person, place, or thing?" Given we are still operating, for the most part, within our human mind; we must come up with ways to use that mind to awaken us to God. One way we can accomplish this is to practice translating things back into thoughts.

Remember, what we think becomes our reality.

Therefore, what looks like a thing "out there" is really just our thought "in here" appearing as a solid object in our so-called material world.

So let's start at the beginning, with thought—and translate these things back to their true origin, into qualities of God. Once we learn how to do this, we will begin to live as part of the wealth and abundance that is Truth.

THOUGHTS ARE THINGS.

Gradually philosophers and scientists arrived at the startling conclusion that since every object is simply the sum of its qualities, and since qualities exist only in the mind, the whole objective universe of matter and energy, atoms and stars, does not exist except as a construction of the consciousness, and edifice of conventional symbols shaped by the senses of man.—Lincoln Barnett, The Universe and Dr. Einstein

Whatever we think becomes a thing. Rather than deal with the thing (effect), let us deal with the thought (cause). Once we really understand this, anything will always be available to us. However, our goal is not things—it is Truth. That is why the First Spiritual Law is "Seek ye first the kingdom of God, and his righteousness, and all these things shall be added unto you."

The way we learn how to understand things as thoughts is to translate the thing back to its qualities. What we are learning to do is translate what we think we need back into thought.

We begin to look for the qualities or value of the "thing."

Qualities are descriptions of true substance and can be stated in one or two words—such as love, integrity, kindness, grace, gentleness, peace, happiness, luxury, joy, and so on. Living in our ruts, we think we want the "thing."

We sacrifice all qualities of true wealth in our lives to accumulate "things." We forget that we work to express the qualities of who we are. In this forgetting, we often sacrifice the quality of time with family or the peace of mind to get the money to buy a thing that we think will provide this for us. Once we begin to see true wealth as a quality we will see that we're drowning in wealth, we just haven't learned yet how to drink it. Our true nature is always available to us. It does not depend on how much we know, but on the quality of our thought.

Practical God First.

TURNING THINGS INTO THOUGHTS.

Pick anything that you're thinking about or desiring to see and list its qualities. For example, let's say that you were thinking about a car. You want the idea or quality of transportation. So how would you like that transportation to look? You might say that its qualities include safety, effortlessness, speed, security, luxury, grace, convenience, and so on.

You have probably phrased this request as something you want or need. However, if you use the words "need" or "want," they imply that you're lacking something. It is a statement of separation. As an expression or reflection of the Infinite One Loving Mind, how could you lack? If you believe that you are lacking, you are.

What we perceive to be reality magnifies, so if we perceive lack, we receive lack. An unlimited Reality cannot lack; therefore neither can you.

You have never been separate from God. In addition, wanting something often involves our ego, or human will asking for it. When we use human will, or ego, we are walking the mental or physical path. We think we are the cause and creator. We believe that if we do enough, know enough, or work hard enough, we can fix the problem. This is not putting God First. It is putting "me first." To avoid this trap of personal ego, which blinds us to the will of God, we ask instead "to see." Since everything has already been created, we are asking ourselves to wake up to what has already been provided.

Steps to making qualities lists.

(Note: Find a link for worksheets and videos for Quality Word lists in the *Resource Chapter* of this book.)

Remember again we are not interested in things here. We are interested in knowing God. Since things are in essence composed of qualities, we translate back into qualities the things of which we desire to become conscious.

Step 1: Take a moment and list 8–10 qualities of something you want to "see". Use one word to express each quality. If you are using sentences, you have not come to the heart or essence of it.

Step 2: There are two kinds of qualities lists: You can either list the qualities of the thing itself, or you can list the qualities of how you will feel when you have it.

For example, let's go back to the idea of buying a car. Your quality list for the thing—or car—might contain ideas such as red, fast, inexpensive, safe, etc.

If you choose to do a qualities list of how you will feel when you drive this car, it might read "wealthy, secure, free, joyful, etc."

If you wish, do both lists. Otherwise, do the list that makes the most sense to you. What you choose to see does not matter, it can be as important as having a home or as simple as setting the table for dinner. It is being conscious of the qualities of these "things" that makes a difference.

Step 3: Now that you have the Quality Word list, the next step is to put these qualities in order.

Why is this important? Have you ever been at a place in your life where nothing happens towards what you want no matter what you do? This is probably because you have a quality or value block. If you have two values that feel equal to you, your core-self will be confused as to which one to provide. Continuing with the car example, let's say you list both the qualities of luxury and frugal. Until you know which quality is first, you'll be stuck and nothing will happen. This is because at first glance they appear to be conflicting. However, once your list is in order you can receive, or become conscious of, all of what you have listed. In an unlimited reality, all has been provided for you already under the law of God's Grace.

You need help to put the list in order. Have someone else take your list and help you. Don't look at your list while this person is working with you, as this will engage brain and logic. What we want to engage is your heart and inspiration.

The person with your list will ask you the following question: "Which is more important to you" and will give you two words on the list to compare.

The person must not give you any other verbal or physical cues. Don't listen to anything except your inner voice, and give the answer it tells you. Don't argue with it. If you are unable to choose one as more important than the other, the person should ask you, "Which one can you not live without?"

Notice that your mind tells you that if you choose one you might not get the other. This is coming from the point of view that there is never enough and that you don't deserve everything you want. Since neither statement is true, just notice these thoughts and move on.

The truth is, once you are clear about what you desire to see, you will be able to see and receive all these qualities. Each word must be compared with every word until you have an ordered list. You will probably be surprised at the order if you have stayed with your heart and trusted your answers.

Now that you have a list, how do you use it?

1. Use the qualities as a filter.

If something appears that you think might be what you are looking for and does not have at least the first four qualities—with the first one first, it is not "it." Think of the time you will save if you can eliminate quickly and easily what is not right for you.

For example, if you find that safety is first on your quality list for a means of transportation and the car you are looking at has a very low safety record, don't buy this car no matter how much you love it. If you buy it, you will eventually be unhappy with it, and somehow you will unconsciously figure out how to get rid of it.

2. See the qualities everywhere.

See the qualities in everything, not just in what you're seeking. Notice that they're always with you in many forms. You have always had and always will have each quality on your list if you just look.

A quality does not have to belong to you. It can appear anywhere. All of what you see is already yours because you can see it. The goal is to notice that the quality you're looking for in an object already exists everywhere, and since you can see it—it exists for you—now.

3. Be grateful for each quality as you see it.

Be grateful for these qualities each time you see them, no matter where they occur.

If the person you dislike most has one of these qualities, be grateful that you have seen this quality in your life. Know that if it is "out there" it was first "within here" and therefore always available.

4. Be and live these qualities yourself.

Now that you have begun to live with God First, no longer is having the "thing" you wanted so important. You have discovered that it already exists as God's thoughts—qualities.

As we express gratitude, we are Living in Grace. The result? Sometimes we realize we don't actually need the thing we were asking to see, or it turns up in another package, or it appears in a way greater than we could have dreamed.

Whichever way this happens, we have begun with seeking the kingdom of God first. That beginning cannot help but produce in our world whatever we need at the moment, because we began with the correct premise. We become conscious of always having whatever we need. We have never been abandoned, nor could we ever be. Looking for qualities opens your eyes to what has always been and always will be yours.

To believe in God for me is to feel that there is a God, not a dead one, or a stuffed one, but a living one, who with irresistible force urges us toward more loving. —Vincent Van Gogh

Happiness is when what you think, what you say, and what you do are in harmony. —Mahatma Gandhi

A human being is a part of the whole called by us universe, a part limited in time and space. He experiences himself, his thoughts and feelings as something separated from the rest, a kind of optical delusion of his consciousness. This delusion is a kind of prison for us, restricting us to our personal desires and to affection for a few persons nearest to us. Our task must be to free ourselves from this prison by widening our circle of compassion to embrace all living creatures and the whole of nature in its beauty. —Albert Einstein

10

— • —

SIX

Repent: *Original meaning: Change completely the way you think. Or: Turn around and walk the other way. Shift!*

Repent [i.e., change completely the way you think: Shift] for the kingdom of God is at hand.—Matthew 3:2, *Bible*

Christ Jesus asked us to "repent for the kingdom of God is at hand." The meaning of this phrase becomes clearer when we use the original meaning of the word—"to change completely the way you think, or turn around and walk the other way".

Lew Sterrett of Miracle Mountain Ranch gives a most unusual and memorable demonstration of the State of Grace and the meaning of repent. He illustrates his points while training a horse. It makes no difference if you know nothing about horses (I don't) or everything about horses; the message is clear to those who are willing to accept it.

As Lew begins to work with a horse it becomes evident that the horse thinks he knows what is good for him far better than Lew. He resists any and all demands made upon him. Fear blinds the horse to seeing the possibilities that could be available to him by simply yielding.

As Lew continues to demand the horse's attention using boundaries and love, the horse responds with anger, aggression, pouting, and stubbornness, not caring if he hurts anyone, including himself, in the process.

Does this sound like what we do when Truth asks us to repent and change our point of view?

As Lew continues to hold to the demands he has made and apply love, the horse eventually learns that bowing his head in humility to his master's desire gives him more freedom than he could ever acquire on his own.

What the horse has done is repent—seen things differently and yielded his personal ego. It is important to note that the horse could not have achieved this state of mind on his own. He needed a "trainer" to assist him in yielding his personal point of view. Our human minds are like the horse. The human mind can never get to the State of Grace on its own. It needs Truth to apply pressure and boundaries.

The amount of time it took and how uncomfortable the lesson was depended entirely upon the horse's attachment to how he wanted things to remain and the level of his unwillingness to yield.

We respond in the same way to God's boundaries and Love. We believe we are the creators and that we know more than God. We are afraid to yield to God who is our Master. Our trust is with the material world and what we can do to manipulate it to our advantage.

Lew knew the fullness of the horse's potential and demanded it of him. He did not enable the horse to stay in a resistant frame of mind because of fear he wouldn't be liked.

He held the standard of the truth of the horse for the horse—until the horse learned it for himself. In humility, the horse came to the State of Grace. The peace and joy that resulted from this yielding was tangible to all who watched.

BECA LEWIS

The State of Grace.

The law was given by Moses, but grace and truth came by Christ Jesus. —John 1:17, Bible

Moses brought us laws to follow so we could be good, wise, and loving humans. Christ Jesus brought us the Laws of Grace. Living from the State of Grace, we can understand the laws of Moses as not telling us what we shouldn't do, but what we actually couldn't do. Jesus revealed in the Sermon on the Mount (Matthew 5:1–48) that Grace is not a karmic law. The doing of "wrong" is punishment in itself. It happens because we have stepped out of the State of Grace.

We act out of a misguided sense, a missed perception. God is not punishing us: God is pure Love. We have punished ourselves by believing in and acting out of separation and duality. As we become conscious of Grace, the "karmic debt" is dissolved. In the Sermon on the Mount, we are presented with the statements of how we think it is—and how it is. It is the new understanding of God that leads us to Grace.

We will find the State of Grace as we bow to the awareness that we are the expression of God, the instrument of God's will. Within the State of Grace, we will find the peace, freedom, and unlimited abundance we work so hard for, and will never receive, while believing in the material world. God's plan for us often involves us doing things we would rather not do. Since everything is a result of perception, all "problems" are a result of our point of view. It's hard to change a problem; it is easier to redirect our point of view.

Doing what we love.

I sat at a table full of successful women a few years ago. Someone asked me what I did and as usual, I struggled for an answer. After all, what was I to say? "I teach people how to transform their lives by rethinking how they view themselves and their world."

That is probably what I should have said but instead I mumbled something and settled back to listen. The talk turned to golf, and one woman asked another if she golfed. "Yes," she responded. "However, even though I keep my clubs in my car, I never seem to do that one thing I really love, which is golf." This prompted the woman next to her to ask, "Why do we do that? Why don't we do the things we love?"

At this point, I burst into the conversation and said, "That's what *The Shift* is about!" Instead of living lives that are only partially fulfilling and focusing on despair, anger or hurt—it Shifts our attention and our emotion to the blessings that are always surrounding us.

When we repent, and use the power of perception to Shift to an expanded sense of what is possible, our life reflects the change. We find ourselves doing what we love and receiving more in life than we ever thought possible.

How did that happen?

How does it happen that we don't do what we love to do? It happens because we decided. Usually we don't remember the exact moment—but we decided not to do the things we love to do.

Decided not to trust again, decided to stop doing things that appear too difficult, decided not to believe in our dreams or decided not to do the work that really excites us.

We tell ourselves stories that go something like this:

- One time I decided to get the job I really wanted, but it made too many people unhappy so I will never do that again.

- One time I took a bus and it was so awful I will never take the bus again.

- One time I played golf and I made a fool of myself so I decided never to play golf again.

- One time I gave a speech and someone laughed so I never spoke in front of a group again.

- One time I was deeply in love and that person left me so I will never trust again.

And that is how it happens. One time—something happened that wasn't just right—and that was the end of that. Isn't that silly? What if a baby said, "One time I stood up and then I fell down so now I don't stand up anymore."

Think about it. Every decision of "I won't do that again," was made when we were younger than we are now and didn't know as much about anything as we do now. In addition, usually the decision was based on circumstances that are no longer true.

Become aware of how many things you have decided "not to do again" by paying attention to how you rationalize to yourself your decisions about not trying something. Listen carefully and you will hear yourself tell the story of the original problem.

Are you willing to live your life based on a decision you made when you were 2, 5, 10, 20, 40—or even yesterday? Couldn't we all just try again?

Example is not the main thing in influencing others. It's the only thing.—Albert Schweitzer

My life is my message.—Mahatma Gandhi

TO TRY AGAIN—PUSH ON THE PAIN.

Years ago, I wanted to learn scuba diving. I did very well. In fact, I did so well when we went out on the boat for the dive no one paid much attention to me. The instructor was busy with the others who seemed afraid. I wasn't afraid at all—until I got in the water and swam away from the boat. As I scanned where I was—in the middle of nowhere—I experienced a panic attack. It took several minutes before anyone noticed my thrashing around and helped me back to the boat.

I wanted to say, "One time I went scuba diving and it was way too scary so I will never do that again." But I didn't.

Instead, I pushed on the pain. At least once a day I would imagine myself back out in the water and I would re-experience the panic. (I was getting a lot of dental work done at the time so waiting for the dentist in the dental chair proved to be a great time to do this, but anywhere will do.)

Every time I pushed on the pain by reliving the experience, I broke out into a sweat and started shaking. However, each time I played the scene over, the panic would subside a little bit more until one day nothing happened at all and I was able to imagine myself back out in the water actually diving and enjoying it.

I booked myself to go out with my original instructor on the next dive. It had taken me six months to feel ready, but the instructor was delighted that I was going to try again. I was still afraid, but with the guidance and support of the instructor and a friend, I made it out and back. I will never forget the feeling of elation I experienced as the rest of the dive group celebrated my personal victory.

Besides pushing on the pain, there is another principle in this story. I asked for help from someone that could and would help me—the instructor and a scuba diving friend.

One of my granddaughters was a little afraid of going in the closed slide at McDonalds. It didn't stop her though. She would approach one of the other kids who was easily going through the slide and say, "I am a little afraid, would you hold my hand?" These perfect strangers always said "yes." Wouldn't you? We can all find that someone who is not afraid of doing what we are afraid of doing and ask if that person will "hold our hand."

LEARN THE LESSON AND DON'T DO IT AGAIN.

It's never a competence problem. It's an ethical, moral crisis. It's a problem of character.—General Norman Schwarzkopf

Sometimes we should not do it again. We should not go back to abusive relationships, not put our hand on a hot stove, not step out in front of a car.

Nevertheless, we may do that same dumb thing again if we just say, "I will never do that again" without any understanding of what happened. The whole event or choice wasn't wrong; it was a part of it that was wrong. After all, we all need to be loved, we all need to use the stove, and we all have to cross the street sometime.

Figure out which part not to do again and then never do it that way again. Decide to love again, travel again, dream again, trust again, speak again, and experience the full, abundant, and free life you were meant to live. Do this all from the understanding that you are the expression of God.

Remember: an error in the premise leads to an error in the conclusion. Start with God First and all that is like God follows.

CHANGE THE FOCUS OF YOUR THOUGHT.

In our era, the road to holiness necessarily passes through the world of action.—Dag Hammarskjold

A few years ago, I found myself feeling quite depressed. Although that was a common state many years ago, nowadays it's something I am surprised to find in myself.

"What started this?" I wondered. "Just a few hours ago I was filled with gratitude and joy. Now I am sad, crying, and tired."

Reminding myself that it was not a problem of being depressed but of a point of view, and that therefore I needed to repent—and redirect my thought—it occurred to me that I had just finished reading (for fun?) a romantic novel.

I had imagined that it would relax me, but instead I entered the culture of the novel and began comparing my life to it. I found myself feeling like a loser because I did not have a romantic man in my life at that moment.

What had changed? Nothing had changed but my thinking. My thought before was focused on feeling free and happy and full of individuality. Now I was focused on what I didn't seem to have—note the word seem—in my world.

At a friend's prompting, I refocused on who I really am, Spirit. I reminded myself that I am always loved and loving, and never lacking. The depression vanished, and joy flooded in to fill the space.

What happened here? I repented. Most of us think that to repent means that we have been bad and must pay for our sins. However, let's look at what the word sin really means.

It means, "missing the mark," I had certainly missed the mark by focusing on a cultural paradigm that did not include the love I was already experiencing. This was not the book's fault, but my own in the way I was thinking about my life. I was missing the mark. I was sinning.

While I was sinning, I was depressed. In essence, I was paying for my sin. As long as I thought that way, I was unhappy. Therefore, I repented. Since the word repent means "change completely the way you think," isn't this the same as Shifting? Once we notice the sin, or the missed mark, we can immediately move to Truth.

Mary Baker Eddy said, "The belief in sin is punished so long as the belief lasts."

I Shifted my thought to Spiritual Reality. I was no longer missing the mark. I was no longer suffering.

REVOLUTION IN THOUGHT IS THE ONLY REVOLUTION.

For any change to be real it must be radical or, using the original meaning of the word—it must be a root change. We cannot pile good thoughts on top of limited beliefs and expect that this will be enough. We must have a revolution in thought. This revolution is based on the following root position: that God is all. Thus, we completely change the way we think. It is not enough merely to state, "God is all." Unless we back this statement with action and understanding, it is simply wishful or magical thinking.

The Shift to Living in Grace requires more than lip service. It is a conscious, constant awareness of God as the only One.

ALWAYS BACK TO ONE.

And verily I say unto you, that whosoever shall say unto this mountain, Be thou removed and be thou cast into the sea; and shall not doubt in his heart, but shall believe that those things which he saith shall come to pass; he shall have whatsoever he saith: Therefore I say unto you, what things so ever ye desire, when ye pray, believe that ye shall receive them, and ye shall have them.—Mark 11:23, Bible

No matter what the situation, in order to see the Truth of it, we must return to knowing only One God.

During the shooting of a movie, when the director wants to run a scene again, the director says "Back to one" and the entire cast and crew go back to where they were originally placed. We must say in every situation—Back to One—One Mind, One Cause, One Creator and Creation, which is Love. In doing this, we are starting from the correct premise.

In *Science and Health: With Key to the Scriptures*, Mary Baker Eddy gives us seven names for God that state God's qualities. She names God as Life, Truth, Love, Principle, Spirit, Soul, and Mind. Each name can fit a particular occasion as we apply the principle of Back to One.

For example: Many years ago, I was faced with a horrible situation. I had left the father of my three children, and in retaliation, he "kidnapped" them and took them to back to where we had grown up. I was lucky; I knew where they were. Even so, the pain of losing them was almost unbearable. I was also dealing with the trauma of leaving him, even though it was necessary.

I asked my dearest and closest friends not to let me return to that situation, as I woke every night in the middle of a nightmare thinking that I would slip and go back to him, if only to have my children again. I also had just begun a full load at college, ten years older than everyone else, as a student in the dance department.

In this state of mind, I was fairly incapable of functioning other than at a basic survival level. To understand God at that time seemed beyond my capability.

What I could grasp was the word Principle. Since God is Love and Principle, nothing but a loving result would emerge for my children and me.

I did not try to visualize the outcome. I did not "tell God" how I wanted it to be. I attempted to stay in the consciousness that God, Love was all that was present, and the result would bless everyone. The result, in spite of all predictions to the contrary and reports that it would be impossible: I was granted custody of all three children—in both states! My daughters returned home with me. My son chose to stay with his dad, as he felt this was the loving thing to do.

I will never forget the feeling of seeing my children again (over nine months had gone by) and the gratitude I felt knowing that, with just a small understanding of Principle, this wonderful result could occur. What had I done? I had Shifted my point of view from a fear-based, limited, lack producing, and small r reality and focused on the qualities of Principle, the qualities of Truth.

I yielded my personal ego. I chose instead to witness the Truth that there is only One Mind. The word Principle was fitting for me on this occasion because I had to continue to remind myself that Truth was fair and loving and consistent. I chose to not outline the outcome, as much as I wanted my children returned to me. I did my best not to be governed by fear, anger, and revenge, but instead by understanding and love. This Shift brought me in alignment with God—and that alignment produced an outward result that benefited everyone concerned.

The biblical saying that, if you have faith the size of a grain of mustard seed you can move a mountain was true for me, and it is true for you.

Practical Repent.

When I was a kid, I used to think that if I cleaned my room every Saturday morning and went to confession right after that, my repenting was done for the week. Now that I know repenting means to shift the way I think, it takes a lot more diligence on my part!

Here is a great way to stay on track—all day, every day: Ponder one of God's names throughout the day. Look for the qualities in evidence each day that represent that particular name. For example: for the name Mind you might see the evidence, or qualities, of order, intelligence, and perfect placement. You get the idea!

Here is a list that you could ponder for each day of the week.

Monday—Mind
Tuesday—Spirit
Wednesday—Principle
Thursday—Soul
Friday—Life
Saturday—Truth
Sunday—Love

Make notes in a journal about what you learn. Pay particular attention to the fact that as you see the qualities of the name and are grateful that these qualities are in your life now, you'll experience even more of each, in a variety of ways.

We must love one another as God loves each one of us. To be able to love, we need a clean heart. Prayer is what gives us a clean heart. The fruit of prayer is a deepening of faith and the fruit of faith is love. The fruit of love is service, which is compassion in action.—Mother Teresa

You might as well not be alive if you're not in awe of God.—Albert Einstein

True religion is the life we lead, not the creed we profess.—Louis Nizer

The various religions are like different roads converging on the same point. What difference does it make if we follow different routes, provided we arrive at the same destination.—Mahatma Gandhi

11

— · —

SEVEN

We have been talking about listening to Spirit's prompting. I call this type of prompting Angel Ideas. Ideas come to us from the One Mind. They guide us to right action. They constitute awareness. They are the Christ consciousness coming to us. These ideas are filled with light and joy. These "angels" are always with us, protecting and directing us to express who we are. They are spiritual inspiration.

THOUGHTS OR IDEAS—CHOOSE WISELY.

What's the difference between Angel Ideas and "thoughts?" "Thoughts" stem from the small r reality point of view. They are culture-impacted points of view. Most thoughts result in feeling a sense of fear or lack. Angel Ideas come from One Mind. An Angel Idea may produce discomfort because it asks us to move out of ruts and habitual ways of thinking, but it never suggests lack and never comes from fear.

Here are two stories about thoughts and ideas that may help illustrate the difference, and the outcome of choosing to listen to one or the other.

Story One: The cord from my laptop charger was bent and almost broken near the connection to the computer. I knew it was. I could tell the connection from the charger to the computer was getting risky to say the least. But instead of dealing with the problem I just kept wiggling and propping up the cord to get the connection.

The thoughts went like this: I don't have time to deal with this, it is going be too difficult, I am busy visiting my family, and of course—maybe if I pretend it isn't broken it won't be, or magically it will get fixed.

One day wiggling the cord was not enough. No power to the computer, only four hours left in my battery. Yikes. I called Dell.

"Sure," they said, "We will send you a new one (free on the warranty)." Bottom line: It would only take a day or two to get to me.

Easy—but two days is a long time when your business is on the computer. In addition, I was getting ready to travel again so I didn't get the part until it caught up with me five days later. In the meantime, my whole business was on hold.

Why didn't I do this before there was an emergency? The cord would have had plenty of time to reach me before I traveled and before the old one broke. It was obvious that I would need a new cord sooner or later. Why didn't I handle the problem before it became an emergency? What stopped me? Thoughts stopped me

All along my inspiration—my inner voice—was telling me to take care of this. The idea of how and when to take care of this was right there with me. The idea or inspiration—or Angel Ideas—gave me an easy solution. But I didn't listen to inspiration or ideas. I listened to thoughts instead.

Story Two: A few weeks after we moved to our new home we stopped by the Senior Center bazaar. At the bazaar, I found a fabulous set of dishes with a place setting for four people for only $5.00. Since most of our household items were in storage, I was overjoyed.

A few days later, it dawned on me I should have bought another box of dishes since we would need a place setting for eight if we were going to have my husband's family over for dinner.

I lamented over this lack of foresight for weeks. All along my little voice, my inspiration—Angel Idea—kept telling me to stop by the Center to see if just perhaps the other set of plates was not sold. Since that seemed impossible, I ignored—once again—my voice of inspiration.

I had thoughts about how hard it would be to walk into the Center and ask the question; how impossible it would be that the dishes would still be there, and on and on.

Nevertheless, one day I was walking by the Center and my inner voice spoke up. "How can you ever write about following inspiration and ideas if you won't do it yourself? Don't be shy—go in!" I walked past the Center and then I turned and walked back, went in, and stumbled through the explanation. The woman behind the counter smiled and said, "Isn't that strange, after the sale we ended up with one box of dishes."

She was happy to get the extra money for the Center and glad to dig the dishes out of storage. I was happy that I listened to the voice of inspiration and Angel Ideas. I grinned all the way home.

Most of us listen to thoughts! We listen to thoughts that tell us what won't work, doesn't work, isn't right, blah, blah, blah. What we should be listening to is—ideas. That is what our inner voice, our inspiration is giving us—ideas. These Angel Ideas are wealth. Ideas lead us to what we want, need, or desire. Ideas inspire. Ideas bring results. Ideas are directions from God.

What voice are you listening to? Is it a thought—limited, old, a common belief? Or is it an idea—which leads you to light and life?

There is another side to listening to ideas rather than thoughts. That is the side of ideas that keeps us safe from doing what we shouldn't be doing. This one is easy: If you have to rationalize what you are doing, you are thinking and not listening to ideas. Ideas almost always demand that we summon courage, but we never have to rationalize them.

Every human being has, like Socrates, an attendant spirit; and wise are they who obey its signals. If it does not always tell us what to do, it always cautions us what not to do.—Lydia M. Child

MESSENGERS

Angel Ideas come to us in many forms. Sometimes they are whispers in our ears. Sometimes they come in the form of inspirations or gut instinct. Often they are revealed to us through the unique expressions of others. Movies, songs, books, overheard conversations on street corners, art, friends, and strangers often deliver the Angel Idea that we need to hear. If we are open to messengers, they will appear.

An Angel Idea appeared to me one day in the form of a taxi driver.

I lived in downtown Los Angeles at the time, and I was walking to my office building about 5:00 a.m. to teach The Shift.

Of course it was dark, but I was used to walking to work in the dark and enjoyed the quiet and solitude. To get to the building I passed numerous hotels and taxis waiting for passengers. At that time of day, the drivers were usually asleep.

I had been contemplating a conference that I had attended the day before in San Francisco. It had been an inspiring and moving conference and someone had casually mentioned to me that we were all messengers of God. I was contemplating that fact, yet also concerned that I would never be as inspirational to others as the people speaking at the conference had been. I started feeling worthless.

As I passed the row of taxis, one of the doors flew open and a man jumped out in front of me. In halting English, he literally shouted at me, "God loves you!" I am sure he saw the tears spring to my eyes as he said it once more, "God loves you!" I smiled at him; he smiled at me and got back into the taxi. I still thank him for carrying the message I needed to hear that day. For me it was an Angel Idea direct from God.

There are two mistakes one can make along the road to truth—not going all the way, and not starting.—Buddha

COMPEL VERSUS IMPEL.

Reason often makes mistakes, but conscience never does. —Josh Billings

He who sacrifices his conscience to ambition burns a picture to obtain the ashes.—Chinese Proverb

Another way to determine whether thoughts or Angel Ideas are guiding us is to understand the difference between the words compel and impel.

Compel means, "to cause a person or thing to yield to pressure; force, oblige, make happen." We often use the word compel when we talk about why we do things. But to compel implies fear or lack. This thinking says that if I don't do this today I will never have what I want tomorrow. It suggests that no matter what it takes to get it, do it now. Often it is a thought that asks us to rationalize our behavior, as in "the end justifies the means." To be compelled may feel like someone is pulling and tugging at us to go a certain direction. If we are paying attention, we will notice an internal discomfort when pushed by compelling thoughts.

Impel means "to set or keep in motion or action; move, actuate, drive, mobilize." It may produce the same action as compel, but with a different motivation. Impel never suggests that there is one way and one way only. It never asks us to compromise our values. It never asks us to impose upon or harm another in search of what we want. When impelled, I feel as if someone who loves me has an arm around me, guiding me, saying, "I am with you and this will be OK."

Thoughts that impel tend to ask more of us. They are more discomforting, more involved and they push us to think and take action. Impel will move us out of our ruts of how it always has been. Compel offers an easy way out. Impel has many layers. Spiritual living is harmonious and easy, but not comfortable.

Comfortable is not the goal.

Sometimes when I really don't know what path to take, I close my eyes while holding out my hands. I imagine holding one path in each hand. My motivation is God First, moving to light, listening for Angel Ideas. When I begin to feel which path feels the most light I choose it, although it is often the more uncomfortable path because it asks me to give up my habitual thinking and move out of ruts.

I grew up in a wonderful town in Pennsylvania. I always knew I wanted to move away when I grew up. I didn't know where. In my late teens, I realized it was California. At that time, it was like moving to a foreign country. I knew nothing about California or why I would want to go. It was totally impractical. I was a young mother; my husband and I had a baby son. Part of me felt compelled to stay home, and get a job. It would have been easier, but it didn't feel right.

I kept thinking I had to go, I felt impelled. I applied to a college in Southern California—still not knowing why, but I figured this would at least give us a reason to go. I was accepted. I still remember exactly where I stood in my kitchen as I read my acceptance letter. I was flooded with joy—and trepidation—as now I would have to tell people we were leaving.

There was not a rational reason to go. I did know that I wanted my husband to pursue his dream of being a professional musician and that California was the place to do this, somehow. We did not know anyone. We did not know what we could or would do once we got there, and we had only $300 (the money we had left after selling all our possessions) and a car. However, all I could see was a lighter path. We took it.

I can look back now and see all the reasons why. We both found what we were looking for by following that guidance, even though in the end it took us on separate paths.

As we listen to Angel Ideas, our desire becomes to make faith, not vice, habitual. We do this by keeping our emotions and thoughts on Truth, by putting God First.

The popular saying, "follow the light" works for practical life. Move towards the light. Listen for guidance. Be prepared to be inspired to action by innumerable Angel Ideas. Don't be afraid, Love will be leading you and those you care about the most. Love has already provided for you. You will become aware of that provision as you follow Spirit's guidance. Remember, the Infinite Loving Mind, the One, is the only Cause and Creator. What we are doing is awakening to what already exists. Eventually you will discover that you are the light.

TRACING THE LINE OF LIGHT.

Throughout history, many people have listened to Angel Ideas and then reported back to us about the limitlessness of life. I have quoted some of them throughout this book.

These people have carried forward the line of light from one generation to the next, from culture to culture. Each has provided us with more insight into the Truth of who we are.

These torchbearers have pointed out that Truth is embedded in each one of us. Although the path we walk to uncover and live this Truth is personal, there is great strength and joy to be found in traveling and sharing with others both past and present.

Many sages have spoken of these universal Laws of Spirit. If we look deep down at the fundamentals of most religions and philosophies and even quantum physics, we find these truths run through all of them.

These men and women are part of the line of light that has carried through time the words and understanding of the One Mind. They spoke in dialects that were appropriate and accessible to the time and culture in which they lived.

In his book *Consilience: The Unity of Knowledge,* Edward O. Wilson argues for the fundamental unity of knowledge and the need to search for consilience—the proof that everything in our world is organized in terms of a small number of fundamental natural laws that comprise the principles underlying every branch of learning.

As the human mind becomes aware that there is more than what it knows and believes, we have begun to step out of the jail of our beliefs and into a world of "what ifs."

Every shift, no matter how small, opens new doors and windows into the eternal All. What we allow ourselves to know (filtered through our point of view) begins to alter what appears, as our material world takes on new form.

What is really happening is that we are finally relinquishing our belief in a material world and beginning to understand that our world is not material, but Spiritual. That understanding dissolves what appears to be material so that its true Spiritual nature becomes visible to us.

UNCOVERING THE EVIDENCE.

We must prove this for ourselves. Taking on beliefs heard but not understood only creates another paradigm or rut. In addition, if we do not bring forward to now the pieces of ourselves that were lost in past traumas and decisions, we become a parody of what God looks like rather than a clear expression of It. If not corrected, in time we are usually worse off then we were before we started our spiritual quest.

The statement about "not pouring new wine into old bottles" speaks of this truth. When that phrase was written in the Bible (Matthew 9:17), there was no way to completely clean a bottle of wine residue. If new wine was poured into this bottle, the wine would interact with the residue—a chemical reaction would take place—and the bottle would explode.

Isn't this a perfect picture of what it's like to pour new ideas into a self that has not truly cleaned out the residue of past choices and traumas?

Just saying "God is All" will not produce good results. However, living fully the true meaning of God as All, and letting go of any limiting point of view that muddies the water, allows us to see the Truth. The result of Shifting our perception to Truth appears to us as good results in our daily life, and we experience the outward symbols of God's activity.

In *Chapter Eleven, Unkink the Hose,* we will learn more about how to collect and clean up the parts of ourselves that we have left behind.

Look for evidence to prove to yourself that there is only One Mind, which is Infinitely Loving.

Take note of the times when you put God First and chose to be conscious of the State of Grace—and then what you needed became visible. Have you ever wished that God would send you an email, fax, or letter and just for once let you know exactly what is True and what you're supposed to do about it? In a very real sense God does this in every moment! But you have to pay attention to see it.

An evidence and coincidence log helps us become more aware of the constant presence of God in our lives. Instead of focusing emotion and attention on what is not working, we begin to look at what is working.

I have a wonderful friend who after discovering the joy of Shifting embraced the value of an evidence log with all her heart. Every day she had astonishing proofs of God's Infinite Love for her and others.

She consistently looked for what was working in her life and focused on the good, true, beautiful, and pure. I loved to get her phone calls. She would begin by proclaiming "evidence log, evidence log," with such joy and enthusiasm that I began to see her as evidence of God in my life.

What to look for? Everything that is good, true, beautiful, and pure. Begin to note the coincidences that are so much a part of our lives. Webster's dictionary defines the word coincidence as "an accidental and remarkable occurrence of events, ideas, etc., at the same time, suggesting but lacking a causal relationship."

Our whole life is composed of coincidences—which are not really coincidences, but evidence of a Divine Intelligence. Think about it. Just to have this book in your hands involved a million different things that had to happen among hundreds of people.

How could you have orchestrated even this small event? You couldn't have. It had to be One Intelligent Mind acting out of Its unfolding and expansion, which coincided within the world as you, reading this book.

Sometimes our evidence comes in the small things that remind us that everything is an activity of God. Here is an example a friend sent me not long ago: "In December 1996, shortly after I began Shifting, I traveled to Yakima, Washington, to give a speech. Before my speech, I went into the ladies' room, and as I was getting ready, I noticed that a thread had come loose on the snap on my pants, and my pants would not fasten in the front.

"It looked terrible. I asked around in the washroom looking for a safety pin. No one had one. I went out to the exhibit area and noticed a booth with a nice lady working it, selling crafts and ornaments. I showed her the problem with my pants and asked her if she had a safety pin. She thought she might. She reached into her bag and pulled out her pincushion. There in the pincushion was a needle and thread, and the thread was the exact color of my pants. We both smiled, and I sewed my pants right there."

Sometimes coincidences take on such a striking form that we are bumped out of our day-to-day living to exclaim, "How could this have happened. What are the odds?"

The more we recognize the hand of the Infinite Loving One guiding our lives, the more we see Its guidance. Writing down coincidences not only grounds them in our mind, it gives us the proof we need on days when we find ourselves momentarily feeling faithless.

I have taken on the habit of writing down evidences and coincidences on little pieces of paper and collecting them out of my pockets every night. Let me give you a few examples. On a recent plane trip, I had four slips of paper before the plane took off. Here's one:

While waiting to board the plane I overheard a mother tell her young daughter that they would not be able to sit together because the plane was full. I started to tell them that I would switch seats with them when I realized that I didn't know where we would be sitting.

Once I was seated in the plane, I was not really surprised to find that the mother's seat was next to mine, and her daughter's right behind me. It was an easy switch. I smiled to myself and thanked the invisible hand of God for proof of Its existence. It's like the wind. We see the evidence of its power but not the wind itself.

Noticing evidence is the practice of being habitually aware of the qualities of One Mind all around us in every moment. This begins to create our own inner conviction of Truth. As that inner conviction gains strength and power, no amount of disagreement from others can suggest to us that there is anything other than Omnipresent Love.

Practicing sounds like work, but it is such a joyful experience, and once you start you will not want to stop. It always produces results. Usually the results appear in ways that we could never anticipate.

Years ago, before I started writing the class called The Shift I was dealing with a major lack of funds. Nothing I did changed the picture (in fact it only made it worse) so I decided to do what I felt was important for me to do and just began to write the class. During that time of uncertainty, I started practicing looking for evidence.

One day I realized that I needed to get some food in the house and decided to walk to the farmer's market. I wasn't quite sure how I was going to pay for it. After inspecting my motives for buying food, I decided that it would be right to take some money from the ATM, even though it would bring my balance to zero, if not below.

When I withdrew the money, I was very grateful that it was immediately available to me and I was grateful for the evidence of Mind's immediate provision. Walking to the market, I decided to practice looking for evidence of Love. I had no ulterior motive, I was not hoping for anything. I just wanted to acknowledge Love's place in all of my life. Here's some of what I saw.

- I noticed Love while watching a man stoop to tie his son's shoes.

- I noticed Love in the careful planting of flowers along the buildings.

- I noticed Love when I saw a businessman stop and chat with a homeless man. I overheard the conversation as I passed by. The businessman was checking on a job interview the homeless man had the day before. He wanted to know if he was going to be all right for the day.

- I noticed Love and Mind in the beauty of the building lines against the sky. I noticed Love in the placing of the streetlights so I could cross safely.

- I noticed Love everywhere, and I was moved by gratitude for Its care for all of us.

When I got to the market, it was crowded, as usual. There were hundreds of people bustling and trying to squeeze by each other. As I inched my way down one of the aisles the crowd suddenly moved away from a center spot. Everyone had his or her back to this center. I was the only one facing it. And there on the floor was a hundred-dollar bill. I picked it up and looked at this gift.

For a fleeting moment, I thought of yelling, "Did anyone drop one hundred dollars?" But I knew that the One Mind had provided it for me at that moment, as It provides for everyone in every moment. As I picked up the bill, the crowd began to mill again. I finished my shopping with an overflowing heart, filled with gratitude and a stronger conviction that Mind, Infinite Love, is always present.

The point here was not the money. The point was awareness of Love. What is needed is already provided. It is our perception of lack that keeps us in lack. Perception produces reality and what is perceived to be reality magnifies.

An interesting coincidence happened one day as I walked home after teaching The Shift. I was contemplating the power of acknowledging One Mind and hoping that I would have many examples to use for the next class.

As I walked past my apartment building, I noticed some bits of paper on the ground and picked up one in order to throw it away. It was a torn picture, and the part I was holding showed a Greek figure and a Greek column. I was still holding it when I got to my apartment.

As I walked in, I noticed a piece of paper lying on my living room couch. I assumed the wind had blown in something from outside (although this had never happened before, and has never happened since).

It was the exact duplicate of the torn piece of picture that I had picked up six floors below. In the past, I might have interpreted this coincidence from the standpoint of a mystical path. Now I understand that the only important symbol of this coincidence is that it is evidence of One Mind.

Whenever I doubt the omnipresence of God, I remind myself of the constant examples found in coincidences that make up the fabric of my life. If there is a time when it seems as if these coincidences are not as evident to me as usual, then I ask myself, am I really following God's plan—or am I being hard-headed and deaf to Angel Ideas?

When I listen to Angel Ideas and follow their guidance, it always astonishes me how much happens in a very short period of time. Recently I stopped to listen, and after yielding to direction I found that within a week's time I had a new source of income, a new home that was better than I could have even thought to ask for, a new car, and most of all, a renewed sense of yielding to the State of Grace and being witness to the outcome.

We are eternally grateful to the invisible hand who has guided us through all the obstacles of this fantastic voyage.—Bertrand Picard and Brian Jones, after completing the first around-the-world flight in a balloon.

Practical Angel Ideas.

We often miss how we have been provided for and how much we do listen to Angel Ideas because we focus so much on what isn't working. Take a moment and write what you have done in the last six months that felt light, or right, to you and what the results were. The size of the event is not important. Small things are what guide our lives. The bonus of doing this is that it puts us in the attitude of gratitude. That thankful attitude Shifts our thoughts to the unlimited abundance of Grace quickly and effectively.

In the past six months, the following wonderful events happened to me:

Its name is unknown: I simply call it Tao. —Lao Tzu

There is only Ati [Spirit].—Chogyam Trungpa

Space and time are not external to consciousness: Our finite system can be accounted for from the basis of an infinite system that is totally mindlike.—Daniel A. Cowan, *Mind Underlies Spacetime*

Truth is one: sages call it by different names.—The Vedas

Tao is the law of all things, of all events. Tao is the common ground of creation.—John Heide, *The Tao of Leadership*

That thou art, other than whom there is no other seer, hearer, thinker or agent.—The Upanishads

I Am that I Am: and he said, Thus shall thou say unto the children of Israel, I AM hath sent me unto you.—Exodus 3:14, Bible

God has no religion.—Mohandas Karamchand Gandhi

La ilaha illa 'illah. There is no god, but God.—Mohammed

I am Brahman, the all in all.—Aham Brahmasmi

I am the Alpha and Omega, the beginning and the ending, saith the Lord, which is, and which was, and which is to come, the Almighty.—Revelation 1:8, Bible

12

— • —

EIGHT

Everything reflected in the mirror called our lives is something we have chosen. However, for the most part the choosing has been unconscious. We choose according to our upbringing and life events, our conditioned culture-impacted paradigm.

Most of the time these choices were made in a split second but have affected years of our lives. We are living lives based on decisions and choices we made when we were young, but as time passes, we continue to live lives based on those unconsciousness decisions.

Some of these early decisions did not even have a "logical" basis. Maybe we were in the kitchen and a can of soup fell on our head. At that moment, we decided we didn't like kitchens, soup, or that time of day—it could have been anything. Other choices seem to have a more "logical" reason for their existence. Perhaps we felt abandoned by someone we love, and chose never to trust in love again. Unconscious choices build and maintain small r reality.

When we are not aware of our choices, we focus on problems in our lives and think that they are problems—when actually they are symptoms.

They are symptoms of our not understanding who we really are and the source of our existence. As we continue to focus emotion on what we perceive to be real, we get more of the same.

Easier and more elegant is to focus feelings on what is True. The message as to what is not true will either bubble to the surface like Magic 8 Balls, or the "problem" will simply wither away without our even noticing.

As we are more aware of Reality, our choices will reflect a more enlightened thought. Following the GRACIOUS steps helps to break out of ruts and paradigms. To Choose Consciously we put God First, Repent, and listen to Angel Ideas. We base our choices on the understanding that we are the reflection and expression of the Infinite Loving One. Our goal is to see and think as the One Mind sees and thinks.

Choose boldly and with commitment.

That the moment one definitely commits oneself, then Providence moves too. All sorts of things occur to help one that would never otherwise have occurred. A whole stream of events issues from the decision, raising in one's favor all manner of unforeseen incidents and meetings and material assistance, which no man could have dreamed would have come his way. I have learned a deep respect for one of Goethe's couplets: "Whatever you can do, or dream you can, begin it. Boldness has genius, power, and magic in it.—W.H. Murray, The Scottish Himalayan Expedition

Nothing explains the results of commitment better than Goethe's statement, "Whatever you can do, or dream you can, begin it. Boldness has genius power and magic in it."

Too many of us stand with a foot on one side of an abyss and a foot on the other side and wonder why we can't move. All we're doing is hoping that the ground doesn't shake so we won't fall in.

We are paralyzed by our unwillingness to commit ourselves to an idea, whether the idea appears as a person, place, or thing.

There is a popular saying, "Be careful what you wish for, you may get it." But of course. So what? Sometimes we can't know that we don't really want something until we get it. Better to get it and find out than to be afraid of asking. Doesn't anyone ever stop and think that we could say, "Thank you, but I realize this must belong to someone else."

When I was in high school, I decided to learn how to play the guitar. I was really just trying to endear myself to my boyfriend, since he was a musician. No matter what the reason, I really, really wanted a guitar. Finally, my parents bought me a one. I practiced on it about two times and realized I just didn't want to play it. My brother did. I gave it to him and he has been happily playing it ever since. In fact, it became his life's dream to be a musician. No one lost anything by my trying the guitar. If I hadn't asked, I could still be wasting energy wanting something I really didn't want, and my brother might never have been the musician he is today.

You don't know how to make decisions? Are you afraid that if you make one you will be labeled foolish for immediately changing your mind should you decide that the first decision didn't suit you? The only foolish thing about decisions is not making them—and not changing them when we learn a better way.

A plane flying on autopilot makes about a dozen small changes in direction every minute to stay on course. That means during an hour-long flight it "corrects course" almost seven hundred and twenty times.

Amazingly, that means the entire time passengers are flying in the wrong direction, but end up in the right spot. Obviously in this case changing course is not being inconsistent. In making a decision you must commit to it, just as the plane commits to flying. You will never know what you really want unless you commit. Only then will your inner voice get your attention as to the wisdom of what you have chosen.

Decisions and logistics are two different things. Making decisions is much easier when the logistics of making it are separate from the act of deciding. Usually we put the two together. For example: moving...anywhere. The decision to move is one thing. If we add in all the logistics like how, when, where, why, what—there are too many variables to deal with. First, make the decision. Then take each logistical requirement as a decision—one at a time. Trust in your inner guidance, be ready to change direction at any moment, and decisions are no longer a stumbling block to "moving on".

When I was a child (I confess I still do this when pressed), I learned that I could easily make a decision by tossing a coin. I told myself I would abide by the coin toss, and I meant it. I would toss the coin, note the outcome, and then quiet my thought. If I found that I was disturbed by the outcome, I knew that the other path was correct for me, and I would then change my mind and go that direction.

You can accomplish the same thing by imagining that you've made a decision. Start taking concrete steps to carry it out. Give yourself a time frame—a week, a month, whatever works. At the end of that time, quiet yourself and listen. What are Angel Ideas telling you?

The answer will be clear if you are willing to listen, and willing to give up control of how you think it should be.

Be committed; trust God's rightful activity and you have stepped into Grace. Evidence and coincidence will bloom around you when you're on the right path. If you find you're not, then change your mind and take another way. Not doing so is just as foolish as continuing down the freeway after you realize that you've missed your exit. The further you travel, the more off-course you will get. Listen continually for Angel Ideas and your detours will be short.

CHOOSE WEALTH OVER RICHES.

For many years I have worked with people and their money as a Certified Financial Planner, and I have I discovered that having lots of money does not necessarily mean that a person is wealthy.

The truth is, we are all wealthy and no one is poor, but that is not what the world has told us. Remember, the Earth state of mind is a game about overcoming the belief of lack. It has created a system of buying and selling, and therefore we must be "sold" on the belief that there is never enough. It really is time be aware of the game and then to know and act from the Truth of One Mind.

As we work through the GRACIOUS steps, we discover that we have always received and always will receive all that we need. As we awaken to the Truth about who we are and the truth that this is not a material, physical, mental, or mystical universe, but a Spiritual one, we will see the evidence of this in our daily lives.

TAKE TIME OUT TO CHOOSE.

I skate to where the puck is going. —Wayne Gretsky

Never confuse motion with action. —Ernest Hemingway

Our days are packed with things to do. If they are not packed, we fill them even if it is just "killing time." When faced with mounds of things to do, we make lists and rush off to accomplish them. We plan our days using every second. We say that we cannot take time off for anything not measurable.

How did this happen? How did we find ourselves in such a state that we think we're doing something while rushing around? The only worthwhile "doing" is expressing who we are. It doesn't matter what vehicle we choose to express ourselves with, but expressing ourselves is what we must do.

Instead, we act out and express at other people. Who have we become when we're so angry that we yell at each other in our cars? When we don't have time to talk to our friends and family? Who are we when we have not chosen to take time to choose—when we do not choose to take time to pray?

WHAT IS PRAYER REALLY?

Desire is prayer.—Mary Baker Eddy

Prayer enlarges the heart until it is capable of containing God's gift of Himself.—Mother Teresa

One day I was attempting to run up a hill. Since it was hard for me to do I unconsciously said something like, "God, help me up this hill." As soon as I thought it, I was stopped in my tracks by the realization that what I had done wasn't really prayer. It was a request for an improved lifestyle. An Angel idea came to me, "What does God know of your need for an improved lifestyle—God is omnipotent, omniscience and omnipresent Love, which is really Heaven here and now?"

I realized that most of the time what is called "prayer" is asking God to understand where we are, and to give us something, or change our circumstances.

I remember two very specific times when I prayed for something. They were quite important at the time. In ninth grade, I visited the church on the hill every day after school to pray that the boy I liked would like me. I was very serious about this one.

A year or two earlier, I prayed in that same church that I would be chosen as a cheerleader. I remembered promising God that I would do a better job of making other people happy if that prayer were answered.

106

In Bill Geist's tongue-in-cheek book Fore! Play he says, "At the Fellowship of Christian Athletes Golf Ministry booth ('impacting the world for Christ through golf'), a representative reminds us that God is all powerful and could definitely help our golf games if He or She so chooses.

"But there are famines, wars, pestilence, floods, and so forth that could distract Him or Her from lending a hand with our putting.

And we reminded ourselves that He or She just might decide to adversely affect our games, too, especially when we're playing on Sunday mornings when we're supposed to be worshiping Him or Her."

Bill may be joking—but isn't this what we all do?

WHAT DO WE PRAY FOR?

We pray for all sorts of things. We pray for health for others, and ourselves, for an improved financial position (again for ourselves and others). We pray for world peace, and we pray, very unselfishly it appears, for enlightenment—so that we may be better people.

Sometimes these prayers are answered, but is it God that answers them? If they are not answered, is it God that doesn't answer them? If there is a God that can be swayed by our prayers, then this God must be like us—human in some way.

Most of us don't believe that God is made in our image and likeness—we believe we are made in God's image and likeness. Depending on the words we choose to say, we believe that God is a Higher Power, One Mind—Spiritual. Yet, we continue to pray for "human" things to change. We are attempting to use God to make our lives better.

When I use God, as the catch-all for asking for things because I think this is what "He" wants me to do, I cannot possibly understand God. What I am doing is saying, "I want a better life for myself or others." Even asking for enlightenment is a request for relief from a limited life.

On the hill that day I realized that real prayer is when we are willing. Willing to let go, willing to do, willing to listen, willing to stop, willing to go, willing to yield. Prayer is not asking, it is not demanding, it is not will-power, it is not a request, and it is not visualizing how we want it to be. It is a willingness to "let go" and let Grace, and truly mean it when we say, "Not my will, but Thine be done." Prayer brings our awareness and perception to God, not God to us.

It is this Shift in our point of view that brings us into alignment with Truth. Once there, we can see what is already, and always will be, available to us on whatever scale we are currently able to perceive. This Shift provides the permanent "answer to our prayers." Not because our lifestyle needs to improve, but because this is the Truth of Being—the unlimited Love of Grace.

The next time I ran up the hill I prayed again, only this time it was different. My prayer sounded something like this: "I am grateful to know that I am not what appears to be a human trying to run up a hill, but in Truth I am a Spiritual being expressing the qualities that are God in every moment. The specific qualities I am grateful to be expressing at this moment are strength, grace, persistence, consistency, joy, ease..." You get the idea. The result—my perception about who and what I was doing—Shifted, so that what looked like a run up a hill became something much more joyous and in a larger sense was much more meaningful.

Prayer sets us in line with God. It does not set God in line with us. It tunes us up to receive Angel Ideas. Prayer lightens our load by enabling—Repenting—directing our thought back to the One Source, yielding to Grace. Prayer brings commitment to what we are doing.

Choosing is prayer when we are choosing to see what exists as beautiful, good, pure, and true. Choosing is prayer when we choose to see what has already been given to us, and to be grateful for the evidence of Love. Choosing is prayer when we choose to express all the qualities of the Infinite Loving One.

When our choices are our prayers, our lives are filled to overflowing with blessings. Take the time to choose, take the time to notice. Take this time first, not after all the running around. The next time you have to choose between getting something done and taking the time for personal prayer, choose yourself and prayer first.

Practical Choosing.

I choose therefore I am.—Amit Goswami, *The Self-Aware Universe*

I wanted to change the world. But I found that the only thing one can be sure of changing is oneself.—Aldous Huxley

Let's look at a way of choosing that will allow your life to unfold easily. We set ourselves up to fail in most choices or resolutions because we don't stop and listen to the internal voice's response to the choice. We stop short of the real choices.

I don't have to remind you, do I, that it is not things that we want; we desire instead a clearer perception and understanding of God. Choosing in this way helps us see what our small-i is telling us, which enables us to focus instead on the Truth of our being

Here's how to choose effectively. Choose something that you have desired, intended to have, or dreamed about. Since many people desire an attractive and healthy body let's walk through how this choice might look. In the *Chapter The Relationship With Our Body* we will take this discussion further. In the meantime, try this:

109

I would first state —*I Choose to have a good-looking and healthy body*.

Now stop and listen. Perhaps the voice says:

"Ha, well sure you may want to have this body, but you will have to exercise to get it."

So I respond:

I choose to exercise.

Listen again. Perhaps the voice says:

"You hate to exercise."

I respond:

I choose to love to exercise.

Listen again. The voice may say:

"You don't have the time to exercise."

I respond:

I choose to have the time to exercise.

The voice:

"You don't have anything to wear to exercise."

I respond:

I choose to have something to wear to exercise.

See how this works? The list can, and probably will, run on for a page or two for just one simple choice. What we are doing by choosing consciously is uncovering, without attachment and emotion, all the hidden choices and beliefs that have kept us from actually doing the thing we thought we had resolved to do. We are shifting our perception.

Take a moment and choose something. It doesn't matter what it is, but it might be fun to try something that you have resolved to do before that never worked. Keep listening and choosing until you feel that release that tells you there is nothing else to uncover.

Now that you have chosen, you can let this part go for now. If you find that nothing happens after a time, go back and choose again. Share with someone you totally trust this dream or choice of yours, and ask that person to let you know when you voice anything that contradicts the choice. Perhaps that person can make a choice and share it with you too. You will become the protectors of each other's dreams.

Take another moment and look back over the past six months. Write in a journal about what you chose. While reviewing, did you discover that some things happened that you did not feel you chose? What were they? What did you learn from those things that you did not consciously choose?

These questions may spark another round of conscious choices. Try doing an "I Choose" page at least once a week. You can never consciously choose too often.

Be sure to only write your response. Not what the voice says. Let's not give it any power.

Find out where to get the free workbook for doing this in the Resource chapter of this book.

Do an I Choose sheet.

In the past six months I chose:

What happened that I did not choose?

What did I learn from what happened?

Now that you have chosen, do a Quality Word list for each choice and have someone ask you "Which is more important to you?" so you can put these qualities in the correct order.

The combination of choosing and knowing the qualities of the choice moves your life towards your spoken and unspoken dreams. Review how to do a Quality Word list by re-reading the chapter, *God First*.

Do a Quality Word list

I have a choice in every moment to keep my heart open or closed, to live in love or fear. More than any other specific practice, I have found that maintaining the awareness of choice is the most important factor in keeping an open heart, for every action, every thought, every moment contains the potential for bringing us closer to either intimacy and healing or isolation and suffering.—Dean Ornish, M.D., *Love and Survival: The Scientific Basis for the Healing Power of Intimacy*

There is a vitality, a life force, a quickening that is translated through you into action, and there is only one of you in all time, this expression is unique, and if you block it, it will never exist through any other medium; and be lost. The world will not have it. It is not your business to determine how good it is, nor how it compares with other expression.

It is your business to keep it yours clearly and directly, to keep the channel open. You do not even have to believe in yourself or your work. You have to keep open and aware directly to the urges that motivate you. Keep the channel open. No artist is pleased. There is no satisfaction whatever at any time. There is on a queer, divine dissatisfaction, a blessed unrest that keeps us marching and makes us more alive than the others.—Martha Graham

Unless this thing is consistent with the highest right, I do not want it; and if it is, I can trust God's law to establish it.—The Lord Thy Confidence (pamphlet from 1912)

13

— • —

NINE

*I*magination is more important than knowledge. —Albert Einstein

Imagination is different from visualization. The word "visualization" implies that we are using our human mind to state what we want an outcome to be. This means we are visualizing within what we already know, and our human ego small-i is the one in control.

Imagination is the ability to allow an internal image to appear that is not present to the senses. Imagination takes us out of our rut or current filter and Shifts to a much broader point of view. Imagination is faith in what we cannot measure. That faith, that imagination, no matter how small, moves the mountains in our lives.

Visualization does have a wonderful place in our lives. Athletes use visualization to perfect their performances. As a dancer, I knew I should never perform until I could visualize every detail of the dance. Thus, I could take every step apart and dance it literally in my sleep. I built and designed furniture the same way. I saw where each cut would be made, where each nail would be driven. Out of that visualization, new and better ideas would emerge because I allowed imagination to be present.

In the same vein, I loved the process of choreography because it was such a perfect way of using visualization to combine music, bodies, and steps. Nevertheless, I could get greater results if I allowed imagination to take over. At this point, steps and ideas I had never before seen or thought would materialize.

Imagination takes us out of life, and ourselves, as we know it. When Einstein rode the light beam in his imagination to discover his famous equation, he was thinking from his imagination. He might have said to himself "Imagine—what if..."

As suggested in this wonderful quote below from Alice in Wonderland, using our imagination seems to be difficult for most of us. We have decided that either what we imagine isn't practical or that it just isn't possible.

"I can't believe THAT!" said Alice.

"Can't you?" the Queen said in a pitying tone. 'Try again: draw a long breath, and shut your eyes."

Alice laughed. "There's no use trying," she said: "One CAN'T believe impossible things."

"I daresay you haven't had much practice," said the Queen. "When I was your age, I always did it for half-an-hour a day. Why, sometimes I've believed as many as six impossible things before breakfast."
—Lewis Carroll, Through the Looking Glass

Have you ever tried imagining six impossible things before breakfast? Think what a difference we would make if everyone stretched his or her imagination muscle daily. We would find answers to questions we had not yet asked. Imagination taps into the One Mind. The result of imagination is the realization that all already exists now and is perfectly and practically possible now. This happens when we are willing to yield to the One Mind.

In Stephen King's book, *Sphere,* the monster tells the humans that the most important faculty we have is the power of our imagination.

Unfortunately, we often use that power to imagine the worst. This is often called worry. Worry disguises itself as a good quality. After all, good people worry because they have a need to make sure everything and everybody is all right. Worry as emotion—and a negative one at that—expands nothing into something. Worry builds molehills into mountains. Worry accomplishes nothing except to make things worse. It keeps our point of view on the negative. Worry is a lack of faith. To walk the Spiritual path we must give up the habit of worry. Imagine: What if God were present—and nothing else. What then?

In his book *The Holy Chariot*, Rabbi David A. Cooper also talks about harnessing the power of imagination. Imagination is the source of all temptation. If we imagine "bad" it can become depression and we will forget our purpose in life. We must fight depression, which is the husk that separates us from the divine. We must use imagination to feel the joy of being connected to God no matter what the outside senses may be presenting to us. Remember they can never tell us of anything True. They only feed back to us what we perceive to be real.

We must learn to imagine the best. Instead of "It's too good to be true," we can say, "It's too bad to be true."

IMAGINE—WITH FEELING.

What makes imagination for good even more powerful is the addition of a positive feeling. If we can imagine what it will feel like as we meet and do our dreams, we are more than halfway to living them.

Once a friend attempting to inspire me to exercise said, "Imagine what it would be like having the body you want, riding down the Pacific Coast Highway in a red convertible with the wind blowing in your hair." I did. I couldn't believe how much that motivated me to live more expressly out of my true self and to express and enjoy myself through all forms of exercise.

Let's stretch our imagination muscle towards the power of good. Let's imagine Love flowing toward, around, and through each one of us—a Love of infinite proportions. This Love is God's Love. This is the Love that is always directed towards each one of us without limitation or qualification. If you could imagine how that feels, how would you be living your life?

Maxwell Maltz in *Psycho-Cybernetics* tells us that our human nervous system does not know the difference between an "actual experience and an experience imagined vividly and in detail." This is a powerful statement. We can turn this information about our human nervous system into a blessing. This is the power of Shifting our point of view to the good, the beautiful, and the true. This is the power of imagination. Rather than holding to what is not working—focusing on fears of the past, present, or future—focus on what is True, and results cannot help but be bountiful. We are focusing, not fretting. We are living expanded rut-less lives.

Imagine all the people living life in peace. You may say I'm a dreamer, but I'm not the only one. I hope someday you'll join us, and the world will be as one.—John Lennon

LOG OFF THE PROGRAM OF SPACE AND TIME.

Often the biggest hurdle we face is that we believe it takes time to change. Let's return for the moment to the symbol (not Reality) of energy and use quantum physics again to make a point. The wave-to-particle phenomenon happens outside of time.

All that occupies time and space is our mental images and our collective agreement that there is a past, present, and future.

Omnipresent, omniscient Mind transcends time and space. When we are conscious of the One Mind, time ceases to exist.

There is no time or space that determines when we will be aware of the Infinite Loving One. Time and space exist only as thought. Depending on our belief about how long things take, that's exactly how long things take. As we become more aware of our immediate-never-separated connection to the One Mind, and express it fully, we will not be tempted to log on to the virtual reality computer of time and space.

When Jesus provided loaves and fishes for the masses, not only did he show that supply is unlimited no matter what the five senses are saying, he proved that it is immediate.

In the absolute realm of Mind, there was no need to go fishing, plant wheat, and wait for it to grow, harvest it, and then turn it into bread. This will be true for us too in varying degrees depending on our current consciousness of the ever- presence of God and on the purity of our motives.

PERCEIVE WHAT IS ALREADY HERE.

I want to know God's thoughts.—Albert Einstein

If you say that you need something, you have stated that you don't have it. You have declared yourself separate from the Source. Not only does this make a sense of lack and separate existence seem real, but also makes the assumption that our personal ego is huge. We have been taught to be humble—but separating ourselves from God is not humility, it is hubris. Aligning ourselves to the only Power that exists requires a surrender of the small-i ego to the one Ego. This is true humility.

Practical Imagination.

I have learned to use the word "impossible" with the greatest caution.—Werner von Braun

Every day for the next week take five minutes and imagine...anything. Let your mind run free. At the end of the week pick five of your favorite imaginings and list what would be different for you if each were true.

Here is a report from someone who tried this exercise:

"At various times during *The Shift*, we have been asked to write down impossible things, at least one a day. So periodically, I will write down something I truly think is impossible. I always write the date, too.

In reviewing my personal diary periodically, I will go through my list of impossible things. I have been amazed at how many things have happened. Actually out of the eighteen things on my list, seven happened and five things took care of themselves in a different way than expected. So, twelve out of eighteen items isn't bad. Nothing is impossible."

TODAY I IMAGINE:

If this were true, what would be different in my world?

Our imagination is the only limit to what we can hope to have in the future.—Charles F. Kettering

What we need is imagination. We have to find a new view of the world.—Richard P. Feynman

A human always acts and feels and performs in accordance with what he imagines to be true about himself and his environment. —Maxwell Maltz

14

— • —

TEN

S hifting is easy. We are continually doing it. Shifting out of ruts and low gear is harder. Habit is aggressive. It doesn't wait around to fill a void; it pushes at us continually to reestablish itself. Have you ever noticed in your life a time when you Shifted to stop doing something and found yourself days, months, or years later doing the very thing you thought you had stopped?

I had established a pattern of working out every morning. I did a different kind of workout each day to keep myself from being bored, and I had been doing this for about a year and half.

One Friday morning I got up to go work out and it dawned on me that I had not worked out all week. It was not because I thought about it and had decided to not work out. I had simply totally forgotten and had gone back into my old pattern of being at work extra early. Shifting to Grace requires eternal vigilance.

Establishing a new habit that more accurately reflects our true nature does not happen by asking ourselves if we want to do it. People often wonder how I get up so early. They think I ask myself each morning, "Do you want to get out of bed" and I answer, "Yes."

The trick is, I never ask my small-i what it wants. That self—Beca—the material self that thinks it is who I am, would probably never want to get out of bed in the morning. Beca definitely wants to stay in bed longer.

Beca wants to stay in all the ruts she has so comfortably established for herself. However, I let my inner true Spiritual self guide me, which means I get up early most of the time.

Every man is where he is and what he is because of his established habits of thoughts and deeds.—Napoleon Hill

OLD HABITS DIE HARD.

Here are two great stories about habits. You probably know the old story of the square roast. A husband was watching his wife cut off the ends of the roast before she put it in a pan. He asked her why she was doing this.

She responded that she did it because her mother did it. "Why" he asked. She didn't know so she asked her mother. Her mother responded, "Because my mother did it." Finally, they asked her mother. "Oh," she replied, "I had to do that to fit it into the pan."

Another great example is the story of why railroad tracks are 4 feet 5.8 inches wide.

Here's the order of how it happened. The people that designed and built the first railroads in America were brought over from Europe. In Europe the width of the railroads is 4 feet 5.8 inches wide. It's simple; they reproduced what they had done before. Just as we all are prone to do.

But why were the rails that exact distance apart in the first place? Answer: Wagon wheels were that distance apart. When the train rails were built, they reproduced what they knew.

Why were wagon wheels always just that distance apart? Answer: If any designer tried to design outside of that width, they ran the risk of wheels not running in the ruts already created by other wagon wheels.

Why were wagon wheels designed that far apart in the first place? Answer: Roman chariots had already caused ruts in the road. When designing updated versions of the chariots—wagons—it was considered easier to go with the width set by the chariots.

Finally, why were Roman chariot wheels that far apart? Answer: We have finally reached the real reason for the choice of 4 feet 5.8 inches. In Roman times, it was an obvious and perfectly practical reason. Two horses pulled the Roman wagons. In order to balance out the chariot perfectly the wheels had to be this strange width to accommodate two horses' rear ends. And now—over 2,000 years later—we are still riding on rails that are based on the width of two horses' rear ends!

How many things are we doing because that's how it's always been? Moment by moment we need to question why we are doing what we are doing. Imagine outside of how it has always been. Live from an infinite Truth and life expands.

TYPES OF HABITS.

Once you realize that the world is your own projection, you will be free of it, a guru told his followers, everything existing around you is painted on the screen of your consciousness. The picture you see may be ugly or beautiful, but in either case you are not bound by it. Rest assured, there is no one who has forced it on you.

You are trapped only because of your habit of mistaking the imaginary for the real.—Aldous Huxley

There are many types of habits. A very popular one is the habit of struggle, which often turns up in another of its forms, the habit of poverty. I realized recently how intrusive the habit of struggle was for me. Although I was no longer always cash poor, I wondered why life had not expanded more fully for me in the area of money.

I didn't attach emotion to this question, but continued to express, as clearly as I knew how, my Spiritual identity as a idea of the Infinite Loving One. While walking down the street one day I had an Angel Idea news flash. "You have a habit of struggle. You have never stepped out of it because you are so good at it."

I am good at it. While raising my three children and being the wife of struggling musicians, I learned how to live well within limitations. I made my own furniture and clothes, I bargain shopped, worked extra jobs, painted, pasted, hooked rugs, and traded services so that I looked like I had more cash than I did.

Someone once said to me, "I wish I had the money you do." If that person had known that I had less than $10 in the bank, I'm sure he would have withdrawn his wish. I learned to enjoy the creativity of making struggle not look like a struggle.

However, I forgot to translate the enjoyment of creativity into a bigger picture that no longer involved struggle, but was simply the expression of infinite supply.

WAKE UP.

Who are you? I am awake.—Buddha

Are we awake? If we're awake we're moving into the state of Grace and waking out of the hypnotic state of the conditioned worldview. When I was in my first year of college, my philosophy class teacher gave us the Four Steps of Hypnotism. If we analyze these, we can see how we have agreed to participate in our own hypnotism, or how we succumb to the master hypnotists, our culture, and the worldview.

It is no exaggeration to say that every human being is hypnotized to some extent, either by ideas he has uncritically accepted from others, or by ideas he has repeated to himself or convinced himself are true.—Maxwell Maltz

1. Agree to play by their rules.

This first step is so important. We agree to participate in someone else's stated rules. This is consent. Consent in any culture constitutes contagion. We know it as the power of suggestion.

In October 1998, Oprah staged a demonstration on her show. She told her audience as they were waiting for the show to begin, they were going to release a strong odor. They were told this over and over again. Although they never did release an odor, some of the audience members gave detailed descriptions of what it smelled like.

We agree constantly to the rules that our families, friends, and the world have made. What makes them true? Nothing at all, except our agreement. We have agreed to play by "their" rules in order to fit in and survive.

2. Agree to something that you know is not true.

The stereotypical hypnotist tells patients that they are sleepy. They agree even if it is not true. How many times on a daily basis do we agree to something we know is not true? For example: An overwhelming number of us have agreed that there is not enough—of anything. We believe and accept the worldview of lack. We don't have enough time, money, love, patience, joy, peace, food, pleasure, understanding...Yes? And yet, in the core of our being, we know this is not true.

Even if we have had only the briefest glimpse of God's State of Grace, we know that there is an infinite amount of everything. In every glimpse of God, we gain a deeper conviction that the Infinite Loving One is All, and as Its reflection, we have all that It is.

3. Turn your thought inward.

This is a surprising part of hypnotism, but on closer analysis, the truth of it appears. What the hypnotist is asking us to do is close our eyes and become alone. When we pull back and turn inward to where we no longer feel the connection to others, we have separated ourselves from Divine Love. In this state of mind, we isolate ourselves, thinking no one would understand.

We hide in our homes and our bodies so that we will not have to participate or come out and play. When things start getting worse, instead of seeking help outside ourselves we retreat, hoping no one will notice. Actually, we believe that no one is noticing and that's why we retreat. Like babies who think they are hidden when they cover their eyes, we think that when we can't see out, no one can see in.

This state of mind keeps us from seeking both physical and spiritual assistance. Hypnotic suggestion gains power when we are isolated.

4. Agree not to do something that you know you can do.

Finally, our hypnotist says something like, "You can't raise your arm." We agree even though we know we can raise it. Think back. What did you love to do as a child that you thought you were pretty good at? Did anyone ever tell you either that you couldn't do it or that it just wasn't done the way you wanted to do it, and you agreed?

When I started college, I thought about being an architect. A counselor actually took me around the college and showed me the rooms where the architects were studying, so that I could see that they were all men. He also reminded me that my weakness was math, and of course, I would need a lot of that. Without a fight, I backed off and switched to interior design.

This turned out not to be what I wanted and I continued to switch majors for a while, looking for what felt right. It might have been architecture if someone had encouraged me, or if I had not already agreed that I could not do it.

Let's wake up to Truth. To correct a habit or move into Truth does not involve more hypnotism. Using hypnotism to cure something is like altering a shadow. It is trying to solve what appears as a physical problem with another even deeper physical problem. Let's add more light to whatever appears as a problem. We are waking out of our darkness and moving into light, not fixing a symptom.

BREAK THE SPELL.

Facts do not cease to exist because they are ignored. —Aldous Huxley

To break a spell, whether cast intentionally or unintentionally, we must first recognize that it is not a spell at all. It is only a suggestion, an illusion. It has no power but the power we give it by believing in its reality. Remember, since there is only One power—God—then there is no reason to fear another power that actually does not exist.

If someone says we can't do something, we don't have to agree. We start first with who we truly are—each of us is the expression of Divine Mind. We listen to the Angel Ideas' guidance as to our motivation. We declare what we know to be True, and the spell is broken.

Sometimes the hardest thing to do is to continue stating and believing that we do know even when it feels like we don't. Repeating to ourselves "I don't know" puts us into the hypnotic mental state of not knowing.

Wake up. State that you do know. Don't continue to fall into the loop of untrue suggestions. In the core of yourself, you know. There is no other Truth.

Since we are the Am in I Am, we do know. When the spell is broken, we will remember.

Do not believe what your teacher tells you merely out of respect for the teacher.—Buddha

VIRUS PROTECTION FOR OUR MINDS.

Evil (ignorance) is like a shadow—it has no real substance of its own, it is simply a lack of light. You cannot cause a shadow to disappear by trying to fight it, stamp on it, by railing against it, or any other form of emotional or physical resistance. In order to cause a shadow to disappear, you must shine light on it.—Shakti Gawain, *Creative Visualization*

As part of my personal commitment to provide perception-Shifting information to as many people as possible I put a lot of information out on the Internet. As a result, my email is in many people's mailboxes. Every time a new computer virus comes out, I am flooded with emails containing the virus.

I have a few choices. First, I could stop participating in the Internet. This choice I can't make because I wish to remain in integrity with God, and because I know one of the rules of the Earth game is to participate and express who we are. My second choice is to protect myself from the viruses. This is the choice I make. I protect myself by being aware of the danger and by always having and using the latest virus protections.

This is a perfect example of the necessity of Being Aware of the difference between signs and symbols of what is True and the reversal of what is True. Jesus told us to be as wise as serpents and as harmless as doves.

Just because we know the untruth and powerlessness of evil does not mean it is smart to ignore it or pretend that it doesn't claim to exist. In this case, it exists because there are those, who not knowing their God-self, are being used as tools for evil to claim its presence. The Internet as a symbol of our Oneness is also a symbol of what can happen when we allow human will and greed to take over.

When human will is in control it is much easier for evil to use us to make itself appear real. Yes, there are some people who seem to love being evil's pawn. Trying to understand why isn't going to help either them or us. As we acknowledge the Truth, we will know how to combat the virus and also free them from evil's hold.

One way that evil maintains a hold on all of us is by using the quality of curiosity to get our attention. Curiosity in itself is a wonderful thing. In the hands of someone who is manipulating our curiosity to get us to participate in evil, it is not.

For example, when the computer viruses arrive by email, the virus protection program asks me what I want to do with it. I can delete it, contain it, or try to "cure" it. Until I knew better I would be tempted not to delete it—just in case I wanted to know what it was. Then, even after it was deleted, the email carrying it would still be in my in-box and I would have to suppress my curiosity to open it before I completely trashed it.

If we remember that the worldview—the conditioned mind, our personality and glittering image—does not want us to know God because that knowledge will destroy it, we will be less tempted to participate in any of evil's attempts to be pleasurable.

How many times do we have to be told?

Success is never final.—Winston Churchill

As in many activities, dance is something that is practiced over and over again. The ballet barre is a perfect example of using repetition to achieve perfection. No matter where in the world a ballet class is being taught, it is taught basically in the same way. As a beginning ballet student, everyone learns the same steps that the most advanced performer is still doing many years later, every day.

Standing at the ballet barre, the students hear the same instructions, over and over. Pull up, straighten your knees, and bend from the hip, stretch out—over and over and over again, from beginner to advanced.

There is a purpose to saying the same thing over and over again. It is to assist the students in building a strong base that will allow them to "fly" later. It is to help learn what is important and what is not necessary.

Beginner dancers use every part of their body to do even a small movement, and that is why a beginner often appears awkward. The polished dancer uses only what is necessary. The grace of dancers shines through in what they are not doing as much as in what they are doing. Doing it over and over again you learn to let go of what is not necessary to achieve the movement. It is learning to balance strength and stretch in order to achieve what looks like effortless movement.

One time I had a revelation while taking a ballet class. After ten years of taking class, the teacher said the same thing she always said, and I heard it differently.

In fact, I heard it so differently that a light bulb went on in my head that totally changed how I approached dance from that day forward.

Why? Because we change our perceptions in every moment, depending on a large variety of circumstances. And it is our perceptions that determine what and how we see and hear and act. I had finally advanced enough, or cleared enough other stuff out, to hear it so differently that I shifted to a completely new level of perception.

It is not a bad thing that we are told over and over and over. It is a good thing. Each telling Shifts us, and each time we act on what we learn Shifts us again and then the next telling brings us higher—in an ever-expanding circle. This is not a circle that brings us back to where we started from, but an expanding spiral that brings us around to hear it again, in a new way.

How many times do we have to be told anything? We have to be told over and over. All lessons are basically the same. Instead of despairing over this, we should rejoice. Someone loves us enough to keep reminding us of our innate perfection. We keep Shifting our perceptions and growing enough to hear it differently. There is no greater feeling than hearing the same thing we have always heard and hearing it so differently that the world Shifts into brighter hues.

No matter what your dream is, it involves the same lessons as a ballet barre. Using what is necessary in each moment and letting go of what is not achieves grace in all areas of life. Going back to how it was...is not going forward. Repetition can sometimes be a beautiful thing. It lifts us up and out to greater heights of awareness. Keep telling and keep listening. Revelation is a shift of perception to what has always been here.

Habit with him was all the test of truth, it must be right: I've done it from my youth. —George Crabbe

BREAKDOWN TO BREAKTHROUGH.

Sometimes we learn the hard way. Sometimes we break down. The choice is ours as to what to do with this opportunity. If we choose to add more negativity to what already feels negative we have entered the "dense zone."

We have chosen to play the duality game. We have attached emotion to the negative. We ask, "Why would God do this to us?" We have made God a creator of "bad." We are thinking that there is both good and bad. We are reverting to the habit of separation.

The only way to overcome this separation is to continually acknowledge that God is present wherever we are, and to recognize that in Reality everything is an activity of God.

If we choose to see the untruth of the breakdown, and use it to reaffirm who and what we are, we enter the "zone of light." With this Shift in perception, the resulting breakthrough will bless us and those we love. We will have become more like the Truth of our being, the expression of Infinite Love. We will inspire and encourage.

Shift what you perceive to be reality. Ask yourself, "What does this situation suggest I believe to be reality?" Then return to placing God First and acknowledging Spiritual Reality.

Seek and ask.

Knowing that God supplies us in every moment with everything we could ever hope for does not relieve us from the responsibility to express ourselves and take action. As we Shift out of our ruts and hear Angel Ideas, we get glimpses of ideas about things to do. These are usually not big things to do, like Joan of Arc's gathering of an army, but smaller, more day-to-day actions.

Such an action may not even seem related to anything we are working to accomplish. It could be as simple as taking a walk to the corner, calling a person, writing a letter, or smiling at a stranger. Although following these Angel Ideas may not always appear to us to have direct results, we can be sure that it does have results. Sometimes we can look and see how taking just one seemingly small step changed the course of our lives.

TAKE WHAT ACTION?

If you don't have the full approval of your conscience and your reason, you'd better not do the thing you're contemplating.—Napoleon Hill, Think and Grow Rich

How do we know which thoughts to follow, after all Maxwell Maltz said we have 50,000 negative thoughts a day. We can all tell stories of following a thought that was not the wisest course of action. In the Chapter entitled Angel Ideas, we talked about the difference between impel and compel, and thoughts and ideas. There is another way we can be Obsessively Vigilant about our actions to more carefully ensure that we are following wisdom.

There are three steps to taking action. As with a three-legged stool, all three steps are necessary for a firm foundation.

• The first step is, allow an idea to appear. These Angel Ideas are true wealth and are always present; we just need to be willing to recognize them.

• The second step is, wait for a positive feeling about the idea. If you have an idea to make soap and nothing moves you from within about this idea, pass on it or pass it on.

• The third step is to know the mission of the idea, i.e., the way to do it. If you have an idea to make soap and you feel wonderful about it, the next step is to find out how to make soap. We don't need to know everything about soap making, just enough to get started. Perhaps it is a trip to the library, or calling a friend.

Wait patiently for each step in the triangle of action and then do it!

The heights by great men reached and kept / Were not attained by sudden flight, / But they, while their companions slept, / Were toiling upward in the night.—Henry Wadsworth Longfellow

SEE MIRACLES.

Universal Law is impartial and unemotional.—Stewart Wilde, Miracles

Sometimes we wait for what we call miracles. Not only is this waiting not a form of action, we are waiting for something that is already always happening. All there is are miracles. That's right, only miracles.

When our perception is in tune with the song of the Infinite Loving One, we are privileged to see more and more proofs in our life that there is only One Mind.

A miracle in the traditional sense cannot be true. This is the miracle that steps in and changes a situation in such a wonderful way that it must be miraculous. It implies that the Laws of God can be broken or sidestepped. This kind of miracle has us praying to a god that arbitrarily grants favors to those he thinks have prayed the wisest and need him the most. This is not Infinite Love in action. This is the result of shifting a personal paradigm that believes that God brings both good and evil and can be charmed into changing and bending his rules for us. This shifted paradigm can often produce the result we are asking for, and we call it a miracle. If health issues are involved, we call it a faith healing.

This is not the providence of One Mind. This One Mind knows nothing about the stories we tell of the illusions we live. Infinite Love just exists. As we shift our paradigms to include this understanding, and begin to take informed action in thought and deed, our world does Shift and produce what others call miracles. In this case these are not miracles, but Reality.

We heal any situation by knowing the eternal perfection of the One Mind. We know that as we align our thought with our highest understanding of what God sees and thinks we will live miraculous lives. Thus the statement "It is too good to be true," is backwards. The statement should read, "If it is good, it must be True." The river of abundance is always flowing. We just have to step in! Miracles are God's Laws in operation, in every moment.

STAY IN TRUTH.

Never let present results dictate the image of what you hold in your mind.—Florence Shinn

As we begin the Shift from rut living to unlimited abundance we will begin to notice people, places and things that are having a problem. As part of that noticing, we may begin to feel that we need to "fix the problem."

If fixing the problem requires us to go down to the problem, we must not make that choice. The wisest way to fix a problem is to apply what we know of Truth to it. If we can begin to see whatever looks like a problem as a reversal of Truth, or a hidden symbol of Truth, the problem will either dissolve or correct.

There is a wonderful story in the Bible in the book of Nehemiah about not "coming down." If we take the rebuilding of Jerusalem's walls as symbolic in the One Mind's language, we can see what the storyteller was trying to tell us.

The storyteller explains how the walls (defenses) of the city (thought) were destroyed by the enemy. Has this ever happened to you? It is a time of great vulnerability. The King's cupbearer (the part of you that is strong and protective of you) goes to the King (the part of you that knows who you are) and asks permission to rebuild. Of course, permission is granted. Nehemiah travels to Jerusalem and gathers others to begin the building. Not long thereafter, a messenger from the enemy, Sanballat, arrives with an invitation. "So hey—let's get together and talk" (let's do lunch).

Now why would the person who has destroyed our city suddenly be interested in talking? Because we are taking our life back, rebuilding our protection. He knows that he had better get to us before the walls are up. Some of us, thinking that it would only be right and kind (to whom?), go down and meet with the enemy.

I cannot begin to count the times I have "gone down" to meet with the enemy. What happened? My walls were broken down once more and I had to begin the repair process all over again. One day, I realized who I must be kind to first. Guess!

Moreover, you must be kind to yourself first, too! Do not go down! In this wonderful story, Nehemiah uses some of his manpower to build and some to protect what they had built so far. Finally, Nehemiah sent his own messenger saying, "I am doing a great work, so that I cannot come down..." (Nehemiah 6:3)

Truth does not go down, it brings up. Those who do not want to let go of limited personal beliefs are often unhappy when we chose to move "up" to Truth. In the seventies, everyone around me was drinking and using some form of recreational drug. Although I wanted to be part of the group, I immediately knew that it was the wrong decision for me. That didn't stop others from trying to talk me into participating. The favorite argument—knowing of my desire to be of service—was, "How will you know how to help others if you haven't experienced their lifestyle?" Carried to its logical conclusion this is absurd since it would mean everyone should live in utter depression and poverty before they are of value to the world. Yet most of us have accepted a version of this argument at one time or another. Do not go down.

However, it is important to take the information that we're learning and apply it to our lives in practical ways. It does not do any good to sit around and think about how wonderful God is while our children are hungry. We are expected to take action while knowing Truth.

I was reminded of this one time when doing laundry. I had methodically piled the coins on my kitchen counter, pulled the laundry together and headed down the hall of my apartment building. It was only after I arrived at the laundry room that I realized I had left the quarters on the counter. Without the money, all my careful preparation was useless.

In the same way, all the studying and understanding in the world will be of no use if we leave it on the counter. We need to take what we know and put it to use. One day we will witness with full clarity that we do not have to die in order to reach Heaven, we are already in it.

In the meantime, utilize what you know now to begin to heal the world within you, the world close to you, and the world that appears far from you. Know the Truth, and it will set you and all of us free. To heal the world, remember you are the world, because what is "outside" is actually "inside." Start here.

Knowledge is of no value unless you put it into practice.—Huber J. Grath

REDEFINE YOURSELF.

The only lasting way to improve the quality of our lives is to improve the quality of our perceptions. The highest perception is to know the Truth about who we all are, and to always base our actions on that Truth.

We will begin to build our own internal knowing that cannot be shaken as we collect evidence and express gratitude for what we have been given. If we are diligent in this process, we can live lives of continuous gratitude in the State of Grace.

Practical Obsessive Vigilance.

One of the greatest gifts we have received is the gift of camaraderie. We can use this gift to our advantage if we join together within small mastermind groups and choose to live the principles of God as we build our lives.

"Mastermind Alliance" is a term Dale Carnegie coined to describe the power unleashed when two or more people are working together in harmony toward a common goal. The goal should be a shared sense of mission.

Pick those whose purpose you believe in and understand and who believe in and understand yours. It is a given that their integrity level must be at least on the same level as yours.

With this group of people that you trust completely, begin meeting to share your dreams and the actions that you are taking to complete them.

Pay attention to habits by using this personal journal and questionnaire:

I noticed the following daily habits.

This is the habit I would like to change.

This is how I would feel if I changed this habit.

The smallest fact is a window through which the infinite may be seen.—Aldous Huxley

15

ELEVEN

When a train goes through a tunnel and it gets dark, you don't throw away the ticket and jump off. You sit still and trust the engineer.—Corrie Ten Boom

Our faith comes in moments. Our vice is habitual. Yet, there is a depth in these brief moments which constrains us to ascribe to them more reality than all other experiences.—Ralph Waldo Emerson

At this point, we have done all the right things. We have put God First, Repented, tuned in to listen for Angel Ideas, Chosen Consciously, Imagined what we wish to see, practiced Obsessive Vigilance and still nothing changes. In fact, it may feel as if things have gotten worse. What is happening?

Have you ever attached a hose to the water faucet, turned on the water and nothing came out? Baffled, you look back at the hose and notice a kink that is blocking the flow of water. This is a perfect picture of what has happened.

We don't need to hook ourselves up to our supply. We have always been hooked up to the Source called One Infinite Mind. We don't need to turn on this Source, since it is always "running." Having understood this, we have stepped out into life with our hose—and still only a drop of water comes out.

This is not a result of God's law not working; it is because we have not shifted our perception to include the presence of God. There is a kink. In this case, the hose gets kinked when we believe, or act out of the belief, that there is more than one power and/or that we are separate from the One Power. This kink takes many forms and blocks our view of Heaven.

Ye shall know the truth and the truth shall set you free. —Jesus Christ

THE WORLD IS THE MIRROR.

To discover the kinks in the abundance hose, it is helpful to know what to look for. Often we are so involved with day-to-day living that we do not really know what our belief system is. An easy way to discover it is to look at the life we are living and then ask: "What does this tell me about what I think is true?"

In this instance, we are using the 2nd and 3rd Steps to Shift. We are Becoming Aware and Understanding Signs and Symbols. The world acts as a mirror. Since everything begins with our point of view, then what we see outside ourselves is what we first believed to be true internally.

We can interpret what our world mirror reflects back to us in two ways. We can ask if it is a symbol of what is True or the opposite of what is True.

If it is a symbol, then you can ask yourself what qualities of God does it represent. Then use this symbol as a guide to help you understand and be grateful for what already exists and is yours now in the highest form you perceive through your current understanding of Reality.

If it is the opposite of what is True, you can easily turn back to the First Law—God First. This will counteract any claim that it may be making as to what is really True.

Turning to God First works for two reasons. First: As we Shift our perception to Truth, that Shift must yield results—as all perception governs reality. Second: As we become conscious of the Truth, our human mind yields to the Spiritual One Mind, which is always present. We have entered the realm of Grace. Then what once appeared as a material world Shifts to appear to us more as it really is, Spiritual.

Let's look at a simple example of these two ways to see a symbol. In the fall we see animals busy preparing for winter. As symbols, they are representing the qualities of diligence, caring, support, and love for themselves and their families.

On the other hand, you may see these very same animals getting into things and causing trouble as they prepare for winter. This would be the opposite of what was True. To correct the problem, go Back to One and see the qualities as they really are.

Both involve flexing your spiritual muscle and thought process. As you do this, you continue to build your inner conviction of Truth.

TEMPTATIONS.

Question whether your automatic thoughts are actually yours.—Alan Loy McGinns, *The Power of Optimism*

What all kinks do is block our view of what is real and eternal and the abundance that is already present. All kinks in the hose have their basis in temptation.

When Jesus was tempted by the devil, he did not accept the temptation as coming from within. Even though the devil spoke in Jesus' voice, Jesus was clear that it was an untrue suggestion and not part of him. His statement "Get thee behind me Satan" explains perfectly what we are to do when faced with temptations.

Before we look at what these temptations are, let's be clear that a temptation is not a statement of fact, but a request to us that we believe a suggestion. Actually, request is much too polite. This suggestion often comes to us subtly, but it is actually a demand upon us to believe a falsity parading as Truth.

Here are some temptations that the voice (claiming to be our own) says to us and wants us to believe. The first temptation revolves around the suggestion that the Principles that we have been learning about don't really work. This is a temptation not to believe that there is an Infinite God, One Mind.

The second temptation declares, "OK so what. Even if there is a God, It isn't here for me." This temptation separates us from God and everyone else. It appears to make our case special.

The third temptation says, "Yes, God's principles work, but not all the time." This statement does not carry one element of truth, since Principle or Law based on Truth always works. It is impossible for it not to work, since God is All-Powerful.

The next set of temptations moves us into different types of ruts. There is the suggestion that it is good to suffer. To some of us this is a treasured statement. We have suffered so much that we hope there's a good reason. But God, perfect Love, could not have made us to suffer.

Our suffering is a result only of being out of tune with Reality. One result of suffering is that it can hasten us to God First and to tune into and receive the blessings that naturally follow from being one with the One Mind. Staying in suffering is not required, necessary, or desirable. Suffering is sin. It is missing the mark. As in all cases of missing the mark—we will suffer only as long as we believe that it is right to suffer.

The temptation to be a victim is similar. We can get quite a bang for our buck with this one in the material world, as we can bend others to our will by claiming to be and acting from a state of victim-hood. However, putting God First and Repenting will immediately eliminate any desire to remain a victim.

And then there is the subtlest temptation of all. It is the temptation to believe that there is comfort in matter. As we become more and more in tune with what is True, as we understand how to change things back into thoughts, and thus live from Infinite Love, our material circumstances begin to change for the better, and this is good. However, as this occurs we are tempted to become comfortable with the results. We are tempted to think that all we were doing was attempting to better our material circumstances. We are tempted to forget that our goal is to wake up to Truth, not to be comfortable in what is not true.

FEAR.

Only the fearless are free.—Guy Finley

A huge view-blocker is fear. Fear is the result of doubt. A basic fear surfaces when we are tempted (more temptation!) to believe that we are not connected to God or that God is not the Only Power. This fear suggests to us that there is no solution to our problem, whatever it is. Or we are afraid that if help ever comes, it will be too late. Sometimes the fear is just that the negative, nagging voice in our head really is our own voice. None of these suggestions are true, because we are never separated from God.

A Sunday school teacher asked her class if they thought they would be afraid if they were in the middle of the ocean all alone. The entire class affirmed that yes, they would be, all except one little boy. When asked why he wouldn't be afraid, he said, "God would be with me."

"How do you know that God would be with you?" she asked. "Because I would be there," he replied.

When it is dark enough, you can see the stars. —Ralph Waldo Emerson

ADDICTION

Those who are unhappy have no need for anything in this world but people capable of giving them attention. —Simone Weil

Addictions of any kind block our view and kink our hose. Addiction keeps us feeling separate. We are all aware of the "big" addictions like drugs and alcohol. However, there is an addiction that all of us fall prey to if we are not watching our thought carefully; it is an addiction to the life we live.

We may not like our life, but we know how it works. We are afraid that if we let go and Shift, things will change, which of course they will. However, for many of us, change means that since we will not know what is coming next, we will not be able to control it. Addiction of all kinds has one cure at its core. It is becoming aware of being connected and cared for by the One Love. Then we can let go and yield as the first Spiritual Law demands of us.

The willing contemplation of vice is vice. —Arabic proverb

ABUSE

People who are willing to give up freedom for the sake of short-term security, deserve neither freedom nor security. —Benjamin Franklin

Abuse blocks our view, whether we are on the receiving or the giving end of it. Sometimes the greatest abuse is occurring within our self to our self. Unless we are observant, we might miss it.

During the time that I was experiencing a drought of cash flow, I had to drop off a document in Beverly Hills. I had exactly one dime and one quarter in my pocket, and parking in Beverly Hills is very expensive. I managed to find an out-of-the-way parking slot. I pulled out my quarter and popped it in, figuring it would be just the time I needed to drop off the document. Then I read what the meter said. I realized that I could have just put in my dime. On this day, I had been practicing listening to the internal "monkey mind" and at that point it went crazy.

The tirade went on for quite a while, but what it said in essence was "How could you be such a complete idiot? Even an idiot knows how to spend money better than you do. You are such a loser and it is no wonder you don't have any money."

Wow! I could not believe the abuse over just one quarter. The only thing that the voice said that had any truth in it was "No wonder you don't have any money." How was I ever going to see the abundance that was mine when I was hosting an abusive voice that told me I was more than incompetent and that there was never enough for me?

I would never have let a person stay in my house who spoke to me that way. I would have been shocked to hear someone else say that to anyone, and would have been quick to defend the one who was attacked.

"How long had this been going on?" I wondered.

I began the process of kicking out the abuser because I knew it was not an Angel Idea. It was not my thought. It was not true. For me the easiest way to rid myself of internal abusive thoughts is to give the voice a form, make it a monster, a person, a dragon, whatever is appropriate for the moment. In my thought I turn and confront the abuser, tell it I will not be spoken to that way nor treated in that manner, and that it is not telling the truth. I then do something to get rid of it, even if it is just kicking it out my mental door.

The first step in ridding oneself of this insidious pest is to listen to what it has been telling us about ourselves for all of our life. The next step is to realize that this is not your voice even if it sounds like it. Of course, it sounds like you. How else could it get you to listen?

Then the next step is to do as Jesus did—command it to get behind us.

SYMBOLIC DOORS.

Anything that requires us to go through a symbolic door to get to God and Infinite Love acts as a kink in the hose. This includes putting our faith in superstition, luck, ghosts, cycles, preachers, people, or channeling to the exclusion of God. It includes the belief that money or time defines the quality of our life. We kink our hose when we accept other people's thoughts as our own, refuse to forgive, or not notice that one door is closed and another is open. Our hose gets kinked when we have a conflict of values, ask for the "wrong" thing, hold on to paradigms, or host depression.

FIGHTING.

If we could read the secret history of our enemies, we should find in each man's life sorrow and suffering enough to disarm all hostility.—Henry Wadsworth Longfellow

At the end of the talk, someone from the audience asked the Dalai Lama, "Why didn't you fight back against the Chinese?" The Dalai Lama looked down, swung his feet just a bit, then looked back up and said with a gentle smile, "Well, war is obsolete, you know." Then, after a few moments, his face grave, he said, "Of course the mind can rationalize fighting back...but the heart, the heart would never understand. Then you would be divided in yourself, the heart and the mind, and the war would be inside you."

It is hard to consistently experience God's ever-flowing Love when we are kinking Love's supply because of conflict. Usually the conflict is within—and it is expressed outwardly to those around us. We handle conflict in three ways:

- By fighting and not listening to each other because we are too busy arguing our points.

- By avoidance, no one wants to talk about it.

- Facing it in a way that will remove the kink by validation—where we listen to each other, validate each other's point of view, and reconcile.

What will never work is fighting. When we battle the human mortal mind, or evil beliefs in any form, we give it the power it needs to exist. If we are fighting we are not aware, or conscious of, the One Love and our emotion is in fear. This is why wars create more of the same problem.

Overcoming whatever appears as evil by understanding Truth, and forgiving those who have become the pawns of evil, at times seems more than we can do. Nevertheless, we can, and we must.

We cannot ask God to help us fight our enemies, as God does not know any enemies. This is trying to use God to get what we want. Not only will it not work, but also in doing so we become the problem. Peace comes to everyone as we declare the Truth of each person and situation.

Men never do evil so completely and cheerfully as when they do it from religious conviction.—Blaise Pascal

Jesus said, "Ye ask, and receive not because ye ask amiss, that ye may consume it upon your lusts." (James 4:3) If we are not getting what we want, we may be asking amiss. But what did Jesus mean? Perhaps we are asking for the thing instead of the understanding of Truth, or the quality. For example:

- We may be asking for something that is only for our material completion or pleasure. Maybe what we want is not right for us.

- We may not be acting or thinking within the Principles of unconditional Love.

- We may not have put God First.

- It may be harmful to others or ourselves.

Another reason you may not be receiving what you are asking for is maybe you are not asking big enough. Have you ever applied for a job and were turned down? Perhaps you thought, "I could have done that job easily." Maybe that was the problem. It wasn't big enough to allow you to grow more Godward.

During my cash flow drought, I finally decided to go back to a day job to supplement my writing and consulting. However, no matter what I applied for I was constantly turned down. I finally realized that I was just looking for a job to pay my bills, the easier the better. I was not looking to express Infinite Mind in any of them. I woke up to the understanding that I had to stretch myself and do what I was really qualified to do, even though at the time Beca was not too happy about it. Of course, I got that job and it blessed everyone, including me.

There are more tears shed after answered prayers than unanswered ones. —St. Teresa of Avila

We are often protected from our choices. During the time I was looking for jobs, I applied for what appeared to be the perfect job for me, and it seemed I was the perfect person for it too. I didn't get it. Since I was positive it was the perfect job for me I couldn't understand what had happened. Years later a scandal broke around the people I would have been working for. Had I landed that job I would have walked right into the middle of it. In fact, the person who held that job ended up in jail. I was protected, even though at the time I thought I was being denied.

Think bigger than today and your tiny day-to-day needs. Pick a dream big enough that it will outlast you. Decide to express the fullest understanding of God's qualities that you know you have.

Here's another list of reasons why you may not be getting what you want:

- You are asking for something that you really don't want, but you feel that you should want it, or it's something that you used to want.

- You have a hidden fear of the responsibility of getting it.

- You already have it but don't see it, as it doesn't fit into what you believe you deserve, or the package it came in looks different from what you expected.

- You succumbed to an underlying pessimism in your thought, or you accepted an outside influence or belief as reality.

Whatever we are asking for must be in line with our expression of God. We must ask with boldness, ethics, and clarity, and then take action.

LYING.

God dwells in you, as you. Everything is a manifestation of that. When you finally realize that, you can't lie to yourself. When you're part of a negative thing—demeaning someone or denying them food or dignity—you know it.—Charles Haid

What is lying? Lying is not telling the truth, as we currently know it. We do it all the time. We lie every day as part of our life. We stretch the truth, don't tell the whole truth, don't reexamine our thoughts and update them. We lie to survive. We lie to get. We protect our "glittering image" our small-i. This is the person claiming to be who we are, acting out, and arranging our life in ways that are not truthful to our Spiritual being. We call this our personality.

This glittering image can ruin our lives if we do not consistently reexamine what we are saying and doing. The "I" that is the expression of God does not need to lie to survive, because it is always overflowing with joy and grace. The glittering image must lie to survive and in doing so kinks the supply hose.

Every once in a while I take a day and really listen to what I am saying, writing, and thinking. I ask myself, "Is this true?" On one of these "lie examination days," I bought a Starbucks Frappuccino, a treat for the week, and went to board the L.A. Metro. On the way into the station, I casually glanced at a sign that had one of those big red circles over a food picture.

"Oh phooey," I thought, "I just bought this drink. It will be okay to drink it while I am getting the ticket, but I will just throw it away before I board the train." That is what I did. I gulped it, not really enjoying it because I had to drink it so quickly, and then threw the cup away as the train pulled in. Just at that instant, a huge Metro police officer appeared at my left shoulder. "Did you see the sign?" he asked. "No," I said. "Well," he said, "You can't drink in the station or on the train, but you can carry it with you to your destination." "Thanks," I said, and he let me step on the train without giving me the very expensive ticket.

I sat down and replayed the whole scene in my mind. I was shocked to realize how many times in a space of five minutes that I had lied—and lied well! First, although I had seen the sign, I didn't read it, so I couldn't follow what it said. Second, I tried to beat the system; whatever I thought it was, by drinking my drink before anyone saw me. Third, I told the police officer that I didn't see the sign at all. Fourth, I got on the train before I could get the ticket—smiling sweetly of course.

So we think these are small lies and not important? Yes, they are small but they are still important. All lies point to the need to hide from Truth because we are not clear that there is only One Loving Mind. They allow the glittering image that is hiding the real "I" to stay in power. The glittering image does not want to die. As we step into the Truth of who we are, it knows it will vanish. In moments of distress, this false self is saying, "Help me, don't let me die." There is no reason to protect or keep alive this false self. When it dies, we do not die—instead we begin to live the life we were meant to live.

We established this glittering image in order to protect ourselves. As we grow Godward, we no longer need it. Thank it for protecting you when you needed it, and then let it go.

We must tell the truth to ourselves about the kinks in our hose and our dreams. We also have to be careful about looking again at our current understanding of what is true. Hopefully, every day we have a clearer understanding. If we are still answering and living from yesterday's understanding, we are lying. Denial kills the essence of who we are. Without Truth, life will become and remain hell.

THE FIRST AND ONLY LIE.

The reason good people suffer, is they think they are people. —John Hargreaves

The devil tells us that all we see is all there is. —Carolyn Myss

The devil can cite Scripture for his purpose. —William Shakespeare

There is really only one thing that we have to combat. That is the belief that there is another mind besides God and this other mind has power. There is not an alternative power. There is only One Infinite Omniscient Mind. That fact does not leave even the tiniest bit of room for anything unlike God. The appearance of another power is the temptation to believe in duality. When we accept duality, we succumb to the temptation to believe that all that exists is just what we can see. We have given the tempter power. Take it back.

The Lord's Prayer asks God to deliver us from the belief in the evil one.

The world, our mirror, gives us symbols to help us understand this truth and to uncover the lie. We know that there is more to life than what we see. We cannot see the wind, or music. We cannot see love, honor, peace, and so on. We do see their effects, so we know they are real. We can also see the effects of knowing that there is only One Mind and that it is good.

Watching for and paying attention to these symbols will lead us to Truth and Grace, which have no paradigm to limit or filter the infinitude of God.

THE PERFECT KINK REMOVER: GRATITUDE.

The person who has stopped being thankful has fallen asleep in life.—Robert Louis Stevenson

If your kink in the hose is not obvious to you, move on to gratitude. A grateful heart always starts the Unkinking process. Sometimes thankfulness is all that is needed to start and continue the flow. If you have ever been depressed, you know how hard it is to move to gratitude.

The part of you that claims to be who you are doesn't want to give up its mood. It gets something from it. Depression is always self-centered. The glittering image, claiming to be you, gets value out of the depression.

Take control of your thinking and your life. Begin a gratitude list. Thoughts have no power to stop your connection to your eternal Source.

The best cure for worry, depression, melancholy, brooding, is to go deliberately forth and try to lift with one's sympathy the gloom of somebody else.—Arnold Bennett

THE FULFILLMENT COMES IN THE SEED.

I am only one, but still I am one. I cannot do everything but still I can do something. And because I cannot do everything I will not refuse to something that I can do.—Helen Keller

Just as an acorn has all that is necessary within it to grow a tree, all Angel Ideas have all that is necessary already provided for within them. All God's paths have the preparation laid. If we find ourselves walking a path that seems barren, there are only two possible explanations.

The first is that is it not barren but we're blind to what is there, because of our state of mind.

The second is that the path does not lead us closer to God. In either case, shifting our perception to the Truth of who we are and what God is will immediately provide the "things" we need.

This Shifting will open our eyes either to the provisions for the path we're on, or to the fact that we must change to a road leading to Truth, on which we will be amply and abundantly supplied.

Practical Unkinking.

Pick someone you like least and write a gratitude list of his or her wonderful qualities. I often do this exercise in The Shift® class, and it is really wonderful to see the results. There is usually someone in class who says aloud what the rest of the class is thinking: "I hate this person! How can I find something to be grateful for, and why should I?"

The first reason you should is that not forgiving is a huge kink in your personal hose. The second reason is we are all one with God, so keeping someone out of that circle harms us all. Do you need more reasons than knowing that blessing your enemy blesses you and them and the world?

How can you be grateful for something about a person when everything about that person seems so hateful? Take the quality that you like the least about this person and flip it to the other side. Is this person demonstrating incredible stubbornness? What a wonderful quality of loyalty this may be. Is he being cruel? Perhaps it is a cover-up for the love he feels towards what he is defending.

You do not need to agree with this person or condone the person's actions; you just need to find the wonderful God-like qualities this person has so carefully hidden from view, and be grateful for these qualities.

Even if all you can be grateful for is someone's sense of order because she ties bows well, you have started a wellspring of blessing both for you and for the other person. Can you live with that?

Even for our enemies in misery—there should be tears in our eyes.—Charan Singh

It is in the silence of the heart that God speaks.—Mother Teresa

I am grateful for the following wonderful qualities in: _____

   1. _____
   2. _____
   3. _____
   4. _____
   5. _____
   6. _____
   7. _____
   8. _____

16

— · —

TWELVE

D ETACHMENT—NOT ATTACHMENT.

Not my will, but Thine, be done.—Jesus Christ

After we have done all that we can, and there is nothing more to do, we turn it back to God. Amen, So Be It.

This is when we practice detachment, not attachment. This is when we put our actions where our mouth is—God First. If we have truly put God First we know that what is good, true, beautiful, and pure will be the result; or more accurately, we will have seen that God is all there is, therefore all is already good, true, beautiful, and pure. We will have relinquished our human will to Divine Will. We will have let go of controlling the results. We will have done this with gratitude, because we are aware that our egos often blind us to the T ruth.

What ties us to this ego is emotion. Our goal is to release emotion, to let it go. This is quite different from expressing emotion or withholding emotion. Correct releasing never has a negative impact. True releasing allows us to open our hearts more fully and to express and receive more love.

Lester Levenson of The Sedona Method has a wonderful technique for releasing emotion to achieve the state he calls imperturbability, which is the characteristic quality of one who is self-possessed and not easily disturbed or perturbed. This is the state of equanimity, calmness, and composure.

He states that all emotions culminate in the following nine: apathy–grief–fear–lust–anger–pride–courage–acceptance–peace. In other words, after identifying the emotion we are feeling, we will be able to see that it is really one of these nine emotions. The Sedona Method takes us through the exercise of asking ourselves what emotion we are currently feeling, acknowledging it and then releasing it. We may ask, "Why let go of the wonderful emotions? "

There are two reasons. First, we must rid ourselves of the lifelong habit of holding on. We must let go of the thinking that whatever we have is as good as it gets. We are afraid to let go of what we have because we worry that we might not get any more.

This habit shows up in many parts of our lives. For example, it could show up in overeating because we are afraid that if we don't eat now we might not have food later. This symptom gets worse while dieting (die-ing). We might also notice this holding-on habit as it applies to other areas of our life like relationships and money. We'll cover more of this in Section Three on Relationships.

The second reason for not holding on to emotions—even wonderful ones—is that in declaring some emotions good, and some bad, we have also declared that there is both good and evil. This may be true in the material or physical and even the thought world, but not in the Spiritual. We desire to enter the State of Grace where there is only One Mind and that Mind is Perfection. The skill of learning how to release emotions plays a vital part in awakening to Truth.

Ask yourself, or have someone else ask you, the four questions at the end of this section. As you do the Sedona Method exercise, you will begin to feel the emotion lighten. Often tears and laughter accompany the release.

This is a great spiritual muscle-strengthening exercise and can be practiced anywhere and anytime. The joy that bubbles to the surface as we relinquish all to God is enough to make us want to learn how to release or relinquish and say So Be It more often.

You may be surprised, as I have been, how often question three prompts a "no" response from yourself. Keep asking the question until you get a "yes."

In the end, we learn that all emotions resolve into only three wants—approval, security, and control. Don't these three sound just like our small-i ego?

Ask yourself:

1. Feel the now feeling.

2. Could you let it go?

3. Would you let it go?

4. When?

A suppressed emotion is one that we have pushed down into the subconscious part of the mind and we have become unaware of it Just know that they are there, and let go of them.—Lester Levenson

THE DANCE OF COMPLETION AND CHANGE.

Why is it that we put off completing things? Everybody knows the inertia of not making the one phone call or visit to the one person he or she really wants to call.

I can remember putting off for months calling the "quality client list" I had as a stockbroker by keeping myself busy with other clients and administrative tasks.

What are we afraid of—that they will say "yes" or that they will say "no?" Perhaps we are afraid of the completion—because completion means we must and will change. Not completing is a passive form of control.

I visited Hawaii many years ago on a business trip that stretched out to two months. I fell absolutely head-over-heels in love with it. At the end of two months, I had to leave. I felt that what happened was due to circumstances "beyond my control."

I missed it so much I could hardly stand it, and tried to make plans to return. However, something always got in the way. I chose to let circumstances and people keep me from returning. Always in the back of my mind I thought, "If it weren't for _____ (fill in the blank) I could live in Hawaii."

Eleven years from the month I left, I returned for a visit. Note this: it took me eleven years just to go back to visit my favorite place in the world—sound familiar? Nevertheless, taking that first step and saying to myself, "I am visiting no matter what. I am not waiting any longer for the whole world to fall in place before I can move back. I will simply visit and not worry about living there," finally got me on the plane.

After making that first choice towards completion, the rhythm of my life became more graceful and abundant. The next year, I returned twice for a visit.

For twelve years, I had kept part of my life on hold thinking that if "things" weren't in my way I would live in Hawaii.

As I returned for the second visit, I had progressed enough to tell myself (and believe it): "You can live in Hawaii if you want to."

On the first day back, I loved it even more than I remembered—and at the same time realized I didn't want, or need, to live there.

Since I was no longer blaming other people and circumstances for not being able to live in Hawaii I could see clearly that my desire was based on not completing my first visit, and thinking that something was taken from me, "outside of my control."

I still want to visit Hawaii as much as possible, but it is no longer necessary or desirable for me—my choice—to live there.

It is like shopping. Have you ever thought to yourself that you really, really, really want new clothes (I know guys, you might not want new clothes, go with tools or something) so you put the money together and go shopping saying to yourself, "You can spend this money on anything you want" and then realized there was nothing you really wanted to buy?

The desire to have what we think we can't have gets in the way of living our life.

Sometimes we think we want a relationship we thought we lost, or someone who doesn't desire us. Or we want a new job, or a new place to live. Not completing what we need to do in regard to any or all of these "wants" is a fabulous way not to live our life by blaming circumstances "beyond our control."

My completing—by taking action—my desire to move to Hawaii and then realizing that it was no longer my desire, opened a brand new door towards what I can choose now.

This is because once something is completed we can move on. It may mean that we do get what we thought we wanted, and it may mean that we realize we don't want it after all. The result is not what is important; what is important is that we complete something, and in that completion, we will find freedom.

For me, this completion means that I can now change my mind and decide to live there after all—or not—but it is my choice. I can stop blaming people, places, and circumstances for not doing what I want to do.

Everyone has uncompleted tasks, agendas, and desires. No matter how small they seem they are important. They are stopping the natural rhythm and flow of our life. When we straddle the fence of incompletion nothing can happen. Once we get off the fence, and begin to take the steps necessary to complete the task, life dream, phone call, book, picture, dream house, dream life...circumstances and events rush in to help us.

Change is inevitable. Change is going to happen whether we desire it or not. Best to make change a personal choice than change that results from having to fix things after the wake-up call that results in broken relationships, accidents, and illness—the list is endless.

In fact, nothing is ever the same from one minute to the next. Try looking at something and then moving just one foot away and looking again. Does it look the same? No. Personal perspective always determines what we see, and personal perspective changes every moment. Change is always happening. We just pretend that it isn't.

The truth is it takes more effort not to complete and change than it takes to let completion and change happen. Not completing and changing is hard work.

Trying not to change is like standing in a flowing stream and trying not to move. How can it be done? We have to hang on, make ourselves heavy, become rigid, and so on. Completing and change takes faith and courage, just like letting go and flowing with the stream, but it is simple once we start. Completing will bring with it a wave of fresh insight and energy and unlimited new blessing we never thought possible and the tools necessary to enjoy and benefit from the resulting change.

As part of the So Be It process, instead of making resolutions or setting goals, take the time to begin to complete just one unfinished dream or task. Don't waste time figuring out which one, just start somewhere. Take that small step and be ready to see the open doors that have been ready and waiting for you to walk through them.

It is the law of the universe to complete and move on, complete and move on, complete and move on. Each cycle is an ever-expanding one. Expanding and emerging is all that is happening. Be Willing. Pick your feet up, and dance with the music of completion and change. You will love the feeling of the dance, once you get started.

START WITH THE SPIRITUAL FACT.

Again, an error in the premise must appear in the conclusion.—Mary Baker Eddy

Any apparent progress that results from beginning with the problem rather than the spiritual fact is a "dangerous resemblance". We can think our way out of problems. We can use our human will to make things happen. We can say, "The end justifies the means."

We can rationalize our actions. However, none of these ways start with God First and with relinquishing our human ego. For a time the result may look the same, but this is a dangerous resemblance.

This resemblance to Truth will try to convince us that we did put God First. However, some day in some way we will be confronted again with what we thought we had solved before, and this time it will be worse.

When I am tempted to ignore Angel Ideas even on a small scale, like not returning the extra penny change, I ask myself, "Are you willing to sacrifice your Life's harmony—Heaven—for this?" If my perception is on lack, how can my perception be with God?

As we awaken to Spirit's prompting, we discover the small and large lies we have been telling, to others and to ourselves. This is not the time to hold on to these lies through feelings of guilt, judgment, remorse or any other emotion that may surface. Here is the time to be grateful for our awakening and to begin to tell the truth, so that we can see more of the Truth. This is an ongoing process. It is a continual awakening, an upward and deepening path.

Another stumbling block to watch for is forgetting why we are Shifting. Once the physical evidence begins to appear, we may be tempted to be grateful for it rather than for the spiritual reality. Misplaced gratitude may open the door to ingratitude about what has not happened.

This is truly missing the point. We are not putting God First to get things. We are putting God First to be more conscious of who we are and to live in the harmony of the Kingdom of God.

Don't get comfortable—choose to keep going to the realm of no paradigm, where we are all with the One God, Living in the State of Grace.

FLY OR DIE—THE LESSON OF THE DOVE.

Attachment is the greatest fabricator of illusions. Reality can be attained only by someone who is detached.—Simone Weil

One of my first greeters in my new home was a pair of doves. For the year that I lived in my apartment on the canyon they constantly visited me at my feeders on the porch, or at the front door as I came home, or outside the bushes of my office. I thought they were wonderful. They were always together and always cooing. To me they were symbolic of my new love relationship.

I was overjoyed when I discovered the female dove was making a nest in one of my planters on our porch in the spring of that year. The only thing that worried me was that we were preparing to move across the country and I wasn't sure what would happen to them and their nest when we were gone.

One day while I was in the office I heard a crash on my patio and when I went to investigate I found my lovely female dove lying on the porch and her companion on the ledge cooing frantically. He was trying to wake her up. I did too. I wrapped her up in something warm and waited for hours for her to revive. She didn't.

I was as heartbroken as her mate. I couldn't understand why this had happened. He mourned for days and then one day he had a new companion.

This made me even sadder as I could not understand why or how he could just move on.

I kept wondering what the dove had taught me. I would only shake my head and say, "I don't know". I was too involved in the grief of it and couldn't understand why it had affected me so deeply. It took many months before I was conscious of the dove's lesson and gift to me. I was sitting in our new house in another part of the United States with absolutely nothing familiar around me and I finally understood.

She had tried to stay—and it was important to go. There was a part of me that was holding on to not leaving what I had known for the majority of my life—symbolized by my lady dove building the nest. The new lady dove knew that it was time to find a new home. She and her friend did not come back to my apartment to live. I only saw them the first day they were together as they perched in the tree and said "good-by" to me.

This is all symbolic of course, as all lessons are. Now that I have let go of so many things I realize another part of the love lesson my dove friend was teaching me. It really wasn't that one dove died and another took her place. The idea of holding on had to die. The part of me that was holding on had to die so that the person I really am—could fly.

Whenever I notice that I am still holding on to some of "how things used to be" I think of my friend the dove and thank her for the lesson about leaving, and I thank the new lady dove for choosing to go so she could continue her life with her new companion and find her wings.

Detach and let go and let God be the activity of your life.

A man can do what he wants, but not want what he wants. —Arthur Schopenhauer

Practical So Be It.

Would you like to practice detachment or relinquishment on a practical scale? Try this following exercise. It might be helpful to share this with a friend in order to support each other in its completion.

Step 1: Make a list of what you do yourself to keep your household and/or your business running during a month.

Step 2: Agree to yourself to give at least three of them away in the next month. Giving them away could mean to stop doing them altogether, or it could mean hiring or asking someone else to do it. There are many ways of detaching. One of the first is to allow others to help. Remember our goal is to express who we are, not to do more to prove our value. Our value is innate because we are the expression of the One Mind.

Step 3: After one month has gone by, make a list of what you actually gave away. Remember the power of habits? Perhaps you meant to give it away, or perhaps you gave it away and then took it back. Pay attention to the underlying reasons why you kept it or why you took it back. Acknowledge yourself for what you gave away then ask yourself why you didn't keep your agreement with yourself if you didn't. Observe the emotion; let it go, and then do it again. You may discover that something you gave away is something you really love doing.

It's okay to take it back if that's the reason, but be sure you choose something else to give away in its place.

This giving away can also involve physical objects that take up space and time. If you feel like they own you or that you are hoarding for the "just in case" moment, think about detaching from them. Remember, thoughts are things. Go back to the quality you are trying to experience by owning these things and see if you still need the objects.

What's the purpose of this process? To practice giving up the lifetime habit of holding on. To begin to tell ourselves the Truth about who we are and what we desire. To begin to simplify our lives so that we have the ability to see the world differently.

Here is an agreement form for you to sign, to prompt you to act from "Not my will, but Thine."

I, _____, am willing to let go of my dreams and goals as I have stated them and allow them to develop through the One Mind. I am willing to put down the burden of making it happen or of being responsible for it not happening.

_____
Signature

I am giving away these three things I now do myself:
1.
2.
3.
What I actually gave away:
1.
2.
3.

What I am still holding on to:

1.

2.

3.

17

SECTION THREE

WALK YOUR TALK

18

· · ·

THIRTEEN

- The Sixth Step To Shift—Walk As One.

Remember the game we called the Earth state of mind? In the Earth game, we must overcome the belief of lack and at the same time be in harmonious and balanced relationships.

There is nothing we can do, think, or say that is not about a relationship. Truth is practical; therefore our expression of Truth will be practical and useful. We apply and use the Truth in every relationship we have, including with our bodies, our supply, our work, and our loved ones.

RELATIONSHIPS WE HAVE AND THE ONES WE WANT.

But relationships are not outside—they are inside of us; this is the simple truth that we must recognize and accept.—Shakti Gawain

All relationships are really a relationship with ourselves. It looks as if we have relationships with family, friends, money, things, and our body: everything "outside" of ourselves. However, in reality, all these "things" are within. As we work on peaceful and productive relationships of all kinds, we are doing the work on our point of view about how these aspects are supposed to behave.

Let's take a look first at our relationship with others, knowing that it is, in Reality, a relationship with ourself.

RELATIONSHIPS ARE SUBJECTIVE STATES.

Relationships are subjective. What does this mean? It means that it is impossible to see other people as they truly are, because we are always filtering and layering in our own interpretation of them.

Pretend you're walking down the street watching someone walk towards you. At first, since the figure is far away, you decide that it is human as opposed to a dog or cat. As it gets closer you determine that the person is tall or short, fat or skinny, graceful or not, male or female.

Closer still, you may have determined the person's approximate age and possible nationality. With each of these determinations, you have made interior judgments based on what you know and have decided about each criteria. Of course, this is a short list. We place people in many more slots than this, all with preconceived ideas attached.

Once the person reaches you, perhaps you choose to meet them and you stop to stay hello. Assuming that this leads to a friendship, can you ever say that you really know this person? What did you predetermine before you met? We barely know ourselves. How can we really know another?

COMMUNICATION.

The concept of "Mondegreen" or the idea of mixing up words so that what is said is not what is heard can often be very funny.

However, the concept of word mix-ups is symbolic of how difficult it can be to understand each other. How many times in a day is there a misunderstanding.

Sometimes it is a simple misunderstanding that seems to harm no one. Other times this misunderstanding leads to major consequences that may take a long time to heal. Nevertheless, all misunderstandings eventually result in a feeling that all of us have had at one time or another, the feeling that "no one understands me."

It is so easy to misunderstand. Many years ago, I was preparing for a date with my boyfriend. I had carefully planned my outfit, but was still worried about it because it was a new "look" for me. As we were going out the door he said, "Boy, you look hot." I thought he meant I had too many clothes on for the season. I was devastated, and very hurt. After a brief pause to take in what he said, I asked him "Do you mean I have too many clothes on?"

He was amazed how easily I had jumped to the wrong conclusion. He of course meant I looked—well just as I wanted to look. We both laughed. What if I wouldn't have asked him what he meant? What if I had brooded all night about my appearance? What if I thought he was rude for saying such an unkind thing to me?

This is what we do, isn't it? We have our own point of view or perception about something—anything—and that colors everything we see, hear, or say about that concept. Do we really hear anything but our own point of view? Perhaps it is true, no one understands anyone.

Is this true for you? What could you do to change it? What could we all do to be in more harmony and balance with each other? Here are some practical things we can try.

- We could stop and pay attention to what we are thinking while we are listening. We could ask ourselves the question, "Am I listening to what is being said, or am I listening to myself comment internally about what I think is being said?"

- We could care more about the outcome for the other person than for the outcome for ourselves.

These ideas will work, and we can all practice becoming better at human communication. At the least, we could learn to laugh at those misunderstandings that do happen rather than taking them too seriously. However, there is a more effective, faster, and permanently better way. We could change our perception to something that would really clear up misunderstandings and would eliminate forever the feeling that "no one understands me."

In the Earth game there is a huge mist-perception. We think we are all separate from each other, with many points of view, many needs, many pains, and many agendas. If we would step out of the game and know what Divine Mind knows—that we are all part and expressions of Love and Truth—then all mist-perceptions and their ramifications would vanish. They would disappear as easily as fog lifts in bright sunshine.

DISSOLVING CONFLICT.

I have learned through bitter experience the one supreme lesson to conserve my anger, and as heat conserved is transmitted into energy, even so our anger controlled can be transmitted into a power that can move the world.—Mahatma Gandhi

Treat people as if they were what they ought to be, and help them to become what they are capable of being.—Goethe

Sometimes we have people in our life with whom we have a conflict. This conflict can be the main source of the relationship or just a minor part of an otherwise harmonious experience. What can we do to either correct the conflict, or when necessary, extract ourselves from the relationship?

A productive way to resolve conflict may be to explain our feelings to the other person. If she or he is receptive and interested in evolving both personally and in the relationship with us, this may dissolve the conflict and move our relationship to higher ground.

However, sometimes this doesn't work because the other person is not interested in working with us to resolve the conflict. At this point most of us make the situation worse by focusing our emotion on the problem. This, we already know, only produces more of the same. Sometimes we really make it worse by bringing the other person's attention to the (our) problem with them. If the other person didn't already have conflict with us, they now do.

There is another way to dissolve that always works, if we are willing to detach from the outcome. Let me give you one example. I once had two relationships in my life where I felt I was doing all the giving and the other person was doing all the taking. They looked to me like they were people who thought of themselves first (and if asked would agree that they did), which left me feeling as if what I needed came second.

I was in personal conflict with both of these relationships because of my feelings of not being heard or taken care of.

They were both very important relationships. One was my husband, one my business partner. I resisted doing anything at first, as I was afraid of the consequences. Then I tried talking to both of them, but this only produced more negative results.

However, I began to realize that to heal the situation and to bless us all; I would have to see them and myself in a new way. I had tried this method before in other relationships and it worked like magic, most of the time in ways I would not have consciously chosen.

Looking back, if asked, I probably would have said that I thought the outcome would be that my husband and I would move towards a more intimate and mutually loving and satisfying relationship, and my business partner and I would separate. I figured she would leave the partnership, leaving me with our other partner, and of course, I just knew that both these things would be best for everyone.

When I recognized the pattern of my thinking and what I perceived as my husband's pattern of thinking, I did two things. I made a qualities list of what I felt a true loving relationship would embody. Once I did that, I realized that my husband was not really displaying most of those qualities in our relationship at that time. I began to question whether I was truly in a love relationship. However, I continued to see both him and myself as we really are—the expression of Divine Love—and to act out of that understanding as clearly as possible.

The result was not at all what I expected. Our relationship became more and more strained.

The more I attempted to do what I felt to be loving the more he pulled away from me and the more I felt his anger. It became apparent that he was not acting from love, but from fear. I continued holding to God's qualities for both of us as best as I could.

The result was that one afternoon I learned of a secret that he had been hiding and lying about for years. After a few days of shock and grief, I was able to feel great compassion for him, but I was not willing to continue the lie and live as we had been. I asked him to leave so we could begin to rebuild our relationship on Truth. This request he accepted by leaving, but never returning.

To my great surprise, in spite of the grief, I realized that a huge weight had been lifted from my shoulders and I was now free to take bigger steps towards the calling I was feeling.

As time went by, I was also able to see my own role in this failure. By continuing to hold to the truth about myself, I finally saw the lie that I had been living. I had lived a duel life. Somewhere inside of what I considered a very independent and capable woman, another woman had been hiding. This woman lived with the belief that she had to have a man in her life before she could do anything. When one man moved on, she focused all her attention on getting a new man. I knew this woman inside me did this. It was quite clear that I had to have a man first before I could get on with my life. I just never questioned the reason or wisdom for this decision.

Now I saw what had happened with all my romantic relationships. I would use my clear focus to find the man of the moment and fall in love. What happened next really wasn't the man's fault for he did not really know me.

He knew the "other woman" who had to have a man in her life. Once the home front was secure, I would emerge. However, in order not to lose the man the other woman had secured for us both, I paid the price of taking care of him. I gave him whatever I thought he wanted hoping he would be so grateful he would never leave.

Obviously, I did not think that I was lovable enough, so I had to bribe him to stay by giving him what he wanted, usually at the expense of what I wanted. Eventually, I would wake up and notice that I was doing all the giving, and the man would wake up and realize that the woman he fell in love with was not the real me.

After my husband left, I began to live my life, feeling and living from the strength and independence I'd always had. I did not look for a man to complete me. A few years after this experience I met a man who also did not need me to complete him. I continue to focus on being who I am, and this man in my life knows and loves the real m e.

The business partnership had a different outcome. Once again, I made a qualities list of what I thought a partnership looked like. I began to act out of this, I thought, and began to see her as an expression of Divine Love. Now, this is the partner that I wanted to go away, remember?

Instead, she stayed and I became unhappier. The more I looked at divine qualities the worse our relationship got. The more I tried to step outside of the role of giver, the worse I felt.

One day I realized, finally, that the problem was within me. I was unhappy over her actions, because I was not doing what I really wanted to do.

She was doing what she wanted to do, and I wasn't. I had diverted my attention to a business that in my heart I knew I would have to leave. Instead of facing this, I focused on my partner's actions, so that everything she did mattered to me.

I changed. I stopped caring about the outcome. Although I did continue to hold to a principle of fairness, I started paying attention to my inner voice, which was telling me that I was not following my soul's path. I knew that I was diverting myself by worrying about a partnership and business that was no longer serving me. I began to tell the truth to both my partners. The result was that the "difficult one" became a friend and ally. We all agreed to a fair solution concerning the partnership that has blessed us all.

Nothing had changed but me. The world outside shifted with my personal shift to Grace. I had to give up being right. I had to give up caring about the outcome. I had to start being kind to myself first—rather than putting others first and then making them wrong for it. The process was only painful when I held on with fear to what I thought I was losing, or when I made myself feel guilty for my role in the past. Neither of these two emotions could bless me or the others involved. I reminded myself that I have always been the expression of the Infinite Loving One, and they have been too. Nothing had ever changed or could ever change that fact. The rest was a story we had lived out and from which we had awakened.

Did I ever tell either one what I was doing? No. I held in my own thought both their Divinity and mine—and acted out of that Truth. I used the GRACIOUS model to shift to Living in Grace.

When we see men of a contrary character, we should turn inwards and examine ourselves.—Confucius

Why did this technique work for me? Most importantly, because I put God First. I followed the GRACIOUS steps.

First, I tried to know, love, and see both my partners as God (Love) does. Next I Repented and changed the way I was thinking. This process demanded of me to listen for Angel Ideas every time I was disturbed by a situation and to go back to Love. I Chose for all of us to have a happy and productive outcome. I Imagined how happy we would all be and were, because we were living in God's Grace.

Of course, I had to keep it up, and be Obsessive about this Shift as my bad habits continually took me back to being upset.

I Unkinked my hose as I held to what was good, beautiful, true, and pure about all of us. I noticed many things that were not good, beautiful, pure, or true about myself and I let them go. I took action, seeking the best way to approach what needed to be done. And finally, I said So Be It and detached from the outcome. All these steps followed effortlessly because I started with God First.

I always prefer to believe the best of everybody—it saves so much time.—Rudyard Kipling

LET YOUR PEOPLE GO.

Love is like quicksilver in the hand. Leave the fingers open and it stays. Clutch it, and it darts away.—Dorothy Parker

Often there are people in our life that we love who just aren't going where we are going. For reasons of their own, they have chosen a different path. If you see them as they really are they may choose to move out of your life rather than face the perceived discomfort of growth. Do not go back and get them. Do not drag them forward. Both of you will lose your focus on putting God First and you may end up staying with them instead of fulfilling your gifts.

There are unlimited paths to the One Truth. Each of us must walk our own and in our own time. We are blessed when we travel together on the same path, but when someone chooses one different from yours, bless that person, and move on.

Sometimes people take the path that moves them away from Grace. However, the wonderful story of the prodigal son reminds us that when one of our loved ones begins the path back of their own volition, we can run to meet him with a wholehearted love.

This is a time, once again, to put God First, not ourselves. For our small-i would like to remind that person of the pain we suffered while he was gone, and of all the sins of the past. But that is what they are—past. This is the time to continue to remind both you and the other person of who you really are, and let the focus on what is good, true, and beautiful become the basis of your life.

In all cases, we must tell the truth to ourselves before we can tell it to others. We will get exactly what we believe we deserve and expect. The Truth is we all deserve to be perfectly loved, and to perfectly love.

FIND COMPANIONS FOR LIFE.

You deserve to be perfectly loved. —Scott Peck and Shannon Peck, *The Love You Deserve*

Within each of us we house both male and female qualities. When we are in tune with our inner voice, we learn how to appreciate the value each aspect brings. As we value our internal male and female we will see in our outward lives friends and companions that fulfill these roles as well as completing these roles within ourselves... The female says, "I feel this." He says, "I hear your feelings. What would you like me to do?" She says, "I want that." He says, "You want that? OK, great, I'll get it for you." And he goes directly to get it for her, trusting totally that in her desire is the wisdom of the universe...Remember now that I am talking about an internal process in each of us. —Shakti Gawain

The Chinese write whole words with symbols. In many cases, two completely unlike symbols are used to complete a meaning that is entirely different from either one of the separate symbols.

An example of this is found in the symbol for "Man" and the symbol for "Woman." When combined, they mean "Good." No wonder we have such a strong drive to bond with another—we desire a relationship that results in good.

However, many of us have not yet found the "one" companion with whom we want to spend the rest of our lives.

Consciously or unconsciously, we scan the horizon searching for "the one." Sometimes we meet the person who seems to be that one, but we find out later that although he or she may have been the one for that moment in time, that person did not wear well as we traveled together.

One way to filter out who is or who is not your companion is to look at the lifestyle that person desires. Does it match yours? Are you making a choice to be someone else, to live a life you would not really choose if you decided to choose this person as your mate? Our goal is to grow and expand our spirit, so choosing a lifestyle to buy affection will not accomplish that primary goal.

Are you not sure of even where to start in the process of finding a companion? Perhaps you could start with noticing who is attracted to you. Are they attracted to the essence that you want to be? Are the qualities you are expressing attracting the quality of the person with whom you might wish to spend your life? If not, choose the qualities that would attract you, and become those qualities yourself. Continue to ask yourself if you are living out of and expressing the values and qualities that you would like others to express to you.

Once we have found the right relationship, how do we keep it? To accomplish an ultimate rapport you must first find the values that you have in common. That means you must take the time to talk to each other, and to learn and share your values.

Once you each know the other, you can use the values you have in common to help with those that are not alike. The second step is to support and fulfill the other person's most important values as much as you can. This is the basis for a powerful, supportive, and lasting relationship, whether it is business, personal, or family. Of course, the opposite is true; if your values conflict there will not be harmony.

We must also commit to the relationship. The word commitment means "the agreement not to run." Although the word run conjures up a physical action like running for the hills, many of us run by withdrawing within our minds and hearts. The result is sometimes worse than physical running, since either party may miss the fact that he or she is now alone.

Another great danger to relationships is comparison. Nobody fares well when we are comparing him or her to someone else. The only comparison that works is comparing our thoughts with what the One Mind is thinking about a particular person, place, or thing (only good). Any other comparison will always result in feelings of unhappiness.

HUMAN LOVE.

Sometimes we pick the wrong life mates because we meet someone and for that moment in time they make us feel loved. But what if that "thing" they were doing that made you feel loved prevailed over all your other qualities and values? The other side of the issue would be, what if someone really loved you and had all the right qualities and values but was not able to make you feel loved?

In the first instance, you might end up with someone you would have never chosen, and in the second, you may lose the person who most loved you just because you did not feel loved.

How do we avoid this? Take the time to observe yourself and your relationships. Ask yourself, what about this relationship makes me feel like the person loves me? Of course, we can do this for all close friends, not just mate relationships.

I used this method effectively when I was dating and noticed that I kept being attracted to men whom I knew could not really be life mates. This attraction was the magnetic, when-and-how-often-can-I-see-you feeling. I stopped one evening and asked myself: "What exactly moves you to this feeling?" I discovered that there was a distinctive sound to the man's voice and the way he looked at me that would trigger this response. From that point on, those two things never grabbed me the same way again. Knowledge definitely is power.

Later, I again asked myself the same question. This time I wanted to know what really made me feel loved so that when I met my true companion I would be clear as to what I would need from him to continue to feel loved so that our love together would thrive over time.

This proved harder than I expected. I realized that I did not really know what made me feel loved because I had fooled myself so many times just to "get a man." To find out, I began to look at everyone in my life that I knew loved me (like my family and best friends) and then I asked myself, "Why do I know for sure this person loves me and what makes me feel loved?" I made a list of these qualities.

181

This was the list I used to filter out relationships I would have otherwise been caught up in.

Try this. It is a powerful and effective tool for finding and keeping true companionship. Of course, this is a reciprocal agreement. What do the people you love in your life—brothers, sisters, mother, father, children, grandchildren, mates, companions, friends—need from you to feel loved? Find out, fulfill it, and bliss is yours. In the end, it is Divine Love that we seek to express and experience. I had the following quote framed and hung on my wall, to remind myself daily what unconditional pure love acts like.

And now I will show you the most excellent way. If I have the gift of prophecy and can fathom all mysteries and all knowledge and if I have a faith that can move mountains, but have not love, I am nothing. If I give all I possess to the poor and surrender my body to the flames, but have not love, I gain nothing. Love is patient. Love is kind. It does not envy, it does not boast, it is not proud. It is not rude, it is not self-seeking, it is not easily angered, it keeps no record of wrongs. Love does not delight in evil but rejoices with the truth. It always protects, always trusts, always hopes, always perseveres. Love never fails. And now these three remain: faith, hope and love. But the greatest of these is love.—Corinthians 13:1–8,13, Bible

Practical Relationships.

(Remember: Check the resource chapter for a place to get a workbook.)

We often don't know what we want in our relationships because we've never stopped to consider the values that are important to us. Take your relationships one by one and determine what qualities and values you want. Don't think of a particular person, but a type of relationship.

The result of using qualities to find and keep relationships will bless everyone involved. Review the Chapter on God First to remind yourself how to make and use qualities lists.

The supreme happiness in life is the conviction that we are loved. —Victor Hugo

In my_____ type of relationship, I desire to be conscious of the following qualities:
1._____
2._____
3._____
4._____
5._____
6._____
7._____
8._____

In my_____ type of relationship, I desire to be conscious of the following qualities:
1._____
2._____
3._____
4._____
5._____
6._____
7._____
8._____

We do not great things; we do only small things with great love. —Mother Teresa

We should measure affection, not like youngsters by the ardour of its passion, but by its strength and constancy.—Marcus Tullius Cicero

There is no closer way to bond people than to align them through their highest values. Common values form the basis for the ultimate rapport. If two people have values that are totally linked, their relationship can last forever.—Tony Robbins, Unlimited Power

My greatest achievement in life—I made one woman supremely happy for 63 years.—Philip Carret, Pioneer Fund

It is more noble to give yourself completely to one individual than to labor diligently for the salvation of the masses.—Dag Hammarskjold

One of the deep secrets of life is that all that is really worth doing is what we do for others.—Lewis Carroll

We are all born for love; it is the principle of existence and its only end.—Benjamin Disraeli

Religion has nothing to do with compassion; it is our love for God that is the main thing because we have all been created for the sole purpose to love and be loved.—Mother Teresa

What you do may seem insignificant, but it is very important that you do it.—Mahatma Gandhi

Constant kindness can accomplish much. As the sun makes ice melt, kindness causes misunderstanding, mistrust, and hostility to evaporate.—Albert Schweitzer

19

— • —

Fourteen

WE ARE NOT IN OUR BODY—OUR BODY IS IN US.

There is no such thing as a material body: There is only a material concept of body. There is no such thing as a material universe: There are only material concepts of the one Spiritual universe. —Joel S. Goldsmith, *The Thunder of Silence*

The human body is the outward expression of thought—just as everything else is—it is a purely mental product and objectification of material sense. —Adam H. Dickey, God's Law of Adjustment

Our body is the outward expression of our thought. It is the holographic representation of our paradigm regarding our life, our parents, our culture, our age, and our belief about all of these.

Remember that a key element of Shifting is discovering the unconscious belief systems or points of view that filter all information to our consciousness. This rut, or paradigm, is what makes up our reality. What we conceive is what we perceive—and what we perceive is what we believe and ultimately receive.

This fact is easier to accept when we are discussing something less substantial than our own personal bodies. However, this truth cannot apply to one portion of our life and not to another.

Once again, we must remember that an error in the premise leads to an error in the conclusion. Always begin with God First.

If we remember to pretend that the Earth state of mind is only a game, then we can also pretend that our body is the marker on the board game of life—nothing more.

TRYING TO FIX SYMPTOMS.

As I wrote this section, I was sitting in front of my computer with a bag of frozen peas tied onto my head. Why was I doing this? Because I was trying to deal with a symptom called a headache.

Besides being an incredibly silly thing to see, the cold from the frozen peas was assisting me in dealing with the pain while I wrote. However, I did not think the peas were curing the reason for the headache.

Come with me as we take a look at a few of the belief systems regarding our bodies and see if we can Shift our perceptions about them.

THE STORY OF THE CURSE.

But there went up a mist from the earth and watered the whole face of the ground.—Genesis 2:6, Bible

The first chapter of the *Bible* deals with the creation of the world as a Divine Thought. In the beginning was the Word. This is a clear description of a Spiritual Heaven present here and now.

In Chapter 2 (Genesis 2:3) we have another story of creation. We can tell it's a story because it begins with a mist coming up from the ground. This is the story of the mist-perception (missed perception) of Truth. If you have ever been confused, you know that it feels like a fog in your head (a mist). The ground, in this case, is the whole perception of Earth. We all know the story of being in Eden and then being quite efficiently asked to leave.

What went wrong? Why were we asked to leave? OK, Eve listened to a serpent. Perhaps we missed a few points when reading this story in the past. Did we notice that she must have talked to this serpent (i.e., suggestion) before, as she seemed quite familiar with him? There is no record of her yelling, "Honey, come quick, there is a talking snake in the grass!"

No, she carried on a conversation with him that she must have carried on before. She trusted him and didn't recognize the lie he was telling. The snake told her that God had said they could not eat of the tree in the garden. He told her what she wanted to hear. There is no record that they were told by God that they could not eat of the tree in the garden. The truth is God had told them that all that existed belonged to them. (Genesis 1:29) Eve had a conversation with the snake about something that God never said in the true record of creation.

What did the snake—or the suggestion of two powers—want Eve to do? Eat from the tree of duality. It is only in the second story—or the mist-perception—that the tree of good and evil, the tree of duality, is found. (Genesis 2:9, 17) God as Omniscience could not have known about another power. Omnipotence leaves no room for anything but Itself.

Eve succumbed to the suggestion that there was both an evil and a good world. Once she agreed with this point of view, and ate the apple, she perceived herself as belonging to a place outside of Heaven, and therefore she was. What we perceive to be reality magnifies.

Where do we want to Shift ourselves? Back to One—the concept that God alone is where we have always been. Since what we believe to be true becomes our reality, what better way to return to the Eden we actually never left—by choosing a God-First Reality?

Now, back to the story. Adam and Eve thought they heard God in the form of a voice that told them they were cursed. The voice could not have been God. God, being One, does not know duality. Adam and Eve were the ones accepting bad and good. God could not have had this thought, since God is Infinite Good. Perhaps it was the serpent? In any case, they felt cursed. The curse for women has been traditionally interpreted to mean that she will always be burdened with women-type troubles, and that men will till the earth forever (i.e., work) with no real satisfaction.

Since there was no truth to the first lie, there is no truth to this one either. Only the power we give to it! Defy this curse! God, as Infinite Love, could not curse Its own children. God as an Intelligence that is only Perfection could not have even noticed that they were accepting duality. No, the voice they heard was the same one we hear disguised as whomever we are willing to listen to, and often it sounds like our own voice. However, it is merely the voice of our personal serpent, once again claiming its power from its only source—the power we give to it. What we perceive to be reality magnifies!

We have readily agreed to this curse because we don't stop to think about its origin. We accept this script and play out the roles, not realizing that it is just a role, not Reality. Everyone knows that actors turn down scripts and roles that they do not wish to play. Turn down this limiting and abusive script—and any other script that limits your ability to live in the here and now Heaven of peace and harmony.

While we are observing the scripts we've accepted without questioning, let's look briefly at the script we've been given on heredity and genealogy.

HEREDITY AND GENEALOGY.

We are not the children of our biological parents, nor did we create our own children. This concept is hard to grasp, but it's an important one. Of course, I can intellectually know that God is the Creator and therefore my children and I are all God's children. However, on a day-to-day basis, I would like to claim that my dad is very brilliant and therefore I too must be, or that my mother is a fabulous, creative cook and so I am. Not to mention my children—how beautiful, handsome, successful, and talented they are—all of which I would like to lay claim to as their mother.

But if I succumb to this way of thinking, claiming myself as a child of humans, and a creator of humans, I also burden myself and my children with the other side of this claim—that of hereditary beliefs.

It is either true or not true that we are the expressions of the Infinite Loving One. We cannot carry forward any limiting beliefs about human personal heredity.

Choose the bigger gift for yourself and for the children who are your guests in this Earth game. Claim and act from the knowledge that we are loved by Love, which cannot include a limited reality. Of course as the reflection of Love we will do whatever is most loving to protect our guests and ourselves. When we start with the Truth of our being, Angel Ideas will lead us to the best solution for any problem

Aging.

For us believing physicists, the separation between past, present, and future has only the meaning of an illusion, albeit a tenacious one.—Albert Einstein

We do not die, we just change worlds.—Chief Seattle

Most of what we experience in growing old is a result of a belief system that says we are supposed to age. Most of us have agreed to a decline in health the older we get. However, symptoms of aging are just that—symptoms of the disease called "old age." They stem from the belief that we live and die in our bodies. These symptoms are not required, necessary, or desired.

If there is actually no time—except of our own making—as physicist Stephen Hawking has stated, then why not stop measuring time altogether—especially when it comes to aging? We could start avoiding age-related thoughts by not celebrating birthdays as age related, which after all are simply measuring how many trips around the sun we have made. Instead, let's celebrate how much we've grown spiritually.

WATCHING OUR WEIGHT.

One of the first problems we have with weight is the mirror we are using. When I was in my mid-twenties I was taking a ballet class. It was my first class after having my third child and I was feeling pudgy. This feeling was not helped by the fact that reed-thin teenagers surrounded me. I was holding my own until I looked in the mirror.

Egad! I thought. Who is that really pudgy person? I could barely take the class as I dealt with fat feelings. I berated myself, I promised myself I would diet until I was thin.

"Just please," I begged God, "don't let me be that person in the mirror."

When we moved away from the barre to begin center work, I was now looking into a different mirror. In this mirror was only a slightly pudgy me. One of the students saw my bewildered look and said, "Oh, don't pay any attention to that other mirror, there's something wrong with it and it's being replaced."

I had to laugh. Ever since, when I catch myself looking into a mirror, real or imaginary, I remind myself of that "wrong mirror."

The only mirror that tells the Truth about who we are is the mirror that shows us as God's reflection, whole, complete, and perfect. If I am surprised by what I see I say, "Thank God that is not who I really am!" I mean this statement in both ways.

Joel S. Goldsmith in his book *Invisible Supply* says, "Everything in your life is an expression either of your consciousness or your unwillingness to let your consciousness express itself.

When you block the expression of your consciousness, you become a blotting paper for the beliefs of good and evil that permeate the world. So you have a choice: you either become a blotter and take it all in and show it forth, or else you become a master of your fate and captain of your soul by an act of consciousness."

We are here to be the activity of God, expressed in our own unique way. When we don't do this our body reflects the result. How long we procrastinate is up to us, but sooner or later we must respond to our calling. One common result (but not the only one) of choosing not to move in the direction of our dreams is the symptom of being overweight.

We must learn to trust Angel Ideas and take action towards our dreams. These dreams stem from our innate knowing of how we can express God best. Support what you believe and think with action. Remind yourself of who you truly are and ask yourself what mirror you are looking into.

The word weight really says it all, doesn't it? What are we waiting for? What weight are we carrying? What heavy thoughts are we harboring? What are we waiting to do or be? Whom are we trying to please?

Whose rules do we follow? Do we listen to internal guidance on what to eat and when, or are we rebelling against what everyone else says we should do? When it comes to food, what unconscious things do we say to ourselves? What power have we given to food?

What words do you say to yourself about food? All the following statements will produce exactly what you say. Do you say any of them either aloud or internally?

- Everything good is bad for me.

- I can't trust myself to eat right.

- My body won't cooperate.

- I'd have to struggle and starve to have a perfect body.

- I'll never weigh what I want to because I am too old, too tired, I've had a baby, etc.

- My body needs to be controlled.

- If I eat even a little of this "bad" thing, I will gain weight.

If any of you find that you accept any of these statements as true, stop now and begin to tell yourself the Truth. There is only One. There is only One of everything, including body. Therefore our body expresses now all the perfect qualities of God. Begin with the right premise—God First.

When we replace the untrue statements with the Truth, it may sound something like this: "I am the activity of harmony and balance. As God's activity of abundance, I have no need to hold onto anything. As an activity of Life's movement I express freedom."

These statements are not mere affirmations. They are Truth. Replace untrue statements with Truth, and you will never worry about weight again.

I have a friend who was burdened by the belief that if he ate a "bad" food he would, within seconds, weigh at least a pound more. I challenged him to prove it to me. We weighed him. He ate a cookie. He got back on the scale and weighed a pound more. Wow! Aren't we powerful beings? Our thoughts do produce the result we expect.

Challenge yourself to stop expecting and producing negative results. My friend and I talked about the truth, that the cookie had not produced the result, his thinking or point of view had kept him from seeing the Truth about himself and the cookie. What did the cookie represent to him? We decided that it represented love, and that Love could never harm him. The problem with food vanished.

Listen to your own personal self-talk about food and ask yourself what each act of eating represents. Choose wisely from what you learn and follow Angel Ideas into a balanced point of view. Then food will no longer be in control.

We are often tempted to have negative beliefs about ourselves that may kink our perfect-health hose. Review the following list and see if any of them sound familiar to you. These are some thoughts that may be going through your mind. Remember these are only temptations to believe that you are something other than the full expression of an Infinite Loving One:

Self-hatred / self-punishment / psychic protection / feeling too vulnerable / fear of being too sexy / fear of being too beautiful / fear of attracting too much attention / fear of being too powerful / thinking that weight equals strength / having a deep need for love / fear of expressing your creativity / fear of expressing your energy and holding it in / fear of emptiness / fear of having your life succeed so that you will have to give up your problems.

Do any of these thoughts tempt you to believe in their reality? Return to what is True. Follow the GRACIOUS line of reasoning. Start with God First, Repent, find another way to see what is happening.

Listen to Angel Ideas. Choose the result you really want, Imagine how you will feel with your perfect health and body, be Obsessively Vigilant while taking action in any way that seems appropriate to Unkink the hose, and when you have done all that you can, give it back to God—So Be It.

EXERCISE.

For most people, exercise is a way to fix a problem or to look better, which makes it hard to do. Exercise is neither of these two things, because there is no outside body to exercise. Exercise is a celebration of the Truth that we are already the expression of perfect health. This changes the whole picture. Instead of exercising to get "better," we exercise as the activity of perfection that is already who we are.

Angel Ideas will lead us to do something that feels like fun and is unique to us. They may lead us to the gym, or perhaps to the beach for a walk, or to take the stairs instead of the elevator. Exercise celebrates God's qualities such as action, grace, happiness, breathing, movement, and harmony. Design a plan that expresses who you are. Stop sitting on your "yes buts" and say "yes" to who you are. The result may look the same, but the motivation is entirely different.

HEALING THE BODY.

All disease is a breakdown in the relationship with yourself and others. It is a result of how you use your mind.—Dr. Jacob Lieberman, *Light Medicine of the Future*

As I was writing this section of the book, a perfect instance happened to me that I would love to share with you so you can see how healing the body fits into The Shift to Spiritual Perception.

Remember the frozen peas on my head? Finally my headache abated, but I was aware of a lingering lack of energy and enthusiasm. Nothing I did relieved this symptom. The problem remained a mystery to me. A few days later, my partners and I went skiing. I had never skied before. I learned how to ski quickly and practiced a few times on the bunny slope.

The practice session went so well that I agreed to go to the top of the big hill and ski down, slowly, with my highly skilled partners leading the way. I really didn't want to ski down that hill and I felt that I had taken on more than I could do, but I managed to get most of the way down.

Near the bottom, I hit a very fast (for me) part and fell. At this point, I heard the Angel Idea, "That's it, you're done." I listened this time. I let the ski patrol come get me, and spent the rest of the day reading while my partners skied.

The next day I woke up unable to move my leg. For the first time ever, I took a taxi to work instead of walking the mile to my office. Now I had a symptom everyone could see and it hurt much more than my headache. I called my spiritual practitioner for help.

She reminded me that Divine Mind is unlimited in its motion. She asked me to forgive the moment and myself for what I was now considering a lack of good judgment. She asked me to take time to fully remember what was going on in the moment that I fell.

I realized that in that moment when I fell and thought I had been unwise, I was really only with God, reflecting perfect Intelligence and Grace. In Reality, the fall had never even happened—because God never conceived it.

The next day I woke up feeling much better. As I walked slowly to work, I reflected on how appropriate it was that I was moving so slowly since that was exactly how I felt in general. "Why," was still a question. I knew it had something to do with my dream of building my writing and speaking business. I had been staring at my work every night and accomplishing about a tenth of my normal output, and feeling no joy in the process.

This day I had a meeting with my business coach. Noticing my melancholy, he began to question me. The outcome of this was that I finally realized that the part of me called "Beca" was saying "no" to the dream.

She was saying no because it was just too overwhelming. She could figure out how to do each part, but the enormity of the idea as a whole meant that there were too many parts to do—and all she had was herself. I'd found the problem, and that was most of the work. Error uncovered is the beginning of the end.

I called my spiritual practitioner again. This time I told her about my lack of energy and the fact that I had also stubbed my toe not long before, so I had been hobbling for a few days.

As we talked, I realized that this had been going on for quite a while. My practitioner talked to me of Truth. She reminded me that God's plan carried the solution and that in essence I have never walked outside of that plan. The pain in my leg vanished immediately.

When I had first hurt my leg I thought I wouldn't be able to dance for weeks. I was able to take a jazz class the very next night.

I continued to think of the I Am—that I represent the Am in the Infinite Loving One. The mental fog lifted and I began to know how to carry out God's plan without worry about the outcome. The "problem" of feeling unable to move forward in life had dissolved and thus the symptoms—headache, stubbed toe, hurt leg, and melancholy dissolved as well.

Practical Body.

How would you feel if you had the perfect body? Imagine, along with what your new feelings will be, and do the two Quality Word lists. Follow up with an I Choose sheet about body.

These are the qualities of how a perfect body "looks"—after putting the list in order:

1. _____
2. _____
3. _____
4. _____
5. _____
6. _____
7. _____
8. _____

These are the qualities of how I will feel—after being put in order:

1. _____
2. _____
3. _____
4. _____
5. _____
6. _____
7. _____
8. _____

I Choose:

I Choose:

20

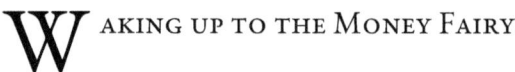

Fifteen

Waking up to the Money Fairy.

The only wealth is life.—Henry David Thoreau

Have you been waiting for the Money Fairy? Have you been wishing on a star, hoping to win the lottery, waiting for your ship to come in? Do you look under your pillow in the morning, praying that the Money Fairy has been there?

Wake up! The Money Fairy is here, has been here, will always be here. Who is the Money Fairy? You, of course. She is the part of each one of us who is conscious and aware of the fact that wealth in all its forms is always immediately available.

When we listen to the Money Fairy within, we remember how to receive wealth. We remember that the money we need is the end result of understanding and living in true wealth, putting God First. She is the awareness that reminds us of Truth. She is an Angel Idea lighting the way to our innate wealth.

ARE YOU AS WEALTHY AS YOU DESERVE TO BE?

Are you as wealthy as you deserve to be? Yes and no. Yes, because you are as wealthy as your current paradigm says you deserve to be. No, because wealth is unlimited, free, and always abundantly available.

Do you know anyone who is demonstrating this Truth all the time? Let the Money Fairy Angel Idea guide you from the small r reality of a limited point of view to the big R Reality, which has no limitations.

WHAT IS WEALTH?

Many wealthy people are little more than janitors of their possessions. —Frank Lloyd Wright

What is wealth? It is not money. It is not possessions. It is selfless, flowing, unlimited love. It is grounded, safe, and secure peace. It is freedom from fear, worry, confusion, or pain. It is the ability to move, breath, dance, and sing without limitation. It is the unshakable awareness that no harm can ever come to you or to the ones you love. It is the knowing that you are loved and loving limitlessly.

This wealth is represented in many forms: companionship, love, shelter, peace, food, money, good health, and a secure future. When we wait for the Money Fairy, we are waiting for a representation of w ealth.

When we awake to the Money Fairy within, we are conscious of true wealth. Thus, we see the representation or symbol. Most of us have it backward. We are working for the result and wondering why it is so hard to get rich (be wealthy).

Money is not required to buy one necessity of the soul. —Henry David Thoreau

Each of us is a tree.

One of my very favorite symbols of true supply is the tree. Imagine with me a tree as it grows its first leaf. Do you think it worries that this is the only leaf it will grow? Is it afraid when its leaves start to fall off, or when someone harvests its fruits? Although we cannot hear the tree's "thoughts" we can easily imagine that the tree never feels lack or fear.

Instead, it "knows" its supply is not the leaf, the fruit, or the flower. It is what they are, their essence—symbolized as sap—that produces the outward symbol of supply. What makes it even more glorious is that those outward symbols bless so many other living things through their shade, their food, their beauty, and the purification of the air.

Next time we worry about spending a leaf, or harvesting our fruit, we would do well to imagine we are a tree and know that the supply within is God Itself.

What does the Money Fairy know?

The Money Fairy stands outside all paradigms. She knows Reality. The Money Fairy is always whispering in the ears of anyone who will listen. She reminds us, that there is a Higher Power, which is Mind, and that Mind is Love, the only Cause and Creator. How simple.

She knows that Spirit is substance, and that what look likes substance is only an outward manifestation of thought. She chooses to know only the One Mind's thoughts and she knows these thoughts are better described as ideas. She knows that ideas are wealth.

Do we know these things too? Of course we do, but we forget all the time. We are in the habit of living in small r reality. We forget that we have a choice. We can shift to the Money Fairy's point of view and begin to experience wealth. The Money Fairy does not deliver money itself, she merely leads us to the well that never runs dry, and sometimes the water looks like money.

The Money Fairy is always willing. She is willing to experience the unlimited wealth of Reality in all its forms. She says, "Yes!" to life. She lives her life in unabashed joy. Nothing can take her joy away. She knows it's the basis of being.

She says "No!" to restricted, unhealthy, selfish, or fearful thoughts. These thoughts do not exist in Reality. She says "yes" to ideas that are open, free, and loving. It does not mean she knows how the things she is saying yes to will happen. She only knows that in order to experience the wealth of Reality, one has to be willing.

We are often afraid to say yes. We make up very good reasons for saying no. We find friends who will agree with these reasons. We can usually prove we're right. But if we're not willing, nothing will change. We'll never find our way home to Reality. Our dreams will not come true.

Have you ever talked to people about a problem they're having, and you can see the solution clearly? You talk, explain logically, and maybe even get mad at them for not understanding.

However, no matter what you say, or how hard you work to make them hear you, they just don't get it. They keep on saying no. They can't see what you can see. It's because you are outside of their paradigm, so the solution is obvious to you. They're inside of their belief system, unwilling to let go to have things change.

Usually when we want something, it is not a big thing that stands in the way of having it. Usually it is a small, simple thought about which we're unwilling to change our mind. Remember the 1st Step To Shift is to Be Willing. No matter how badly we may desire improvement, or dream of having everything we've ever wanted, unless we are willing to have it, we will not.

How do we know what we're willing to have or to do? How do we know what our current belief system or paradigm is? We can look into our life-mirror. It will reflect back to us exactly what we think is true.

The world gives us direct, tangible evidence of who we think we are and what we think we deserve. This doesn't make us, or it, good or bad. It is just how we think things are. Wanting something better is the result of hearing the whisper of the Money Fairy—that there is more to life than what we call reality.

Sometimes we are not willing to change our point of view until many things happen to us that we do not like. Finally, we can do nothing more, and we whisper, "Help me." If we are willing, we will be helped. If we have moved ourselves out of the way; if we have said "I might be wrong about how things are;" if we have realized that we are not the One in charge; we will have become aware that we are the essence of God.

The endless I Am knows no limitations, has no judgments, no prejudices, no time. It is wealth. When we are willing to yield to it, our dreams unfold. If we have become humble and loving—we have become willing for the One Mind to guide our lives.

Our task is to get our human or small mind to consent to get out of the way. If the human mind could get better it probably would, but it can't.

All it can do is step aside and yield to the One Mind. Don't waste your time trying to change your mind—release it instead.

Do not wait; the time will never be "just right." Start where you stand, and work with whatever tools you may have at your command, and better tools will be found as you go along.—Napoleon Hill

FOCUS ON ABUNDANCE, NOT LACK.

To have and not to give is often worse than to steal. —Marie Von Ebner-Eschenbach

All that we are arises with our thoughts. With our thoughts, we make our world. —Buddha

Most of us, when faced with a problem, worry over it. We try all sorts of ways to fix it. One very important thing the Money Fairy knows is that if we are having a problem, such as not enough money, that is not the problem. We think it is. We focus all our attention on it but the problem gets worse.

We have already learned that a problem is a result, not a cause. It is a result of a choice, or a set of beliefs that we have in some area of our life. We know that where we focus our attention is where we get the result. In other words, it is our emotional thought that produces the result.

For example, we can believe intellectually that we are all wealthy and that money is always available. However, when there's not enough money in the bank to meet our bills, fear takes the upper hand. Our emotion is a sense of lack.

Remember, what we believe to be reality magnifies, and it is emotion that does the magnification. Therefore, when we allow emotional fear to have the upper hand—we perceive more lack.

WHAT IS MONEY?

Money, which represents the prose of life and which is hardly spoken of in parlors without an apology, is, in its effects and laws as beautiful as roses. —Ralph Waldo Emerson

If money be not thy servant, it will be thy master. The covetous man cannot so properly be said to possess wealth, as that may be said to possess him. —Francis Bacon

All achievement, all earned riches, have their beginnings in an idea. —Napoleon Hill, *Think and Grow Rich*

Money is an object. Money is a representation of wealth. It is an object that can carry out a purpose without us being physically present. This object extends our love to everyone it touches as we express gratitude for its assistance in demonstrating that love.

When you spend money, are you thinking about gratitude and love? Or are you hoarding it because you think it is your wealth? If there is not currently enough of this object to accomplish what you want, do you let that perception become the truth for you? Does the outward picture become the inward?

Money is an emotion. We may think money is logical but it is emotional. As a Certified Financial Planner, I spent years listening to people asking me about their money. They all wanted to know the facts. What many were not willing to do was face the truth that facts have almost nothing to do with money. Money is nearly all emotion. Investing money with logic produces one kind of result. Investing money with feeling produces another.

Learning which emotions govern our spending gives us control. What we focus our attention on is what we will get. If our emotion is lack, lack will multiply. What we perceive to be reality magnifies—so Shift to true wealth and accelerate into abundance.

Money is a symbol. The weakest motivator is money—though you wouldn't know it to look at the world as it is today. We bid for the highest salary. We stay in work that we hate because it pays more. Companies offer money bonuses while treating employees as cogs in the wheel.

However, we must look deeper to find the real motivator. The only thing we can control is what we accept as Reality. Once we replace limited thought with God First our world changes. To be wealthy we have to stop thinking that we are working for money, and become aware of what we are really working for. Once we do that, we won't make the foolish choice of working twelve hours a day to provide for our family while losing them in the process.

I used to say routinely, "I want to be rich and famous." I couldn't understand why that wasn't happening. One day I realized that neither one of those statements was true for me.

I discovered I hardly cared about money, and could not get motivated by traditional ideas such as the being the biggest producer or getting the year-end bonus. And the thought of being famous actually scared me. What was going on? I was repeating what I thought was true, that we all want to be rich and famous. However, I had to find out what I really wanted.

There are four qualities money represents for most of us. These are Security, Power (Prestige), Freedom, and Love. When you have completed the worksheets at the end of this chapter, you will see where you spend your money—in other words, you'll know which quality motivates you the most. At this point, you can ask yourself, is this really what my work, or lack of work, is providing me? Am I working for money and sacrificing the quality? Which quality it is doesn't matter. It is the knowledge of what's important to you that makes the difference. Do the worksheets and find out for yourself.

One result of completing the worksheets is that you may find you have a value conflict. This happened to me.

Although I had been using these worksheets in my "The Truth About Your Money" workshops, I had not filled them out myself for years. While writing The Shift class I transferred the worksheets to class notes and decided to do them again myself. Since I was struggling with money supply at the time, I was willing to do anything to uncover what was blocking my progress.

The result showed me that freedom and security held equal place in my mind. We already know when we have two equal values, or qualities; our core-self does not know which one to give us. We have to put the qualities we want in descending order. At that point, we move forward.

I understood the value conflict immediately. Valuing freedom, my days were my own and I did not have to report to anyone. Valuing security, I wanted enough money to pay my bills and have enough left over to play.

However, in my case, at that time, putting freedom first meant that I was not secure; I did not have enough money to pay my rent or to play, and so I was not really free either.

I recognized that I had been ignoring the Angel Idea that had been knocking at the door of my mind for over a year—to return to the work I knew and did well (financial planning) and provide security for myself first. Then I could find freedom. I realized that I was not being practical or loving to myself by continuing to struggle at something that could not yet provide for me. I was not going to give up my dream, I was just going to provide a measure of security in order to be free to create and think instead of worry.

During this thought process, I discovered hidden fears about what would happened to my internal values, and my life, if I returned to the business world.

I confronted these fears by knowing that Love always provides a place for me to be myself and take care of myself. The result was much better than I imagined, and by returning to the business world, I became more valuable to others as well as to myself.

Because I was clear about what I wanted to offer, at no point did I have to compromise what I believed in.

WORKING FOR ALL THE WRONG REASONS.

Whatever you think having more money will give you—aliveness, peace, self-esteem—is the quality you need to develop to become more magnetic to money and abundance. View money and things not as something you create to fill a lack, but as tools to help you more fully express yourself and realize your potential.—Sanaya Roman and Duane Packer, *Creating Money*

At any point that you begin to substitute money as a goal, as a motivating factor, for the more important things in your life, you may end up in pain.—Michael Phillips, *The Seven Laws of Money*

I was talking to a couple about their desire to purchase a vacation plan that would last them through their lifetime and their children's and grandchildren's. We spoke about how much the children would like it, and how they might use it to travel more. While we talked, I questioned them about their family. It turned out they had five kids, but they rarely saw each other as an entire family, never had meals together, and the dad was feeling badly because he hadn't seen his oldest son for a few weeks. They were missing each other because of their schedules.

The dad worked a huge number of extra hours at his job. Why? The company requested it. He had just spent $14,000 for a tractor to mow his lawn. However, when the decision came down to purchasing the vacation package he turned it down. Why? Not enough time to take a vacation (he didn't want to disappoint the company) and he didn't want to spend the very small amount of money the membership would cost.

If he would have been willing to tell me what he loved most and the qualities most important in his life, I am fairly sure he would have answered—my family and their happiness. Yet, everything he did said otherwise. He was working for all the wrong reasons and missing the whole point.

Things that matter most must never be at the mercy of things that matter least.—Goethe

POOR IS A STATE OF MIND.

The majority of people who fail to accumulate money sufficient for their needs are generally easily influenced by the opinions of others.—Napoleon Hill, Think and Grow Rich

Poor is a state of mind, broke is a temporary condition.—Michael Todd

Poverty is a contagious disease. There is no value in being poor. Poverty is a sin in the real meaning of the word: We are missing the mark of who we really are and what we already have.

Don't accept the common point of view that there is not enough. We live in an agreed-upon perception, or paradigm, that idealizes a sense of lack.

Not just lack of money, but lack of time, lack of love, lack of patience, and lack of courage.

The news reports lack. Friends report lack. Advertisements want us to feel lack so we will buy their product. Break this cycle. Shift out of this low gear that grinds uphill and state the Truth.

As the expressions of the Infinite Loving One, we are already and always the expression of wealth. Since God is omnipresent supply—where is the lack?

Each of us has all we need in every phase of our lives. Make wealth contagious by listening to Angel Ideas, and then take action on the ideas and gifts they bestow.

Remember, to receive you must first give. However, be cautious. Don't give so much away that there's nothing left. This type of giving also causes poverty.

UNKINK THE MONEY-HOSE.

When your money-hose is kinked and instead of a stream you are getting a trickle, ask yourself whether you are tempted by thoughts or ideas in the list below. All of us to some extent have one or more of these thoughts rumbling around in our minds. However, once we see through them they begin to dissolve. Remember, these suggestions are not our own thought, just temptations to believe in duality.

- Not understanding or acknowledging what is true value.

- Not understanding or acknowledging another's value.

- Being afraid that there is not enough.

- Remaining in the habit of "thinking poor."

- Harboring thought patterns such as hate, bitterness, and despair.

- Having feelings that the world owes you a living.

- Wanting it our way.

- Believing that we are separated from the Source.

- Believing that there is something else besides the One Mind.

- Believing that we are the creators—for good or evil.

- Not putting God First.

- Thinking that poor is a divine quality.

- Believing the misconception that to be wealthy people have to compromise their values.

- Not wanting to accept the responsibilities of wealth.

- Afraid of "doing better" than those we love.

- Believing in the role of our gender.

If there is not enough cash flow, it may be because of one of the following reasons:
- Believing money is something we have to earn.

- Believing supply is an outside representation.

- Forgetting it's the product, not the purpose.

- Believing in the myth of lack—of all kinds.

- Stockpiling and not circulating. This applies to everything, including money.

- Not completely living up to our highest sense of integrity.

Once we uncover a negative thought pattern, return Back to One—to the One Mind. We do not claim these thoughts as our own. Relinquish and release.

Fear of poverty is a state of mind, nothing else! But it is sufficient to destroy one's chances of achievement in any undertaking. —Napoleon Hill, *Think and Grow Rich*

THE PRINCIPLES OF THE LOAVES AND FISHES.

As I have mentioned before, there is a wonderful story in the Bible that illustrates true supply, the story of the loaves and the fishes (John 6:1–14).

Instead of thinking that only someone as wise and as evolved as Jesus could accomplish this "miracle," let's look at what he may have been trying to tell us. What Laws of Spirit was he demonstrating?

Jesus was teaching a multitude, a crowd. He was so interesting to listen to that as he walked, the crowd followed. Towards the end of the day, Jesus realized that the crowd must be hungry. Love is practical. While teaching about eternal Love and endless supply Jesus did not expect the crowd to go hungry.

The disciples, thinking there was no way to feed everyone, told Jesus that he was not responsible for making sure they were fed. He had been teaching Truth all day, what more could he do? They suggested he send the people home to eat.

Since there was no handy-dandy fast-food restaurant nearby, Jesus thought that this would be unkind.

Love is indeed practical. Taking care of human needs while we learn of the Truth is both wise and necessary.

What happened next? Andrew, one of the disciples, noticed that a lad had a few loaves and fishes, but he was not sure how they could feed the crowd.

Jesus had no doubts. He did not believe what his eyes were telling him. For us this might translate into not believing the checkbook, but turning to God First.

When something looks impossible, we know it seems that way because we are seeing the situation through a material lens.

The story continues. Jesus thanked God for what He had already provided.

Three points:

- Jesus never doubted at that moment that he was personally provided for.

- He also knew that everyone in the crowd was already provided for.

- He was grateful for this understanding.

Once he received the loaves and fishes from the lad, Jesus had the disciples begin to feed the crowd. What points was he making? First, there was no time delay. The seeds did not need to be found and they did not have to wait for the seeds to grow to harvest the grain to turn it into dough and then bake the bread. There is no time factor in God's provision. Second, he expected and knew that Mind's (Love's) provision was always available and demonstrable.

The last point is one of my favorites. After everyone was fed, there was an abundance left over! Most of us operate from the belief system of having just enough to get by. This story demonstrates to each of us that we should expect to receive an overflowing abundance at all times. There is no waste. It is our heritage to have more than we need.

WHAT IS DEBT?

But by an equality, that now at this time your abundance may be a supply for their want, that their abundance also may be a supply for your want, that there may be equality. —II Corinthians:8:14, *Bible*

Debt is a gift from someone who believed in you enough to lend you money. When you repay debt, you are repaying a gift. Our bills are a form of a gift. The utility companies provide light, water, and phones before we pay for them. What a gift! It is a belief in our future selves.

At some time, most of us either lend or borrow money. How we approach either side of this process either blesses us or kinks the hose. Each of us at different times in our lives has more to offer than someone else. Sometimes this giving does not come in the form of debt but through a wise business transaction.

When I first began in the financial planning industry, I sold life insurance. I had a great deal of trouble with the word "sell," because I didn't want to manipulate people into something they really didn't want to do. Eventually, I learned that my purpose was to let them know what I had to offer as truthfully as I could, and then give them a safe place to make the right choice for themselves. This reasoning helped me through the first hurdle of selling.

One day, I discovered another hurdle. I was in the middle of a divorce and really felt that I needed a life insurance deal to close so I could move my children and myself to a new home. I found I was afraid to close the deal. I didn't want to impose my own sense of lack upon the women I valued as a friend.

Then I read the quote above from Corinthians about equality and I saw the deal in a new way. I realized that at that moment, my friend's abundant money supply could provide what she needed in the form of life insurance, and I could provide that "right idea." It was equality. I was not less because I didn't have enough money. We were both blessed by the transaction.

If we approach the repayment of debt of any kind with the thought, "Oh no, I have to pay this," we are kinking the money-hose. If you have a debt that you do not want to repay, you may end up not receiving any money at all just so you won't have to pay it.

If you aren't receiving enough money and you have debt, ask yourself:

- Am I choosing to not pay?

- Am I withholding Love from anyone?

- Am I withholding forgiveness from anyone, including myself?

- Am I not expressing gratitude for the gift I have?

Here is one more thing to ponder. Before choosing to borrow, make sure that you are not using debt simply to escape what is going on now, while giving your future self a problem. Remember, debt is either a gift or a burden to your future self, so make sure you are borrowing for the right reasons.

Goodness is the only investment that never fails us. —Henry David Thoreau, Walden

Practical Money.

Ask yourself, "What is wealth to me?" To get the wealth we expect, we must keep our focus only on wealth. Be grateful for the overflowing abundance of ideas—true wealth—that supply us moment by moment. Don't forget that it is okay to expect and receive money as a form of wealth. List here your qualities of wealth and have a friend help you put them in order. (See the Chapter God First for a reminder on how to do Quality Word lists.)

Then do an I Choose sheet on what you want to see. The combination of a qualities list and an I Choose sheet is very powerful.

21

— • —

SIXTEEN

- Check the Resource chapter for the link to get the money worksheets, and then follow the instructions. This is an important exercise. Don't skip it!

The best effect of fine persons is felt after we have left their presence.—Ralph Waldo Emerson

The questions, "Who am I?" and "Why am I here?" fly around the back of our heads and bang on the door of our minds. When we open the door, we can get interesting answers.

THE DUCKS SAID STOP!

We are put on this earth to reflect what is best about ourselves.—Charles Haid, *Drama-Logue*

One time some ducks admonished me for not knowing the answer to these questions. It happened one day when I was running. I was going through a change of marriage and career and wasn't quite sure where I would go next. I got into the habit as I was running of asking myself "What shall I do? Who am I?" My running route took me by the harbor, where I would often have to pick my way through a flock of ducks. One day as I ran through the ducks I heard them say—really!—"You are driving us crazy with this question. Why don't you just be yourself? We never ask 'should we be ducks?'—we are just exactly what we are and we don't waste time wondering if we can be something else."

You think I didn't hear this? I did, or at least I knew that was what they were saying—and it stopped me cold. I realized the truth of what they were telling me. We all bloom as the plant that we are. I could care for myself as if I were a rose knowing I am a lilac, but I could never stop being a lilac.

What I needed to do was just be who I am and take care of myself as that person—and stop pretending, or wishing, I was someone else. And that is all you need to do, too. That is your purpose, to express who you are.

I long to accomplish a great and noble task, but it is my chief duty to accomplish small tasks as if they were great and noble. —Helen Keller

Our stumbling block comes into play when we think it matters how we express ourselves. When we think that some callings are more important than others, we may not think ours is important enough. That is far from the Truth. Each flower in the field, each duck in the harbor, each person is a unique and necessary part of God's expression.

As we listen to Angel Ideas, we begin to know who we are and what we love to do. This is the key, loving what we do. Let's do an exercise that may help us determine what we love and how we would like to express it.

Throughout this book, we have done many qualities lists so by now you're quite an expert. Take a moment now and review your lists. Make a new list of the top 8 to 10 qualities and values that you feel you must have in your life. For this exercise, they do not have to be in order.

The qualities and values that mean the most to me:

1. _____
2. _____
3. _____
4. _____
5. _____
6. _____
7. _____
8. _____
9. _____
10. _____

Now comes the fun part. Trust your inner voice to speak while you do this. In other words, get your logical mind out of the way. Take these 8–10 qualities and make them into not more than three sentences that describe you and your life. Be sure to include emotion and action.

What have you done? You have written a mission statement that can be used as a yardstick to measure your actions and decisions.

In *The Shift* classes where I use this, some people know they have written something wonderful, and others think they have written something less than wonderful. You know what? Everyone always writes something wonderful, because it gives a clearer picture of the heart, and the heart is the first place to begin your life and purpose.

In the fabulous movie *Pleasantville*, as the inhabitants expressed an inner value of their heart they each transformed from black-and-white to full color.

The hero stayed black-and-white until he expressed the value he thought he most lacked—courage. When he expressed it through a selfless act, he discovered it had existed within him all the time, just as you will.

BECOMING YOURSELF.

You have certain mental images of yourself, your world, and the people around you, and you behave as though those images were the truth, the reality, rather than the things they represent.—Maxwell Maltz

We use electricity every day. Have you ever stopped to think that when we plug in a lamp it is the lamp that "decides" how bright it is going to be? The electrical wiring in our house doesn't know of the lamp's choice. It could be a 20-watt bulb or a 120-watt bulb. The electricity is just being electricity. The lamp is expressing the electricity; otherwise, we would not see it.

We are like lamps. We are all connected to the Source of One Infinite Love. How bright we choose to shine is up to us. Why not choose to be a 120-watt bulb?

In his famous "I Have A Dream" address in 1963, Martin Luther King Jr. said, "In a real sense all life is interrelated. All men caught in an inescapable network of mutuality, tied in a single garment of destiny. Whatever affects one directly affects all indirectly. I can never be what I ought to be until you are what you ought to be, and you can never be what you ought to be until I am what I ought to be."

MEETING OBSTACLES.

Ah, it seems so easy. Just plug into the Infinite Mind and express It through our illumination. Why don't we? What seems like a difficult question has a simple answer. It is because we believe that we are human, and acting out of "human nature," instead of knowing we are Spiritual.

Easy not to do.

The reason people fail or wallow in mediocrity is not because of what they don't know—it is because they refuse on a daily basis, to put into practice the things they do know. The natural inclination is to gravitate to the line of least resistance. That which is easy to do is easy not to do!—Matol Training Handbook

When I was in my twenties, my mentor tried to tell me why people wallow in mediocrity. I would nod wisely at her and think that I understood. Only recently have I really understood what she meant. It is our "human nature" to think life must be hard. When we were growing up there were things that we did that came very easily to us. We loved doing them. Somewhere we decided that since they were so easy to do they must not be important. Definitely they were not how we were going to "make a living" because "making a living" was supposed to be hard. For most of us, the easy thing to do slipped away. It was even easier to let them go.

This also pertains to not doing what we know how to do. We already know how. However, our small mind says, "Well then, there must be more to know." Doing what we know would be too easy and therefore no longer important.

The key to loving our life purpose is to take back the easy thing. Go back and find it, and then move forward with what you love to do. Shifting may sometimes be uncomfortable, but not hard. Doing what you love may make you uncomfortable, but it will feel joyful. Take each day and do something you already know how to do. It really is easy to Shift out of low gear into high gear when the car—you—is moving!

It seems to me that those songs that have been any good, I have nothing much to do with the writing of them. The words have just crawled down my sleeve and come out on the page. —Joan Baez

WHAT WILL PEOPLE THINK?

The reasonable man adapts himself to the world; the unreasonable one persists to adapt the world to himself. Therefore all progress depends on the unreasonable man. —George Bernard Shaw

What does it matter what people think? People will think anything they want to, no matter what we do. They will misquote and misunderstand us even when we do the best we can to fit into their paradigm. Given that, why not be doing something that makes you happy? It will surprise you how many wonderful new friends you will make who will support what you are doing, once you begin. What people think is their business, what you do with your life is yours.

BREAKING HABITS.

The secret of success is constancy of purpose. —Benjamin Disrali

No one can possibly achieve any real and lasting success or get rich in business by being a conformist. —J. Paul Getty

A foolish consistency is the hobgoblin of little minds. —Ralph Waldo Emerson

Hello—isn't this crazy? We hang on to "less than best" just because we know what it looks like and how to deal with it. Crazy but true!

We know what our life looks like now. Why change? We hold on to cars, relationships, and lives that aren't working, because at least we know how they don't work. We can adjust to fit into what will happen, when we get home or start the car, because it happens that way all the time.

Change is the universe's request to stretch and shift. Either you will follow the gentle request, or it will begin knocking and then pounding, until one day you finally wake up and begin expressing your unique version of the Infinite Loving One. After all, look what happened to Jonah when he did not follow his inner prompting from God. The whale swallowed him, depositing him forcefully where he had been prompted to go in the first place. The world needs each one of us to be ourselves. When we are doing something not ours to do, we are in the way of the person who needs to be expressing himself or herself in that place. And if we choose not to express our essence, everyone else loses the wonder and value of us.

For a man to achieve all that is demanded of him he must regard himself as greater than he is.—Goethe

USING CARGO CULT RELIGION.

In his book, *Surely You're Joking Mr. Feynman,* physicist Richard Feynman describes a group of South Seas natives after World War II. During the war they had seen airplanes land with lots of good things inside, such as clothes and food. After the war, they wanted those things to appear again. So they built runways, lit fires and made a wooden hut. A man sat in it wearing two wooden pieces on his head that looked like headphones. Then they waited for the planes. Of course, nothing ever happened. They had the form, not the essence. He calls this "cargo cult religion."

We do the same thing when we merely worship symbols and rituals and magic to get to God. We pray for miracles when we are the miracle. For the planes to land, we must build real runways, with real substance. This takes work—and the willingness to let go of who and what we think we are. Shifting is not a magic bullet; it is a process.

THINKING THINGS ARE DIFFERENT WHEN THEY'RE NOT.

Have you ever thought that what was bothering you had magically transformed into something different, a better picture, and then discovered it had not? Have you ever seen that something wasn't working but just "knew" that if you waited long enough it would change?

Tell the truth—you know these are both lies, don't you? And we know that lying, especially lying to ourselves, is a huge kink in the abundance-hose.

Sometimes we think things are different only because we are looking at them from a new angle. I had an example of this one day when I was roller-skating at the beach. I normally followed the same route each day. At one point the path had a fork in it. I would always take the left path. This path took me by the bay and then circled back around a park. One day I was lost in thought while skating.

Suddenly I realized that I had never before seen the bay that I was looking at. For a moment, my heart froze. I thought I was lost. Where had this bay come from? I had skated the area for years and I had never seen it before. I stopped skating and stood looking at the bay. Soon I recognized a familiar landmark and I suddenly knew what had happened. I had unconsciously taken the right-hand loop. I was seeing from the opposite direction.

Later that day I applied this insight to a personal relationship. I had been dating a new man whom I thought was very different from the last one. I had left the previous relationship because it had become emotionally abusive.

This new man looked different, he came from a different background, and therefore I felt he treated me differently. I stopped by his office to pick him up, but for some reason I found myself extremely irritated and upset with him. I excused myself and went to the bathroom. As I looked into the mirror, I remembered the skating incident from that morning. A light bulb went on in my head and I realized that although this man seemed different, he was not.

I was in the same type of situation from which I had just freed myself. Nothing had changed at all. I had merely been imagining that the situation was new.

Pay attention to those things in your life that you think will get better, or that you think have gotten better even though you have not done any changing yourself. For things to "change" we must face the truth about what they are and what we want, and not be afraid to move on if necessary.

EXPRESS YOUR PURPOSE THROUGH WORK, JOB, BUSINESS, CAREER.

Your soul doesn't care what you do for a living—and when your life is over, neither will you. Your soul cares only about what you're being while you're doing what you're doing.—Neale Donald Walsch

"Everyone does God's work in their own way," Wright told a rival, "You do it your way, I do it in His."—Frank Lloyd Wright

The more we live by our intellect, the less we understand the meaning of Life.—Leo Tolstoy

Trust thyself, every heart vibrates to that iron string. Accept the place the divine providence has found for you, the society of your contemporaries, the connection of events. Great men have always done so, and confided themselves childlike to the genius of their age, betraying their perception that the Eternal was stirring at their heart. —Ralph Waldo Emerson

Although we often express ourselves through our work, we do not own our work. We don't succumb to the temptation to say, "This is my work."

No matter how wonderful that work is, when we claim it as ours it now owns us and we have forgotten to put God First. Our "work" is to express God's love and express the unique qualities that make up our individuality. Since this is who you are, you are never "out of work." This is nice to know because it makes unemployment impossible.

If we find ourselves out of human work, the need is not to heal an adverse situation. The need is to practice what we know—that our work is to express who we are. On a moment-by-moment basis we acknowledge the evidence of Love, and Love will provide the ways and means to supply us with our human needs.

Principle, One Mind, does not analyze symptoms such as being out of work. It simply perceives Its own presence and power. To us this will appear as ideas accepted and to be acted upon.

We can always experience strength, security, and stability if we will look away from the prevalent and pervasive claim that we have no value, and instead remember that there is no other power to resist Principle. All activities are the activities of the One Mind and those activities are what we call "business."

During one of my "job searches," I kept wishing that God was much more direct in sending messages to me. I wished It would just send me a fax and let me know what the heck I was do. Finally, I got that fax, and I am passing it on to you:

Dear Loved One,

You have been reassigned to a new position. It is the one I have been telling you about for many years. It meets all the criteria that you asked for. In addition, your pay scale has been elevated to meet your new understanding of your worth.

I have been holding this position open for you for quite some time, since you are the only one who can do this particular job. I felt that you were ready a few years ago, but as we discussed, you felt that you had other things to do, and what you wish is what I want for you.

Today I rejoice that you have finally agreed to accept this new position. As you are performing your tasks, please remember that the ease and enjoyment you experience are sure signs that you are doing a wonderful job.

Please call on me at any time for assistance and encouragement, or if you wish to extend your job description. You may also contact me if you desire to increase your salary, which will be my pleasure to do.

Your ever-loving employer and Father-Mother, God

LOVE WHERE YOU ARE.

To affect the quality of the day, that is the highest of arts. Every man is tasked to make his life, even in its details, worthy of the contemplation of his most elevated and critical hour. —Henry David Thoreau, Walden

Remember that marvelous TV Show *Quantum Leap*? The show revolved around the premise that the main character had somehow perfected time travel. The problem was he couldn't get back to his own time.

Instead, when he traveled in time he would "leap" into someone's life, become that character until his assignment was complete, and then "leap" into another time and person. Sometimes he would think that he had completed his assignment but the leap wouldn't happen. At that point he would look again to see what he had missed and continue to live that life as well as he could until the issue was truly resolved—and at that point he would leap.

Sometimes we are stuck in a place that we really don't like and nothing seems to get us out of it. The emotions of hate or dislike are like glue, and won't let us go.

As a young mother, I lived in a town that I had grown to dislike very much. I thought about how much I wanted to "get out of there," but no opportunities or money presented themselves to make the move. With each day that went by, I counted more reasons why I didn't like where I was. One day I drove the car I disliked (because it too reminded me of the place I lived), to the store. As I was pulling away from the curb, someone pulled up behind me and hit my car. I got out and looked at the person who had run into me and started to laugh. He represented everything I disliked about where I lived. I had finally gotten the message from my Angel Ideas, even though they had to be pretty graphic and hard-hitting for me to wake up.

I went home and decided to make where we lived as beautiful as possible. Since I was short on funds, I took my shovel and dug up the entire front yard by hand—and replaced it with a brick walk, fencing, and flowers. I then did the same in back. I soon loved where I was living, and when I did leap to the next place I had forgotten how much I disliked the old one.

A calling is a messenger of change.—Greg Levoy, Callings

You miss 100% of the shots you never take.—Wayne Gretsky

WHERE IS YOUR FOCUS?

It is not enough to stay busy. So, too, are the ants. The question is: What are you busy doing?—Henry David Thoreau

The idea of Shifting is easy. Even the doing of Shifting is easy. Why we sometimes remain in low gear is that we simply forget the basics. If you ever find yourself in a place where you need a quick visual to Shift out of low gear, try this picture.

Pretend you are at the movies. All of a sudden the movie on the screen starts to sputter and fade. Eventually you can't hear or understand anything. At that moment, does anyone in the audience jump up and run to the screen and try to fix the picture? No, the whole audience turns around and yells at the person in the projection room, "Focus the projector!"

We are all sitting in the movies watching our lives unfold. When we do not like the picture, there's no point in running to the screen (our life) and beating on it. Instead, stop and focus the projector (your thinking).

This focusing will change the picture. And if you yearn to be everything that you've dreamed of and want your life to unfold with meaning and joy, focus your projector on the image of the Infinite Loving One—and your life will overflow with peace and abundance.

Eventually you will notice that you are not the movie, the projector, or the One who does the focusing. In the meantime, Shifting to God First will start the wheels moving, and the power of perception will take you where you want to go.

Practical Purpose.

Here is one last worksheet for you. Write out what you want your purpose, as expressed in a life career, to feel and look like, after starting with a Quality Word list. Finish up with an I Choose sheet and then give it back to God. So Be It.

Once you have completed the qualities list put the words into a story about how you want to spend your life. Be sure to include people, places, things, activities, and feelings.

The qualities I desire to express in my career are:

1. _____
2. _____
3. _____
4. _____
5. _____
6. _____
7. _____
8. _____

This is a story of how I want to spend my life:

22

—·—

SEVENTEEN

- THE SEVENTH STEP—CELEBRATE WITH GRATITUDE

At the end of each ever-expanding circle of our increasing awareness that we live in the Kingdom of Heaven, we celebrate with gratitude—for what we now know, understand, and have put into practice, of Truth.

Our gratitude is unending for the understanding that as we Shift to Spiritual Perception and focus on Truth, what is untrue is revealed and easily dissolved through the understanding that all that has ever happened or will happen is the activity of the One Mind.

We remind ourselves that the purpose of the Shift to Spiritual Perception is not to change the outside picture, but to know and experience and be the activity of God.

Use these following statements of Truth as guidelines to stay on the Spiritual path: I know that *what I perceive to be reality magnifies.*

Therefore, I am willing to choose to magnify only GRACIOUS.

- God First: I will put God First in everything that I say, think, or do.

- Repent: I will change my thinking and Shift to Spiritual Perception.

- Angel Ideas: I will listen for, and take action on, the constant guidance of Angel Ideas that reveal light, love, and abundance.

- Choose Consciously: I choose to be conscious of the good in my life that has already been provided through the activity of the unlimited Mind of God, the only Cause and Creator.

- Imagine—What If: I will imagine only the feelings of what is beautiful, good, pure, and true.

- Obsessive Vigilance: I will be obsessive about only one thing: Shifting to GRACIOUS.

- Unkink The Hose: I will Unkink the constantly flowing abundance-hose by releasing negative habits, limited belief systems, and personality.

- So Be It: I will give it to God when I have done my part; and having done all I will stand in Love.

- I acknowledge in gratitude and joy that all of my life is in the constant care of a loving, all-good God.

- So Be It.

Although you will see some worksheets at the end of each chapter, it might be easier to download the PDF workbook to use over and over again.

Here's where you can find the workbook, the money sheets, and even a copy of all the quotes used in this book

And if you would like more of *The Shift Series* books where I explore some of the ideas found in *Living in Grace i*n greater detail, you can find them all at:

23

RESOURCES

Although you will see some worksheets at the end of each chapter, it might be easier to download the PDF workbook to use over and over again.

Here's where you can find the workbook, the money sheets, and even a copy of all the quotes used in this book: perceptionu.com/the-library/workbooks

And if you would like more of *The Shift Series* books where I explore some of the ideas found in *Living in Grace i*n greater detail, you can find them all at: becalewis.com/books/shift-series

24

— • —

Author's Note

Writing this book was a culmination of having people ask me for advice throughout my life, based on my point of view. This point of view "came with me," but has been refined through practice and thought and by reading every book about God and spirituality and philosophy that I could lay my hands on, driven by my deep need to search for Truth.

It was the urging of friends that prompted me to solidify what I was telling them and to begin to offer a class called *The Shift*, and it was friends who then said, "Please write this down in a book," and that's how this book, *Living In Grace* was born.

It was a long gestation period. It took over eight years to write. It was originally published in 2002. I have updated a few things each time it has been republished, but nothing that most people would notice.

If you like what I write, you can help spread the word, and keep my work going, by "liking" my books, anywhere the option is offered. I would be honored if you would also post your honest reviews of the book. This will help other readers decide whether it is worth their reading time.

In today's world it is the reader that spreads the word about books they like. If you like mine, anyway you choose to spread the word will be so helpful and appreciated. I thank you in advance for all that you do!

I hope this book has helped you discover more about the Truth of yourself, and that your life will expand in wonderful ways because of this knowledge.

Join my mailing list at to find out what book(s) I am giving away for free.

Don't forget to pick up your free workbook and money sheets. You can find the information in the Resource chapter of this book.

I am looking forward to getting to know you!

-Beca

THE FOUR ESSENTIAL QUESTIONS

WHAT OTHERS SAY

What Others Are Saying About The Four Essential Questions

"R eading Beca Lewis is very much like sitting down for a quiet chat with a wise, close and trusted friend. In The Four Essential Questions Beca shares examples from her own life; her own experience; her own knowing, as she guides us to rediscover the Divine in all things and gently prompts us to examine who it is we truly are. Highly recommended."—Greg Willson, co-editor, Cultivate Life! Magazine

"Beca Lewis makes heaven feel so down to earth! Her writing is clearly inspired, yet practical, provable, and proven by her as evidenced through the wise yet humble stories she tells about her own experiences. The Four Essential Questions definitely helped to open my eyes to some unseen limits I may have been accepting for myself or in denial about, and at the same time brought a sigh of relief that I could be free of them!

Her message comes with honesty and conviction, yet no preachiness or judgment. The book feels just like a warm and ongoing conversation she has been having with God, which we have been made welcome to sit in on. Very comforting, inspiring, and FUN to read! I would highly recommend this book to fellow seekers and I know I'll be reading it again!"—Laura Moliter, CS, Author of The Key to the Kingdom: How a Change in Perspective Can Make Your Earth More Like Heaven and the e-book, Inspiration and Exultation: Healing Ideas for Every Day

"Beca Lewis has written a thoughtful and deeply felt spiritual guide to dissolving the material habits that keep us from our spiritual nature. It is a calming meditation that will help you move through the daily cacophony to a place of deep inner peace and love. Bravo, Beca! Thank you for this." —Chellie Campbell, author of *The Wealthy Spirit and Zero to Zillionaire*

"You put a wonderful book together. I loved how you organized it, how you positioned the profound with the concrete, and your honesty. I haven't seen a book quite like this, Beca. I stayed up late to finish it. It was unput-downable. I really, really loved this book!"—Gloria Wendroff, Godwriter, author of *Heavenletters, Love Letters from God*, Winner of Chelson 2004 Inspiration Book Award

Dedication

To my husband, Delbert Lee Piper, Sr., whose inspiration, feedback, support, and love have made all the difference, and whose influence is seen everywhere in my life, including in this book.

25

— • —

FORWARD

U se this book as a handy life guide.

I think of a guide as something, or someone, that keeps us aiming in the direction we want to be going. A guide has traveled ahead of us and has seen the dangers and the glories of the road that lies ahead.

Knowing where we want to go, it keeps us on track, and leads us away from danger, so we can enjoy the journey and arrive safely at our destination.

Sometimes a guide can do that gently. A simple whisper and a soft nudge is enough. Other times a yank on the arm or a shove in the back is necessary to keep us from falling off the cliff towards which we are blindly walking.

For a guide to be effective, we must be truthful to it. If we lie to the guide about what we want, who we are, and where we are going, we will end up in the wrong place.

As you read this book, tell the truth to yourself.

Use these questions to readjust the direction you are traveling based on what you learn.

Let *The Four Essential Questions* become your personal guide so that you remain safely on the path to your destination.

26

— . —

Preface

*H*abit with him was all the test of truth. It must be right: I've done *it from my youth.* —George Crabbe

We all have habits—some of them work in our favor. However, the ones that are formed through unknown and unconscious perceptions always work against us without our knowledge. In order to eliminate these dangerous habits, and replace them with spiritually healthy habits, we have to drill down into our thinking and perceptions.

We will use *The Four Essential Questions* as the drill. Once the way is cleared, we can consciously choose the habits that work for us; not against us. In this book, you will find the tools you need to continue to check, and eliminate, the habits that are no longer wanted, and build spiritually healthy ones.

When drilling into a deep piece of wood, it is necessary to continually pull the drill-bit out so the sawdust created lifts out of the hole.

Otherwise, the sawdust compacts and makes it harder and harder to drill. On the other hand, when we keep on drilling, and clearing out, at the end, the drill bit breaks through, and the last of the sawdust falls through easily. The hole is clear and ready to be used.

If we don't completely drill the hole the whole way through there are two results. The obvious one is that it was a waste of time to do all that drilling because without a completed hole nothing can be done with it. The other, not so obvious, is that the hole will, over time, fill up with "stuff."

This also happens when we dig a hole for a plant. Of course, we know that the dirt must be taken out of the hole, in order to be even called a hole. However, if we don't fill the hole with the intended plant, it will eventually fill up with something else.

We dug plant holes one year expecting to plant trees, but never got around to it. The next year, the holes had to be completely cleared again in order to be ready for the trees.

This same idea happens with ruts. My husband Del sees this all the time when working in the woods. If a machine has gone through and caused ruts, and they were not filled in again with soil, eventually they fill up on their own.

Perhaps this seems okay, but it isn't really, because they don't fill up with solid dirt. Instead, they fill with loose things like leaves and grass. This makes them invisible to someone using the path or road, and causes a dangerous hazard for anyone who steps, or drives, into them.

This is the same with uncovering habits. We are really drilling down into our thinking, but if we don't go the whole way through, the empty space will simply fill up with unwanted, and unknown, "stuff."

That is why it is important in drilling down into our perceptions to continue the process of clearing unwanted habits. If we experience a small amount of freedom, or life changes a bit for the better, it will be tempting to simply stop and go no further. However, if we stop before completion, then like the uncompleted hole in the wood, the unplanted hole in the dirt, or the unfilled rut, we have an even worse situation than we had before.

Sometimes holes are easy to drill, dig, and fill in. Other times they are not. However, if the going sometimes seems to be too hard, or even boring, because it isn't happening fast enough, keep going anyway. Use the questions in this book to help you through it; to make it easier and even to make it fun.

The reward is far greater than the apparent effort.

Just as when we finish drilling a hole and the last of the sawdust simply drops out, if we keep on going, the last of the unwanted perceptions that have caused the habit will simply drop away.

There are only two mistakes one can make along the road to truth: not going all the way, and not starting. — Buddha

27

— • —

CHAPTER ONE

A *human being is part of a whole, called by us the "universe,"*
a part limited in time and space. He experiences himself, his
thoughts and feelings, as something separate from the rest—a kind of
optical delusion of his consciousness. This delusion is a kind of prison
for us, restricting us to our personal desires and to affection for a few
persons nearest us. Our task must be to free ourselves from this prison
by widening our circles of compassion to embrace all living creatures
and the whole of nature in its beauty.—Albert Einstein

Since we were very young, inside all of our heads, a voice suggests
something to each of us. That suggestion is usually in the form of
a question, which is why I call it a *life question*. We are rarely aware
of our life question, and since we are unaware of it, it runs our life,
because of the perception it creates.

Seneca Elder, Twylah Nitche, said, *If you are not getting the right*
answers, you are not asking the right questions. Obviously, we must
discover our own personal life question and break its pattern in order
to live the life we want to live and to be free of its grasp.

To discover our life question, we have to listen, and observe, our
own conversations, and our own life. Once we discover it, the next
step is learn how to face and replace it with a statement that works
for us, not against us.

243

We see the results of these life questions when we begin to notice that life isn't working as well as we know it could work, and that the path we are on is not taking us where we thought we wanted to go.

The good news is, there are only a few of these life questions, and we all say, or ask them, with a variation or two.

Perhaps yours is like one of these:

- I don't know.
- Why do I have to live up to everyone's expectations?
- Why is life so hard?
- Why is life so unfair?
- Why am I this way?

It is possible that you don't recognize these questions for yourself immediately, but if you listen to your external and internal conversations, you will begin to hear, and recognize, the one that you have been saying and asking all your life. This question, or statement, is currently the guide of your life.

Do you really want to be guided by the perceptions, "I don't know, Why do I have to live up to everyone's expectations, Why is life so hard, Why is life so unfair, Why am I this way?" Of course not!

The Four Essential Questions we will ask in this book will break the pattern of that *life question* which is really a *life-sentence*. Breaking that pattern is the key to living the life that we want to live, were meant to live, and desire to live; not sometime in the future, but here and now.

Of course, we all know the definition of insanity as spoken by Albert Einstein: *Doing the same thing over and over again and expecting different results.*

Ask these *Four Essential Questions* and answer them truthfully, and you can absolutely expect different results!

PERCEPTION RULES

What we perceive to be reality magnifies.—Beca Lewis

In the world of marketing, one is supposed to come up with a "catch phrase" or USP (unique selling proposition). Many, many, years ago I condensed all that I was trying to say into this phrase: What We Perceive To Be Reality Magnifies.

Years later, I am still using it because it is the clearest way to explain that what appears as reality—is not. Perception is reality. This is different from what is meant by the saying, "What we focus upon creates reality," which implies that we are creators or at least co-creators. It's easier than that, because perception is reality. However, the big question is—whose perception, and can we shift ours and thereby shift what appears as our world? The answer is "yes," but first we need to know and understand how perception works, or rules.

On the TV program *60 Minutes*, a General spoke about war as a perception. While working as a Certified Financial Planner, I learned that the stock market is an agreed-upon perception. The worldview that governs so much of our lives, is an agreed-upon perception. Everything that the five senses tell us is a perception—not a real thing, but a perception. Nevertheless, these kinds of perceptions block from view what is big R Reality.

Cleaning up perception is not creating a new world. It is seeing the world as it really is, completely and irresistibly, perfectly spiritual.

Then what is spiritual? Is it a cleaned-up material view that attracts what we want to us, and creates a perfect lifestyle? Is it measurable energy that can be manipulated and used to benefit us?

No, that is a material perception. Spiritual, Spirit, is not measurable. Spiritual is not measurable by the human senses. It is not related to dogmas or human opinions. It is the seven nouns of God in action—Soul, Mind, Spirit, Love, Life, Principle, and Truth*. It is the logic behind it all. It is the essence and power of unconditional Intelligent Love.

As we become aware of the thoughts, ideas, beliefs, and perceptions that color the world we see, we can choose whether we want to continue with the limited, chaotic, often cruel, and never fixable perception of the worldview, or the elegant, logical, entirely loving, always supportive, One Intelligent Mind, God's perception.

Since what we perceive to be reality magnifies, why not choose to magnify what God sees and knows? That perception is the perfect one, containing all that is, holding every element of Its idea called world, man, universe, animals, plants, every blade of grass, and every grain of sand as Itself in action.

The proof that there is a God, is that you and I, and all that we know, exists. All questions about why and how are distractions. If our intent is to know as God knows, then let's forget the human questions; and instead practice seeing as God sees.

Of course, this involves discovering, uncovering, eliminating, dissolving, and letting go of all perceptions that block our sight to the One Perceiver. Assuming we are all willing to do this, because our intent is to see as God sees, then the next step is to become aware of what we believe to be reality and see if it is in alignment with the Truth of One Cause and Creator.

This is not a judgment time; this is simply an awareness of the misperceptions that we have held dear. This is what will result in a life shift.

This is doing dirt-time and deep practicing. As we make that shift, and awareness begins to creep into our life, lots of "stuff" appears that is not necessarily what we wanted, or expected, to see.

It's like moving. As we take things out of closets and drawers and decide if we want to move it to the next place, or throw it away, we are amazed to find that we have not paid attention to what has been accumulating in our home.

It's the same with a state of mind. We hide past actions, hurts, and sorrows in boxes, and drawers, and closets in our mind. As we move from the past state of mind to the next one, we get to decide what to take with us and what to discard.

When we move from a physical home, we touch physical objects to make the decision about what to keep.

If we get emotional about why we have it, thinking that it can't be replaced, get mad at ourselves for not noticing it before, or practice any other form of judgment, then we can be stuck in that moving process forever. It's not necessary to do this.

In the same way, as we examine our perceptions, ideas, and beliefs that we have accumulated, it is not necessary to understand the why and how of each one.

It is not necessary to beat ourselves up for the mistaken points of view that have lived in our thoughts. If we did this, we would never move. That point of view would be our mental home for a long time.

What we can do instead is choose whether the object in our home, or the perception in our thought, is how we want to live now. We can let go of anything that isn't the highest understanding we currently have of the perfection of Love.

As we clean our home, what has always been there becomes visible. As we clean our perception, what has always been present becomes visible.

If the doors of perception were cleansed everything would appear to man as it is, infinite. For man has closed himself up, till he sees all things thru' narrow chinks of his cavern. —William Blake

Let's stop trying to perceive what is real through the narrow chinks of our cavern. Let's choose to see as God sees—Infinitely. Then there is no need for a secret on how to create and achieve, because it will be clear to us that all we need is already present, and all that needs to be done has already been completed, in big R Reality.

Yes, perception rules.

There is no getting away from it. It is like the ever-present air that we breathe, or the force that keeps us from floating off the planet. It exists as a law, so it is best to make friends with it, understand it, and learn how to use it for good, and in this way the habits we form will be from this new perception. The results are almost unimaginable.

*Synonyms of God as stated by Mary Baker Eddy

Two Modes Of Perception

The only real voyage of discovery consists not in seeking new landscapes but in having new eyes.—Marcel Proust

We know now that *what we perceive to be reality magnifies.* Perception is our reality. What we believe and perceive within, is what is seen without.

There are two modes of perception: *state of mind and point of view.* We get to choose both; this is the meaning of free will. Our choices do not change big R Reality, they simply allow us to see and experience more or less of it in our daily lives.

To live congruently, our *point of view perception* and *state of mind perception* must be in sync and harmony. This is much harder to do, than to say.

This is why an unknown life question can be so devastating to our life. It means that without our awareness, it has created a point of view that builds the life we are experiencing, which in turn builds an unhealthy habit. Dissolving that question through awareness, we can consciously choose our own point of view and corresponding state of mind.

It is important to know that I am not talking about positive thinking, or even mind over matter. Both of these ideas exist in the small limited realm, or small r reality, and only work by using human will power, or human strength. I am talking about letting go of the illusion, the misperception, of humanness, and stepping into the unstoppable force called Love, or Mind, or God.

Perhaps you don't care to access this Infinite realm. So be it for now. It doesn't really matter at this time, because all I am asking you to understand and accept is that perception is reality, and as we shift ours, the world shifts with us.

THREE HABIT STORIES

Story One:
For over 6 years, I had eaten peanuts in the shell for breakfast. This may be a crazy breakfast, but I loved it all the same. However, every time I cracked a peanut, little peanut pieces flew around which required some careful cleanup afterward. Then one day Del decided this was the day I could learn the easy way to eat peanuts. Instead of breaking them in half I just had to look, or feel, for the dimple in the top of the peanut, give a slight push and the peanut opened easily, with very little flinging of pieces.

I was amazed to learn I had been cracking peanuts the hard way for years. However, that was the easiest part of the lesson. Ever since then I have to remind myself constantly, "Not that way," as I crack instead of push, "this way." I am still working on eating peanuts the easy way.

Story Two:
When we used to go to an office, some mornings we had to use a swipe card to get in before the doors were officially unlocked. The office had three doors, two of which are right beside each other. One day, another person and I reached the two doors at the same time.

I swiped my card in the one door as he swiped his in the other. As I did so, he turned to me and said, "What? This card works on that door too?"

He had worked in that office for almost two years and had taken the longer route to his office all that time because, obviously, the first person who had shown him how to use the card showed him how to open the side door. For two years, he had never thought to try the card in the other door, or even noticed that other people entered through different doors.

Story Three:

We had two cars, therefore two huge car keys to carry around on our key chains. I had taken one set of keys off my chain since I never used the other car. I kept the keys in a bowl by the door. Then one day we decided that I best put the keys back on the chain. I looked in the bowl and they weren't there.

I remembered that I had thought of taking the one set with us when we were traveling and I decided that I must not have returned it to the bowl afterwards. I searched our traveling stuff and it wasn't there. For the next few months, every time I thought about it I would look for the keys. In the car I would look under the seats, in the glove compartments, in desk drawers—anywhere I thought I might have put them.

One day, Del decided to take the Thule off the top of one of the cars. He went to the box where we keep keys that we rarely use to get those specific keys and—yes— you guessed it, there were my car keys. I remember that when I was cleaning months before, I had put the keys in the box for rarely used keys.

Why didn't I look there? Because, as soon as I realized they weren't in the bowl I assumed that I had not returned the keys to their proper place after traveling, because I had accepted that I am a person that misplaces keys.

Imagine what would have happened if I would have said to myself instead, "There is only One Mind and that Mind is intelligent and never misplaces anything. Therefore, this mistaken belief about myself is not true and cannot affect my world."

Changing patterns, or habits we don't want to keep, to the spiritually healthy habits that we want, takes five steps:
- It must occur to us that there is another (and easier) way.
- We must be willing to learn this new way.
- We have to learn the new way.
- We have to actually do the new way
- We have to remember that we learned it!

This is what we will do together in this book: learn, practice, and remember that we learned how!

28

— • —

CHAPTER TWO

I cannot imagine a God who rewards and punishes the objects of his creation, whose purposes are modeled after our own—a God, in short, who is but a reflection of human frailty.—Albert Einstein

Hasn't everyone wondered, at least once, how God could allow the suffering, death, and intentional evil in the world to exist? How could he let wars continue? How can he be on both sides of a controversy?

Of course, we have also looked at the other side. We have observed the harmony and beauty of a flower, the flight of a bird, the majesty of a mountain, and we have wondered where all that could have come from, if not from an Infinite Intelligence.

In the long-standing debate over "is there a God" or "isn't there a God," we can agree with both sides.

The answer is: "no," there isn't a God that allows evil to exist; and "yes," there is a God that is the Principle of Life.

Perhaps part of the problem is the word God. Depending on what framework of perception we grew up within, and have worked out for ourselves, either we love this name of God, or we hate it.

If we could drop our preconceived ideas about what the word God means, perhaps we would find that we are all in agreement. Perhaps we would also find a way to resolve our own internal struggle with why evil appears to exist if God is Love.

What if we stopped seeing God in terms of a powerful human that knows both good and evil, and can be swayed by human prayer and opinion?

What if instead we saw God through a scientific and Spiritual Perception as the Mind Fabric of what we perceive as the Infinite Universe?

What if God were The Infinite Intelligence that both creates and holds it all together? What if God is not in any way human, but instead is like the principle of math, the Principle of Life?

Don't most of us blithely say that God is omnipresent, omniscience, omnipotent, and omniaction? Have we stopped to examine what this means and implies? Isn't this a scientific statement that leads us to the evidence of God as the Principle of Life?

Could this God, the Principle of Life, be both good and evil? Wouldn't this idea of duality negate omni? There can be no debate. Either God is completely good, or God is completely evil.

The original meaning of the word God is Good. Makes sense doesn't it? Because if God is evil, it stands to reason that eventually, it would destroy itself. Therefore, thinking logically, there cannot be a God that knows evil, or is on both sides of a controversy. There can only be a God that is the Infinite Principle of Life.

However, what about what we experience as evil, lack, sorrow, and ill health? All these are present in the worldview, the human god's world, but not in the big R Reality that is the Principle of Life, all moving in perfect harmony. Anything that doesn't appear as Good is a distortion of Truth.

Here's where we exercise what we call our free will. **We choose**. And our choice determines our experience. We can't be on both sides of the fence, or serve two masters. We get to choose the perception of Infinite Good,—and when we choose and live this perception, and make it the basis of our thought and actions, then what isn't true will dissolve, revealing what Is.

Much evil is done in God's name. However, that doesn't make it God's fault. When we interpret God as if It were human, this assumption will inevitably lead to both good and bad consequences. One side will win and one side will lose.

We can always tell when we are living from the human god idea. We start working hard at fixing things, making things better, being right, getting healthy, getting rich, or just getting by.

Our thoughts are filled with either worry, or competition. The human god starts with duality, and knows both good and evil. Everyone knows what the results of this looks like in our lives, and in the world. It's not God that lets evil exist. We let it exist in the only place possible, in our acceptance of duality and a human god. It only exists in the same way that darkness exists before we turn on the light.

Again, the answer is "no," there is no God that knows good and evil, and "yes," there is a God that is omniscient Good.

The more we begin with this Truth and live in it, the more we make it the premise of our being, and the more it will dissolve anything that is blocking the view of the unlimited good and abundance of the omnipresent Infinite One.

When we make this choice, we will experience our own personal evidence of the existence of God as All.

So make up any name you want to for God, because God by any name is still All There Is, and It is Infinite Intelligent Good.

CONCENTRIC CIRCLES OF LOVE

Love is the only currency that can never be devalued. We only need to share and receive it freely.—Beca Lewis

The great artist Van Gogh said to his brother Theo, "I tell you, the more I think, the more I feel that there is nothing more truly artistic than to love people." I wonder if Van Gogh would mind if I took away the word *people* so that his sentence would simply end with the word *love*.

Wouldn't this expand the picture? Instead of thinking that we can only love those people, places, and things that look exactly like us, we could expand the idea of love to include everyone and everything.

As I write this, on our dining table is a dish with rocks and water in it. Sitting on top of those rocks and water, are some blooming narcissus bulbs. Every time I look at them, I marvel at their beauty and their promise that spring isn't that far away.

It is a concentric circle of love.

The dish by itself would have been empty and fairly boring. Filled with rocks and water, it still would have not been much to look at. Add the bulbs to the dish, rocks, and water, and they now all have a purpose. At the same time, without the rocks, water, and dish the bulbs would not be blooming.

This is an example of how that concentric circle of love supports and expands. As we see the flowers, we are filled with joy at their beauty, and we pass on those lovely spring feelings to each other, and then to another, and another, and another.

We are all like a stone thrown into the water, concentric circles expanding to include, and touch everything.

Recently I saw a video of a crow that loved and cared for a kitten who could have died without him; and the kitten reciprocated by loving him back. This love continued even after the kitten turned into a cat and found a home. Each morning the crow waited for him by the door, until he came out to play.

What if the crow would have looked at the kitten and thought, "He doesn't look like me, and don't cats normally kill birds?" Instead, he showed love and got love back, and that shared love has been a continuing expanding circle to everyone who sees and hears about it.

One Christmas, my husband gave me a whole pack of DVDs that he called "happy movies" because each of them ends with *love*. One of the movies is called, "Stardust." In this movie, the heroine shows the hero that true love does not need proof of its love. It doesn't require sacrifice and sorrow. It doesn't love for prestige. As they lived this truth, the world they found themselves in transformed.

In another movie "Enchanted," the heroine is so infused with love that her point of view expands into, and through, everyone and everything she meets. She shifts the world into which she was un-lovingly banished. Without blame, and by being only love, she too transforms that world around her.

Concentric circles of love. We are all at the center, and the cause, of concentric circles.

We get to choose whether that circle will be one of love, or of the multitude of other names for what is not love. The opposite of love hides behind words like sorrow, blame, despair, upset, anger, or revenge, but it is always just the opposite of love, and only has power because we choose it instead of love. That concentric circle does not end well—for anyone.

In order to be a concentric circle of love we have to start with the love of ourselves. Starting there it is easy to be a stone of love that begins the circle of love that expands to transform the world.

Like the crow that loved the kitten, we have to begin by being happy with ourselves, content with who we are. We love by not looking at what we don't have (how does a crow feed or hug a kitten?), but by what we **do** have. We have the capacity to love because that is the essence of our being.

None of us can do anything alone. Like the flowers in the dish, we must have each other's support and encouragement. Without each other, we will feel empty and unfulfilled. Try as we might we cannot stop the concentric circle that extends from what we do and say. It is our choice whether we expand love, or the opposite of love.

As we choose love, that concentric circle will bring into each of our lives the fullness of what it means to love and be loved, and together we can enjoy the sweet fragrance of each of our unique blooms.

It doesn't matter if we are the cat or the crow. The crow had to give love to something he wasn't supposed to love, and in return, the cat had to accept love from something he wasn't supposed to trust. If they can do it, we can too! Like the women in "Enchanted" and "Stardust" we can transform the world we were "sent to" into the world we know it really is—Love in action.

STEP INTO THE GOOD

When love and skill work together, expect a masterpiece. —John Ruskin

Our garage was stuffed full! We had just moved and the building that would house Del's workshop wasn't ready yet. So we had moved all of his work equipment into the tiny garage, plus the things that we hadn't found a place for yet in the house.

It was so full I couldn't find anything, so Del arranged it enough to get an overview of what was there.

It was better and we were grateful, but I knew Del longed to be able to get to his equipment easier.

Later that day, two of our kids came over and asked if they could help with anything. "Yes," I said, and pointed to the garage. "Can you make it any better?" A few hours later, they had the garage completely clear in the middle, with everything in order all around the sides. I stared speechless for many minutes. It was amazing and completely unexpected.

In anticipation of Del seeing the garage, we all ran out to meet him as he drove up in his truck. "Look," I said as I pointed to the garage. No reaction. He backed up right to it with all three of us pointing and saying, "Look."

He looked, but had no real reaction. He got out of the truck and looked in; still no reaction; then he walked into the garage and saw it.

He stood in the middle of all that good, as speechless as I had been. In his mind, there had been no way it could have looked like that, so no matter how many times we pointed, he had to get out and actually walk into it to see how amazingly good it had become.

It was a perception, a preconceived perception. We all have them. Things can only be so good, can only look a specific way, and can only come to us in a particular way. It's a locked-in paradigm in our own minds.

Good could be sitting beside us, chatting us up, and we would miss it if we didn't know enough to walk in and look.

However, how do we look for good when we have no idea what good to look for?

Actually what we need to do is step into good, and then we'll see it. Here's an example how that looked to me on a speaking trip.

While waiting for the plane, I was contemplating how much I had recently let human perception become my focus rather than Spiritual Perception.

With nothing much else to do, I decided it was as good a time as any to start practicing Spiritual Perception with more diligence.

I took the phrase, *Since God is One and All, everything that is present is present as God only,** and started practicing what that means. I continued practicing Spiritual Perception, which is seeing good, or God, in place of what the five senses report. I looked at the people around me, and tried my best to see through what looked like people and see the qualities of God.

I looked at my chair, my computer, the ticket in my hand, and tried to see the qualities of God. I saw beauty, kindness, order, practicality, safety, and comfort. After just a few minutes of doing this, I heard my name called to come to the ticket counter, where I was told that I had been reassigned to a business class seat, so that a family could fly together.

I hadn't been practicing Spiritual Perception to get something. However, as I practiced, I stepped into the good, and the outcome was something that made my trip much more pleasant.

There is one more part to this story.

After getting the upgrade, I had to calm down my personal sense by reminding myself that I wasn't practicing to get, but to understand. So I continued looking through what appeared to be a person, place, or thing, and attempted to see God instead. As we were all lined up to board, I heard two men talk about how hard this flight was going to be for them. I didn't hear why, but I did have the fleeting thought that it didn't have to be that way.

Within moments, the same ticket guy called their names and handed them both upgrades. Spiritual Perception was revealing good for all, which of course is the way it is, since God is One and All. Spiritual Perception reveals that there is nothing going on but God, Good.

Instead of thinking that there will be a time that the tares will be separated from the wheat, we know that as we gain spiritual awareness, what appears to be tares are not something that must be destroyed, but simply wheat misperceived, and then that misperception will completely dissolve what appears to be tares.

Step into the good by practicing Spiritual Perception, and reap the benefit of the constant ever-providing harvest of the Infinite.

This is a practice that will benefit everyone. It doesn't take special equipment, or the perfect time, or money, or personal ability. It is available to each one of us at all times

We can begin now, and never stop stepping into the good, by practicing Spiritual Perception in each moment.
*John Hargreaves—*The Indivisibility Of The Infinite*

RIGHT THINKING

The smallest fact is a window through which the infinite may be seen.—Aldous Huxley

Since it is a law that perception rules, and what we perceive to be reality magnifies, the most important thing we can do is to learn how to think rightly, or practice right thinking. There are seven steps to right thinking. Practice these correctly every day, and you will marvel at how fast life will change for the better for you.

Following these seven steps is the perfect way to start your day, or to heal any situation. I have used some personal examples to get you started.

Step One: Set Your Right Intent

This Book Intent: To give you clear and easy tools that you can use to discover and eliminate useless, destructive perceptions, and in doing so reveal your and Unique Spiritual Blessing.

My Personal Intent: To be more loving in every area of my life.

What is your Intent?

Step Two: State Your Right Premise

This Book Premise: There is only One Infinite Power, and it is Good.

Accepting this premise doesn't mean we have to believe or understand it at first. We simply have to accept it, and let ourselves move to an increasingly clearer understanding of it.

There are many names for this power; many of us call It God. Mind, Soul, Principle, Life, Truth, Love, and Spirit are also names for this One Infinite power. Because this One is omnipresent, omniscient, omniaction, and omnipotent, there is no room for any other power. This One's power is rooted in, based on, and operates from, the Principle of Intelligent Love.

This One is spiritual. We misperceive people, places, and things as material, or grounded and created in matter, when actually they are the ideas and reflection of the consciousness of the One power, or Mind.

This means that what we perceive as matter, and a material universe, is a misperception of a spiritual universe. There are not two universes, just one: God's.

As we begin this journey together, we are going to make this premise our starting point. Instead of thinking of ourselves as humans with imperfections, let's begin with the premise that within the truth of big R Reality we are much more: we are the idea of God and Its glorious reflection.

Let's begin with the premise that we are perfect now, and we have only to uncover and dissolve our misperceptions to live in the happiness and harmony that is already present. This book isn't about why this is true. This book is based on that fact.

Let's relax into the Truth that we are not what appears to our five senses, and we are not what we have been trained to believe, within the small r reality.

We are much more; we are the idea and action of the One Infinite Divine Intelligence. It doesn't matter what name you use for this Intelligence, it is still, and always, the Principle of Love.

My Personal Premise: God is Love and fills all space, and is visible to us in what appears as people, places, and things.

What Is Your Premise?

Step Three: State Your Right Identity

My Personal Right Identity: I am the action of Love.

It's actually easy to say, or state, a spiritual premise, but harder to place ourselves within it. As we step onto this spiritual path and take on the right perception of ourselves, we also must relieve ourselves of any guilt, judgment, and story that may want to attach itself to us.

Remind yourself that you are the Light of Love, and everything you discover on this journey is either leading you to that awareness, or has been trying to hide it from you.

We are letting go of what we don't want, and embracing what we do want. Laying down our ego and taking up the Truth of our Being is a joyous event, and one we can share together.

Instead of justifying why we think we are human, let's rejoice in the fact that we are more than that, and embrace what we perceive as human within the arms of Infinite Good. This way, in our everyday life, we are not questioning how we are doing humanly; instead, we are glorifying God in the way that we live.

What Is Your Right Identity?

We have laid the foundation of our perception. We have stated a right intent, premise, and identity. Now we come to the "work."

Step Four: Right Resistance

When we declare the Truth, both of God and our being, what is not true becomes more visible and often much noisier.

Since we are making a break away from ideas that have blinded us from the Truth, that lie will begin a campaign to change our minds.

Everything that we have ever heard within our head will get louder. It will try to dissuade us from our intention, premise, and identity.

One suggestion that it will make is that if we are spiritual and perfect now, that negates our human experience.

The suggestion will come to us that all that we experience within our lives is a lie, and if we fully accept the premise of One power now, all the good we see, and all the good we do does not mean anything.

The lie will remind us that we seem to experience two powers. One is the power of Love, or God, and the other is the power of evil, or the devil. Both appear to exist here in the place we perceive as separated from the Infinite One. We call this place the universe, or more locally, the earth.

The Bible records these two powers in the two stories of creation. In the first story, God, within Its consciousness creates (knows) everything, and it is Good. In the second story the but appears out of the mist and presents a second power and life where both good and evil are known.

Most of our daily lives are lived within the context of the second but story and all that stems from knowing, and accepting, both good and evil. Within the second story, most of us attempt to be good humans—and we succeed, some of the time. However, we are always confronted with, and confounded, by that belief in another power other than Good.

Instead of resisting the Truth, which is the intention of the lie, we must resist the lie. One very powerful way to do that is to use right reasoning to reason our way back to Truth.

Step Five: Right Reasoning

Let's reason rightly with the lie that says that if we start with the premise of only One power which is infinite, Intelligent Good, we negate our human experience. Beginning with the premise that there is only one power, does not negate what appears as a human experience.

Why? Because there is not a material and a spiritual universe, there is only a spiritual one. All that is present is present as God only. Our life, the world, the universe seen as two places, with two powers, is not so much an illusion as a misunderstanding. God could not know about a misconception of Itself. It is Infinite, omnipresent Good. Where is the place It knows about evil or even shades of good? Obviously, it is nowhere.

The fact that the Infinite is All-Good does not mean we don't provide comfort, food, shelter, love, and care for ourselves and each other. On the contrary, in doing so we are demonstrating the Truth that Good is omnipresent, seen in these moments as "us" in action, as Love Loving Itself.

We do not have to live with the *but* story. Instead, we can say the word *and* which will take us to the first story of perfection.

When we acknowledge the omnipotence, omnipresence, omniaction, and omniscience of God we can say, "And that means my daily life is within that context.

As I understand, live, work with, and practice this premise, the mist rises and dissolves revealing what I have perceived of a human life as Life, God, expressed and lived as me."

We can embrace the and, and release the but.

It is our awareness of the omnipresence of Good that shines through our misunderstanding of what we perceive as a human life that results in what appears as an improved human condition. It is our confusion and misunderstanding that blocks the continual awareness of continual Good. We do not cause it, we do not create it; we are only temporarily blinded by it.

The river of Good is constant. The shining of Good is omnipresent. Accepting this premise brings a sigh of relief. It is the path of freedom. It does not take away, or create, what is real, but reveals it.

If we say, "It's all an illusion" and use that as an excuse to not participate fully in life, we are in error. It helps to say instead, "This is a misperception of what is really present and going on," and know that all action we take within our highest understanding of God is God Itself in action.

This way of thinking dissolves the boundaries between us, and lifts the confusion.

We can look at both the theories of evolution and intelligent design, and see that the Truth resides in both. Instead of fighting for a human way of life that lives with two powers, we can live as we are: One.

Instead of separation, comparison and judgment we find the intimacy of One—and our eternal and distinct spiritual identity is revealed.

Step Six: Right Practice

Ask yourself this question as we reveal your true spiritual identity and as you practice this shift, "What are the possibilities, and where is my focus?"

It takes deep spiritual practice, and using what we know, in order to grow. We can't attend to it in just an hour or two a week and hope that we will understand, and that things will change.

Spiritual Perception is a moment-by- moment decision to be aware of the Truth, or essence of Life, and to dissolve any lie claiming anything but Good is always present.

Step Seven: Right Action

Do we have to give up something to experience this? Yes we do. We have to give up the ego that protects the but story.

This is easy to do when we realize that we are not giving up the essence of ourselves, and that it is not negating our life; it is validating it. Selling all for the pearl of great price is what we are doing.

Releasing our beliefs that may have served us well in the past, but are no longer needed, is not a sacrifice, it is a gift.

When we experience joy and love, we are experiencing Truth breaking through our fog of misperceptions, just as the sun breaks through the clouds. It is always present; all we have to do is shift our perception, and let go of what blinds us to the presence of Love.

29

CHAPTER THREE

I slept and dreamt that life was joy. I awoke and saw that life was service. I acted and behold, service was joy.—Rabindranath Tagore

She was always-on-call. I wanted to be like her, but I had no idea how I could handle what she did with such apparent ease. Any time of the day or night, any time of the year, she was always on call for those that needed comfort, or understanding, and yes, healing.

I remember the time that I called her in the middle of the night because my baby was having convulsions, and I knew I could turn to her. I was hysterical. She answered the phone with no tiredness in her voice, present and available. She told me the Truth about my child. She reminded me that my little girl was in Reality the child of God, was Light itself, and that there was no room for anything else. I calmed down, and within minutes so did my child, the child of Light. It was over and never returned.

Always-on-call, how did she do it? Thinking I was not capable of this feat of love, I chose other ways to live. I thought about "disappearing" where no one could find me or need me. I tried not to influence people in case I did something wrong that hurt them forever. I disappeared into my busy work, my business, and sometimes my sorrow.

I knew my friend had things to think through, and I felt privileged to be someone she spoke to when she wanted to share. We had lunch together and talked about our kids and her grandchildren. I organized her papers, I knew what she needed to resolve. However, through all that, she was always present and on call for others no matter when, or where, the need appeared.

Eventually, I realized that we are all always-on-call, whether we want to be or not. We can run, we can hide, we can lie, and we can wait, but none of these actions will take away the fact that we are always on call—because that is a function of being alive. The question is—are we on call in a way that pleases us and brings happiness, or on call in a way that constricts and imprisons us?

Did I tell you that I never knew her not to be happy? Always-on-call, and always happy is a way of life that all of us can achieve.

As we go through The Four Essential Questions together, I know that you too will discover that always-on-call is not a burden, but a source of constant pleasure, and the blessing of our lives.

What Is Our Responsibility?

Always-on-call sounds frightening. When do we get time off? It feels as if the burden of responsibility would be overwhelming. Why not run, hide, lie, and wait?

I grew up with an intense feeling of responsibility, as I suspect most of us have. After all, it is what we were taught and trained, to be responsible, and of course we must be. But under what point of view?

If we take full responsibility, as if we are the cause and creator of all that is going on, then the burden is crushing. Who can survive under that? Well, some of us do for a while by "being strong." However, one day, that strength ebbs and we can't take it anymore. Many symptoms of this false responsibility are present in all of our lives. These symptoms range from physical sickness, to monetary distress, to unhealthy relationships.

"It's all my fault," is not a mantra we want to encourage no matter how many times we are told that it is. We may say it out of the desire to be humble and good, but ironically it makes us ego-driven, because we have given ourselves the power of Life itself.

"It's all my fault" also means "it's all my doing." Really—all of this is our doing? We, who cannot answer even the basic question of how the universe began, must accept responsibility for everything?

Yes and no. We are responsible, but not for what we have been trained to believe. We are responsible for thinking, choosing, and being aware of what is really going on. We are responsible for our perception, our point of view, and state of mind. We are responsible for our choice of perception. We are responsible for the act of shifting that perception.

Choosing and shifting perception changes the sense of the burden of responsibility. Responsibility then resides where it belongs, with that which is the only cause and creator, God. Our only responsibility is to be who we are intended to be. Our responsibility is to become aware of our running, hiding, lying, and waiting, and then to choose to let it go, and to live fully as our Unique Spiritual Blessing, our eternal spiritual identity.

We will go through The Four Essential Questions together, and together witness how they can relieve us of the false responsibility of cause and creator and return us to the true responsibility of choosing the correct perception and staying there.

RIGHT OR WRONG

Do not condemn the judgment of another because it differs from your own. You may both be wrong. —Dandamis

As we ask ourselves these Four Essential Questions, it is important to know that the answer is neither right nor wrong. The intention of asking is to become aware. If we are running from a bear chasing us, then asking ourselves "Am I Running," is a good question to ask, and will make sure that we are moving.

If we are running from living our life, that's different. Then we must ask, "Why am I running, and what am I running from?"

If we are hiding from someone trying to hurt us, then the wisest answer to the question "Am I Hiding?" most likely will be, "yes!"

If we answer "yes" because we are hiding our light under a bushel so no one can receive the benefit of that light, then the answer gives us a new awareness of how we are living our life.

REACTING TO ILLUSIONS

Men who are devoid of the power of spiritual perception are unable to recognize anything that cannot be seen externally.—Paracelsus

Standing in the shower, I glanced up and saw what I thought were drops of water leaking from the top of the shower structure.

Since our days in our new home had been about "fix and repair" my first reaction was, "Oh no, not another thing to fix." Then I looked again and saw that what I was seeing was the reflection of the shower hooks on the ceiling. There was nothing to react about; the problem was an illusion.

Here's the thing that we often forget. All problems are an illusion. Uh huh, I know. We all know the many ways that problems do not feel like an illusion. However, just because they don't feel like an illusion, doesn't make them real.

This includes the often said, but usually misinterpreted, statement, "There are no accidents." It depends on how this statement is interpreted as to whether it is a True statement or not.

From a Spiritual Perception, this statement is correct because there are no accidents. They are an illusion, a misperception.

On the other hand, this statement is wrong when it is interpreted as something God would allow in order for good to result from the accident.

Of course, when what appears as an accident occurs, we have a choice of how to respond. When we remain in our highest understanding of God, Love, when confronted with the story, then that learning, that growth, that awareness, can, and often does, lead us to Good.

However, an illusion is an illusion, whether it is drops of water on the ceiling, or an accident, or mistreatment, hunger, lack, or sickness.

They are all illusions.

In each case where an illusion tempts us to believe that it is real, we have a choice of reaction or replacement. We can react to the illusion or replace what the outside is telling us to be true, with what we know to be True.

Where does the statement that "anything that is not good is an illusion" come from? It comes from the Principle that God is Love, and Love is omnipresent and omniscience. This statement, this Principle, leaves absolutely no room for something other than Love as the only Reality.

The question is, "Doesn't Love give us these accidents and bad things in order to teach us?" The answer is, No! Omnipresent Love couldn't know anything other than Love. It doesn't know us as humans needing to be taught a lesson. Divine Love isn't a glorified human personality.

It is a human interpretation of love that Love punishes, denies, or takes a break. Divine Love, as a Principle of being, knows nothing about anything other than Love Loving. This means that if we are not seeing direct evidence that Love is omnipresent, then we are being hypnotized by an illusion that Love is not omnipresent.

Feelings of fear, anger, hate, discouragement, despair, not knowing, lack, unhappiness, and doubt all stem from that illusion of the lack of omnipresent Love.

In the shower, I looked again at what appeared as something "bad" and saw my mistake. In life, we need to look again at the illusion representing itself as real, and see that right there is the evidence that it is an illusion.

It takes practice, but that is only because we have practiced so long in the illusion of lack that we have to rebuild our awareness of Truth. Within each of us is an already-present awareness that right where lack appears to be, is the direct experience of Love Loving Itself.

Either Love is omnipresent, or it isn't. Since what we determine and perceive as Reality is our personal reality, is what we experience, then whether we actually believe that Love is omnipresent, or have a direct experience that It is, or even if we don't believe it, why not go ahead and choose anyway the perception that It is.

WHY BOTHER?

Take your heart out into the vast fields of light and let it breathe. —Hafiz

What's the point anyway? Why bother to ask ourselves these questions? Why bother having more awareness?

There are esoteric answers, and practical answers. Here's an esoteric answer: Doing so helps dissolve misperceptions, including the main one, that we are separate from the divine Source. Here is a practical answer: Doing so increases our ability to live a happy and full life.

Both of these are certainly reasons for becoming more aware. However, the biggest reason will be that as we practice awareness, we will find ourselves. And not only that, we will find that we are wonderfully gifted, creative, resourceful, and loving.

Knowing that this is all about awareness, and then choosing what to do with that awareness, let's explore The Four Essential Questions, starting with the first one, "Am I Waiting?"

Make an agreement to yourself that no matter what you discover, you will not let the answer either dismay or excite you, but instead you will allow it to give you a strong basis upon which to make clear choices and set strong intents.

Are you ready? Let the exploration begin!

30

— · —

CHAPTER FOUR

In our age the road to holiness necessarily passes through the world of action.—Dag Hammarskjold

Waiting is sometimes a good thing, and sometimes a bad thing. How do we know the difference? Once we have figured out the answer to that question, we will then need to know if what we are now ready to do is the right thing to do, or not. If we have all that straightened out, we will then need to know the right time to do it, because the right thing done at the wrong time makes it a wrong thing to do.

No wonder we have a habit of waiting!

If we use the example of reading this book, it is obvious that to read the book we have to begin, and the right thing to do is to read the book.

Obvious and easy, but still there are those of us who will put the book down at some point and then wait for a time, before we will pick it up again.

How long that will be depends on the reason why we put the book down in the first place.

It's apparent that there is more to waiting than meets the eye. To understand the mysteries of waiting, let's explore the subject further by asking ourselves these questions:

- How many ways do we wait?
- Who or what are we waiting for?
- Why wait at all?
- When is it the right choice to wait, and when it is it a stalling, or survival, tactic?
- How can we tell the difference?

STALLING

I had to laugh at myself while writing this section on waiting. I got to the paragraph above and "something" suggested I check my email. Once I did that, I then decided to answer people who had written. Then I "had" to clean out emails I didn't need any more. From there, I decided to take action on what some of the emails suggested I do. It was over an hour later before I realized I had stopped doing what I intended to do—write about waiting for at least one page—and had managed in the process to create a perfect symbol of the stalling form of waiting!

As I wrote those words, I realized I felt a little chilly, so I got up to put on a sweater, then I noticed that the phone was dusty so I went and got something to dust it with—stalling again. Why do we stall?

There are so many reasons for it you and I could probably spend a day listing them, so rather than figuring out the why of each one, let's come up with a way to minimize stalling, or perhaps to eliminate it all together.

Here it is, so simple we might think it useless, but it is a cornerstone of our actions. Become aware of it! Then treat it the same way we treat a distracted child. Gently, but with a clear focus, bring ourselves back to our stated intent.

Stated intent—what is that? We did a brief review of the idea of intent in the section of this book called *Right Thinking*. Let's pause now, (not stall), for a moment, and discuss the meaning and value of intent.

INTENT

The definition of intent revolves around purpose. This definition of intent—The state of a person's mind that directs his or her actions toward a specific object—is closely related to how we want to apply the concept of intent in our work together.

Intent is always present, but usually our intent is hidden from us, either because we are not aware of our unconscious choices or desires—which translate to intention—or because we have never learned how to consciously be aware of our intent.

I have often said, Whoever has the clearest intent wins, and this is absolutely true. By winning I mean, "leads the way." Since the way of those with a stronger intent may not be the way we thought we were going, or wanted to go, then all the more reason to be aware of, and to be present with, our own intent.

Intent is in every detail of life, so when we ignore it, we can lose our way in every situation in life—from what we buy at the store to how our life plays out. When we go to the store with the intent of only buying what is on our list, but end up buying the impulse item at the checkout counter, the store had the clearer intent.

When our intent is not to spend past our budget, but then we see something we want and put it on our credit card, then both the seller of the item, and the credit card company, had the clearer intent. At least one of them did not have our best interest at heart.

If we apply this idea to the more important parts of our life, it becomes obvious that it is always important to be aware of our intent.

Our intents are often formed by what we have been trained to believe is true, or right.

This means that it is important to be aware of the intent of those who are training us (schools, media, peer pressure, religious teachings, and political loyalties). Once we are aware of another's intent we can easily choose who, or what, we want to believe, because as we remember, what we perceive (believe) to be reality magnifies!

When our primary intent is to be what we really are, and to live our lives from the principles of good and happiness for all—beginning within our own lives—then we are less likely to be influenced by, or waylaid by, intentions that are false for us.

Using the advantage of the law that *perception rules*, we can stop trying so hard. We can stop powering our way through life. Instead, we can rest in our intention as we bring our state of mind and our point of view into harmony.

Squirrel Intention

One animal that truly represents clear intent, and intention, is the squirrel. Anyone who has ever put up a bird feeder knows that eventually it will be necessary to outwit the squirrels. We have watched squirrels study a bird feeder, and know that it is only a matter of time before its intention, and its skill in carrying out its intention, will win over our intention to stop it.

The squirrel doesn't feel guilty for having such a strong intent. It is not focusing on winning anything; it does not carry any personal grudges, or feel competition with anyone else, including us humans. It is not out to hurt anyone. No, it simply has a clear idea of what it is, and what it wants to accomplish.

If I could get inside of a squirrel's thought, I am sure I would find that it also never doubts that somewhere, somehow, there is a way, and it will figure it out. A squirrel doesn't stop trying because it falls off the feeder, or makes a fool of itself. A squirrel demonstrates patient intention.

I watched a butterfly trying to get out from under the canopy on our deck. It fluttered and flew everywhere. I tried to direct it to fly down to get out, but it was much too busy trying too hard. It had a strong intention to get out, but it was not a patient, and wise, intention.

If the butterfly could have borrowed a page from the squirrel, it would have paused, and watched. It would have looked around and discovered the many avenues of escape. It would have known that it got in, so there must be a way out. I watched it for over an hour and it still had not escaped.

Sometimes it was just a quarter of an inch away from edge of the canopy. A short pause there, feeling the breeze, listening to direction, would have released it in that moment.

This kind of frantic intention that the butterfly demonstrated, is not based on wisdom, but on fear. We want to set our intentions just like the squirrel's; patient, wise, confident, and skilled. Since we have the ability to do so, we will also add the extra quality of looking at the big picture. We can ask ourselves the question, "Will this be good for all for now, and into the future?"

FIRST INTENT

There is a theme running through the show, *Battlestar Galatica*, that relates to this idea of first intent. The idea is that once you find, and accept, your role in life, the ego drops away and life really begins. Or, said differently, once we recognize that our first intent is to be the intent of the Divine, because we are Its idea in action, then we begin to discover the unique expression of our life.

There is a segment of the TV show *So You Think You Can Dance*, where dancers who are in the "bottom" perform a quick solo that is designed to show exactly who they are, and what they bring to dance. It's called, "dancing for your life."

They are encouraged to bring all of themselves to that dance, reveal their heart, share their passion, and be entirely present in those moments, so that all that they are is visible to others.

When they are willing to set that as their intent, and they fully sink into that intent, their solos are beyond description. And the audience can tell when they don't.

If we can tell the quality of intent of a performance on stage, in an area most of us are not trained to observe, imagine how easy it is to tell when people are not "dancing for their life" in their lives.

We, of course, know when we are not. In the dance world, this is called "marking." Just marking the moments, standing where you are supposed to be, giving a rough estimate of how it goes, using as little energy as possible, this is marking. Most of us live our lives this way, just marking it, marking time, using up time, so that we don't have to "bring it on."

I could put this section on intent under every question, but I think it fits best under waiting. At least in the dance world we could claim to be saving our energy for an upcoming performance. However, what performance are we waiting for in our life?

It doesn't work anyway. Marking a dance doesn't build the strength, or commitment to the movement, that is needed for a brilliant performance. Marking life, waiting for a performance that isn't even scheduled, is tragic. We have been designed to bring the unique blessing that we are into every moment. Make that your first intent, and see how fast the false habit of waiting for what is already present melts away.

In the TV show *Lie To Me*, there is a young woman who demonstrates a natural talent for the work. In one scene, she complains that she is not getting enough recognition, while at the same time she is doubting her ability. Her boss says to her, "You still don't get it yet, do you? You have a talent. And guess what. It's not about you. It's not about me. And the talent, and what you do, are not just for you anymore."

This is true for each of us.

We each have a talent, and it is never about us. It is what we are designed to do. Instead of intellectually talking about ideas and doing nothing, it is time to take action. This willingness to be who we truly are, to live as we have been designed to live, as the action of the Divine, and to take our place in the world is our first intent.

It's Just Too Much

"It's just too much, I am overwhelmed and under appreciated. No matter what I do, it doesn't give me any satisfaction, and it is never good enough." Do you ever think, or say, something like this?

In today's rush-rush-rush world with its speeded up technology, and information overload, combined with the appearance of lack in so many lives, "It's just too much" is a common feeling among us all.

Sometimes it is hard to remember the reason why we do anything. Our society focuses on the rich, famous, and the beautiful—or how to get there—and rarely is the contentment to lead a simple, loving, and fulfilling life, celebrated.

Here, in the midst of this false sense of what life is about, we must find our own awareness of what happiness is for us, and learn how to live that elegant, and contented, life. This means that we have to step out of the worldview of what we thought we are supposed to do, and by listening within, find the path we are meant to walk, and then get up, and live our life fully.

There is always much to do; that is what life is about. Can you imagine if the force we call Life, would suddenly appear depressed and overwhelmed? Plopping Itself down in front of the TV, It would declare, "It is just too much, I can't do this anymore." Of course, this would never happen! Life is always about being Life and Love. It is not waiting for someone to notice It, (we rarely do), or appreciate It, or enjoy It. It just does what It does.

The joy is in being fully what we are, and living the simple beauty of life by letting go of what we no longer need. The trick lies in revealing to ourselves who we are, and that is exactly what we are doing together as we ask ourselves The Four Essential Questions, and then listen honestly, and without judgment, to the answers.

LIFE JAMS

Have you ever been in a traffic jam? Once traveling from Connecticut to Ohio, Del and I were in three of them. Two of them lasted long enough that we turned off the car and waited for an hour or more before being able to move on. In all of them, we never saw the cause even though the result was over 10 miles of stopped traffic. However, once the cause of the jam was removed, the traffic flowed as if it had never happened.

Did you ever sit by a little stream of water after a rain, and put sticks in it to watch the water back up? Of course, we have all seen big streams of water backed up as one log, or other obstacle, gets stuck and backs up more debris until the stream stops running, and begins to flood.

Life jams work the same way. One thing gets stuck in our mind, and a life jam begins. It can feel like nothing is moving in our life, or it can be an overwhelming flood of feeling that it's just "too much."

We react to this life jam in many ways. We can feel angry, depressed, tired, manic, confused, or even live in a state of "who cares." Since life jams are not visual, like a traffic jam or a blocked stream, we often don't understand what has stopped the flow. We just know that our life is not working.

The good news about all jams is that all it takes is the removal of the first obstacle for the traffic, stream, and our life to begin to flow again. But, how do we find the cause of our life jam? Often we already know the cause, but haven't believed it could be so simple; or the problem could feel too hard to let it go.

Years ago, I was in a life jam. Nothing I did worked. Nothing happened. I worked hard, tried hard, used all the ideas I could think of that always worked before, but they didn't work this time. However, all along I was hearing an inner voice telling me that I wanted to paint.

Nevertheless, since nothing was working in my life, I had "reasons" why I couldn't paint. No money, and no time, were two of them. I felt that I had to get out of the jam I was living in first. Finally, out of ideas, I decided to listen to the inner voice again. It said, "Paint." I said "No money, no time." It said, "Paint."

I thought that meant I would have to buy an easel, paints, and brushes. Eventually it occurred to me that I could afford a can of wall paint, and a brush, so that's what I did.

Within days of my beginning to paint my walls, my life started to flow again. In this case, my life jam began by my wanting things to go my way and by not honoring an inner desire that I had because I felt that I didn't deserve it. I was listening to a belief, a committed thought pattern, not to my intuition.

Life jams are also caused by not wanting to, or not knowing how to, do something. Or having too many things to do without knowing what to do first.

The answer is again: listen. Perhaps the thing we feel we have to do doesn't really need to be done, or can be done a different way. Ask for help for the thing you don't know how to do.

Take one thing—anything—and lift it out of the jam either by doing it, or by getting rid of it. Your life jam will loosen by doing one thing at a time, just as a tangled knot in a necklace unfolds by taking out one knot at a time.

Sometimes it takes someone outside of ourselves to see the cause of our life jam.

Often in speaking to clients, I hear them state the cause, but they still can't see it themselves. If I can guide them in a way that opens their eyes to their thought pattern, they can easily release that thought, and the actions, or the non-actions, that follow from it, and let life flow again.

Spirit always flows.

It's our thoughts, and the perception that follows them, that cause life jams. Our belief systems, past and present, are as solid as matter. In fact, what appears as our life and matter is our firm commitment to what we believe to be true. Unless it is based on big R Reality, it is always a misperception of what is actually happening.

MATCHING REASONS TO ACTIONS

You miss 100% of the shots you never take.—Wayne Gretsky

Sometimes we wait because we can't figure out why to take an action. Sometimes waiting is a good thing; we call this kind of waiting "pausing." Other times there is a direct need to take action now, but we can't get ourselves to move, and that kind of waiting is what we want to eliminate. One way to stop waiting, and start doing, is to find enough reasons to take action that mean something to you. This takes some self-observation, but that is exactly what you are doing as you ask The Four Essential Questions and observe the answers.

Here's what I learned when observing myself while looking for how to match reasons and actions. First, I realized I need a curtain-opening scenario in order to get myself motivated.

When I was taking ballet as a teenager, I got bored with it, until my teacher announced a recital. Suddenly, for me, there was a reason to go on, and all thoughts of quitting vanished. In fact, I remember that performance like a gem in a crown of my life.

As part of the promotion, the producers of the program had a picture of me taken because I was the Sugar Plum Fairy.

The photographer said to me, "You will remember this time and this picture for the rest of your life." That proved to be very true. Although for the next 16 years I was part of many performances, and loved them all, that one has stood out to me. The picture taken that day hangs on my parents' bedroom wall, and my children, and now my grandchildren, have asked me about that time.

What's important about this is that I discovered a reason that motivates me. However, since performing is something I no longer desire to do, it may appear I can no longer use that as a reason and motivation. The opposite is true

To bring that reason up to date, instead of focusing on the outside picture called "performing," I looked at the essence of what was happening at that moment, and realized there was something more than just the performance that I loved. In fact, I loved it even more: It was the community of performers. It was the anticipation of something marvelous, and slightly scary, that we prepared for together, and that together we would experience. When I design something, and I am thinking of doing it around these same ideas and principles, I am on the road to doing what I want to do, instead of stalling or waiting.

Another key element in doing a performance is the idea of a curtain going up. Standing backstage, we would peak out at the audience, and feel the tingles of anticipation knowing that there were people out there waiting for us to appear.

We hoped that we were prepared. Of course, we had to be, because the curtain was going up! It didn't matter if we were the performers, or the technical crew running the show, we all had to be ready, no excuses, because the show had to go on.

Applying this idea to the life I lead today, I noticed that there was a correlation between the feelings of too much to do that seem like a task, and not a joy, and therefore causing inertia in me, and not having a curtain going up type of deadline.

So I began to set deadlines that I knew would stretch me, but I also knew I could meet. To make it a curtain going up deadline I needed an audience on the other end, so I set up expectations. I let people know when to expect things from me.

These expectations range from when I reply to emails, to what day the new website will be unveiled, or to what day people will be coming to the house for a party.

When I am really stuck in the waiting mode, I use another way to motivate myself; it may sound morbid, but in reality, it is based on love. I ask myself, "What if you died today; how would you feel if this weren't done?" This is useful for tiny things, like leaving the house picked up when I walk out the door, and larger things, like writing this book, or putting my papers in order.

I have found other reasons that I can use to move myself to take action.

I have discovered that if I feel that what I am doing will change lives, I am motivated to take action. To get into this mode, I often ask myself, "Does someone need for me to do this? Is someone waiting for someone like me to make that phone call, write that book, or go to the store and pick up groceries?" If the answer is "yes," I am much more likely to take action.

Designing a system is another motivation for me. And if it is a system, or tool, that I can leave behind for another to use to improve their day-to-day life, then the excitement of this idea impels me to action. If I combine these ingredients—the community, the rise-of-the-curtain deadline, how would I feel if I didn't do it, is someone waiting for me to do this, and a system that will make a difference—then I am highly motivated.

Another trick I use is this: I never ask myself this question when I am in a stalling or waiting mode: "Do you want to?" This may sound opposite to what I am talking about, but it is exactly the same thing. The reason I don't ask that question, is the answer will always be "no." "No I don't want to get up, no I don't want to exercise this morning, no I don't want to write today, no I don't want to call anyone, no I don't want to do my work, no and no and no!"

Instead, I give myself reasons that inspire me to get up, exercise, write, call, and work. The person we ask, "Do you want to," when we are in the waiting-stalling mode is not really who we are.

In fact, it is the counterfeit of ourselves, whose intention is to stop us from fully living our lives.

Just as we do not give credence to children throwing a temper tantrum, or listen to people whom we know mean to do us harm, we do not listen to that voice that is not us, because it does not have our best interest at heart, and it is always lying. You can read more about this voice in this book under the heading What Voice Is Yours?

Now it is your turn to listen within, and observe your life, to find what reasons motivate you to take action. Find inspiring ideas, and they will help lead you out of the quicksand of waiting.

WAITING FOR OTHERS

I never teach my pupils. I only attempt to provide the conditions in which they can learn. —Albert Einstein

How many times have we all waited for someone before going on with a part of our lives? Pardon me if you are a man, but speaking to the women reading this—how many times have you waited for a man? I suppose it's our training. After all, there was a time when all we were supposed to do was find a man, settle down, and let him take care of our many children, and us, for forever after.

Oh wait, was it so long ago, or are we still on that page? Witness shows like *The Bachelor.*

We are not that woman anymore, are we? On the other hand, perhaps we are, just not so obviously. I am not advocating that we do not choose to please each other, but many of us make choices based on the counterfeit *what if* factor. Instead of the *what if* of imagination and allowing our ideas to flow, it is the *what if* I do this, will it win his, or her, love and respect? Or the *what if* I do this and I lose him or her?

Then there is the *I can't* factor. How many times have we all said 'I can't, until I have someone to help me?"

We often make standing still choices based on the *what if* and *I can't* beliefs. We sacrifice our time and our desires while waiting for the "perfect someone." Sometimes we think that someone is already in our lives, but that person is choosing to live a different way, while we wait, or table our desires, so that person can be fulfilled.

In one of my long-ago relationships, after noticing that once again my waiting for him did not stop him from living his life the way he wanted to, without a glance at what I might desire, I said to myself, "Beca, it is time to get a life." It took the breaking of many old habits, and sticking with the first intent, but today, I do have a life—my life.

Say this to yourself, "It is time to get a life!" No more waiting for a person, place, or thing. Take the step forward that moves you into the life that is waiting for you. It is in that life, and only in that life, that those that you wish were present now can find you.

GIFTING YOUR FUTURE SELF

Instead of giving our future self a problem, wouldn't it be more fun to give our future self a gift? Future self, as in who we will be tomorrow, later today, next year, or ten years from now. We all do gift our future self sometimes.

We make enough in one meal to have it later. We save some money to spend it later. We mow the grass during the week so that we can go away on the weekend.

However, more often, we give our future self a problem instead of a gift. We spend more money than we have, we don't clean up our mess, we cover up problems, we don't take good care of ourselves, we don't learn new skills to keep up, we don't read the instructions on something we are putting together, we don't listen when someone is telling us something.

Oh yes, this list could go on and on.

Instead of making resolutions about what we are going to do, which for the most part is giving our future self a chance to feel guilty because we don't do it, why not switch it up and think instead, "How can I give my future self a gift?" Of course, we will be asking our future self to pass it on to its future self. These gifts are not designed to make our future self into something less, but to enable it to be m ore.

Since not gifting our future self is often our habit, I developed a few ways for breaking that habit. For example, I notice that I often give my future self a problem because I put things off until there is enough pressure to get it done, either external or internal. Noticing that, I use the methods described in the section of this book called Matching Reasons To Actions to help me break the habit of waiting, and instead put it back under my own choice of when and how.

"Have a place," is an example of another method I use for making sure I am thinking of my future self. Packing for trips is a good example of how this works. As I think what I need for a trip, long before I go on it, I drop what I need into a bag that sits on top of my suitcase. A few days before the trip I open the suitcase, and the bag, and as I go about my days I willy-nilly toss into it whatever occurs to me that I will need on the trip. The day I actually pack, most of what I need is already there.

There are many more ways to provide for our future self. The interesting outcome is that as we gift our future self, we find that we are gifting our current self too. We live more in the moment, not the past. We find ourselves less stressed and more excited about life.

How does this all fit into Spiritual Perception, which is of course always the theme?

Here it is: Love providing for Its future "Self" is the Principle of big R Reality. It's not how our five senses report it to be, but how we **know** It to be, using both logic and internal awareness. God—I know I am temporarily making God "human like"—lives as the moment of "curtain going up" and "having a place." God has to have every star in its right place, bird feathers attached, insect feelers operational, flower buds prepared, tree roots anchored, and every hair on our head numbered at all times.

As we gift our future self with small and large acts of kindness, it is a constant reminder that we are the recipients of Love gifting Itself in all Its unique forms and ways. Not because it has to, but because that is how it works. Knowing this, and living from it, is the best gift we can give our future selves. As an outcome of this gift to ourselves, we give to everyone our lives touch. Gift your future self by living in your present self, and pass it on.

WHAT ARE WE WAITING FOR?

I thought it would be interesting to put some of the things people wait for in the form of a list. Why not put a check mark beside the ones that mean something to you? Then notice which one happens today. Noticing gives us power to make conscious choices.

For example, the first word on this list is clarity.

It might seem as if we want to wait for clarity. However, waiting for clarity just might take a lifetime. Why not pause for direction, take a step forward, and pause again for more awareness and focus. Pause, and listen, for the still small voice for what action to take—take the action—and pause again. We call this POL (Pause, Observe, Listen). Then act, and do it again.

Here's A List: What Are We Waiting For?
- Clarity
- Focus
- Enough reasons
- To know what to do
- For the time to be right
- For the right age
- For enough: money, time, knowledge, etc.
- To be out of debt
- Until we can do the whole thing at once
- Until we can do it perfectly
- A partner
- A team
- Friends and family to agree with us
- Until we live someplace else
- Funding

Why not add to this list? Then when you ask yourself, "Am I Waiting" you will have a "cheat-sheet" to help you uncover what you are waiting for. This awareness is the beginning of freedom. Here is an example of waiting, written by a member of The Shift® Community, Diana Cormier:

"While reflecting, the thought of waiting came to mind. If I look back on my life, it seems if I were to attach just one word to summarize my life that word would be waiting. Waiting for life to start, waiting for love, waiting for the right job, waiting to graduate from school, waiting for a vacation, waiting for happiness to start, waiting for, waiting for, waiting for. A definition of the word wait from Webster's is to remain inactive or in a state of repose, as until something expected

happens (often followed by for, till, or until): to wait for the bus to arrive. (Repose = absence of movement.)

"*If we find ourselves in a constant state of waiting, aren't we implying that good is only something in the future? Or perhaps we are looking back at a good time in our lives and then we are believing that good is only in the past. To be in a constant state of waiting, and therefore implying that good is ours only in the future, and only if a certain chain of events takes place in a certain way, is limiting our experience now. Mostly because this constant "wait state," in nature, never becomes the future. To wait for good means that we are deprived of good now. To be deprived of good now means that we believe it is possible to be deprived of God's expression now, and that we are an expression of Divine Love only in the future, but not now.*

"*We never have to do something, or wait for something, to be Love's expression. God's reflection is now and always. God isn't waiting for something before expressing Itself. Divine Love is always expressed, and that expression is us. We are now and always the manifestation of God's perfect Infinite expression, full of nothing but perfection and good.*

"*I don't need anything or anyone to rescue me from another person. That other person is an individual expression of Divine Love as much as I am. Love is reflected in love.*

"*I am not governed or controlled, either energetically or mentally, by another person. My energy and my well-being is protected and governed by Divine Love. Two ideas of Love—two people—can do nothing but support, enhance, and bless each other.*

"*What blesses one, blesses all. I am free of any dependence. My happiness, love, energy, and experience is dependent on God alone, not on any other person. I don't have to wait for inspiration in order to heal; I am the inspired expression of God. My thoughts are God's thoughts; God's thoughts are the only thoughts I can have.*"

Thank you, Diana, for this example of moving on from false waiting!

OK, now for the rest of us, what are we waiting for? Start now! Don't wait to learn the next three questions, or until you finish the book, or after you take a shower, or until the first of the month, or until you have someone to do this exercise with you, or until you know everything. Start now. Ask yourself, "Am I Waiting?"

31

— • —

CHAPTER FIVE

Yesterday we obeyed kings and bent our necks before emperors. But today we kneel only to truth, follow only beauty, and obey only love. —Khalil Gibran

As we discussed earlier, there are no right and wrong answers to these questions. The questions are designed to do two things; help us become aware of what we are thinking and doing, and to assist us in making clear, conscious choices.

Of course, there are times we may choose to run because that is the wisest thing to do at the time. To get out of an abusive marriage, I chose to run. However, eventually I had to stop running, go back, and collect what I could of what I had to leave behind when I ran. Perhaps if I hadn't been hiding from the truth of what was happening for so long it may never have escalated to running, and instead I could have dealt with it in a way that was less difficult for everyone involved.

If I had asked myself *The Four Essential Questions* way back then it absolutely would have changed the lives of many people. Now, instead of running from the memory, I choose consciously to forgive myself and everyone involved; we were all blinded at one time or another by our misperceptions.

Let's look at some of the ways that we run.

Running From The Past

There are obvious ways that we run, hide, and lie about the past; like moving away and rarely or never going back home because we don't want to face what we have run from. Let's look at some of the less obvious ways we run, and how we can choose to stop running, replacing the issue instead with something we can live with.

Here's an example: I spent many years working as a Certified Financial Planner. For a few of those years, one of my clients was a large municipality that allowed everyone who had a 401k to trade their own account. This meant that my phone rang all day long. On the other end of the phone were people I barely knew, and who were not following any of the ideas that my "real" clients would follow, such as patience, wisdom, and holding on to what was good.

These people were day trading, and for the most part did not know what they were doing.

I hated that phone ringing because I knew I would be talking to people who wanted something quickly, and that wanting would more often than not lead them to losing their money, because they were not interested in listening to my advice. Now, many years later, I still don't like the phone ringing very much.

You could say that because I have set my life up so that phone rarely rings, that I am running from the phone. That would be true except for one tiny difference. Instead of running, I consciously set up my life this way. I am willing to let the phone ring while at the same time providing ways to talk to people in other ways. This means that when the phone does ring, it is for all the right reasons.

When we say that we can't do something because it reminds us of the past, we are running.

The problem with running away from something in the past is that it keeps us from seeing what is present now. A state of mind of disgust, or fear, or any similar emotion, blinds us to what is right in front of us.

When we face a task filled with resentment, or sorrow, or anger, or simply the statement, "I won't do it," we are running, and most likely running from a memory of the past. There are two interesting things about memories—one, they are always wrong, and two, (which supports number one) they can always be changed.

I have a vivid memory of a time when I lived in Venice, CA. In this memory, I would walk out my back door, walk up the bank at the side of the house, and go paint pictures at a friend's home. It's a lovely memory. For years, I saw this vision in my head, when I recalled that time.

However, one day I realized this was a merged memory, because I never left by the back door, and there was no bank on the side of our house in Venice.

Although I did paint with a friend when we lived in Venice, the memory of the bank on the side of the house existed from the home we lived in when I was a teenager. I actually can't picture where my friend's home really was in Venice anymore; it has been replaced with a false memory.

Our memories of the past are a mixed bag of some things that happened, some things that didn't happen that way, how we were feeling about it then, and how we feel about it now. Talk to someone else about that time, and they will have a different memory of that time than you do.

Therefore, we can now choose to have different feelings about any event in the past. Why is this important? Remember that perception is what determines our reality, and if we really want to live abundantly in every area of our life, it's time to reframe our past perception, and choose one that more closely matches what we know and desire now.

Perhaps you are not interested in living abundantly. Maybe you like the excuses why you can't do something. Okay, then keep running from what never happened. Eventually you will have to do this shift work anyway, so since you are thinking about it now, why not now?

Not Looking

Have you ever not opened your snail mail, not read your email, not answered the phone, or not opened a package? What a great running technique. It's a funny one though, because when we do the "not looking" behavior, most of us are clueless why we are doing it.

What do we think? That if we don't open the email, it doesn't exist? As much as we may try to tell ourselves that it doesn't exist until we look at it, (like Schrödinger's cat) the truth is, as we well know, that it does. Therefore, it weighs on us. In the back of our mind, we know there is much unfinished business. People have written us and they expect a response from us.

Each time we run, and don't look, the urge to run and not look gets bigger because of the built-up pressure of not doing what we know we "should" or want to do.

Here are some steps to use to stop this particular running habit. First, become aware of this behavior. Next, pay attention to what you think will happen if you look.

Will something more be expected of you than you think you can handle? Is it just one more thing on a very full plate? Do you think you won't know how to answer? Are you punishing the person for something? Are you afraid of that person? Do you think you will say the wrong thing?

Don't judge the answers, just notice how you feel. Accept that it is okay to feel that way. However, recognize that the not looking isn't solving anything, and then put into practice a step-by-step approach that works for you.

One Step At A Time

Sometimes we run because there is just too much to do, or we don't know what to do next.

Here's a way to stop that practice—one-step-at-a-time. We have all heard of this concept before.

We know what it means, see the big picture, but don't be overwhelmed by it. Instead, take one-step-at-a-time and you will arrive at your destination.

It's an easy to apply tool to add to our perception shifting basket, and one that makes life so much easier if we utilize it.

It is easier to take one step at a time running up a hill than it is to look up and notice how much further there is to go. One-step-at-time, one foot in front of another, and the top of the hill arrives almost without noticing it.

I saw evidence of how powerful this concept is even if you are as light as a bird, because it was bird feet that demonstrated it to me.

We have a railing that goes around our deck, and after a snowstorm the snow on the railing was over 12 inches high. One section of the railing is a landing area for the birds as they fly to the feeder hanging under the roof of our porch. These are little birds that barely make a mark in the snow when they touch down.

The next day, after the snowstorm, the snow on the railing was still over 12 inches high except for one section. The section where the birds land was packed down to only a few inches. It was bird feet that did this, one tiny foot at a time, one little light step at a time.

Within each of our hearts, there is a calling to do something.

Too often, we are overwhelmed with the idea of it and stop listening, walling it off, hoping that it will disappear, and then we start running. This never works, does it? Because the desire and calling never disappear. Like the water behind the dike in the Little Dutch Boy Tale, there will always be a leak, and it will flood out into our lives.

Or we will stand there with our finger in the hole in the dike, not being able to do anything else.

Instead of running, we could take a cue from the birds. The reason the birds land on the railing is to get to the food. In a very real sense these birds have a calling to find food. The calling we are hearing within our hearts is the same thing. It is our food, hanging there, safe under the roof, ready to feed us forever.

We don't have to know how to do all the details of what is calling us. We don't have to understand where it will lead. We don't have to qualify; we don't have to earn it. We just have to be willing to put one foot in front of the other and accept it for what it is—the essence of what we call God—calling us to bloom as our Unique Spiritual Blessing.

This calling carries with it all that it needs to support and sustain it. We can trust in this Truth. Instead of fighting who we are, we can love it. Not love the small personality, or ego that we think we are, but instead we can love the God qualities that we represent. We can enjoy them, and we can share them. If we don't love them, we can't say we love God, can we?

Loving ourselves is not an ego trip. It is a step into humility when we recognize the Truth of ourselves. In this state of humility and Love, we can get out of our own way and step forward into what is calling us, because it is simply our awareness of God becoming present as our lives.

We can take those little steps, no matter how small, no matter how light, because each step does make a difference. All that is required of us is to be the active awareness of Good. And in Truth, what could be easier than that? One-step-at-a-time, it's that simple.

LEARNING SOMETHING NEW

An Age is called dark not because the light fails to shine, but because people refuse to see it. —James Albert Michener

We often run from the idea of learning something new. I should actually say that adults run from the idea of learning something new. Children are in the constant business of learning something new—exploring, discovering, and open to adventure.

I often hear adults say "I don't want to grow up," and in the same breath they say, "I don't want to learn that new thing, or new idea." Well then, act like a child and learn new things! Better yet, retain that childlikeness while choosing to grow up, because growing up is a glorious event. As a grown up we have the means and wisdom to constantly learn new things, and in doing so we will open up to ideas and worlds that were hidden to us when we chose to run from the n ew.

Yes, I know that in the information-overload era that we live in, everything can feel like a learning curve we can't meet, and the more we feel we have to learn just to keep up, the more we are tempted to run from learning.

In my writing and consulting business I always have new software programs to learn, and upgraded computers to purchase. Each time I have a choice—either run from the learning, stall as long as possible, or put aside time to learn, grateful to see so many symbols of the Infinite Intelligence of the divine Mind. This is the same choice that we all have. We are the representation of Infinite Intelligence, and therefore already contain all that we need to know to live our life productively.

FROM WHO YOU ARE

Our deepest fear is not that we are inadequate. Our deepest fear is that we are powerful beyond measure. It is our light, not our darkness that frightens us.

We ask ourselves, who am I to be brilliant, gorgeous, talented, and fabulous? Actually, who are we not to be? You are a child of God.

Your playing small doesn't serve the world. There's nothing enlightened about shrinking so that other people won't feel insecure around you.

We were born to make manifest the glory of God that is within us. It's not just in some of us, it's in everyone. And as we let our own light shine, we unconsciously give other people permission to do the same.

As we are liberated from our own fears, our presence automatically liberates others.—Maryann Williamson

This famous poem by Marianne Williamson says it all. We all, at one time or another, have run from our light. Some of us have kept on running.

The other side of this equation happens when we are dealing with a relationship issue with someone.

If we hold the Truth in our thinking about the person we have the issue with, and treat that person as if they are a child of God (not angry, spiteful, depressed, incapable, etc.) then one of two things will happen. Either the person will move closer to us because of a willingness to live as the child of God, or that person will move away from us.

Sometimes we are that person, running from the Truth of ourselves.

We may run to the easier path, to those that will treat us as we are used to being treated—because it feels familiar to be treated as if we are a victim, or angry, or depressed, or incapable. On the other hand, we may simply run away from everyone, just in case someone might see the lie that we are living.

You know that saying, "You can run, but you can't hide." This is certainly a true statement, which makes it a perfect lead-in to the next question.

32

— • —

CHAPTER SIX

Let yourself be silently drawn by the stronger pull of what you really are. —Rumi

Many of us refuse to reveal ourselves to anyone. Perhaps we feel this is an invasion of privacy. This makes complete sense. We do need to keep things private that need to be private. On the other hand, we live in a world where one fast Google search will reveal massive amounts of information about us. This kind of visibility isn't going to go away.

The question is, how are we choosing to be visible? Of course, it is wise and prudent to hide from view many personal and financial details. We can monitor what is being said about us, and do our best to make sure that what is being said is accurate.

However, many of us hide from those who would benefit us if we would just let them into our lives.

Hiding behind a wall from those who would help us, not only does not serve us, but it also doesn't really work. We live in a world of constant visibility, and yet we hide the most important part of ourselves, our essential expression, our Unique Spiritual Blessing, from everyone—beginning with ourselves. When we ask and honestly answer the question, "Am I Hiding" we can make conscious choices, rather than hiding "just because."

ISOLATION

Call it a clan, call it a network, call it a tribe, call it a family.
Whatever you call it, whoever you are, you need one. —Jane Howard

When I am struggling with something, I have to force myself
to not withdraw and hide. Hiding when we are troubled, and
isolating ourselves away from those that could, and would, help us
is a dangerous choice. This type of isolation is the perfect breeding
ground for the dark, and unlikable thoughts, that got us there in the
first place.

A friend called this false isolation. As I thought about that idea,
the image of a pack of animals running away from a lion entered
my mind. As I mentally watched, I saw how the lion separated one
animal from the pack and then easily tired it out, hunted it down,
and killed it.

This sounds rather gruesome, but in many ways, it is an accurate
picture.

When we are struggling, we need protection and support,
not isolation.

The solution is to join a pack. Get yourself a circle of angels. It's
amazing how many of us call ourselves a loner. I certainly have. Yet
we are never alone anyway. We are all part of the whole.

I watched a documentary about how DNA works. The
commentator described the division between those that believe we
have evolved and those that believe that God created us all in seven
days.

I visually, and emotionally, stepped back from that division and
listened instead to the symbol of DNA. Instead of seeing it as a
divisor, I saw it as a symbol that proves both theories, when we begin
with the premise that we are all One.

To make this overly simple doesn't negate the idea, so here goes. We all have the same DNA. There are two factors that make us different, the ordering of the particles, and the timing of switches. For example, we all have the possibilities of patterning. It is the arrangement of particles and the timing of switches that determines if we will have the spots of a leopard, the coloring of a fish, or freckles.

Starting with the correct premise that God is the intelligent creator, and all that we see is the outcome of Its creation, do you see the magnificent symbol of DNA, and the oneness of both ideas?

Understanding DNA as the symbol of the intelligent creator and abundance of living creatures as the outcome, evolution becomes just a variety of ways that the One Painter has painted Its ideas.

Let's go back to the idea of finding ourselves a circle of angels. To do this, find a group of people that see and value you for who you are—not for how you act, for what you have, or for what you say—but for the essence of yourself.

Find a group of people that want you to bloom in your life without any personal prejudice of what that will look like. Find a group of people who are willing to take action.

Band together in a pack and connect with them. Get organized in a way that works for all of you. Stay together. Protect each other. Honor and respect each other. Always be present for them, as they will be for you.

When we are tempted to isolate ourselves in times of trouble, let's remember the picture of the weaker animal that is easily hunted down by a predator. Then picture an elephant tribe that circles around a member of their group that is in trouble, and protects it from danger until it is strong again. Join a pack, join a circle of angels, and protect and be protected.

It is true, United we stand, divided we fall.—Aesop

SILLY REASONS

One of the happiest times of my life almost never happened because I didn't like the idea of going out at night, and I didn't want to miss a rerun of my favorite show at the time, Perry Mason.

Go ahead, laugh, but seriously, those were my reasons. I had to force myself past these two issues to do something I knew would take up every extra minute of my life, which I didn't feel I had many of, for the next few years.

But I did it. I started a dance company while attending college full time, raising children, and working at least one part-time job to support my family.

I had many excuses that were even better than not wanting to go out at night, and missing Perry Mason, but my human sense of myself tried to stop me from experiencing full happiness with something that silly. I could have used any of the other reasons, and anybody would have understood, and agreed with me, that I was too busy, but when I listened within, I found those two excuses were the real reasons I was stopping myself.

Once those hidden reasons were revealed, I had a choice of accepting them as real, or setting them aside and doing it anyway, which is what I did.

The result of choosing what looked so hard to do was a time that everyone involved still recalls as a brilliantly happy experience, full of priceless memories.

I heard a woman explain why she was not fully expressing herself by saying, "I guess I am delaying my happiness." Don't we all delay our happiness at least some of the time?

Why we do this isn't important. We could take lots of time and drill down into our human situation and find perfectly acceptable reasons for delaying or never accepting happiness, with and as, our life.

However, why waste time with the why we aren't happy, when knowing why we are not happy is not necessary to be happy.

In fact, this is often another excuse for delaying happiness. Instead, let's move to happiness now by stepping out of the human why and why not. Let's go to where happiness is a quality that always exists, and can never, ever, be replaced by sorrow.

Where is that? Not in the human duality point of view. Not within the state of mind of not being good enough, or it not being the right time, or in feeling guilty, feeling superior, feeling old, or feeling useless.

It is not found in the thought that we are the wrong sex, wrong height, wrong weight, or lacking intelligence or skill—no—nor it is found anywhere within the human duality point of view.

The *where* is here and the time is now. It is within the understanding that what we call the force of life, the substance of being, is Mind Itself, the Infinite intelligence of Love, Loving Itself. Here is where happiness is the substance of our being. Not something that must be attained, but what is, now.

There is no need to plead that the love of God shall fill our hearts as though He were unwilling to fill us...Love is pressing around us on all sides like air. Cease to resist and instantly love takes possession. —Amy Carmichael

We can see it everywhere, a baby's laugh, a bird song, a tree in the breeze, a flower blooming. These are the symbols, the signs, the proof of Love as the only cause and creator.

We will see more of these outward expressions only as we begin within the Truth of being and stay there.

What appears without will become closer and closer to the essence of Truth, not because we are creating it or making it happen, but because we are lifting the veil from our eyes, or more accurately our perception. The mist dissolves, revealing Life Living Itself.

Happiness cannot be stopped from being the essence of our lives by those seemingly logical reasons that the dualist worldview gives when we see those claims for what they are—lies.

We can never change an outward appearance by remaining unhappy, but when we choose an inward happiness, it will shift what appears without in ways far beyond any human outlining.

We can choose to be happy now, even when we are surrounded by people who are not happy, and who have good reasons why they aren't. If we really want to help them, we must step out of that story and light the way for them by revealing happiness, in and as, our life now.

It doesn't need to take years, months, days, or even hours to be happy now. When we stand in Truth, the Truth will set us free.

I am still determined to be cheerful and happy in whatever situation I may be, for I have also learned from experience that the greater part of our happiness or misery depends upon our dispositions, and not upon our circumstances.—Martha Washington

Hiding In The Noise

Many of us hide in the noise. You think not? That's only because you might be thinking I must mean the noise of sound. Yes, that is one kind of noise. We live in a noisy world anyway, don't we?

However, here are some ways we make it even louder.

We talk all the time. We all know people like this. What they say they have already said—repeatedly. It is always the same discussion. It often contains some form of a phrase that points to the faults of others, rehashes the bad breaks of the past, and laments the unfairness of the world. Talking too much, without listening to others, or ourselves, is a very easy place to hide.

We hide in the noise of clutter. Even the most orderly of us have clutter. We all keep things that don't work, clothes we don't wear, objects we don't like, and stuff we don't need. However, some of us stack those things up so much that we can't think straight at all. Clutter drains us.

We lose things, and we have no space. We pay money to store things away that we never look at, but remain within our lives taking up room, and making noise. The noise of clutter is a fabulous place to hide from ourselves, and others.

The noise of busyness is the disease of our era. How busy can we keep ourselves? If we aren't making ourselves busy, we let others do it to us. To add insult to injury, we often use things in that busyness that make lots of noise.

I used to live where lawns were at a premium, and then I moved to where huge lawns are standard issue. Lawns are noisy. Lawn mowers and leaf blowers are noisy in loudness and time.

I am in full agreement with this quote by William Henry Hudson: *I am not a lover of lawns. Rather would I see daisies in their thousands, ground ivy, hawkweed, and even the hated plantain with tall stems, and dandelions with splendid flowers and fairy down, than the too-well-tended lawn.*

Imagine the stillness of lawns planted as fields. Imagine sitting quietly in nature just listening to the silence. That isn't as farfetched as it seems. However, first we have to ask ourselves, "Am I hiding in noise," and if we are, begin the process of eliminating it.

Practice sitting quietly in active meditation. Listen within to the still small voice, and then take action on what you hear. Pause, Observe, Listen, and take action.

In the *Preface* we talked about the symbol of pulling the drill out to clear the sawdust. This is the same as using the Pause, Observe,

Listen (POL) tool. Within a pause we can easily let go of what is no longer needed, making it possible to continue drilling down through habitual habits.

HIDING IN BUSYNESS

Let's talk more about busyness, because not only does it often create a lot of noise in which we can hide, busyness all by itself is a wonderful hiding ground.

In an age when things were supposed to be easier, and we would have more leisure time, the opposite has occurred. "I'm too busy," is a phrase we all have said to keep from doing something we want to do. In busyness we don't have to think too much or make radical changes, because we are too busy.

Try taking an hour off, without electronic interruption, and spend that time quietly with your thoughts. As they occur, watch them go by like clouds. Don't hold on to them or judge them, just watch them go by.

Listen within, listen without, and listen to the silent rhythm of the universe.

Feel yourself melding with the rhythm of where you are, whether it is in a chair or outside in nature. Feel the non-busyness, yet profound living of life that is always going on. Listen to who you are, listen to your heart's desire, listen to the still small voice within guiding you to living your life fully. In this hour off, notice that the world did not end because you were not rushing around making things happen.

Make this time off a spiritually healthy habit.

My husband has always taken quiet time the first thing in the morning. He sits in the dark, drinking his morning drink, and listens. And then we sit together and do the same thing. As you make this time off a habit, take more time away from being busy. Eliminate those things you are doing because you felt you had to, but actually they have nothing to do with you.

The interesting part of no longer hiding in the busyness is you will find that you are actually more productive. What needs to be done gets done with more ease and grace, and as you stop hiding, your life expands. That expansion takes place within the context of your preference of how you wish to live your life. Most of us do not desire to jet-set around the world, or to be famous enough to be known as we walk down the street.

However, even if you do find yourself that well known, that is still no excuse to hide in the busyness. Whether our days are simple, or complicated, we can still learn not to hide in the busyness of life.

Did you know we are trained to be busy so we won't think too much? Our schools were first designed to keep us in line with the religious beliefs of the Puritans. Their premise was that we are all sinners, especially the children.

Because many of the first settlers in America were English, much of our education system is patterned on the systems they brought with them. The Puritans, strict fundamentalist Protestants, believed education was necessary in order to read the Bible so that one could receive salvation.

This was in line with the beliefs of the Protestant Reformers. Schools made no distinction between religious and secular life. They inspired children to endure the hardships of a life in the New World through religious devotion.

The first compulsory education laws were passed in Massachusetts from 1642-1648. They were specifically oriented towards a segment of the population (non-Puritan) that was not, in their view, providing their children with a proper education.

Religious leaders were concerned about the rapid growth of the non-Puritan population and took these steps to maintain Puritan religious beliefs. The first act, called the Massachusetts Act of 1642, made education a state responsibility. Although the schools were not yet funded or required, education itself was, and all children were supposed to learn how to read and write, or parents would risk loss of the custody of their children. This law was amended and strengthened in 1648.

Children from poorer households received a minimal education, and slaves from Africa only learned what was necessary to attend to their masters. Later, during the industrial revolution, schools focused on teaching us how to sit still and follow directions so that we could be good factory workers.

Today the educational system is often too focused on passing tests, and only a lucky few learn how to think, and reason.

Perhaps if we don't think too much, we won't question the workings of governments, or the injustices brought about by just a few people, because they are keeping all the rest of us too busy.

Therefore, even if you think that you can't afford to stop hiding in busyness, do it for the rest of humanity.

Imagine a world filled with thinkers and imaginaries, and we were one of them. How many of us would then agree to the world's many inhumane practices, including wars, that we now let slide by, because we are too busy hiding?

Not Listening

We all know someone who literally can't hear, and chooses not to wear a hearing aid some, or all, of the time.

What a great way to hide. Not knowing what is being said, we can pretend that there is nothing for us to do, or to know.

Of course not wearing a hearing aid is obvious, but what about just not listening? When someone is talking, are we planning what we are going to say next?

Or perhaps we are not listening at all. Instead, we may be designing our home, thinking about our next date, or work, or our vacation—all wonderful hiding mechanisms for not listening when someone else is talking.

There are other ways we don't listen.

We don't listen to the signs of our lives, or we don't read the instructions, or we don't read what is written to us—the ways of not listening are numerous, and we are guilty of all of them at one time or another.

When we recognize them as a hiding technique, we have begun the real process of listening. We will start listening to what are we being told, and in the process discover that there is much to hear, either through literal words, or through signs and symbols. The more skilled we get at listening, the less likely we will answer "yes" to the question, "Are You Hiding."

Checking In On Others

If you can see your path laid out in front of you step by step, you know it's not your path. Your own path you make with every step you take. That's why it's your path.—Joseph Campbell

Checking on others is a great way to hide. It is widely accepted, and it may even make you look like a good person. This is the one where you notice, react to, and try to do something about, someone else in hiding, lying, waiting or running.

We can easily see someone else's faults, and unwise habits. We can make a living at doing so.

In fact, there are professions where this skill of noticing is required and many a hider, liar, runner, and waiter has done a good job of hiding within their ranks.

Whew! You may be thinking, she means a profession like psychology, and that eliminates me.

Not so fast.

How about professions like teacher, mother, police officer, actor, father, banker, salesperson, coach, life guide—yes this list could include all of us.

If in our daily life we spend time observing others in order be good at what we do, then this is an easy place to hide.

The most dangerous way to hide in the checking-in-on-others scenario is by being a friend. In the name of friendship, we can point out others' faults, and consider it a demonstration of being a good friend.

Here is the key question to ask ourselves to keep us on track. Are we using these professions, and skills to hide ourselves?

We must be observant, wise, and aware. Leaving ourselves out of the observations, or observing ourselves as hiding but doing nothing about our own habits, is a habit that will someday boomerang back to us in ways we usually don't see coming. It's back to perception again. What we see in others is actually going on within our own perception.

We will become better at every profession we are a part of, if we begin with the correct premise about ourselves and others. We are not superior to others just because we see their faults.

It's a fact that we can't see what we don't already know. This works both ways. We can't see good unless we learn to look for and support good, and we can't see the "error" in others if it is not already something we have experienced ourselves.

CONTROL AND PLANNING

When I do good, I feel good; when I do bad, I feel bad. That's my religion. —-Abraham Lincoln

We know who we are, don't we? If I say, "control freak" raise your hand if it sounds familiar. I understand. I am giving up controlling and controlled planning myself, so I understand that it is a hard thing to walk away from.

However, once we begin to understand how miserable it is to always have to be in control, and to have everything planned, we can finally begin to give it up.

It certainly doesn't fit into the idea that God is the only cause and creator, or follow the guidance of "not my will but Thy will be done." Instead, it is the perfect place to hide.

There are many ways to control. There are those who feel as if they have no control over anything, so they take control over something that they feel they can do, like eating. Or perhaps control over others.

Some people plan everything so much that the joy of discovery and unfolding is lost in the details of getting it right. There is nothing wrong with being good at managing, or planning—in fact it is a delightful and necessary skill. However, only if it is based in the right premise; the premise that we are the action of the Divine, not a lone operator.

It's easy to spot controllers and controlled planners who are not only controlling and planning their own lives, but other lives as well. They always have to run the show, they change what other people have set up because it doesn't match what they want, and they punish others, in a variety of ways, for not going along with their plans.

None of us want to live that way. Let's give it up, and step out from behind the control curtain and get to know ourselves.

A tree doesn't control; it grows and shares itself, blessing all that get to know it.

One morning I woke up with these words ringing in my ears as if someone had spoken them to me. "Don't plan; share." I pass this idea on to you. It has helped me immensely in seeing the difference between controlling, and being, the action of Love.

HIDING IN THE STORY

Hiding in our story is very handy for many of us, because we have collected great stories. They give us wonderful excuses for our current behavior.

They usually begin with, "When I was," and continue on about life as it was when we were younger, how our parents treated us, what school was like, how our friends behaved—the list is endless.

Some of these stories are not so bad, and some of us have absolutely horrible stories to tell. Either way, when we use these stories to hide in and away from our current life, we keep ourselves away from living the blessings that life is offering us here and now. On the other hand, it is possible to use these stories to learn about ourselves and move on into life with a brave, and open, heart.

If you think you are stuck with your stories, think again. Go back and read the section on Right Thinking in this book. It will help reset that story in your memory so that it takes its proper place. I am using the idea of story on purpose. It is a story, and nothing more, and only occurs and occurred within our own perception of it.

Now is the time to talk about accepting guilt and responsibility for our stories, and then hiding in that pain. Why do we do this? Because we think that we, or another, created it and caused it. This is not true.

Please know that we do not create the situation or story line from our actions, or our thoughts—either from our current life, or from what some people call karma. Remember, there is only one cause and creator, and It tells only one story. That story is about unfolding and expanding good, equally, for every one of Its ideas. There is no one left out of, or separated from, all that is good. Because God, Good, is omnipresent, that is not possible.

Therefore, the story, or stories, that appear to be in and about your life are misunderstood events. Yes, they may have happened. Yes, they were either lovely, or horrible, or somewhere in between.

However, no story actually happened within big R Reality, the Reality of God, Good, who knew—and knows—nothing about it. Therefore, our True Being, our essential eternal identity, does not know anything about it either. Nothing has removed us from the Good that is God.

When we dream, we see many stories, yet we wake up from the dream, knowing that it was a dream. We often learn from those dreams, but we don't live from those dreams. What appears as our everyday life is the same as those dreams. As we wake up into the awareness of our true being, then the dream of human life and worldview begins to fade, and will correct itself based on our new awareness.

We are all aware of the illusion of dreaming. We don't wake up from a dream and then base the rest of our day or our lives on it. Perhaps we will look for the symbols found within the dream in order to become more aware of what we are thinking and perceiving, but it will not become the basis of all our actions. The stories found within our lives are nothing more than stories, like dreams. And like dreams, the stories and the story teller are one.

What we perceive to be reality magnifies. Magnify the story, continue to give it full power, and yes—it is a great place in which to hide.

However, I ask, "Why stay there?" Wake up! The big R Reality holds more possibilities than we can possibly imagine—all of them good—and everything will get better and better the more awake we become.

HIDING IN VICTIMHOOD

Yes, I could have put this under the heading of Hiding In The Story because being a victim begins by believing a story. However, it deserved its own category because we all do it almost automatically, at least once in awhile. Oh, I know, we all know someone who really plays up the victim story, but when we look closely at our own lives, we are doing it too.

There are many ways to hide in victimhood, but the one that has us sacrificing for others so we can remain a victim is particularly unlovely. In this one, we claim to be acting out of love for others, but in reality, we place a burden on them. They, of course, could then use this scenario to choose to hide in victimhood themselves.

We are not required to sacrifice the essence of ourselves, our desires, and our hopes so that others can have theirs. Many of us do give up a dream, or two, or three, so that our children can have theirs; or we work at jobs that may not be our first choice so that the family can be fed. This does not have to be chosen as a sacrifice; and most certainly we must not choose to act the victim in these cases.

If we do so, we have negated all that we have done for others; we have made them responsible for our unhappiness. Instead, we can lean back into the provision of Love. We can choose to do these things with delight, happy to have the chance to serve, which is not sacrifice. Instead of burdening others with our victimhood, we release them to live free of the guilt of our sacrificing for them. Guilt is a terrible burden to pass on to anyone.

It is easy to give to others so that we don't have to give to ourselves, but this is hiding. Be sure that what you are choosing to do is not based on victimhood.

You will find that there is a more elegant, and marvelous, idea for you to choose from for your life. Infinite Love does not take from one to give to another. Take action from this premise, and watch life unfold perfectly for you and the ones you love.

Another way to hide in victimhood is hiding in ill health. This is not a discussion of whether ill health is real or not. We are going to stay away from that issue for now. Instead, let's look at using ill health to get the attention we crave.

It could be ill health in terms of a disease or an injury. When we take the time to examine our motives for giving power to either of these situations, we will often find that they provide the perfect motive for not participating and for getting something we desire—from attention to income.

We have all probably tried the "I'm not feeling well" gambit to get out of going to school, but that habit remains into adulthood unless we become aware of it, and send it packing.

Here's a personal example of battling with the temptation to give in to victimhood, in this case an injury.

It was a beautiful day so I decided to walk longer, and explore a new way home. The ice had melted on the streets—or so I thought—so I had removed the chains on my shoes (yes, they exist and yes, they work) and I was happily striding down a new side street enjoying the view of the lake.

Suddenly I felt myself falling sideways. I hit the street with a huge thud as I fell directly on my entire side. As soon as I hit the ground, I got back up because I knew that it would not be wise to succumb to the belief of falling.

That was the easy part. Then the war began.

I knew that if I could hold to a Spiritual Perception that I—in God's image and likeness—had never fallen and if I could choose not be tempted into believing in what the senses were telling me, the result would be "no result" from the illusion of a fall.

I imagined how wonderful it would be to have direct proof that everything is only thought, and to know without doubt that maintaining a Spiritual Perception, and letting go of anything unlike Love, would immediately dissolve any negative situation.

That liar, which does not want us to know who we are, didn't let me alone for a second. It reminded me that I had fallen very hard and was lucky not to have broken something.

It told me I would be sore, unable to move my shoulder and hip, and that the bruising would be extensive. It suggested that I could "use" the injury to get a bit more attention from anyone, anywhere. It would give me something to say to people that they could commiserate with. I could fit in.

It was a war between what I knew to be True and the temptation to believe the worldview and what it was saying to me about who I was, and what had happened.

The barrage of tempting thoughts continued for days.

The fall was no different than any other event that tempts us to use the negative to achieve a positive, to succumb to something we know is not true, just to get a bit of love, or attention; to give into the idea of lack in any form, to accept the lie of separateness from Divine Love in whatever way it decides to make its appearance.

It is still the same lie.

What defeats this lie? Always the same Truth; there is only One, and it is Spiritual, and we are Its Being.

The result of the fall was "no result," and "no result" is what we want from any lie. Let's all resist the temptation to be part of the worldview so that we can fit in. This is not where we want to fit anyway. What we really want is to become aware of, and experience, Divine Love's infinite Oneness. In this Oneness, we always fit in.

It's much easier to give up material things, and pleasures, than it is to give up material worldview habits and thoughts, but imagine the result of giving up the habit of hiding in victimhood.

WHAT AND WHERE IS SELF-LOVE?

There are many paths to enlightenment. Be sure to take one with a heart. —Lao Tzu

Recently I started thinking about the idea of self-love. I begin wondering what the difference is between the self-love we want, and the self-love we don't want. Because on the one hand we hear we should learn to love ourselves, yet on the other hand we hear that self-love is selfish. It turns out, the word self-love can mean the exact opposite depending on who is saying it, and how it is used.

My mentor used to say this to me, "Self-love is more opaque than a solid body."* I often thought, "huh" when she said it, and decided she must not be talking about me, since I was so often down on myself. Where was my self-love?

Yet, looking back, I know she was trying to tell me something about myself. Now I see that being down on myself was the negative version of self-love. I was often attempting to find something I needed, by giving to others, so I could have what I thought I lacked. It was still really all about me.

That is what the negative self-love is about; it is "all about me." It rests in the human personality, and ego of self, and not surprisingly, it does not ever bring permanent happiness.

I wasn't trying to make life all about me. I was trying to be a good wife, mother, daughter, employee, and service provider. I was trying to do the right thing, all the time. However, because I didn't understand that loving myself meant not loving the human personality self, but loving the qualities of God present as me, I was often in need. This meant that without realizing it, life was often all a bout me.

Do we need self-love? Absolutely, but which kind? Jesus' admonition to "love thy neighbor as thyself" states clearly that we had better love ourselves well if we are going to treat our neighbors well too. This is tricky, I know. Same phrase, entirely different meanings, and entirely different results.

Perhaps the first step to seeing the difference between the two kinds of self-love is to begin with the question, "What premise is our self-love based upon?"

Is it self-love beginning with the premise of a human personality and needs—where we take care of ourselves through will power, positive thinking, control, destructive behavior (which is actually inverted control and will power), and hard work?

Or is it self-love beginning with the premise that we are the presence of Infinite Intelligent Love, which eliminates need of all kinds?

With the second form of self-love, we love ourselves because we are the reflection and expression, of God.

We observe the qualities of God that we uniquely express, and cherish their presence as us. We care for ourselves within the context of caring for the gift that we are to each other.

As knowledge of ourselves as the qualities of divine Love increases, so does our self-love. This is an easy love to have. This self-love removes ego. It eliminates fear. It dissolves being stuck in negative descriptions of ourselves. We learn to love, and treasure, the qualities we express. We give thanks for who we are. We find life flows from this kind of love, and we no longer need to use any form of human control.

It's easy to tell which self-love we are practicing.

In the human version of self-love, we experience need. We have all experienced this kind of self-love need. It is a need for anything we feel we don't have—from love, money, health, or time. Needing is not a good experience, or feeling.

Within Divine self-love there is no need, there is only the experience in each moment of the qualities of who we are, present and being lived as us. In Divine self-love, we find plenty of everything, and our love for ourselves flows to our neighbors equally without effort.

In human self-love we ask, "Notice me, help me, give to me, and take care of me." In Divine self-love the I Am is present. Within this self-love our personality and ego step aside so that we can be seen as we are—the reflection and expression of God.

Self-love within a spiritual context is a marvelous way to live. Opaque means not being able to see through something. Through the lens of human self-love we are unable to see the Truth of any situation.

However, as we are willing to know ourselves as the qualities of God, the opaqueness fades, and in the resulting clarity, we find our freedom from need. We experience instead the joy of divine self-love, which is always overflowing, filling our lives full of blessings without measure.

* Mary Baker Eddy—*Science And Health With Key To The Scriptures*

HIDING IN THE PAST

It is not life and wealth and power that enslave men, but the cleaving to life and wealth and power.—Buddha

Let's consider what we believe is the past, and family history, past and present.

At a family gathering a few years ago, we shared our favorite family memories. For some it was easy, for others, not so much. In fact, when I asked Del if he had a favorite family vacation memory (since that was mostly what everyone picked) he didn't have one; not only because he doesn't have good family memories, but also because his family never, ever took a vacation.

However, if you ask any of his children, they have a multitude of favorite family memories. I know, because they share them all the time.

We can either take our past and learn from it, or be buried in it.

As we traveled that week through family history, it was easy to see the frozen attitudes; stuck states of mind, and points of views. Not just in others, but in myself. The first night at our family gathering, I didn't sleep at all, because I was caught up in the same feelings and emotions that haunted my childhood—self-loathing and depression because I had felt misunderstood and disliked.

And even though many years had gone by, and much shifting, the intensity of the experience reminded me of how that felt, and it took some doing to shift away from that so I could let go, and enjoy the trip—which I surely did!

Yet, we must do more than just shift from bad memories to good ones, or let slide those things we don't like and embrace the ones we do. We have to let it all go. Our family history must all be re-seen as God in action, as shared love, as the unfolding of grace—with not one trace of ownership or heredity.

As we look at family, past and present, let's see what is actually present and let go of our self-will and justification—both on the good side and the bad side. It's all in the small r reality room, where everything is seen as material and measurable.

We can step out of that room to the Spiritual Perception of family, and consciously experience ourselves as the unique essence of Light that we are. We can embrace what appears as family members not as limited editions of themselves, but as a unique essence of Light.

Flow Like Fire

During one of our early morning talks in the dark, with our favorite morning drinks, we sat watching the fire in our stove.

The fire was doing something we had never seen before. It would quiet down so that all that we saw were very hot logs, and then a spurt or whiff of fire would rise and immediately blink out, as the entire roof of the stove would suddenly be alive with flame. Within moments, it would quiet down and repeat the process, but never the same way twice.

Fire is like that, it is never the same way twice; and yet the essence of it is always the same. Everyone knows fire when they see it, even though it has an infinite variety of ways to express itself. This made me think of plans and making lists.

Yes, I know that on the surface it appears to be a strange connection.

However, just a moment before we had been talking about plans and lists, and the fire's show that morning was the perfect symbol of the difference between how we think things should be, and how it is when we are aware of how life flows.

I thought, "What if we were more like fire when we made plans and lists?" What if instead of saying this is exactly how my day, my work, my party, my dinner, my life— my anything—is going to go, what if instead we accepted that the essence of our plans will always be perfect, and then let the outcome be expressed in a variety of interesting, and beautiful ways.

WHAT IF WE FLOWED LIKE FIRE?

Then instead of feeling remorse, or guilt, or anger, or emotion of any kind when our plans do not go as we expect, or when we don't finish our to-do lists, what if we flowed like fire and lived within the awareness of the beauty and uniqueness of each moment?

What if instead of seeing ourselves as limited humans, we saw ourselves as a unique expression of divine Mind? Then no matter what happens, we would be aware of our innate, individual perfection of being.

When we study fire, it is easy to see that no matter what shape it takes, it remains fire. We can see the same thing with anything in nature. A tree remains a tree, and a squirrel remains a squirrel.

It is when we get to ourselves that we often stop having this basic awareness. We think if we haven't done this or that, or the situation we are in is not as we planned, that we ourselves have been affected adversely and become someone else.

However, the Truth is, we remain who we have been and always will be. Even if we don't know who we are, it doesn't change who we are. As we let go of expectations, fears, and judgments, the view of ourselves begins to clear up. When that happens, we may think that we have changed, but we haven't.

Instead, we have begun to see the face of our own fire—the Truth of our being.

In his excellent book, *The War of Art*, Stephen Pressfield makes the point that we must always be about our work. Yes, we must. Just as fire must be doing fire, we must be doing who we are. However, if we make the mistake of measuring that idea in human, linear, and stilted terms, we miss the fact that when we are aware of the essence of ourselves, like the fire, whatever we are doing, we are still doing "our work."

I love making lists and plans. I have a list by my computer I check every hour. I have plans for today and plans for next year. However, if my plans change in either the next moment, or the next month, it will not change who I am. And if I don't let emotions cloud my awareness, it will not change the quality of my day, or of my life.

As we strip off expectations and judgments, and discover the infinite ways that we express the essence of our being, we discover that we have always been an individual expression of the Divine Mind.

We are like the fire. The only real plan of fire is to be fire. Like fire, we flow into and as our life, in an infinite variety of ways, while always remaining ourselves. We will become increasingly aware of this fact when we let joy be our guide, and allow gratitude to light our flame. Then our lives become what they are—a spectacular show of infinite expression. Never the same, always beautiful.

33

—·—

CHAPTER SEVEN

*N*ever, *never be afraid to do what is right, especially if the well-being of a person or animal is at stake.*—Martin Luther King

It's easy to tell when we are lying. At least it is easy when we are paying attention. It's easy because of the way it feels. Only those who don't know they are lying, either through innocence, or through depravity, don't feel the result of lying.

Of course, all lies begin within ourselves and to ourselves, and if we get too good at lying to ourselves the consequences are very dangerous.

Therefore, when we ask ourselves, "Am I Lying?" we mean not just to others, but first, "Am I lying to myself?" Sometimes it may be justified to lie to another, if the moral law of protection dictates it, but most of the time it is best to tell the truth.

However, lying to ourselves is always a dangerous and slippery slope. I first saw the results, and dangers of lying to oneself in a childhood friend. When we were young, everyone in school knew that his dad was going out with other women, and even young girls, because he was cruelly blatant about it.

However, my friend's mom pretended that it wasn't happening, which of course affected her life. It was worse for my friend. As he got older, he refused to speak about it. He would even say that it wasn't true. I watched as that lie ate him up and consumed the boy that he was, and hid it from view. He started acting like his dad, and lying to himself, and others, about it. Because he knew that he and his dad were wrong, and he couldn't face the truth, he started closing himself off. In time, he became bitter and angry, and acting in ways he once would have hated.

I can easily look back and see that if he had just been willing to admit there was a problem with his dad, and worked through that problem for himself, none of the rest of what followed was likely to have happen.

He is not alone in this behavior. We all lie sometimes to ourselves and to others to protect our ego, or because we don't think we can survive telling the truth. Sometimes we don't call it lying, we might call it exaggeration, but it is still a lie. Unless we pay very close attention to what we say, it is easy to fall into this trap.

Our human ego is always playing a game of one-upmanship, because it believes that doing so is necessary for survival.

Because we are, in big R Reality, a reflection of God, we can defeat this habit by first setting our premise to our right identity, and then as we notice the lies, either big or small, we can choose to correct them. As we dissolve and eliminate habits like these, because we are basing our behavior on the true essence of ourselves and others, there is another lie that will often show itself. This is the lie that it is necessary to heap guilt and judgment upon ourselves for what we have done.

Although it is always necessary to notice, and then eliminate behavior that does not reflect our True nature, it is not necessary to punish ourselves once that behavior is gone. We don't punish our children in their teens for what they did when they were two. This same kindness, and clarity, needs to be extended to ourselves. If we do not do so, it will cloud our view of the goodness of God, and of our own spiritual identity.

I said it was easy to tell when we are lying. It is. When we refuse to look at the facts, when we rationalize our behavior, when we are angry, and judgmental, or depressed, there is a lie waiting to be exposed.

Yes, exposing our lies to ourselves is painful, but not nearly as painful as losing our loved ones, and ourselves.

When we lie to ourselves it is inevitable that in some form, we will lose ourselves, and those we love.

TELLING THE TRUTH

We do not need magic to change the world, we carry all the power we need inside ourselves already: we have the power to imagine better.—J. K. Rowling

Of course, the opposite of lying is telling the truth. Obvious isn't it? Or is it?

Most of us feel that if we don't say anything we are not lying. Perhaps. However, we are also not telling the truth either, and that is the point of the question, "Am I Lying" after all.

The Twelve Step Program of Alcoholics Anonymous deals with this issue of lying in a few of their Twelve Steps—let's look at two of them.

Step Ten, states: "Continued to take a personal inventory and when we were wrong promptly admitted it."

This requires a constant monitoring of the internal lying that goes on in all of us, and then demands that instead of festering a lie, the truth must be told.

Step Five states: "Admitted to God, to ourselves, and to another human being the exact nature of our wrongs."

This is a crucial step in this process. We can tell ourselves that if we know the truth it doesn't matter if anyone else knows it. This step demands that we say it aloud, that we fully face our fears. Why do this? It is certainly not to embrace our fears, but to release us from the prison of lying.

The poet and scientist Piet Hein wrote:

The noble art of losing face
May one day save the human race
And turn into eternal merit
What weaker minds would call disgrace.

Our fear is that if we tell others what we have done wrong, or admit to the mess we think we have made, we will lose either our friends, our loved ones, our reputation, and our pride, or maybe all of these, all at one time.

However, not one of these is as valuable as losing our soul, or the essence of our being.

For what is a man profited, if he shall gain the whole world, and lose his own soul? Or what shall a man give in exchange for his soul?—Bible, Matt: 16:26

The glorious part of telling the truth is the reward. One woman in our *Shift* community wrote about how many wonderful opportunities were flooding into her life as a direct result of telling the truth about a situation, and taking action on what she discovered; opportunities that she could never have expected, or tried to make happen.

She said, "I just want to say that this has really all opened up since I dared to share with you all the traumas I was experiencing post house sale. Just letting you all in on my deep secret of possible short sale/bankruptcy/whatever on the house has seemingly opened the floodgates. Yesterday I saw a branch of the bank and said a little prayer of gratitude as I was waiting to cross the road!"

It is a lie that says to us that we will lose our friends, our loved ones, our reputation, and our pride. Instead we regain our pride, find our true friends and loved ones, and rebuild our reputation as someone who can admit what is happening, and work through and out of it.

MAKE IT APPROPRIATE

Telling the truth to both ourselves and to a trusted friend, or advisor, is different from releasing information over everyone and requiring them to bear the burden of our truth telling. Choose wisely to whom you share.

And for heaven's sake, don't be one of those people, who after deciding that they might as well tell the truth, start spilling out details to everyone. This is a good way to hide from the feelings, and a wonderful way to run from the responsibility.

Actually, it is another form of lying; thinking that spilling your guts to anyone who will listen is actually truth telling. Once again, lying is going on.

I once wrote a truthful letter to two people I love, and instead of destroying it after writing it, I sent it. Although the letter did speak the truth, as I personally saw it to be, it was my self-indulgence that wanted them to know about it.

I look back now and wonder, "What did I want to come of that letter," because there was absolutely nothing positive that the letter could, or would have, ever done for them. Instead, it caused a riff that although long ago forgotten, and forgiven, by them, remains a point of sorrow for me, because I know how painful it was for them to receive that letter. I caused it by telling the truth inappropriately, and only as I saw it, and not as it was for them.

SELF-AWARENESS TESTS

Each of us is an integral idea of infinite Mind. This means that it takes all of us, expressing our Unique Spiritual Blessing, to be the full completeness of the I Am.—Beca Lewis

I often have people I work with take a test, or two, designed to help them understand both their life preferences and the way they make decisions.

It helps me understand them better, but most of all it helps them understand themselves better, and enables them to design the life they really want to live; not the one that someone else wants, or wanted, for them.

Since this request has the outcome of freeing them from hidden habits, and false beliefs, about themselves, it is always interesting to note that everyone, me included, feels like lying on the test.

Why? Because as we stare at the questions, there is an underlying theme going on within ourselves. It says something like this:"If I choose this answer it probably means I am a certain kind of person and I don't want to be that kind of person."

Once again, this lying is to ourselves about ourselves. No one else ever really needs to know what we wrote on the test. The glory of this knowledge is, if we really find out who we are, we can choose to be that without the walls and limitations built up to protect a false belief.

Why would we think one kind of person is better than another? It is those pesky perceptions again, brought on by words spoken directly to us about ourselves, or ones we have read.

For example, the first time I took one of those personality tests and I turned out to be a D. I was horrified when I read what that meant. All I could see were the negative words; "Bossy, demanding, unthinking, driven."

I wanted to be soft, lovable, and helpful. I couldn't see how I could be that D person and also be soft, lovable, and helpful.

So I would try to lie on the tests. However, really I was always lying to myself, and that made it worse. Because, when I was not aware of who I was, I did act very bossy, demanding, unthinking, and driven.

Once I accepted that a D had a profile I could embrace, and consciously chose to use these qualities (that untamed, and untrained could appear negatively) I was able to behave more as my heart desired—soft, lovable, and helpful. I embraced, and applied the positive aspects of a D, dissolving the negative ones.

No individual is better than another. In Truth, we are all the qualities of God, and so these tests are not defining our limitations, but displaying our unique strengths. We are all unique ideas and individualities of the divine One, the Principle of Love. Instead of lying about who we are, we embrace it. Experience the joy of living as yourself, without the lies, and without the deception.

Choosing

We often lie to ourselves, and others, when we make choices. One way we can tell if we are lying is to ask ourselves if we are rationalizing.

The funny thing about rationalizing is that it can argue on both sides of the same issue. Thinking choices through can make it appear as if both sides of the choice are good sides, so how can we come to a choice that is in our best interest?

We can start with our intent. First, we begin with the big intent, the intent of our life, and then keep bringing it down to the choice itself.

Choices following the still small voice within often feel like the harder choice. However, in the end, it is the easier one. Sometimes when we make a choice, we feel relief. This is because we have chosen the path of least resistance, and we are not really heading down the road of our true intention.

Asking ourselves constantly, "Am I Lying," and then being willing to hear the answer, will solve most of our choice problems. Of course, we lie the most to ourselves, and then come up with a good reason why we have made that choice to those that are affected by it.

The good news is, we can always change our mind, and usually must, in order to end up where we mean to be going.

I watched a video clip of New Orleans Saints quarterback Drew Brees throw a football at a target. He threw ten times, and ten times hit the center of the target. However, when the film is slowed down it shows the ball nose making subtle corrections the entire trip to the target.

Another example we all know is that of the bumblebee who flies to its destination by making hundreds of directional switches. Like the bee, and the ball, we can easily re-choose if we keep our eye on where we intend to be going.

THE ART OF PERCEPTION

The spiritual life is a call to action. But it is a call to action without any selfish attachment to the results. —Eknath Easwaran

I love this idea. That Life Itself is a call to action. However, there are two pitfalls that often cause us to fail at this idea, and do the opposite and take no action. Not the action of conscious non-action, but no-action.

The first pitfall is that as humans we think we know better than infinite Life Itself. The second pitfall is that we think we are human, and as such we are co-creators, and creators.

Taking action without being attached to the outcome is a science and an art. It is a scientific fact that there is no intelligence in matter and the only intelligence is in Infinite Mind. Physicists have proven this fact, although they are often reluctant to call it Mind, as in Spirit.

The art of it comes into play as we attempt to live what appears as a human life while knowing that we aren't human, we are the idea of God.

This surely is an art, isn't it? Isn't this a portion of what Henry David Thoreau meant when he said, *It is something to be able to paint a particular picture, or to carve a statue, and so to make a few objects beautiful; but it is far more glorious to carve and paint the very atmosphere and medium through which we look. To affect the quality of the day—that is the highest of arts.*

It is this part of the quote—*to carve and paint the very atmosphere and medium through which we look*—that carries with it a significant message, because it is a statement about perception.

If we begin with the perception that we are a human, creator of our life, well, we all know the amount of pressure and stress that results from this point of view. It is inescapable. No matter how many pressure, and stress reduction techniques we learn, they will only damp down the underlying fear that this point of view produces. How can we affect the quality of our day, if we have not been an artist with our own perception?

Choosing the perception of a human, it may appear that it is possible, with a lot of work and a bit of luck, that we can create a life that we love.

Choosing the perception that we are Life Living Itself, we experience an immeasurable difference.

One carries with it stress; the other releases us to the freedom of living as our USB, our Unique Spiritual Blessing.

Our thinking does not create the life we experience. It is our perception about life that makes up our experience of it. This is a subtle difference in statement, but it makes a huge difference in the outcome. One produces many emotions, and drama, much stress, and guilt, or complete denial. The other brings relief, because we know that what may appear one way is only that way because we are seeing it that way, through our habits and the lens of our perception.

We can shift our perception in every moment, and affect the quality of our day. We can be an artist with our perception, and in any moment choose the highest understanding we have about the fact that all that is ever going on is "Life Living Itself and Love Loving Itself." Imagine that. Just imagine what this means!

I implemented this type of shift of perception as we searched for a home, and went through the process of buying one. Most of the time, I was able to stay within the point of view and state of mind using "I Am" statements. I said statements like, "I Am Home Itself, and therefore there is no need to worry about this outcome or try to make it happen."

Sometimes, I could feel the fear and stress rush in, and the lies would tell me it would never work.

Then, when it looked as if it was going to work, I still had to stay in the "I Am Home" perception, or the fear of, "Oh my gosh, what have we gotten ourselves into" would rush in.

That human habit of lies is always waiting at the door of our mind. It may hide in the bushes, but it is there, and at the first crack in the doorway, it will push its way in and try to settle into every corner of our consciousness.

Nevertheless, it can be removed immediately by a perception shift, and Truth can fill the spaces of our consciousness so there is no room for fear to sit down or hang out.

To be an artist of perception takes practice, just as being an artist of any kind takes practice. However, one day we will all witness that the artist is actually Love, Life, Mind, Soul, Spirit, Principle, Truth—Living and Loving Itself—and that we are the consequences of that action.

Action is the movement of the spiritual essence we call God. Therefore, action is what we are, too. It's easy to allow ourselves to take action when we know that even though the outcome is not ours to decide, it will be better than we imagined.

WHEN LYING SOUNDS SO TRUE

Here is a story I have never fully shared before. I have told bits and pieces to one person, or another, but never the whole story to anyone. I am willing to tell this now, because it will make clear the point I want to make, because it is imperative for us all to know the lie that sounds so true.

I used to be terrible at picking romantic relationships, but this was one of the worst of all.

It started right after a divorce. A friendly divorce, but still a divorce. However, I was not unhappy. In fact, my daughters and I had moved to a beautiful townhouse with a very affordable rent. We were the first ones to occupy this townhouse, as it had just been built, and my income was "luckily" low enough to qualify for a low-income housing rate.

It was an adjustment. I had to sell my house, move the girls to a new school district, and I was sleeping in the living room, and on the balcony, in order to let them have their own bedrooms. I was happy doing so. I was surrounded by new and felt free for the first time in ages. Sleeping on the balcony in California felt like a gift, and not a sentence.

Then I started dating a man I knew from a business connection. I was smart at first. Instead of having him pick me up, I met him when we went dancing, and came home alone, happy as a clam.

However, he appeared to offer me something I hadn't realized I always wanted: A business partnership as part of the relationship. I realized that I wanted to speak, write, and teach with someone who thought, and believed, the same as I did.

He had all the right words. He was a part-time minister after all. He appeared to have the right connections and right ideas, and I was tempted.

However, once when he came to pick me up at a dance class, as I saw him approach I heard a small quiet voice ask, "Why are you dating a wolf?" I ignored the message, because I wanted what he was offering. So I let him into my life more and more. Soon I lost my perspective, and I was hooked into his lies.

We started going to conferences, and events, together. He knew how to ham up our relationship there so everyone would talk about it. I didn't notice I was paying for it all, because it appeared to be what I had always wanted. In retrospect, I see it as a dangerous counterfeit.

After a few months, he said we had a job in Hawaii. I had put on my wish list a trip to Hawaii, a trip to Hawaii paid by someone else, just months before I met him.

"Wow," I thought. "It is coming true." I had the enough presence of mind to ask my mentor what she thought.

However, at the time she was coming from the same erroneous belief system, as I, so we discussed that it was too bad women needed a man to get ahead in the business world, but since we did, why not take this leap?

I went to Hawaii with him. We worked, but not really together, because instead of being partners, he kept me out of the loop. He asked me to marry him, and I accepted. Looking back, it was ridiculous because I was not happy at all. I had not yet discovered that just because something on our wish-list comes true, doesn't mean it is because of Love. This too was a dangerous counterfeit.

My two daughters were living alone in our beautiful townhouse, and I missed them terribly. However, the pull of that dream and his lies were keeping me locked into that counterfeit situation. I came back home to pack. I spent four days packing his house, and mine, and putting them in storage. I shipped my car to Hawaii. I paid for everything.

When I look back at this time, guilt and regret really tries to kick in. My daughters were alone. One went off to college, and the other went to live with her dad. That lasted a very short time. The older daughter had to come get her, and move her to a friend's family who took her in.

Finally, I realized that his entire goal was to keep me unhappy and needing him. Awareness started to break through. Yes, I wonder too, "What was I thinking?" I wasn't.

I was lying to myself the same way he was lying to me. How do I know? I rationalized everything.

One day I was speaking to my mentor on the phone. She knew only a tiny bit of what was happening, but she did know that I wasn't happy. She asked to speak to the man. He gladly said "yes" and proceeded to give her his charm act. She asked to speak to me. As soon as he handed me the phone she said, "Leave now!"

I trusted her. We had both been wrong, and I knew I needed to follow her advice. I gathered the people we were working with and laid out why the venture they were planning would never work. Effectively I closed the business.

The partners were grateful. He was not. I was offered a week away at a retreat on a nearby island by a friend, which I gratefully accepted.

After that week, I left Hawaii with much less than I had brought with me. I carried a suitcase small enough for me to put in the airport locker. I spent the rest of the day walking on the beach, waiting for the plane to leave. I had spent all the money I had earned from our home sale, so I had to leave all my possessions in Hawaii, including my car. My children were living elsewhere, and I had nowhere to go. All that I had left was in my suitcase.

A friend picked me up from the airport and took me home, and let me sleep for days. Another friend offered me a small rental she owned that had just opened up, and I moved in.

Another friend paid my bills for two months until I could think again. Another friend called and gave me a job. Many years later when I was trying to understand what love really acts like, I remembered this time and saw clearly the truth in the statement, "Love always shows up."

I started writing, and I went on a talk show and exposed him, but not to himself. I discovered that the entire time I was living with him, he was carrying on a long-distance relationship with his girlfriend that he had supposedly given up when we met.

All of this because I believed that someone—a man— outside myself could give me what I yearned to be. He was lying, and I was lying, to myself first, and then to everyone else in the situation. Notice that in spite of all these mistakes, I was never abandoned. My true friends were always there and cared for me. Love remained. I just had to step into Its flow, and accept Its gifts.

How could all of this have happened in the first place? I had **not** set a clear intent about love and relationships. I certainly was not coming from the correct premise about partnerships, love, or family. Because I did not do that, I was always vulnerable to an idea that was almost right, but not based on truth.

Many, many people are smooth-tongued liars. They know all the right words, they have all the right answers. Pay attention. Make sure that you don't become one yourself, because you have lied to yourself first.

Never allow someone to be your priority while allowing yourself to be their option.—Kelly Angard

Sing—Knowing You Have Wings

For as long as I can remember, one of my favorite poems has been Victor Hugo's poem, *Be like the bird that, passing on her flight awhile on boughs too slight, feels them give way beneath her, and yet sings, knowing that she hath wings.*

Isn't this poem beautiful? It sings about the principle, and the perception, that no matter what appears to be happening, when we know who we are, we can sing, knowing that we have wings, and knowing we can easily fly up, and away, to safety.

Once, while walking in the woods, I watched a hawk's nest high in the tree, swaying in the wind, and felt the meaning of this poem even more deeply.

Having felt for myself the bite of fear while sitting high in a tree while it swayed, I thought of what it would feel like to be that high and ride through the blasts of wind that whip the tree limbs around so freely.

I imagined that if it were me, I would worry that the limb would break, and then what would I do?

And then I laughed out loud, startling a few wood creatures I am sure, with the realization of what the *knowing that she hath wings* means to a bird. If the limb would break, they would simply fly away, singing as they always do, with the joy of the freedom of flight.

Notice that my thought about falling began with a *what if* question that made me feel afraid. Of course I would be afraid I could fall, if I didn't find peace in the knowledge that there is always safety, and always a solution, and this knowing will act as wings, always flying me to freedom and safety.

Victor Hugo's life's work was profoundly influenced by his awareness of the social injustice, inequality, suffering, and uprising that was the underlying theme of France in the 1800's, the place and time in which he lived. His writings, like *Les Miserables*, were directed at pointing out, and bringing to light, what was wrong within the system, so it could be corrected.

Yet, he wrote a simple, and elegant, poem on how to escape, without harm, the mess that the worldview dualist system makes. He wrote about how the bird, faced with a weak and falling branch, sings, knowing that she hath wings.

Not only does she fly away as the weak branch breaks, she sings. She sings **before** the need to fly. She sings in the morning in celebration of a new day. She sings in the day, not because she must, but because she can.

A Chinese proverb says, *A bird does not sing because it has an answer. It sings because it has a song.*

Are you singing your song? Until we are all aware of, and acting within,the awareness of the oneness of what appears as mankind—aware that we are within the circle of One, and not without it—aware and acting from the Principle of the Infinite Intelligence known as Love—social injustice, inequality, and suffering will appear within the times we live. Yet, we do not have to be part of the suffering, we can sing, knowing that we have wings. We can sing as the bird does, because we have a song.

No matter what we call the voice of the system— worldview, predator, devil, or monkey mind—this voice is belligerent and loud, but subtle. It demands that we listen to it. It brings with it all the emotions that begin, and end, with fear and its tag-along friends called doubt, anger, discouragement, frustration, sadness, despair, and the rest of these life-hope-stealing companions of the what if negative voice.

Since we do live in a thought Universe, we must be able to recognize who is asking the what if question, and who is doing the thinking. It's hard to sing when we are within the grips of the what if voice of fear. However, there is another what if voice, and it sings the song of the Infinite Principle of Love.

The still small voice within brings gifts of love, with its corresponding comforting feelings of hope, encouragement, possibility, joy, and the rest of its friends that encourage us to sing, knowing that we have wings.

Sometimes this comforting voice also says *what if*, but the *what if* it asks is not loaded with fear, it is loaded with hope and possibilities. It sings to us that there is always an open door—there is always a solution—we are never separate from the gifts of Love. There is no one who has more than another within the Infinite provision, and equality, of the Divine.

To hear this voice we must pause and listen to the stillness within the peace of Love. To hear this voice we have to stop agreeing with the what if voice of fear. It may still be making noise, but we are giving up the habit of listening to it, because we have the thought-wings of awareness of the omnipresence of Love.

What isn't love is loud and insistent that we pay attention to it, like a petulant child, or a bully, or even a terrorist.

That doesn't mean we bow down to it and give in to its demand to be afraid. Instead, we pay attention to the peace, beauty, and love that is all around us, when we do this, what to do about the bully of fear becomes evident.

If we attempt to fight fear, it has us in its grip.

Instead, we sing knowing that we have wings, and rise above it, watching it dissolve itself as it battles with itself, which is all that it knows how to do.

Sing, knowing that you have wings, sing with celebration, sing with gratitude. Share your song, sing of joy, sing of good, sing of the evident abundance in your life. Sing, because singing of these things reveals even more goodness. Sing because it dissolves the blinders imposed by fear, and reveals the consistent care always present for y ou.

Sing of the abundance of your neighbors and friends, show it to them, and share it with them. We cannot be rich without all being aware of their richness.

Are you afraid that your clients can't afford you, or your employment can't keep you working? Sing, knowing that your clients have wings too, sing knowing that abundance does not come from people, places, and things, but appears because we are present, because we are the representation, and idea, of abundance itself.

Keep singing when the wind blows, or if the limb you are on begins to break. Sing, that there is nothing to fear, because we are One within the One of the I Am.

Gather your thoughts to this place and keep them there. Let the illusion that threatens dissolve itself into the nothingness from which it came, never touching you, or your loved ones.

34

CHAPTER EIGHT

E very one of us has said, "Yes, I am Waiting, Yes, I am Running, Yes, I am Hiding, and Yes, I am Lying," some of the time. We are all uncovering unwanted habits. The point is to dissolve them as quickly as possible into spiritually healthy habits.

Sometimes it is very simple to do this. Asking these questions, and answering them truthfully, brings awareness, and awareness often does the dissolving without any extra work on our part. If we would keep asking these questions all day, every day, many issues that have clogged up our lives would simply dissolve away.

Instead of living life with a bag over our head, or our head stuck in the sand—either one of which leaves us completely vulnerable since everyone else can see and we can't—we are at least observing our life. This means we are more likely to do something other than wait, run, hide, and lie.

Sometimes we have to do more than become aware. Sometimes we have work to do, and actions to take. Which returns us to the idea of perception—point of view, and state of mind. Since *what we perceive to be reality magnifies* then it seems entirely logical, and very wise, to choose the most abundant, joyful, infinite perception possible.

This actually is easy to do. The idea that there is a Divine Principle of Love that is omnipresent, omnipotent, omniscient, and therefore omniaction, is a cornerstone of much of the world's agreement. It is certainly mine.

Who wouldn't want the outcome of living from that perception?

I really think the answer is, nobody. The only reason it is not consciously chosen by everyone is we doubt that there is such a Divine Intelligence. However, for the moment, it doesn't matter whether there is or not, because it is perception that determines our own personal reality, so why not choose this one?

Of course, there are the pundits who will say that this is not a fact. "Prove it wrong then," I suggest.

See if you can prove that what you *perceive to be reality* does not magnify. In the meantime, while they waste their time, you are asking yourself these questions and you are choosing to stay awake, alert, and aware. In doing so, you will experience it for yourself.

I therefore suggest, for your own sake, that you try this experiment. Choose the best perception you are willing to accept as true, and let it lead you into a better life.

However, just choosing a better perception, or the Infinite One, as your *point of view perception*, will not actually move much of your life into what you desire.

The culprit is the second half of the perception rule, our *state of mind perception*. Sadly, it is our state of mind that we are most unaware of, and what must be addressed in order for things to change for the better.

We can choose a wonderful *point of view perception* like, "There is only Love." However, if our *state of mind perception* says something like this: "I know that's not actually true, and I can prove it because I don't feel loved or loving, and bad things always happen to me. Besides, what is so loving about what goes on in the world," then this *state of mind perception* diminishes, and sometimes completely negates, our *point of view perception*.

If our *point of view perception* is that the Infinite is Abundant, and yet our state of mind perception is in fear and doubt, it is hard to see the Truth, that yes, the Infinite is Abundant.

So what do we do? We have to shift both our state of mind, and our point of view, and bring them into harmony with each other.

This takes us back to *The Four Essential Questions*. When we answer, "Yes, I am hiding," then we begin the process of shifting. One way we can do this is to use a logical progression of thinking. It might go something like this, "I notice I am hiding, but since Love is omnipresent I can never hide from Love. Since the Truth of my being is that I am the expression of Love, then this hiding is a lie about myself."

As we state this kind of Truth, the fear that is causing the hiding begins to fade away. Is it this simple? Yes, and no.

Yes, it is this simple in concept. No, because we are so locked into our own prison of beliefs that escaping them can sometimes be daunting. However, if we are willing to let them go, it gets easier and easier.

I often ask people, "What is stopping you from living happily, and freely, abundant?" Often that answer is, "I doubt myself."

We can easily see that this doubt is a state of mind and a point of view all rolled into one.

Doubt and discouragement are the devil's tools.

They are easy to use because we are so willing to pick them up and claim them as our own. It seems right. After all, we can all say to ourselves, "Look at what I can't do, or what I have done, that never worked out."

The question is, "Do you want to live in that state of mind and point of view? How badly do you want to escape the outcome that this perception produces?"

No one can escape your perception for you. In fact we are all too busy escaping our own. We can help, support, guide, and walk together, and we can celebrate the shift of perceptions together, but we can't do it for you.

You have to decide. Once you do, the solution is easy. **Shift your perception, and keep it there**. Seriously. That's it.

Yes, I always write about shifting perception. How could I not when that is the answer? Do you want me to make up a false solution just to bring about another useless theory that distracts, and disrupts, the world?

There are many false solutions. If you are not yet ready to move out of the prison of human beliefs, you can surely find a *point of view perception*, and *state of mind perception*, that matches the quality of life you want to live.

Or instead, you could believe all the stories based on a human viewpoint that make life sound more exciting. Stories are good. I love a good story, but that doesn't mean I want to *live* in it.

Eventually, we will all find that stories are not freeing us from the real illusion—that we are human.

If not human, then what are we? We are idea of the One Infinite Mind.

I am fully aware that this makes no sense to a human point of view. Neither does the fact that the earth goes around the sun, or that railroad tracks don't converge in the distance.

Again, it doesn't matter if you believe the point of view that we are all the ideas of the One Infinite Mind in order to experience the outcome of shifting to this point of view.

Let's return to *The Four Essential Questions*. Yes, this is the ultimate use for them; to shift perceptions. As we notice that we are waiting, running, hiding, and lying, we also notice the point of view and state of mind that has produced this response. Then we have the chance to make a conscious choice to choose another perception, and let that shift cause a change in our behavior.

The worst thing that could happen is that your life will get better. The best thing, well heck I don't know, because the Infinite One-and-Only Creator is surely in charge of that, and for that fact I say, "Thank God."

Ask, Is It True?

We have answered, "Yes I am lying, or hiding, or running, or waiting." Now what? Add this next question, which is actually a two-part question. We are going to ask, "Is it true, lower case t," and then ask, "Is it True, upper case T."

Here's the difference.

Asking, "Is this true," lower case, is asking within the context of what our five senses know. Is it true that no one has ever been kind to you, loved you, or helped you? Absolutely not. Someone somewhere has done all those things for each of us. There is nothing true about any absolute statement within the small r reality, or everyday life.

Because we know that shifting perceptions changes everything, asking this one question, and then listening for, and accepting, the answer, can change everything. Just asking any of these questions, and then continuing on our day as if nothing happened, isn't useful at all. Ask the question, then Pause, Observe, and Listen.

Often this means that we will have to give up cherished reasons for believing what we do, and behaving how we do. Here's a question to ask yourself, "Which one do I most want? To be right, or to be happy?"

Once we make the decision to be happy, and all that happiness entails, it is time to move on to the second way to ask that question. Asking, "Is this True," upper case, means we are asking is it True within big R Reality.

Big R Reality is the Reality that the One Divine Mind is, and knows. We are not talking about the god that is human like, that doles out punishment and knows about bad. We are talking about the spiritual idea of God that is all there is, and is only good, so therefore only knows, Good.

Does this God, or It, the Principle of Life, know about any of our actions within the small r reality? No. For some people this is a huge disappointment, because they think this means they are not personally loved or cared for, and that their prayers are not heard.

True, those prayers are not answered in the conventional sense. However, when we pray, it begins our alignment with the omniscient One, and this process will reset our perception to the Truth of our being, bringing us back to the Big R Reality.

Yes, we are personally cared for in the same way we care for ourselves, God cares for us, because we are the reflection and idea of God.

How To "Snap Out Of It"

One grateful thought at a time, just like one snowflake at a time, changes the landscape. —Beca Lewis

Have you ever said to yourself, had it said to you, or said to another, "Just snap out of it!" This statement supposes that we have the ability, knowledge, and desire at that moment, to do so, but this is often not the case. Therefore, this little solution is dedicated to all of us for those times when "snapping out if it" sounds good, but feels impossible.

Of course, we all know that the first step in "snapping out if it" is wanting to. When we are deep in joylessness, discouragement, despair, or doubt we may feel abandoned in this state of mind. The question then is, "How do we become willing?"

Here are two quick ways to get over the *why bother* feeling and begin to be willing to "snap out of it" and be happy again.

1. Pause and remember a time you were happy. To remember might take some deep recalling and imagination.

Compare it to how you feel now. Really feel the difference. Were you more comfortable physically, and mentally, when you were happy?

Keep feeling the difference until you catch that glimmer of "willingness," and hold on to the feeling. Think of it as a tiny flame you have to keep alive.

2. Do it for someone else. In everyone's life, there is someone else, or a cause, that we love enough to choose to do something for them, if not for ourselves. Albert Einstein said, Only a life lived for others is worth living.

Be willing to snap out of it so you can "do" for someone or something else. (Not sacrifice ourselves for someone else—don't get confused here, these are two different things.)

3. The next step is easier than discouragement would want us to believe. It's the step of gratitude. Everyone knows that being grateful is the perfect "snap out of it" remedy. However, exactly how is that done?

Have you ever told yourself to be grateful and heard the answer, "No I don't want to!" Of course you have! Why would discouragement want you to leave it?

We are going to be grateful in spite of it! How are we going to do this? Repeat steps one, and two, if necessary and focus on that willingness flame. We are going to get it to burn brighter by blowing gratitude on it—but how, and for what?

Most of the time when we have fallen into a funk, it is not just one thing that has taken us there.

Usually, it is that one little extra thing that happens and we finally say, "I can't deal with it!" Uncovering all that has taken us down might take forever, and often keeps us there, as we ruminate over it like a cow chewing its cud.

Instead, let's begin with a premise, a point of view, that happiness is something we have a right to have, and that it is actually the by-product of the Divine Order of Good running the universe. Yes, in the funk we say, "Yea right," and that's okay. Let's prove it to ourselves anyway, because remember, it is more comfortable for everyone when we allow ourselves to be happy.

Here are a few examples of how to be grateful in a way that resets the internal system back to its original state of joy, and happiness.

In today's climate of uncertainty and change (which is always present, just more promoted now than it has ever been), it may appear even more difficult to step away from it. Don't believe it. Snapping out of it now is just the same as it was thousands of years ago, and as it will be in the future, because the lie is always the same. It's just that the story is told in a variety of ways.

Let's take one of the lie's variations that pops into everyone's mind when in a funk, and see what we can do with it. How about the thought, "Nothing I ever do makes a difference, and no one really cares anyway."

This thought, if true, would mean there is an aspect of the Divine Order that is not working right. This is impossible. Therefore, our perception shift will be to prove this fact to ourselves so that we can once again experience happiness.

To do this we will need to notice those things that do make a difference. Notice that when you smile at people it lights up their face. Notice the dew sitting on the grass makes it sparkle. Watch a baby smile, a bird sing in the tree, or the sun rise in the morning.

Avoid the thought that none of this is because of you, and instead translate what you are seeing back into qualities for which you can be grateful.

Perhaps it goes like this. "I am grateful that someone is happy, I am grateful for all those sparkles, I am grateful for the innocence of babies, I am grateful for birds singing, I am grateful that the sun always rises." Feel the Truth of this!

Keep going—the flame is starting to grow: "I am grateful for the order expressed in the stars moving smoothly in the night, I am grateful for the beauty of a flower, I am grateful for the ability to see all the evidence of the Divine Order, of which I am an integral part."

Keep going—fan the flames with more gratitude for the power of Love. Become immersed in the feeling of it. "I am grateful that trees send down roots, for the bulbs that bloom in spring, and for the clouds that scuttle across the sky.

I am grateful for the presence of light in all its forms, for the laughter of children, and for the hugs of my friends."

As we fan this flame of willingness with gratitude, we will rise out of any state of mind that hides happiness from us. Translating things back into thoughts, or qualities, we find the spiritual joy that opens our eyes to the infinite power of Good, and Love, that is the ground of our being.

We are not required to swing between joy and sorrow. Within the Divine there is no shadow of turning; there is only the eternal now of ever-present Joy. Happiness is a by-product of this awareness, and we can always choose to return to it.

Next time you hear "snap out of it" you can say, "Okay, I know how to do that!" And you know what? Sometimes that statement is all it takes!

Be thankful for what you have; you'll end up having more. If you concentrate on what you don't have, you will never, ever have enough.—Oprah Winfrey

Stuck, Inertia, And The Fire Within

Knowing trees, I understand the meaning of patience. Knowing grass, I can appreciate persistence. —Hal Borland

We installed a wood burning stove in our living room that we use to heat our home. It works wonderfully well, and it continues to provide guidance as well as warmth. Watching it one morning, it demonstrated to me the difference between *inertia* and *stuck*—and how to dissolve both.

I never had a wood burning stove before. I thought that it would be just like a closed stove. However, a wood burning stove has an airtight glass door on it so you can see the flames. You can also feel the heat the same as a fireplace, but because of its design, the heat is not dispersed up the chimney, which makes it many times more efficient at heating.

This means that you can't just throw wood on the fire. You have to open the sealed door, which then allows the oxygen to flood into the fire. Therefore, you have to pause before fully opening the door so that the fire does not build too quickly from that rush of air.

One day it had warmed up outside so I hadn't put any new wood on the fire during the afternoon. That evening, as I prepared to build the fire again, it appeared that all that was left were a few very small embers. On this same day, I was thinking about the difference between inertia and stuck.

Because it appeared that there was no fire, I wasn't as cautious as usual when I opened the door. The moment I did so, the fire literally exploded into flame. "That," I thought, "Is what becoming unstuck looks like."

Like those embers, all it takes is the swift infusion of oxygen or, in our case, Truth, and what has been silently and steadily burning within will burst into bloom. It doesn't take much.

On the other hand, there is inertia. This can happen when we have let the fire go out completely. Then it takes a lot of small tinder, coaxing, and a build-up before the fire begins to burn efficiently again. That is what inertia looks like.

We often think of inertia as not moving. However, *inertia is either a state of rest, or a state of motion, that is resistant to change.* We see this in our everyday life in our habits. It is the way we have always done it, whether we are doing something, or just standing still.

To change our state of being, like the fire, takes an outside force proportional to how ingrained the habit has become. How dead the fire is beforehand determines how much force, or fuel and oxygen, is needed to start it burning efficiently again.

Approaching this from the right premise of Spiritual Perception, when we are in the state of mind of inertia, it will take more awareness and discipline of thought to change a bigger, or more ingrained, habit of thought than a smaller one.

On the other hand, when we are stuck, the desire and intent is already burning.

Then it takes just a small amount of outside force, or awareness of Truth flooding into our consciousness, to propel us out of stuck and into Life.

Of course, these two ideas are intertwined. Both states of mind, called stuck and inertia are misunderstood perceptions of the True nature of Life, which have become habits of thinking and acting. However, understanding the difference between the two may help relieve the frustration we sometimes feel when we have been steady students of Truth and yet it feels as if the fire of our life has not yet begun to burn efficiently.

There is great comfort and relief in knowing that the Infinite Principle never experiences inertia and never gets stuck. It is never even aware of our misperception. It is always operating in the harmony and perfection of graceful unfolding.

This means that as we add the fuel of awareness and perception, and diligently tend to the fire within, what appears as stuck or inertia will dissolve into nothingness. Either state does not exist in the perfection of the Truth of Being. As the mist dissolves, we will experience our current highest awareness of Love Loving Itself in practical ways, far beyond our human design and planning.

Open the door of your fire within, and let in the Truth of who you are. It doesn't make any difference whether this action explodes your life into bloom, or if you have to diligently build the fire first.

Sooner, or later, the **illusion** of stuck or inertia will dissolve, and the infinite abundance that is you, will stand revealed.

WHAT VOICE IS YOURS?

Voice? What Voice? I always find it a bit alarming to know that there are people declared insane because they hear voices. It must be a matter of degree that makes the difference, because we all hear voices.

These voices come from many places, and the ones we listen to (perhaps this is the key in the insanity issue) determine the outcome in our lives. Therefore, it is imperative that we take the time to determine what's up with those voices.

I'll cover three types of voices.

The first one is *outside voices*. This should be the easy one. We can all tell when an outside voice is speaking to us, can't we? We should all be very capable of deciding whether those voices have our best interests at heart.

We should be good at it, but often we are terrible at recognizing that many of those voices are only for, and about, themselves and that they intentionally spread the disease of fear.

You know those outside voices; they can appear as our friends, family, and the media.

Even those voices that perhaps mean us well, are often not the best voice for us to listen to. It is too easy for us to forget that we don't have to believe what an outside voice is telling us. Often, instead of thinking it through, we assume that because they say so, it must be true, and therefore it must be true for us too. Therefore, we accept an outside voice, and what it is saying as true, and as if it were our own voice. It's not.

The second type of voice is the *voice in our head*. We all know this one very well, because it is constantly speaking. What we may not be aware of is that the voice in our head is always, always, always—yes, always, putting us down in some way. We are never good enough, we never have enough, and we are always doing something wrong. We are stupid, or lazy, or a combination of every negative quality p ossible.

If that voice were an outside voice, most of us with any sense at all, would not only not listen, but never allow it in our lives again.

Not so with this voice in our head, because this is the voice that we **think** is our own voice, speaking to ourselves. After all, it speaks in our language, talks as we do, uses terms we understand, and we can see that it has a point. Nevertheless, this is not true.

This is not our voice. It is the liar's voice disguised to sound like our own.

Its lies are built on a teeny-tiny piece of what we feel is true, so we decide the whole thing must be true, and of course, since it sounds like our voice, we think we have to listen.

Listen to me now.

Here I am, an outside voice that not only has your best interest at heart, but also knows the Truth about you, and wants you to know it too. That voice inside your head is **not** your voice! No! Not ever!

This means you can stop listening to it, you can stop paying attention, you can stop letting it ruin, and run, your life. I am not saying it will stop talking, because it won't. However, you will learn not to hear it, and the volume will be turned so low you will sometimes forget that it is there.

The only way to get to that peaceful place is to begin now to say to it, "I know you are lying, I know you are not my voice. I know you don't care about me at all. I know your intention is to keep me from living a full and productive life. So from this moment on, you are on your own."

You may have to repeat this many times before you— not it—get the message, but for the sake of your permanent freedom, don't give up.

Now for the *good voice.*

Yes there is a good one. You know this one too, but if you have been listening to all the other ones, you may be out of practice in hearing it.

The other voices may be so loud that you have to really work at hearing this good voice.

The only way to hear this voice is to be quiet. It is that still small voice within.

This is the voice that guides you gently and with care and kindness. This voice is direct from your Self, the real self. This is your voice, because it is from the One, the eternal divine essence of Love.

You can trust this voice. This is the voice that says, "The real you has never done anything wrong. You are the loved of Love. You are the action of intelligence." This voice speaks the Truth.

Listen to it, follow its guidance, and all will be well.

FACE AND REPLACE

Don't wait for the last judgment. It takes place every day.—Camus

Here you go—a technique to use for shifting perception that works everywhere, anytime, and gets easier with practice. Face and Replace is so simple children can do it. In fact, they are better at it than most of us adults.

Remember, *what we perceive to be reality magnifies*, so whatever we are perceiving to be reality becomes more and more real to us.

Our senses do not create reality; they report to us what we believe it to be. Good and faithful servants, they tell us exactly what we expect, and often want, to hear.

One morning two things happened to me that demonstrated quite clearly the idea of being aware of what is going on.

I was preparing to do an exercise program that involved putting in a video, and following along with it on my exercise machine. I turned on the TV, and inserted the disc. Before I could switch over to the exercise program I was caught up in an infomercial for skin care. Although I clearly know all the manipulation tricks used, I was still intrigued. I sat at the edge of the bed, and watched, thinking how wonderful it would be, if what they were saying were true.

I left the DVD in the open tray, and went to my computer to check out the product. If I hadn't already set the habit of *pause before buying*, I would have ordered the very inexpensive trial offer even though I knew it meant I would be on a monthly installment plan for more. But, I didn't. Instead, I decided to Pause, Observe, and Listen, and I headed back to exercise.

All was well for about thirty minutes. Then I got tired, and bored. Having done this program many times, I started thinking about what was coming next instead of just being present.

I managed to keep my focus for a few more minutes when, without thinking, I turned it off.

Even though in that moment I unconsciously shut off the program, I knew that I was not quitting for good. I knew I would return. Why? Because I knew that it is only a false belief about myself that sometimes stops me in the moment. However, because of my underlying intent to express myself in movement, I will continue to return to it.

The problem arises when we take those momentary "I don't want to" messages as a truth to follow, when they are actually very much like the manipulation of an infomercial—in reverse perhaps. It stops us from doing something, rather than getting us to buy something.

Here's how *Face and Replace* worked for me in this instance. I faced the fact that I wanted to buy that product to fix my wrinkles. I replaced that desire with a simple pause. I paused to listen within to see if this was the right choice for me. There was nothing esoteric about it at all. Just a simple stop and listen. In this case, I got a very clear awareness that it wasn't the right thing for me to do.

In the second instance, I faced the fact that I was tired and bored, realized that in that state I had stopped the process. Instead of blaming myself, and feeling guilty, I simply replaced those ideas with the statement that I would return, and then trusted myself that I would.

I have a third example. A few minor events occurred one day that for some reason took me to the panic room. You know the one where it starts to feel as if you don't know anything, you can't do anything right, you are totally misunderstood, and all your work will never pay off because you can't do it right, ever—I could go on and on, as I am sure you could too.

It was as if a robber had broken into my home (my consciousness) and was stealing my peace, and happiness.

When I found myself in that room, I immediately closed the door behind me, to keep the robber out. Of course that meant that the robber was still waiting for me outside the door. I knew that eventually I would have to come out of the panic room and face what was terrifying me.

I knew there was no real danger, because it was my thought that was causing the panic, and that it could be stopped in the same way. Therefore, I faced each incident that was bringing on the fear, and replaced it with Truth. In this case, it was the Truth of a Spiritual Perception.

It went something like this.

First, I became aware of the fact that all my fear stemmed from an outside point of view. I was trying to make something happen in the world, on the outside, and I was getting outside feedback.

The next step was not to run from what I was hearing, or from the emotions it brought with it, but to look it squarely in the face and let it know that I "saw" it.

Then, instead of fighting where it wanted me to fight, or run away, I chose my own arena.

I went to the room, into the state of mind perception, where all the wonderful Truths I have learned are housed, and I pulled them out, one by one. Within myself, I faced each outside lie, and said in effect, "You can't scare me because you have no power."

Yes, I went back to the fact that omnipresent Love does not contain fear, or sorrow, or lack. Therefore, the fact that all of those appeared to exist for me was just an illusion. A very vivid illusion, but still an illusion.

Maintaining the *point of view perception* that Love Loving Itself was all that was really going on, meant I also had to bring my emotions into check, or my *state of mind perception* into harmony with that *point of view perception*.

I went for a walk, I read a book, I listened to words of wisdom, I breathed in a quiet space, I watched the birds outside my window, I stepped outside and smelled the air and I did a few stretches—all the while maintaining the best point of view that I could. Eventually the panic was dissolved, and I returned to my work.

Sometimes *Face and Replace* takes a split second; other times it take minutes, or hours, and sometimes days. Nevertheless, Love, Truth, God, always carries the day, because It is the only power. The other power is a lie that only needs to be exposed and replaced with the

Truth. No matter what lie it appears to be telling, it is actually only ever telling the one lie: that there is an absence of Good, Truth, or God.

THE BIG MELT

Where we live, in the winter, snow covers the ground most of the time. As spring approaches, I wait with anticipation for the emergence of green shoots that I know are preparing themselves beneath the snow. However, in order to see those shoots the snow must melt.

Every day, I look out my window to see how much more land has been revealed. In the same way, our coverings must also melt to reveal what is sprouting beneath. As we let go of running, hiding, waiting, and lying, the beauty of our lives, and or our unique self, is open for us to experience, and for all to see and appreciate.

As snow melts, it provides necessary water for the plants beneath, but it does not feel pain in the process. As our icy coverings melt, we do not need to experience pain either.

We can allow what we have learned to feed, and sustain, what is emerging.

VISIBLE AS MYSELF

As we let go of all the evasion tactics, and we find a blissful rest in the assurance that Good, God, is all there is, then the Unique Spiritual Blessing that we are begins to emerge, and our life begins to reflect our true spiritual nature.

It is glorious to wake up, even a tiny bit, to the concept that what we consider a human, a person, is in Reality God seeing Itself. We are reflecting God, divine Mind, Love, Truth, Life, Spirit, Soul, and Principle and It is saying, "Here I Am, Visible As Myself."

Today you are You, that is truer than true.
There is no one alive who is Youer than You.—Dr. Seuss

THE 28 DAY SHIFT TO WEALTH

35

— • —

THE 28 DAY SHIFT TO WEALTH

*I**f ye have faith as a grain of mustard seed, ye shall say unto this mountain, Remove hence to yonder place; and it shall remove; and nothing shall be impossible unto you.*—Matthew 17:20

This *28–Day Journey* you are about to take is based on *The Shift System* and the understanding of the law that what you *perceive to be reality magnifies.* This means that what you think or believe is reality will become the day-to-day life that you will experience.

It is not possible to break this law and there is no way around it.

This law can produce terrible cycles in our lives, because the more we believe the worldview, the more we appear to receive it.

If you are experiencing a lack of any kind, unless you break out of the thinking pattern and habits that are producing the movie called Lack, the more lack you will experience.

This law would be scary and discouraging except for one thing.

When your perception shifts to the big R Reality of Divine Love and abundance, the darkness of lack must and will disappear. All belief of lack can be dissolved because it is just a mist—a missed perception—that has no truth other than that we believe it and act out of that belief.

Sometimes we harbor unconscious beliefs that must be uncovered so they can be dissolved, and this book will assist you in doing so.

Your perception does not create anything (good or bad) it just keeps you from seeing what has already been provided.

You are not either a good person or a bad person if you are experiencing lack. Fear of lack and the lie of material sense holds many of us in its grip. But fear can be dissolved forever through the Truth and Principle of Divine Love.

There is no material problem to heal. There is only a belief of a problem. When many people hold that belief, it may appear to be more difficult to dissolve, but it is still just a belief, and can be stepped out of forever.

Sooner or later, we must all escape from the cycle of lack and the worldview of not enough. Sooner or later, we will all have to choose to come out of the belief in a material world and live instead as we are—a Spiritual Being.

In this *28-Day Journey,* each day's lesson follows the word **W E A L T H** and includes: a short reading, a mini writing exercise, and a discipline to do for the day.

You can call this work prayer, or meditation, or tasks for the day. It doesn't matter. What matters is that you start the day from the correct premise—the Reality of Good and Abundance—and practice this thinking throughout the day.

You should be able to complete all of this in under 15 minutes a day. The rest of the day is the practice of staying in the point of view and state of mind that you have created in those fifteen minutes.

This practice will shift everything!

If you would like to explore in more depth, the concepts that are mentioned throughout this book, you might like my other books in *The Shift Series.* You will find them listed at the end of this book.

36

— · —

DAY ONE

R eading For Day One
Understand that wealth is something you already possess.
Yes, I know, it rarely feels that way, especially as the worldview is set
up to encourage all of us to fear that there is not enough.

Most people succumb to this fear at one time or another,
and become obsessed with finding ways to get more—usually
money—since that is the currency we most associate with as wealth.

Have you ever noticed that when you are in the fear of not enough
and working hard to have enough, there is never enough?

We are going to start from the premise that the *not enough* is a lie.
Why?

Because *what you believe to be reality magnifies.* If you and I agree
with the worldview that there is not enough, there won't be—for
you, for me, for anyone.

To release ourselves, and others, to wealth we all need to: Wake Up!
Wake up—Wake Up—the W in W E A L T H.

To see and experience **your** wealth and prosperity, the key is to
decide to focus on the wealth already present in your life. Not money.
Wealth.

Money will follow when you decide to eliminate any thought that
is not about what you and others don't have.

Instead, let's focus entirely on what you do have.

Writing For Day One

Start your *Wealth Journal* today. Spend the next two minutes writing in a journal or this book all the wealth that you can see right now that is already yours to use. Look around, what do you see?

For example: your computer, desk, chair, rug, walls, windows, cup, drink,—keep going!

Discipline For Day One

Did you notice that there is so much wealth right in front of you that you can't possibly write it all down in two minutes!

This is your disciplined thought for today. Repeat to yourself—out loud if possible, as many times as you can—this statement:

"I am awake to wealth!"

How about saying this at least one hundred times today! How about two hundred times? More—yes—you can do it!

Say it while working, playing, brushing your teeth, talking on the phone, watching TV, and driving the car. Turn on the light with this statement. I am awake to wealth!

That's it—simple. You can do it—all day!

"I am awake to wealth!"

37

— • —

Day Two

Reading For Day Two

Are you looking for wealth in all the wrong places?

Perhaps you are looking for wealth in your paycheck, your daily sales record, checkbook, bank account, stock market, business, employees, clients, bosses, husband, wife, lottery, or inheritances?

Looking for wealth in these places is like looking for your reflection in the mirror without first standing in the front of the mirror. Obviously, your reflection is only there because you are there.

In the same way, lasting wealth in any form cannot appear until its true substance is seen.

Without knowing its true substance, the wealth you see is only a mirage.

So today let's begin to wake up to the true substance of wealth. This is the wealth that has always been yours and can never be taken away. We are going to start understanding this lasting wealth by beginning the practice of turning things back into thoughts; this is where true substance is found.

How can you do this? You will start by discovering the qualities of the things that you see.

Writing For Day Two

In your *Wealth Journal*, take one thing that you noticed as wealth in your life yesterday and translate it into its true substance by noticing its qualities, and then listing them in your journal. Describe each quality in only one, or maybe two, words.

For example: I could translate the chair I am sitting on to these qualities—useful, comfortable, beautiful, perfect height, well designed, well crafted etc. You are not limited to writing for just two minutes. You can do this for as many things and for as long as you feel like!

Discipline For Day Two

Today, you are going to add extra words to your disciplined thought from yesterday.

You are going to keep this thought in mind, body, and spirit all day: "I am awake to the true substance of wealth!"

You can say it, shout it, or whisper it—just keep it going! If you feel impelled to dance, jump, hop, run or twirl, do that too!

Keep it up—in every moment!

"I am awake to the true substance of wealth!"

38

---·---

DAY THREE

Reading For Day Three

As you practice turning things into thoughts, you are not trying to alter a belief. You are not using your mental powers to change physical situations. You are not attempting to blend body, mind, and soul into one.

This is not an exercise in self-will, will power, or even "knowing the truth."

What is it then? It is waking up to the Truth that there is only One Mind—Omnipresent Intelligent Love.

Isn't this a relief producing idea?

Since there is only One Mind, it means that the only creator is the One Mind. It means all-good exists now, everywhere and forever, for you—as you.

Surrender to the One Mind. Give up the struggle. Relax and let yourself experience that you are the Loved of Love.

Writing For Day Three

Today, let's begin the process of discovering what is wealth to you. In your *Wealth Journal,* make a list of things that you believe you want and need in order to feel wealthy. Don't be embarrassed. No one will see this but you. This is not the time to withhold information from yourself, either. Let's get it all out in the open!

Take as long as you want making a list. Not a quality list. We'll get back to that later. Today just list things like cars, homes, clothes, food, money, office items, trips, classes—list it all.

While you are doing this, have fun.

What I don't want you to do is get attached, worried, upset, fearful, depressed, or entertain any negative thoughts about what you don't seem to have while you are making this list.

Pretend you are simply writing a story list, which in fact you are. Play!

Discipline For Day Three

While you are going about your day, notice how many ways the things you have listed that you want already appear in your life.

As you notice them, say this (change the wording to fit for you):

"Thank you for this _____ in my life!"

You may not own most of what you see. It doesn't matter. Be grateful anyway. If you can see it, the idea of it is already present in your awareness. This is where we begin.

Say: *"Thank you for this (car, dress, money_____ all that is on your list) in my life."*

This will be a busy day saying thanks—have fun!

39

— • —

Day Four

Reading For Day Four

Are you responsible for making money, finding supply, getting things done? No. Can you really do any of this? Can you make things happen? No.

However, the worldview certainly pressures us to think and act as if we can. The worldview proclaims personal achievement as the goal and working hard as a necessity for getting ahead.

But you are stepping out of the worldview.

You are standing apart from all these beliefs. The worldview of personal power and personal responsibility can not hijack your thoughts, so that all you can think about is a material and physical outcome.

When it feels as if you are responsible, then it may appear that you don't have the time, energy, or desire to practice disciplining thought to God First, which is what we are doing in this course.

But you are awake! You know that your only responsibility is to know Truth and to take action, but only after starting with the correct premise of One Mind.

Instead of being responsible, you are the observer and receiver of the unfolding of all that God Is.

Writing For Day Four

Do you have a wonderful list from yesterday of things that you want? Great! Look at that list and close your eyes. Imagine how it would feel to have all of those things, without work, worry, or responsibility. Imagine that they are present for you now to do as you wish. Then write a quality list of those feelings.

For example:

I would feel:

Free, safe, secure, excited, joyful, etc.

Discipline For Day Four

Pick one of those quality words and say them in the phrase: I AM.

For example:

"I AM freedom."

"I AM safety."

These I AM exercises you are doing are not an affirmation. They are a statement of Truth. There is only One Mind—omnipresent, omnipotent, and omniaction.

When you say I AM, you are speaking as this One Mind. You are waking up to the Truth of yourself.

Note: You can find more about quality lists and how to do them in my book *Living In Grace: The Shift To Spiritual Perception.* or come to and look for the how-to-do page.

40

———— • ————

Day Five

R eading For Day Five

The 'E' in W E A L T H stands for *enthusiasm*. It is an essential ingredient to seeing and experiencing your wealth and prosperity. The original meaning of the word Enthusiasm is "divine inspiration," or "a god within."

As you have been doing your quality lists for the last four days, you probably have begun to feel divine inspiration.

In essence, you are being Truth by focusing only on what is good, pure, and beautiful.

This is so much easier said than done, especially in the beginning of our practice, because we are all so used to going with the flow of the worldview perception and agreeing with what we see, hear, taste, smell, and touch rather than staying in Truth, which cannot be seen with the five senses.

The key to always seeing and experiencing your wealth and prosperity, is to have a variety of ways that corral your wandering thoughts that drift off to the worldview of lack, limitation, and fear and bring them back to Truth, and what you wish to experience each moment of the day.

Today, you are going to do this by focusing entirely on your qualities of wealth. You are going to *practice seeing the invisible.*

As you do this, expect to feel the divine inspiration of this practice. In fact, practicing seeing the invisible is the most fun you can experience once you get the hang and the habit of it.

Writing For Day Five

Go back to the list you made in your *Wealth Journal* for Day Three.

Pick something on your list. It doesn't matter which one and then turn it into qualities. You are getting to be an expert at this, aren't you?

Make a list of eight to ten qualities. Then write that list on something that you can carry with you for the next few days.

Discipline For Day Five

Take one word on your list and look for examples of this quality in every person, place, or thing that you see today. Start writing these observations in your *Wealth Journal*.

For example:

If the word *love* is on your quality list, you are going to look for the variety of ways that you see love expressed today.

The idea is to expand your awareness of love, to see that it exists in infinite forms and is always available to you, when you are awake to seeing it.

Be prepared to experience enthusiasm as you do this.

Enthusiasm is you!

41

— • —

DAY SIX

Reading For Day Six

The enthusiasm that we are talking about is not the "jump up and down" kind—although it may inspire this behavior.

It is the internal enthusiasm that comes from divine inspiration. It comes from the internal knowing that no matter what appears in your life, if it is not a result of unlimited Love—it is not Truth.

When those moments, or days, of doubt or fear enter your thoughts and you wonder if there is something wrong with you because you are still in lack of some kind, think about it this way. If you were working a math problem, but just couldn't find the answer, would you assume that the principle behind the correct answer was wrong? No.

In the same way, when Divine Love does not appear to be expressed as abundance in your life, that doesn't make the principle of what you are learning wrong.

As evidence grows in your life that the Principle of Divine Love **does** work, even when it doesn't appear to be working for you, you will still feel Enthusiasm because you know that the Principle is correct, and you will experience the outcome in your life. It only requires faith the size of a mustard seed.

Writing For Day Six

For your two minutes of writing today, simply write about how you are feeling about where you are in life. Express yourself truthfully. Remember, no one will see this but you. Don't worry if some of it is about the negative things that may be going on.

Remember, untruths sometimes have to be uncovered to be dissolved.

When you are finished writing, read what you have written and add a written comment to yourself about it at the end. This observation is critical, so please don't skip this part of the writing assignment.

Discipline For Day Six

Yesterday, you noticed a specific quality in every person, place, or thing. Today, using the same quality word, you will continue to look for this quality with an additional twist.

Every time you notice this quality, express gratitude for its existence in your life. Do this even if it seems to have nothing to do with you. If you noticed it—it does.

Use your own words, but it might sound something like this if love was your quality word:

"Thank you for the love I see expressed as that mother kisses her child, or the love I see as someone tends their garden, or opens the door for another, or" ...you get the idea.

The list is endless, as is Love.

42

— ● —

DAY SEVEN

Reading For Day Seven

Although you were probably not aware of it, in this first week of your 28–Day Shift to Wealth, you have been practicing the first two steps to *The Shift*.

Those first two steps are:

1. *Be Willing*

2. *Become Aware*

When you began this course and started to practice these concepts, you **demonstrated the willingness** to let go of what isn't True and to understand and live Truth.

As you practice the quality words, you **have become more aware** of Divine Love.

One of the most important beliefs we must be willing to let go of is the idea of personality. Any personality; yours, mine, the people in the news, at work, your children, friends, celebrities—everyone.

I know, the worldview holds personality in high esteem. However, personality is what binds us to lack and limitation. Personality is a limited material sense of each one of us. *Be Willing* to let it go.

Become Aware instead of the true essence of each person as the qualities that they uniquely express.

Writing For Day Seven

In your *Wealth Journal,* describe some of the wonderful examples that you have seen of the quality word you are working with and how it felt to be grateful for the experience of it—even when it appeared to be outside your own life.

Discipline For Day Seven

Continue with the same quality word practice not only seeing it everywhere, but practice being it everywhere.

For example: Using the quality word Love:

Ask yourself throughout the day, *"Are my thoughts loving towards others? Are my thoughts loving towards myself? Would Love do this to Itself?"*

43

— • —

DAY EIGHT

R eading For Day Eight

How often does your personality declare to you that you have a right to be sad, miserable, discouraged, depressed, fearful, angry, withdrawn, apathetic, unhappy, listless or any other quality that is the opposite of enthusiasm or joy?

After all, it declares, "Think what you have gone through in your life. Remember how badly this worked out? What about the love you lost? What about your savings that are now gone? Remember how that person betrayed you? Oh yes, what about the people you know who always get ahead but are "bad people?"

See, I don't even have to know you personally to know that some—if not all—of these thoughts occur to you.

Why? Because I know personality, and that personality suggests all these thoughts to each one of us, although perhaps worded differently depending on what style of communication we are used to receiving.

Sure, you can come up with lots of reasons to entertain those kinds of thoughts. People will understand. After all, it makes you "more like them." But succumbing to this temptation won't get you any closer to your desire to understand and experience the enthusiasm of knowing wealth and prosperity.

Just remember, **you are not your personality; you are so much more,** and that is what you are discovering.

Now—feel that joy!

Discipline For Day Eight

Today you are going to *Become Aware* of whether or not you are *being* the quality word that you have been working with the last few days. Once again, using the quality word of *love* for an example: observe your thoughts and actions throughout the day and ask yourself: "Am I acting as love? Are my thoughts loving towards others? Are my thoughts loving towards myself?"

Be an observer only. No judgment—after all, judgment wouldn't be love, would it?

Writing For Day Eight

This writing takes place after the discipline for the day has gone on for at least a few hours.

Write your observations of how successful or unsuccessful you have been being the quality word of the day.

Write and observe. That's it!

Be Love!

44

— • —

DAY NINE

R eading For Day Nine
Today is the third letter of W E A L T H in *The 28–Day Shift to Wealth*.

The A in W E A L T H stands for Angel Ideas—those marvelous ideas that seem to pop out of nowhere, bringing light to any situation.

These angel ideas are always immediately available.

In fact, they are ready for you even before you ask for them. They wait for you to listen for them. When you do, they bring you the solution to a problem, an idea for something new, a way to see something differently, and joy to the moment.

Angel ideas are different from human thoughts.

Thoughts can keep us in the worldview by repeating back to us only what appears to be true and then making it appear even more real by giving us a rationalization for why it must be true.

Nothing about human thoughts releases us from our current point of view.

Angel ideas lift us above and out of the worldview. For those people who don't honor angel ideas, they seem "impossible, silly, never been done, how will that work, can I really do those" kinds of ideas.

For those of you who expect, honor, and love angel ideas, know that they are pure wealth.

Discipline For Day Nine

Listen, and expect to hear, and be moved by, innumerable angel ideas.

Expect to revel in the delightful, brilliant light that they bring to every corner of your life. Expect them to dissolve all limitations in the process.

Remember the phrase we all learned before crossing the street when we were kids? "Stop, Look, and Listen." What a perfect reminder. So, before doing anything today—"Stop, Look, and Listen" for angel ideas. They are there—always!

Writing For Day Nine

After you spend the day listening, jot down some of the ideas, and thoughts that come through to you in your *Wealth Journal*. Don't worry about figuring out whether they are thoughts or ideas. We'll address that issue in the next few days. For now, just be a scribe and write them down!

45

— • —

Day Ten

R eading For Day Ten

How can you tell the difference between an angel idea and a thought?

Although thinking and thoughts are obviously useful, for our purposes, we want to distinguish between a thought of what to do, and an angel idea of what to do.

An angel idea is what is often called "inspiration."

It appears outside the bounds of what seems possible. A human thought of what to do starts with the premise that you are a material being, and material laws govern your life and control your wealth.

An angel idea will stretch what you think is possible for you.

It will take you out of your material personality and its limitations. A thought of what to do fits what you already know, and in most cases will simply be a band-aid to fix the immediate situation.

An angel idea is not always obvious as to the why of doing something.

In fact, it can be completely unrelated. For example: You begin wondering about how to buy a new house, and the angel idea comes to you to call a friend and find out how they are, or go for a walk in the park, or shine your shoes.

These angel ideas do not seem to relate to the situation. But an angel idea will lead you on a path that will provide in ways you could not think of on your own.

However, this is where it can get tricky. These may be thoughts that are a distraction to keep you from studying and understanding Truth. However, you'll be able to tell the difference as you continue working with quality words.

Keep listening and practicing. As you do so, you will be better able to hear angel ideas and know the difference between them and fear-based human thoughts and distractions.

Writing For Day Ten

Keep writing the angel ideas and thoughts that are coming to you. It's okay to write them both down. Your *Wealth Journal* is a place to record all that you are thinking about.

However, you are also writing how you feel about each Angel Idea or thought, and this will begin the process of uncovering which one it is.

Discipline For Day Ten

Today, would you keep this idea at the forefront of all that you do?

"I am listening and being guided by Angel Ideas."

That's it—you can do it!

46

— • —

DAY ELEVEN

R eading For Day Eleven
      As you practice using quality words to turn things back
into thoughts, you are practicing tuning into angel ideas.

This process brings your material thinking into the realm of
thinking as One Mind. Then, when you need or desire something,
an angel idea will be an enlightened message based on Truth.

When you begin with qualities, the objects, the work, your loves,
and the people that appear in your life will be more abundant as their
true spiritual nature shines through the belief that they are material.

Because angel ideas call for some form of action on your part, the
A in W E A L T H can also stand for *action*.

**It may be a form of action in which you do something, or it
may be a form of action in which it appears that you don't do
anything, which I call "active not doing."**

Once again, you may ask, "How do I know if it is an angel idea, or
a thought based on a material perception?" One way to know is to
ask yourself if you feel impelled or compelled. Impel means "to set
in motion, move, actuate, drive, mobilize" which is the way an angel
idea will guide you.

On the other hand, compel means to "cause a person or thing to yield to pressure, force, oblige, make happen." Compel may cause you to take action based on a material perception.

The action may be the same, but when the basis starts from an angel idea, the outcome will be harmonious and lasting.

Writing For Day Eleven

In your *Wealth Journal,* make a list of actions you have taken in the past that, in retrospect, you can now discern whether it was an Angel Idea or a material perception that motivated you.

Remember to not judge, or succumb to guilt or the "I wish I would have done it better" syndrome.

This is observation only!

Discipline For Day Eleven

As you take action and make decisions, pause first and ask yourself, "Do I feel impelled or compelled?"

Take action only on an impel feeling, never on a compel feeling.

47

— · —

DayTwelve

R eading For Day Twelve

Angel ideas are pure wealth because they instantly connect us to the Truth of our being.

Although we have been talking about angel ideas as if they are telling us to do or not do something, in their purest form, they are statements of Truth; and in that form, they ask nothing of us but to acknowledge Truth.

For example: You are looking for something you misplaced or lost. The angel idea, in this instance, may be the absolute understanding that God is omnipresent.

You might then reason. "How then, could anything be misplaced? How could an omnipresent Mind forget something? Could there ever be a place that omnipresent Mind is not? Therefore, nothing is misplaced or lost—ever."

This idea of omnipresent Mind is the angel idea revealing God.

The result may be a flash of inspiration where the supposedly misplaced object is, or you will see it where it has always been, or it will be replaced or appear in a different manner.

This is inevitable because the material symbol is never the Reality of the object. It is the quality of God represented by that object which, of course, can never be lost or misplaced.

Writing For Day Twelve

Have you ever lost or misplaced anything?

Turn it back into qualities and write the angel ideas that come to you about the Truth of this thing in your *Wealth Journal.*

Discipline For Day Twelve

Your disciplined statement for the day is:

"I AM omnipresent Mind and Mind never loses or forgets."

Remember to say to yourself as many times as you can; you can write it, sing it, dance it, run it. Just keep this angel idea in the forefront of your day.

48

— • —

Day Thirteen

Reading For Day Thirteen

It seems obvious, doesn't it? If we have love, we are wealthy. But often we *do* have love and still don't feel wealthy or prosperous.

There is something you can do to increase both Love and your experience of wealth.

You can love.

You can refuse to do anything but see and be love. No matter what the person, place, thing, or situation looks like, you can find something good to love about it. You can refuse to be tempted to discuss, think about, or be afraid of anything that does not appear to be good.

As I wrote this, I was sitting in an airport, and just as I wrote—*you can see only love*—I noticed a woman walk by with her two children and bend to kiss her daughter on the forehead. Love!

Earlier in the day, I experienced a room of over two hundred people extend love—without thinking of anything but love—to a man in trouble. Love was the tangible feeling in the room, and love healed the situation.

If you think about it, you know anytime love is acknowledged, it becomes obvious that love is the only power, and in the moments of experiencing love, you know W E A L T H without measure.

However, instead of seeing love, we are in the habit of discussing the "story of what doesn't, isn't, or won't work."

No longer! You are done with the story of lack, and you are now living only the Truth of love.

Discipline For Day Thirteen

Since you are going to be thinking only about love, you are actually going on a thought diet—instead of a food diet.

Today, you will avoid all those thoughts that are bad for you.

"Magically" it will also affect anyone else within the radiance and radius of your thought.

Imagine that! Others will have the benefit of your diet.

Don't worry about how this thought diet will bring you wealth and prosperity. In fact, that worry is something that you are dieting from today. In this Love diet you can love every second of the day. Don't hold back. Stuff yourself with love.

Writing For Day Thirteen

Feels good to be full of love, doesn't it? Spend some time today noticing love and writing it in your *Wealth Journal*. Also note what happens to you and your day when you are only full of love.

49

— · —

Day Fourteen

Reading For Day Fourteen

I have heard it said that the person you love the least is how much you understand of God—or Divine Love.

This must be true because if we really understood that everything is the creation and outpouring and expression of, and thought of, and love of LOVE—then what is there not to love? How can we say Divine Love is omnipresent and then turn around and see someone or something that is not love?

It can't happen, but it seems to. There appears to be many unloving, unkind, and perhaps evil people doing unloving, unkind, and evil things. In fact, as you continue to live and see only the qualities of love, what is not love will become more apparent.

This is a good thing.

Why? Because what is not love is coming to your attention so that you can dissolve it with Truth.

This doesn't mean you should hang out with it, hoping to cure it. It means you dissolve it by knowing that there is only love. Any action you take from this perfect standpoint will result in the perfect solution to the situation. Listen to those angel ideas—they will guide you.

You are still on the Love diet, so continue to Love—accepting nothing but Love in yourself and others.

Writing For Day Fourteen

Consider the word love and write all the qualities that you can think of that are love to you.

Discipline For Day Fourteen

Here are your two statements for the day. Please say: *"I AM Love"* and then take one of the qualities of Love and say that too. "I AM _____"

All day in every way! Love *is* you!

50

— · —

Day Fifteen

Reading For Day Fifteen

The second commandment is: "Thou shalt love thy neighbor as yourself." Do you?

Yourself, I mean; do you love yourself? Because, if read correctly, this statement means your neighbor is yourself. So before you can truly love what you perceive as your neighbor, you must love yourself. As you become more and more aware of the fact that you are Love Itself, this loving yourself becomes easier.

In actuality, you are Love Loving Itself.

It sounds nice, doesn't it? Although it is True, if we aren't living it moment-by-moment, it is as illusive as the words on this page. Our intent is to be living Truth.

So today, let's uncover what you **don't** love about yourself. How? By listening to the voice in your head and what you say to yourself.

Before you start this process, know this. **The voice in your head is not you.**

It sounds like you, speaks the way you do, tells you what you think you would say to yourself. But, it's not you. It's the tempter deceiving you into believing something that is not Truth.

Of course it sounds like you because otherwise you wouldn't listen.

This fact will separate you from what it says. However, if you don't know what it is saying, you can't dissolve all of it.

As you listen today, stay in Love. If you do that you might find yourself laughing at the absurdity of the tempter's lies.

Discipline For Day Fifteen

Listen to what the voice in your head is saying to you, and what you say out loud to yourself about yourself, or how you describe yourself to others.

Writing For Day Fifteen:

Write in your *Wealth Journal* what you hear yourself say or think.

Remember, when you discover what isn't good, loving, and pure in yourself and others, always remain an observer knowing this is not Truth about you, or them.

51

— • —

DAY SIXTEEN

Reading For Day Sixteen

Today, let's gather wisdom about love from the words of a poet long ago; substituting the word love for the word charity to arrive at the original meaning.

"And now I will show you the most excellent way.

If I have the gift of prophecy and can fathom all mysteries and all knowledge and if I have a faith that can move mountains, but have not love, I am nothing.

If I give all I possess to the poor and surrender my body to the flames, but have not love, I gain nothing.

Love is patient. Love is kind. It does not envy, it does not boast, it is not proud.

It is not rude, it is not self-seeking, it is not easily angered, it keeps no record of wrongs. Love does not delight in evil but rejoices with the truth.

It always protects, always trusts, always hopes, always perseveres. Love never fails. And now these three remain: faith, hope and love. But the greatest of these is love." — Corinthians 13

Discipline For Day Sixteen

What a perfect description of love. As you can see, this passage states the qualities of Love, and the action of love, based on these qualities.

Make a list of the qualities and actions of love found in the poem and put the list where you can see it today.

Throughout the day, ask yourself if you are acting as love in all these ways.

Also, be aware of those who claim to love, but are not being, or acting, from these qualities.

Once again, be an observer only and stay with the Truth of being in every instant.

Writing For Day Sixteen

Write a *love letter* to yourself!

Make it a wonderful letter full of appreciation and acknowledgement and all the qualities found in the poem we are reading today.

Put the letter in an envelope and date it a year from now. Put it somewhere you will see it next year so you can read your Love letter from yourself, or perhaps have someone mail it to you.

52

— • —

DAY SEVENTEEN

R eading For Day Seventeen

What a privilege to be able to say *thanks,* but how often do you do it? Very seldom! I know this to be true, because there are so many things for which all of us forget to be thankful.

I'll prove it.

Stop right now and look around you. Really look. No matter where you are, there are countless things that have been provided for you.

For example: I know everyone of you is reading these words. Think of that. Think of the millions of events that have taken place that have made it possible for you to be able to read this message wherever you are, written by me on my computer, wherever I am living.

Imagine what has been provided for you in order for this to happen; the electricity, the software, the paper, the printing, etc.

Think of the dedication, energy, love, and care that so many people have given to each element of what we all so casually use.

You could spend hours giving thanks just for the things you are aware of within the circle of your arms.

I know another thing that you are not thankful enough for—the talents that have been given to you.

No matter how good you are at giving thanks for them, I know you have missed a few. Most of us have missed almost all of them. To rediscover your talents, start small.

Once again, start where you are sitting. What are you doing?

Think of the gifts and talents you have been given that allow you to do that.

Expand out into your day, then your community.

Notice how you express unlimited talent and gifts each second of the day.

Writing For Day Seventeen

Take time to list in your *Wealth Journal* all the talents you have noticed.

Don't forget to say thanks for each one! When you are done—think again—I am positive there are more!

Discipline For Day Seventeen

Give *thanks* today.

Give *thanks* out loud when an Angel Idea moves you to speak.

Give *thanks* inside for everything. Remember, we are seeing what has been given, and today we give *thanks*.

I am giving *thanks* for you and your unique gifts and talents that you share with the world.

Thank you!

53

— : —

DAY EIGHTEEN

Reading For Day Eighteen

Amid the claim of lack—which produces worry, anxiety, and fear—we can be thankful that the claim of lack is a lie. We can be thankful that in Truth there is only One Creator and One Power, only one Intelligent Loving Mind and we are the Loved of this Love, and all that It is and has, we are, and we have.

We can say thank you for the Truth, even if there are times it doesn't appear to be true to us. We can do this in the same way we can say thank you for the fact that the earth is round although appearing flat, for the fact that railroad tracks don't merge in the distance even though it appears that they do, for the fact that all that we see is mostly space even though it appears solid.

All these material symbols show us that what we see, hear, taste and touch is not Truth—it is perception.

We can therefore be grateful and give thanks for the fact that no matter what current material perceptions may suggest, we know that spiritual perception will reveal all our needs provided for, before we knew we had a need.

It's a spiritual law. *"Seek ye first the Kingdom of God and his righteousness: and all these things shall be added unto thee."*—Matthew 6:33

We can be thankful that our desire is to *Seek ye first the Kingdom of God* and rest in the assurance that all these things have already been provided. We can be thankful for the Truth that we can and will perceive their presence now.

Writing For Day Eighteen

Spend your two minutes today beginning a gratitude list, and writing a thank you note to Divine Love.

Discipline For Day Eighteen

Stay in gratitude and thankfulness for your permanent, unlimited wealth, no matter what the temptation is to believe otherwise.

54

— · —

DAY NINETEEN

R eading For Day Nineteen

Does it concern you that there appears to be lack for others? Is this one of the thoughts that has been binding you to the belief of lack?

There appears to be a tremendous amount of poverty in the world, and we hear about it all the time. It appears in the news about other countries, or on the streets of our hometown. Sometimes this poverty strikes closer to home as it appears in our children, parents, and friends.

These pictures of poverty, whether on TV, the news, a phone call, or a letter from a loved one, touches the emotions of our heart and pulls us into the worldview of lack by suggesting that poverty exists for them.

If it doesn't exist for you, it doesn't exist for anyone—anywhere—anytime. Whenever these pictures of poverty appear—in whatever form—we must be diligent in rejecting them. **Not ignoring them. Rejecting them!**

Think of it this way. If you were in a theatre watching a movie and someone you know was an actor in the movie playing a homeless person, would you then rush home to see what you could do to make sure they were clothed and fed? Of course not. You would know that in Truth they were secure and safe.

In the same way, when we are presented with the movie of poverty and lack for others, we can know this is a material perception and therefore not true. Using spiritual perception, we can know that all the people we see in poverty are really, just as you are, safe, secure, and lovingly provided for by Divine Love.

As the mist dissolves, the worldview of lack will also dissolve.

In the meantime, when you start with the correct spiritual perception, any action that you take to express love to those who appear to be in need, will not only be practical, but will also bring the spiritual light which can lift them too from the illusion of lack.

Remember, what you see is really what you believe. The dreamer and the dream are one.

Think how wonderful it will be as we begin to perceive as Divine Love perceives!

Writing For Day Nineteen

You have been writing about what you are grateful for in your life. Today spend some time writing a gratitude list for what has been provided to others.

Discipline For Day Nineteen

When presented with the illusion of lack, for anyone, do not agree with it.

Do not sympathize with it.

While bringing empathy to the situation, stay in the knowledge of One Mind—Divine Love pre-providing all that each person needs or desires.

55

— • —

DAY TWENTY

R eading For Day Twenty
Have you ever stopped to realize that **you** are supply?
Think about all that you are and all that you do and how much you
are a supply to others.

It's not just that you may be bringing an income to a family; it is
much more than that.

It's a smile, a touch, and an acknowledgement. It's your kindness,
attention, hugs, and readiness to help.

Your unique expression of Divine Love and the One Mind is
endless supply in a multitude of ways. This is something for which
you can be thankful.

Be thankful that your purpose is innate, that you are invaluable
and an inevitable supply, without trying to make it happen. Be
thankful that there is nothing for you to do except surrender to being
your unique expression and take action as directed by angel ideas.

Writing For Day Twenty
Today write in your *Wealth Journal* in what ways you are supply
for others. If you really don't know—ask!

Discipline for Day Twenty
Your statement for the day: "I AM supply." As the day's events
continue around you, stay in this thought: "I AM supply."

56

— • —

DAY TWENTY ONE

R eading For Day Twenty-One

When I first heard the angel idea of using the word WEALTH, I thought the H was for *help others*. When I listened again, I realized that the H in help means: "Help yourself first."

Before you can effectively help others, you must help yourself.

You are now. You are taking the time to redirect your thinking—to shift your perceptions, to know the truth about wealth, because if you understand wealth, you will have it and be able to share it.

But what about other times?

Have you ever found yourself distracting yourself from your true wishes and passion by helping others before you helped yourself? Isn't this action one of the most draining, stifling, and ultimately wealth stealing things you can do?

Yes, it is, and in the end, you have nothing left to help others with—no desires, no motivation, no resources. Sometimes we use this lack as a weapon against others. (For example: 'I gave up all my dreams for you.')

So today, you can ask yourself first, *"How can I help you?"*

Helping yourself first may take just a moment of thought shifting, or it may take many days, weeks, or months. However, when you start with helping yourself first, you will find you will naturally move out into the world and ask, *"How can I help you?"*

You will be so filled with wealth that sharing and using it will become your nature. Your desire to help will expand into a dream bigger than yourself that will become the motive of your days and will outlive your personal time on earth.

Therefore, no matter how much you help others now, stop and help yourself first, and then let that flow out of you into whatever action angel ideas lead you to do.

Discipline For Day Twenty-One

Your disciplined thought for the day is to ask yourself this question: *"How can I help you?"*

Writing For Day Twenty-One

When you hear the answers to that question, write them down in your *Wealth Journal*.

This will be an invaluable aid in remembering that supply is you.

Helping yourself first is one of the primary ways to say "thank you" for the gift of wealth that is you.

57

— · —

Day Twenty Two

R eading For Day Twenty-Two:

Have you ever needed help but not asked for it? Why?
Perhaps it was because you were embarrassed, ("I should know
better") afraid, ("they will be so angry or upset with me"), indifferent
("what difference will it make anyway"), "good reasons" ("I don't
have the time, money, patience, knowledge, contacts etc.").

Do any of these reasons sound like an angel idea leading you to
light and love? No, they sound like the "tempter" lying to you about
who you are and what is true wealth.

Help is a built in provision of supply and wealth.

Look at the many symbols of this idea of supply found in nature.
The sun helps us all, the wind spreads seeds and clears the air, the
rain supplies needed moisture for all life.

It's a reciprocal law of being.

When you ask for help someone is now free to give you that help.
Perhaps their greatest wish is to be of service, or perhaps they have
yet to learn of the gift of service.

Either way, your asking for help allows them to be supply, and you
to surrender your personality to your true nature as an expression of
Divine Love.

Discipline For Day Twenty-Two

Ask someone for help. Simple. No rules—just ask.

Writing For Day Twenty-Two

Sometimes this asking for help is to make use of services, ideas, classes, meetings, and gifts already available to you.

Make a list in your *Wealth Journal* of any kind of supply of help that you already know about, but haven't yet used. If one is appropriate for your current need, then go get it and use it.

58

— • —

DAY TWENTY THREE

R eading For Day Twenty-Three

If you asked for help yesterday, someone responded. Did
you notice?

Did you remember to give thanks for their help? Giving thanks is
a vital part of the circle of reciprocal being.

**Give thanks with what you have, knowing you have an
unlimited supply.**

Now that you are helping yourself first and are in the habit of
asking for help—you are aren't you—you can move on in the circle.
You can pass it on. You can be of help and service to many. You don't
need an acknowledgement or reward for being of service.

**You are not giving help to be a good person, but to express
yourself as a spiritual being.**

However, when you help others, you are not providing a way
for them to continue in any behavior that does not serve them.
The first step in helping others is knowing who they really
are—Spiritual—and then treating them as if that was true.

True help does not keep anyone in a position of helplessness.

Help supplies the need with love, and with the expectation that
their need is temporary. The greatest help you can give another is to
hold to the unwavering knowledge about their true spiritual nature.

No matter what they believe about themselves, you can know and love them as they truly are.

Discipline For Day Twenty-Three

Your disciplined thoughts for the day are:

"I am aware and grateful for the abundant help that I am continually receiving. I am aware of the need of others and I am grateful to be able to provide it as the expression of Divine Love."

Writing For Day Twenty-Three

What help have you received in the last twenty-four hours?

Think about it.

Help arrives in a multitude of ways, if you will but look. This could be an ongoing list in your *Wealth Journal.*

Thank you for helping others as you help yourself!

59

— • —

Day Twenty Four

R eading For Day Twenty-Four

What is the best help you can give to yourself, and therefore to others today?

You can step outside of the material picture.

You can choose to not identify with any suggestion of lack in yourself or others.

No matter what the material picture is telling you about what you don't have, or what you need, you can choose to remain in the internal knowledge of the truth of constant, loving, and practical supply.

When human hope fades, you can help yourself by remembering good is the only power. You can remind yourself how often you have proven this to yourself in your own life, and heard and read about the proofs of good in other's lives.

You can help yourself by remembering the power and truth of Elisha's statement, *"Fear not: for they that be with us are more than they that be with them."*—II Kings 6:16

You can help yourself by remaining constantly aware of the still small place within—listening only to the voice of wisdom found in this stillness.

You can help yourself by letting go of how you think it "should" be and know only that God is in control and has already provided all that you need.

You can help yourself by not listening to, reading, talking, or entertaining any thoughts that do not declare the eternal, omnipotent power of Divine Love Loving you as Its own.

Discipline For Day Twenty-Four

Today your eternal and still thought is: *"I Am the Loved of Love."*

Writing For Day Twenty-Four

Look back on your life for proofs of good and spend your two minutes today recording them in your *Wealth Journal.*

Write: *"I Am the Loved of Love"* throughout the day on whatever is nearby to write on.

60

— • —

Day Twenty Five

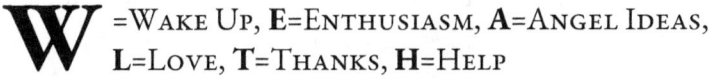

W =Wake Up, **E**=Enthusiasm, **A**=Angel Ideas,
L=Love, **T**=Thanks, **H**=Help

Reading For Day Twenty-Five

Yes, we have covered all the letters in the word
W E A L T H!

**But there is one more step in the process. And that is the
vital step of practice.**

While writing this section of the book, Del and I moved to an
apartment in town for the summer. While making arrangements
with the landlord, I noticed that it looked as if a garden had once
been planted around the house, but had become choked with weeds.

When I mentioned this to her, she suggested that perhaps I would
like to take care of the garden for the summer. After a bit of
negotiation, I got the job.

At first, it looked as if it would only take a few hours to clean the
garden. But I was wrong. It took a very long time, and it was very
hard work.

As I hoed and weeded, it occurred to me what a perfect metaphor
gardening is for what we are studying.

Underneath all the weeds, it was possible to see that someone
originally cared enough to buy expensive and beautiful plants. And

then they neglected them so that most of them died, or became the bare bones of what they once were, showing very little beauty.

For the past twenty-four days, you have taken precious time and care to plant a beautiful *thought garden.*

But without continued, constant care, it too will be overgrown with the weeds of the old habits of perception and aggressiveness of the worldview.

When our landlord first planted the garden, it must have looked beautiful. But she stopped too soon. If she had taken just a bit more time to cover the soil with the weed stopping fabric or cardboard, and then mulch, not only would very few weeds have grown, but the plants she wanted would also have thrived, providing enjoyment for all—and eliminating all the work of restoration.

In the same way, you must cover the soil of your thinking with the protective understanding of Truth and continue to mulch and water your thoughts with the nutriment of Divine Love.

It takes constant practice. But you know that practice is as important as planting in the first place.

Writing For Day Twenty-Five

Imagine what you have been studying for the last twenty-four days is a garden and describe it to yourself in your *Wealth Journal.*

Discipline For Day Twenty-Five

Notice if any old thought habits have crept back in, and uproot them immediately, before they have time to make deep roots.

61

— • —

DAY TWENTY SIX

W =WAKE UP, **E**=ENTHUSIASM, **A**=ANGEL IDEAS, L=LOVE, **T**=THANKS, **H**=HELP

Reading For Day Twenty-Six

The premise that this W E A L T H Course is based on is that there in only One Mind and it is omnipresent, omniscient, omnipotent, omniaction. It is all Intelligent and all Loving.

It is the only Cause and the only Creator.

On the surface, it may appear that you are studying this *Wealth Course* because you want more money, love, happiness, peace, security, time—all the things that most of us never seem to have enough of.

And it is a good thing to expect to have all that you need at all times.

However, you must remember that these things will be the inevitable result of choosing and living the spiritual perception of One Mind. Your desire is to release all the beliefs that hold you in the material world so that you can experience—here and now—heaven on earth.

When you fully realize that what appears as the outside world is really your own perception of reality and the worldview that you have agreed to believe, it makes absolute sense to spend time understanding Reality—first and foremost during every moment of the day.

Easier said than done! But it **must** be done!

I have come up with a few ideas that help me remember to practice during the day so that I don't reach the end of the day and wonder where my thoughts have been.

One that works well is an *oven timer day*.

I spend time studying spiritual perception and when I am done, I set the oven timer, or phone timer, or computer time for forty-five minutes in which I do other things that I feel need to be done. When the timer goes off, I stop whatever I am doing and study some more. Do this for a day or two and notice the difference in the quality of your day.

Discipline For Day Twenty-Six

Use the *oven timer* day method, or choose a method of your own, but stop whatever you are doing every forty-five minutes today and remember that there is only One Mind. This could be a quiet meditation, a time of study, or a moment of prayer.

Writing For Day Twenty-Six

Write in your *Wealth Journal* what attempts to distract you as you take your time to remember? Do you easily stop what you are doing? Awareness is the first step in releasing and dissolving all that is not One Mind.

62

— • —

DAY TWENTY SEVEN

W =WAKE UP, **E**=ENTHUSIASM, **A**=ANGEL IDEAS,
L=LOVE, **T**=THANKS, **H**=HELP

Reading For Day Twenty-Seven

Does practice mean that you are practicing being a better human? Does it mean that you are practicing to "get more spiritual?" Does it mean that you have to make something happen, get better at something or do something to be sure everything works out?

None of these reasons are why you are practicing.

Right now, you are perfect.

Right now, you are a spiritual being with no humanness at all. Right now you are the effect of the One Cause and Creator. Right now you are the embodiment of all that God is. Which means of course that right now you are all the varied forms of wealth that you desire to experience.

So why practice? Until every moment of our day is the expression of this Truth; until our thinking is only God's thinking, until we have only the perception of Reality, we practice. We practice to wake up and to keep our thinking in Truth.

What a glorious awakening it will be when this is no longer necessary because we are fully awake and aware of who we really are: the effect of divine Love and the Infinite One Mind.

In the meantime—we practice—and experience the joy this brings, and the tag along result of what appears to be an improved human experience, which is in reality the veil of mist-perception rolled away and Truth revealed.

Discipline For Day Twenty-Seven

Your constant statement, thought, and motivation for action today is, *"I am the effect of Divine Love and the Infinite One Mind."*

Writing For Day Twenty-Seven

As the effect and embodiment of Divine Love and the Infinite One Mind, write in your *Wealth Journal* how life *really* is for you.

63

— • —

DAY TWENTY EIGHT

W=Wake Up, E=Enthusiasm, A=Angel Ideas, L=Love, T=Thanks, H=Help

Reading For Day Twenty-Eight

For the past twenty-eight days, we have practiced together. We learned how to use the word W E A L T H as our guide.

During these last twenty-eight days, you have increased your understanding of **True Wealth**.

You have done this because you know that when you understand this wealth, you will never worry about lack again. Now that you have started this process, don't stop!

Continue to practice the Truth about Wealth, just as you practice any other skill. Some days will feel easier than others, but the results will far outweigh any discomfort along the way.

What this practice will reveal to you is the treasure that can never be taken from you. A treasure that you can spend with the assurance that it will never be depleted.

Never worry about the outcome of what you are guided to do.

That is not your job. You can't control what other people say, think, or do. Your job is to start with the correct premise in your own

419

thinking and to constantly pay attention to your motive for all the actions you take or don't take.

If you discover that you don't always walk in True Wealth (none of us do yet) be thankful for that awareness and then let it go.

Never hold on to those things you discover about yourself that are not beautiful and loving. Don't say to yourself, "this is who I am," don't beat yourself up for your mistakes, big or small. Let them go.

Set yourself free to be and experience True Wealth.

I know that you are walking now in the light of the Truth about Wealth and I am privileged to have been able to spend this time with you!

Wealth is You!

Discipline For Day Twenty-Eight

Today your eternal thought is: "*I Am Love Loving Itself.*" Repeat this constantly to yourself throughout the day.

Writing For Day Twenty-Eight

Look back on your life for proofs of good and spend your two minutes today recording them in your *Wealth Journal.*

Write: "*I Am the Loved of Love*" throughout the day on whatever is nearby to write on.

64

— • —

Keep Going

It's so easy to forget or slip back into the worldview of lack and limitation. There is so much agreement about *not enough* or *not good enough* that it takes a conscious, consistent commitment of thought to stay in W E A L T H.

Without that conscious, consistent commitment of thought and action—habit takes over.

If habit were a person, it would be someone who waits outside your door every minute of the day, and when you open that door just a tiny bit, it uses all its force to push its way into your home.

Then it moves your stuff around the room to suit itself, sits down in the most comfortable place in the room, and starts telling everyone else how it is going to be, starting now and forever.

If you find that habit of accepting the worldview of lack making itself at home again in your thinking, there is only one way to get it out.

No—pushing or begging won't work. Arguing about what is True won't move that habit.

Although arguing for what is True can be useful because it increase the strength in us to do the only thing that will banish that habit.

And that is to **turn on the light!!**

It's easy, isn't it? Because what's hard is remembering to keep the door shut and remembering to turn on the light. Habit makes us forgetful.

So two thoughts for today: **Keep the door of your thinking shut to the beliefs of lack and limitation and keep that light shining!**

It takes a complete, conscious commitment to **not** become hypnotized by the continuing demands of lack, to believe in it whichever form it takes. No matter how loudly the voice of lack may scream, it can be silenced by knowing its power is your reaction to it and your belief in it.

Use the W E A L T H system to shatter these dark thoughts with the power of light.

This is not a passive state; it is an active state. Now is the time to join the millions of people who desire to see peace and wealth for every individual.

Lack screams loudly to get a reaction from us. When we do not react at all, but instead shine the light of Truth with calmness and Love, the results are amazing.

It doesn't matter how big the problem seems to be, or how little. It is the same problem. It is the belief that we are separated from our source, and that there is a power other than Good.

Don't believe it. It doesn't matter if, at the moment, we don't understand this, but we don't have to believe the lie. This is imperative in your personal life. It is imperative for the planet.

Will you take a moment today to see yourself as Light?

Pretend that you are unzipping your human covering and inside is Light. Unzip and let it pour out. Let it dissolve any darkness it touches.

Send that light to shatter any dark beliefs that you find existing in your thought or the world's thought.

You are the light!

THE INTENT COURSE

65

— . —

INTRODUCTION

B efore we begin these twenty-eight days together, I would like
to explain why this is a course on *intent,* rather than *intention.*
The answer lies in the definitions of each. Intent implies a sustained,
unbroken commitment or purpose, while intention implies an
intermittent resolution or an initial aim or plan.

Right away, you can see why we have chosen the word *intent.* We
want to be able to sustain our commitments, and not get distracted
or manipulated into changing them in a way that does not serve our
life's purpose.

Intents are the underpinnings of everything that happens in our
life, and to our life. Whether it is an intent as big as a life purpose, or
an intent on how we want to spend our evening—what we intend it
to be, will set the outcome in motion.

There is another reason why it is important to cultivate this skill of
setting intents. If someone else has a clearer intent than we do, his or
her intent wins, or prevails over ours. In other words, we will follow
what they have decided is important whether it is in our best interest
or not.

While perfecting the skill of how to set clear, conscious intents
during this course, you will also perfect the skill of noticing what
other people intend. This gives you the chance to decide if you want
to follow their lead or not. Knowing that intent underlies all action,

you can immediately see how dangerous it is to not know what your intent is at all times.

In this book, you will find the *worksheets* and *tools* that will enable you to become a master at setting and reading intents. This skill can, and will, change every experience in your life—if you are willing to do the work of knowing yourself.

This book is designed to be completed in twenty-eight days. However, you can choose your own timing. After all, it is your intent how you want it to work. It is also the perfect book to use in a mastermind group of two or more like-minded people.

Say yes to what moves you and life becomes the outcome of your clear, conscious, and grace-filled intent.

I also have a free workbook for you, in case you don't wish to write in this book, or you are reading or listening to this book digitally. You can find the links to the workbook and the online evergreen course and a community where you might find others to be in your mastermind in the resource chapter at the end of this book.

66

— . —

THE IMPORTANCE OF INTENT

Have you ever stepped into a room to get something, and then couldn't remember what it was?

Have you ever stopped in the middle of a store and forgot why you were there?

Have you ever found yourself wondering what the meaning and purpose of life is in general, and yours specifically?

Have you ever found yourself doing something for a few minutes, or maybe a few years, and realized it wasn't what you wanted to do at all?

Have you ever been in a relationship that you realized was not a good one for you?

Have you ever bought something and then wondered why you spent the money for it?

Some results of these *have you* questions are relatively harmless. Others are annoying or expensive.

Some of them have been downright dangerous.

How can you avoid these negative results? By knowing the *why* of every action before you take it.

This may sound impossible, but it's not. In fact, it is imperative for living a life of ease, harmony, love, and abundance.

The trick is to know your intent. Most of us don't have a clue what our intent is even for simple things like going to the store, let alone our intent for our life.

However, it is actually easy to find out once you learn how, and that is what this book can do for you.

Let me give you a simple example.

You are going to have lunch with your best friend. What is your intent for the lunch? Does it revolve around money, food, or connection?

Let's say it is money and your intent is to stay within your preset budget. However, once you sit down, you realize there is nothing you love to eat within your budget.

A range of emotions may follow from disappointment to anger, which overrides the joy of the meeting.

This means you have missed the opportunity to explore a different solution for food, and the connection with your friend.

On the other hand, if your intent is the food, and it turns out the food is not very good, what happens? Perhaps you experience disappointment or anger about spending money on not very good food, and once again, miss the connection with your friend.

However, if your intent is clearly defined as *connection,* then neither the budget you have set, nor the lack of good food, would spoil that connection.

You would keep your focus on the true intent of the lunch, and the rest would fall into its proper place in importance.

Actually, any of these intents—money, food, or connection—are perfectly fine, as long as you know which one it is. If you choose it consciously, you will remain pleased with the outcome.

A clear, conscious intent for every area of your life will give you the ability to set goals, or resolutions, that you enjoy doing, and will accomplish with pleasure.

Without a clear, conscious intent, momentum can carry you down a path faster than the blink of an eye, and it just might not be the direction, or path, you want to take.

Without a clear, conscious intent, you are easily distracted, and someone else with a clearer intent than yours can manipulate you in every area of your life.

With a clear, conscious intent, your purpose in life becomes bigger than the small human ego and provides you with a path to walk that is filled with life's endless rewards far beyond your daily expectations.

As with all things, the key is first to be willing, and then to take clear, conscious action.

In this book, you will find a well defined set of actions to take to discover your intent in every area of your life, including the overall *Master Intent* for your life, which is the most important of all.

Once you set the primary intents for your life, the rest of them will be easy to discover.

Soon you will find it a breeze to discover your intent for everything from cleaning your house, to what schools to go to, what person to date or marry, what clothes to wear, or what car to buy.

The basis of this system is a spiritual one, meaningful and important to you, not someone else.

Using this system, you will know what you want, why you want it, and how to have it.

67

— · —

BEGIN AT THE BEGINNING

As you begin *The Intent Course* become an observer of your life. Pay attention to your actions and choices. **Don't judge—just observe.**

The Intent Course is divided into sections as if you were doing a four-week intensive shift. You could do this at the end of one year, or at the beginning of another to set the year into intents that will serve you, rather than hinder you.

Or you could use *The Intent Course* anytime you feel you need to have an awareness wake up. Whenever you use this course, be ready to shift to a new, different, bright, shiny, happy, light, brilliant awareness of life!

Each of the four-week sections have assignments for you to do. *They are important, so please take the time to do them.* If the voice in your head—which is not you—tries to tell you that they not important, or that the work is for someone else, it will be lying (as it always does).

The truth about *The Intent Course* is that this is all about and for you! Of course, we all know how much it will benefit everyone else if you take care of yourself first—if you need to remember that point in order to be completely present for yourself, go for it.

Begin by finding thirty minutes every day for private quiet time.

I will be expanding on this as we go through this program, but you may want to take out your calendar now and decide where those thirty minutes can come from.

Do it, even if it means thirty minutes less sleep, because you get up thirty minutes earlier to sit quietly. You'll experience the beneficial results of this immediately. If you are doing this course with a partner or within a mastermind group, be sure to make all these commitments with them.

During the next four weeks, you will set your intent for the following areas of your life:

Home—Family—Mental—Life—Health—Relationships— Spiritual—Wealth

In each section, you will be making *Quality Word* lists for each one of the words assigned for that week. The lists you are doing in this course will be on how you would feel.

If you love doing these lists, then you can do another list on how it would look. You will learn more about Quality Word lists later on in this book.

You might be wondering why we don't start by setting goals in this course and begin instead with intent.

There is nothing wrong with setting goals, but setting them *before* we fully understand what we intend means we are likely to set goals based on an outside picture of how we, or someone else, thinks it should be.

Letting goals be the driving force of our actions will eventually fail because we are beginning from the wrong premise.

The result of not knowing our intent first will not be what we ultimately desire. If for some reason we actually accomplish our goals, usually through shear will power or by luck, we won't be able to enjoy them, or maintain the results of what was often intense labor.

Accomplishing goals from the wrong premise does not bring permanent happiness. Goals set after intents are set become the outcome—or action—of what we began within.

Setting our premise on the spiritual awareness that Divine Love is the only cause and creator, and then acting from that awareness, will always result in increased happiness and harmony.

The work is in *The Shift of Perception*, not in the use of human willpower.

Ready? Here we go!

68

— · —

THREE QUESTIONS

To begin this course, ask yourself these three questions.

Don't answer them the way you think you are supposed to answer, or how you think it should be, or how you think others want you to be. Instead, begin by listening within, and answer these questions honestly.

Remember, *The Intent Course* is for you, and only you. Be honest with yourself. It's the first place to begin anything.

Although these are important questions, don't take too much time to think about them, just go from the heart.

Even if you do this course over and over again, answer these questions again. You will be at a new point in your life, and these answers will change.

As you do this shift of perception for yourself, I promise you that everyone and everything in your life will benefit from the choices you make from your clear intent.

Be patient. Trust in the fact that the universe has your best interests at heart, and is always ready to fulfill your intents. Pay attention though, because often it will look different from you thought it would look, but it will always be the perfect outcome.

1. In a few sentences, describe how you see yourself.

2. How do you think others see you?

3. What do you most want to get out of this intent course?

69

— . —

COMMIT TO YOURSELF

The peak efficiency of coming from pure intuition and pure intent makes conflict and disharmony altogether unnecessary and not existent. — Delbert Piper, Sr.

Are you ready to begin? Make a commitment to yourself that you will fully do each week's assignment.

This will be the first commitment of many commitments you will make for yourself. We will spend the next twenty-eight days setting completely conscious intents that will last a lifetime.

As you make these commitments, you will discover how you feel about requirements. Just observe and keep notes about those feelings, remember no judgments, just observe.

Begin by setting your overall intent for this course.

Begin with the intent and decision that this is for you, not for anyone else.

You are not doing *The Intent Course* to get good grades, pass tests, make someone proud, prove yourself to anyone, or any other reason that we tend to do things, especially when taking classes.

This is for you. It is all about you. Yes, I will keep saying this, that's how important it is!

Stop now and write the answer to this statement:

This Is My Overall Intent For *The Intent Course*:

Now that you have stated your intent, we can begin.

Pause a moment to realize that you can expect to experience a fuller, happy, and more peaceful life just by shifting your perception, and that is what you will be doing in this course.

If you are working with a partner, or partners, in your own mastermind, please share a little about your intent for this course with each other. Share what you learned about yourself just by deciding to do this course and by writing your intent.

If you are doing this course by yourself, write a note to yourself as if you were sharing with someone else.

70

— • —

PERCEPTION AND QUALITY WORDS

The shift that we are doing in *The Intent Course* is a perception shift. It's very important to have an understanding of perception, so let's take a moment and talk about it.

There are two modes of perception—*state of mind and point of view*.

Once we understand that all we have to do to change the quality of the life we experience, is shift both our state of mind and point of view perceptions, our lives become much easier—or not—depending on how much we love our current state of mind and point of view perceptions and how willing we are to part with them.

Point of view and state of mind are intertwined. We can't have one without the other. However, there are some generalities that we can make. If our state of mind is in an *emotion* (as opposed to feeling) then it will be harder to shift our point of view.

Since the law is *what we perceive to be reality magnifies,* then determining, and then shifting, what we perceive to be reality becomes a priority.

In this book, we will uncover some points of view that have limited you. In addition, you will find a variety of tools that you can use to shift your state of mind. If you wish to spend more time in the area of shifting perceptions, I have other books that may be helpful that you can find at .

For this book, we will focus on one of the most powerful tools you can use to shift both your point of view and state of mind at the same time. It's simple, easy, and extremely effective. We are going to make and use, Quality Word lists.

This leads to the question, what are qualities? In our small r reality they are the description of what we want in our lives narrowed down from many words, to one or two words.

For example: Let's say that we want a new car. Usually, what we think we want in a new car is determined by someone else's intent, either unintentionally or intentionally, as in advertising.

This time, instead of just popping on down to the nearest showroom and buying what we think we want, let's begin with quality words, and that will lead us to a more conscious intent and a far better outcome.

If we choose to do the Quality Word lists on how we would feel if we had our car, we might list words like: happy, wealthy, safe, calm, excited, adventurous, secure, etc.

The next step is to put the Quality Word list in order. This is just as important, and maybe even more important, than making the list in the first place.

This is because when we first make our Quality Word lists, the words will arrive willy-nilly off the top of our heads—engaging our intellect, or our thinking mind. This thinking mind is what the worldview has trained us to pay attention to first, and that training has it backwards.

In *The Shift*, we first pay attention to the inner voice, the still small voice, the heart, the gut, our intuition, or the feminine principle, and then engage the thinking mind. This will lead to an action that organically grows from beginning within.

437

This is why we always need someone else to help us put our lists in order. It allows us to listen and feel, not think.

If we don't get the list in order, then our thinking will run the show, which is almost always counter to our true feelings. As you can imagine, this will not bring lasting happiness.

After making Quality Word lists, we often discover that we really don't want what we thought we wanted.

Once I did a list for a new car, and after putting my list in order, I realized that all the qualities I listed were really met by my walking, which is exactly what I happily did for the next four years.

In the big R Reality, quality words are actually describing God, divine Mind, infinite Love, Soul, or Spirit. No matter what you call It, the substance of It is qualities.

This awareness is exciting, because it means that as we focus on turning what appears to be things—which exist outside of ourselves—back into thoughts, we are actually becoming aware of their true substance, the substance of the Divine.

Please note: Quality words are never comparison words. We don't use them to compare what we have, or don't have now. We always develop quality words from how it would feel to have the perfect idea. We always begin from the inside out.

71

—— • ——

TOOLS FOR SHIFTING STATES OF MIND

We have a few phrases that you will encounter as you work through this course that need a bit of explanation.

DIRT TIME

This is a phrase developed by my husband, Del Piper. All lasting shifts take place within the framework of doing the work, getting dirty so to speak, by being willing to uncover, uproot, and discard.

Dirt Time is just like weeding a garden. As thoughts arrive into our thinking that do not state and represent Truth, we weed them out.

We practise *Dirt Time* as we practise *Replacement Thinking*. This is where we replace all thoughts that do not begin with the correct premise of One Mind, with those that do.

PAUSE OBSERVE LISTEN OR POL

This is exactly what it sounds like. Take the time to pause, observe, and listen. This is not about judgement, it is about awareness and observation. Observation does not lead to judgement but to dissolving.

If what you observe is not in line with One Mind, which is Love, then it is not True. The trick is to continue to stay in Truth while observing what isn't true, and then to throw Love and Truth on it until it dissolves like the wicked witch in the Wizard Of Oz.

This is not positive thinking! Positive thinking covers up and hides negative thinking. *The Shift* uncovers and dissolves.

439

As we dissolve what isn't true, we can hear the still quiet mind instead of the monkey mind that runs human thinking. As a result, we experience more and more of the true peace and harmony of Life.

Del tells the true story of a young man whose dream was to see a fox in the wild. He practised Dirt Time and used tools like Pause Observe Listen to still his mind and eliminate human worldview thinking.

One day while he was walking a trail in the forest, a grey fox jumped out of the bushes that lay ahead on the trail.

The fox shook himself, looked down the trail and began walking toward the young man as if he wasn't there.

Keeping a still, quiet mind, the young man continued down the path toward the fox.

Just as they passed each other, this young man had the beginning of the thought, "Wait until I tell ..." Just as he had this thought, the fox stopped in his tracks, turned and looked at him with bared teeth.

As he began to think, the young man became visible to the fox.

With many hours of Dirt Time behind him, the young man was able to immediately replace that thought with nothing but a calm, still mind. As he shifted out of thinking, the fox no longer saw him and they both continued down the path.

Stop thinking, and end your problems. —Lao Tzu

CALM STABILITY COUNTDOWN

This countdown is also what it sounds like. It is a tool used to calm yourself down or calm your state of mind.

It sounds simple, but is often hard to do because of the many distracting thoughts residing within, and as, our thinking. The monkey mind will become easier and easier to dissolve, the more we practice this technique.

You can do this in a quiet spot, or in any situation you find yourself in, from traffic to conversations. Start with a ten-to-one countdown.

Begin by breathing in, not with your shoulders, but with your diaphragm and through your nose. As you breathe out, say to yourself, "ten." Breathe in, breathe out, and say to yourself, "nine." Continue to one. If at any time you are distracted, start again.

360 DEGREE SOFT VISION

This is another of Del's state of mind tools for you to use. Once again, it can be used in your quiet time, or anytime during the day. The intent is to be able to see and feel, all around you at all times.

Hold your hands outstretched to the side of you and move them to where you can just see them while still looking forward. This is your side expanded soft vision. Imagine doing the same over your head and down under your feet.

This is a skill that Indian Scouts perfected. They were able to see everything going on around them at all times. When something caught their attention, they would switch to a focused view to see what it was, and then back out to the expanded view.

We are trained in tunnel vision or automatic vision. We can only see what is right in front of us, or what we expect to see, or have always seen. We miss everything else.

Using the 360 Soft Vision tool, you will begin to see what is already present. You will expand your point of view while stilling your state of mind.

As you practise this, you will discover that what was hidden becomes present and practical in your life.

You will see what was already present, but were blind to it because of your perception. Expecting to see what is already present becomes a habit that reaps practical results.

One of our coaching clients was practising 360 Soft Vision while calling on one of his clients. As he went to meet him, he realized that although he had the paperwork he needed, he didn't have a pen.

Using Replacement Thinking, he immediately stated the Truth that everything he needed was always present. At that moment, something caught his eye. He noticed that the plant he was standing beside had a pen stuck in the dirt. He pulled it out, wrote with it, and returned it to the plant for someone else to use.

I had something just like this happen to me. I was going to a client, and had forgotten a pen. Instead of being upset with myself for being disorganized, I went back to the correct point of view, that there is only one infinite Mind, and It is always providing.

I had the idea to stop at the post office to pick up my mail on the way to my appointment. In the mailbox was an envelope with a pen in it. It even had my company name on it since it was an advertisement for ordering the pen. It was perfect. It was immediate, and it was very practical.

72

— · —

Week One Assignments

O K, we are ready to officially begin. We are beginning with a Quality Word list for *home* and *family*. Settle into a nice quiet place and get ready to shift!

Dirt Time Assignments

1. Do Quality Word lists for home and family. You will find the worksheets after this assignment.

2. After completing the lists, find a partner to put each of your quality words into order.

No, you can't do this yourself. Someone else has to ask you the questions. Read the next chapter in this book called *How To Do Quality Word Lists.*

Then complete the worksheets by putting the words in order on the lines provided.

3. Combine the two top words from your quality lists into an I am statement. You would say this: "I am _____" completing this phrase with the top two quality words from your list. For example, *I am joyfully ordered.*

Repeat this sentence to yourself multiple times during the day. *Feel* what it means.

4. Use all your quality words to help write the story of your life as if you were living fully from your intents.

5. Do one thing every day that you don't want to do. You will find lots of ideas as you do your homework sheets.

Don't think too hard about this. Just find one thing to do and do it. Put your clothes away, make a phone call, take a walk, complete a task. Anything that you have been putting off, go do it—now!

6. Practice: Calm, Stability, Countdowns from Ten to One.

7. Practice: Pause, Observe, Listen. Do this often during the day.

8. Begin a new habit of 360 Soft Vision to replace automatic vision or tunnel vision.

9. Take thirty minutes a day to sit quietly and practise these tools.

10. Take action from that calm, still, inside, insightful state of mind.

Notes:

73

— • —

How To Do Quality Words

The point of doing Quality Word lists is not to get more things. Why? Because things are the outcome of what we perceive within and will appear as needed in our lives as we learn how to listen, and follow the guidance from within first.

Our intent is to understand more about the true substance of what appears as people, places, and things. Since everything in big R Reality is composed of qualities, we must learn the skill of translating back into qualities the things we desire to see, or have, in order to become conscious of what is already present.

How To Do Quality Word Lists

Step 1: Take a moment and list eight to ten qualities of something you want to see, or have. Use one word to express each quality. If you are using sentences, you have not come to the heart of it.

Step 2: Choose the style of list you will do. In this course, you are concentrating on making lists of how you would *feel* if you had the perfect expression of what you want.

However, there are two kinds of Quality Word lists. You can either list the qualities of the thing itself—how it looks—or you can list the qualities of how you will feel when you have it.

For example, let's pretend you want to buy a new car. Your quality list for how this thing—or car—would *look* might contain words such as red, fast, inexpensive, big, compact, spacious, etc.

If you choose to do a Quality Word list of how you will *feel* when you drive this car, it might have words like wealthy, secure, free, joyful, and so on.

In the beginning, just do how it would *feel* lists. Use the *how it would look* list as additional information.

Step 3: Now that you have the quality list, the next step is to put these qualities in order.

Why is this important?

Have you ever been at a place in your life where nothing happens towards what you want, no matter what you do? This is most likely because you have a quality, or value, block.

If you have two values that feel equal to you, your core-self will be confused as to which one to provide. Continuing with the car example, let's say you list the qualities of luxury and frugal.

Until you know which quality is first, you'll be stuck and nothing will happen. This is because at first glance they appear to be conflicting. However, once your list is in order you can receive, or see, all of what you have listed.

You need help to put the list in order. Have someone else take your list and help you. **Don't look at your list while this person is working with you, as this will engage brain and logic.** What we want to engage is your heart and inspiration.

The person with your list will ask you the following question: "Which is more important to you?" Then they will give you two words on the list to compare.

It is imperative that the person asking not give any verbal or physical cues, or pre-decide in their own mind what your answer will be. This is the time for both of you to practice a still, calm, state of mind.

When answering, don't listen to anything except your inner voice, and respond with that answer. Don't argue with it. If you are unable to choose one as more important than the other, the person should ask you, "Which one can you not live without?"

Notice that your mind tells you that if you choose one, you might not get the other. This is coming from the point of view that there is never enough and that you don't deserve everything you want.

Since neither statement is true, just notice these thoughts and move on.

The truth is, once you are clear about what you desire to see, you will be able to see and experience all these qualities.

Each word must be compared with every word until you have an ordered list. You will probably be surprised at the order if you have stayed with your heart and trusted your answers.

How to Use Quality Word Lists

1. Use the qualities as a filter.

If something appears that you think might be what you are looking for and does not have at least the first four qualities—in order—it is not "it."

Think of the time you will save if you can eliminate quickly and easily what is not right for you. For example, you find that the word safety is first on your Quality Word list for a means of transportation, and the car you are looking at has a very low safety record; don't buy this car no matter how much you love it.

If you buy it, you will eventually be unhappy with it, and you will consciously or unconsciously figure out how to get rid of it.

2. See the qualities everywhere.

See the qualities in everything, not just in what you're seeking. Notice that they're always with you in many forms. You have always had, and always will have, each quality on your list if you just look. A quality does not have to belong to you. It can appear anywhere. All of what you see is your world.

The goal is to notice that the quality you're looking for already exists everywhere, and since you can see it—it exists for you—now.

This practice expands your concept of what the quality actually means, and as a result expands the potential outcomes.

3. BE GRATEFUL FOR EACH QUALITY AS YOU SEE IT.

Be grateful for these qualities each time you see them, no matter where they occur.

Even if the person you dislike the most has one of these qualities, be grateful that you have seen this quality in your life. Know that if it is "out there" it was first "within here" and therefore always available in the most appreciable form for the moment.

4. BE, AND LIVE, THESE QUALITIES YOURSELF.

Now that you have begun to understand the substance of qualities, no longer is having the thing you want so important.

You realize that it already exists as ideas—qualities.

As we express gratitude, we are living within divine Grace. The result? Sometimes we realize we don't actually need the thing we were asking to see, or it turns up in another package, or it appears in a way greater than we could have dreamed.

Whichever way this happens, we have begun with seeking the kingdom of God First. Beginning with this perfect intent cannot help but produce in our world whatever we need at the moment. We have always had it. We have never been abandoned, nor could we ever be in the future.

Looking for qualities opens your eyes to what has always been, and always will be, yours.

Note: This chapter on Quality Lists is an excerpt from the God First chapter in my book *Living in Grace: The Shift To Spiritual Perception*. And if you would like to hear and see how to do a Quality Word list, check the resource chapter of this book to find where you can do that.

74

—·—

HOME QUALITY WORDS

I desire to be conscious of: *My perfect idea of home*

These are the qualities of how it would *feel* if I were living in the perfect home:

1. _____
2. _____
3. _____
4. _____
5. _____
6._____
7. _____
8. _____
9. _____
10. _____

Get together with your partner and put this Quality Word list into order.

These are the feel qualities of *home* in order

1._____
2._____
3. _____

4. _____

5. _____

6. _____

7. _____

8. _____

9. _____

10. _____

Dirt Time Assignments

My top quality word for home is:

Is this currently my intent for home?

Take your top quality word and write a sentence using this word stating your intent.

Take the second quality word and write a sentence using this word stating your intent.

What are three action steps that you can take for your intent for Home?

1.

2.

3.

Take one of these action steps and write three to do's for it.

1.

2.

3.

What is stopping you from living from and as your intent?

Write a story about your life as if you were living fully from this intent.

75

— • —

FAMILY QUALITY WORDS

I desire to be conscious of: *a perfect idea of family*

    These are the qualities of how it would *feel* if I had the perfect family. (Don't think of the family you have right now, or one you know. Just list how it would feel to you if you had the perfect family.)

1. _____
2. _____
3. _____
4. _____
5. _____
6. _____
7. _____
8. _____
9. _____
10. _____

Get together with your partner and put this Quality Word list into order.

    These are the feel qualities of *family* in order

1. _____
2. _____
3. _____

4. _____
5. _____
6. _____
7. _____
8. _____
9. _____
10. _____

Dirt Time Assignments

My top quality word for family is:

Is this currently my intent for family?

Take your top quality word and write a sentence using this word stating your intent.

Take the second quality word and write a sentence using this word stating your intent.

What are three action steps that you can take for your intent for Family?

1.
2.
3.

Take one of these action steps and write three to do's for it.

1.
2.
3.

What is stopping you from living from and as your intent?

Write a story about your life as if you were living fully from this intent.

76

— • —

WEEK ONE FOLLOW UP

*W*e've all been conditioned to believe the external is more
important than the internal. Now we know it is just the
opposite. —Bill Bryson, *A Short History Of Nearly Everything*

After completing this first week, there was a common thread
among many of those who took *The Intent Course* with Del and me.
Almost everyone felt discombobulated, or weird, or disconnected.
This may happen to you as you begin to completely shift your
perception.

Here's a short story that may help explain this phenomenon.

While I was in college (way back when) my ballet teacher suggested
that we should all be Rolfed, which I did.

In each of the ten sessions, a different area of the body is deeply
massaged to break down and dissolve tension and scar tissue. For me
it was symbolic of dissolving the pain of past history, just as we are
doing in this *Intent Course.*

When I returned to ballet class after every Rolfing session, I was
a completely discombobulated! I would jump up and literally fall
down—splat onto the floor, run into walls, bump into myself. All
the muscles had rearranged themselves and it took awhile to live from
this newly arranged me.

It's the same thing with shifting. You are totally rearranged! You will see people, places, and things differently, and will respond to them differently. Stay in the awareness of the One Intelligent Mind and keep your intents, and soon the world outside will rearrange itself to fit the new you.

It is helpful to know this is not how it will always be when you shift. Today, I get Rolfed periodically and experience none of these side effects. Soon shifting will become the way you live, and that makes all the difference.

There is a common pattern of getting relief and then getting stuck. Always go back to Truth, otherwise habit will kick in to "fix" the stuck in a not-so-divine way. Complete relief comes from Truth. It's true as stated by Jesus the Christ, *And ye shall know the truth and the truth shall make you free.—Bible:* John 8:32

It's easy to act as if you are a weather vane, always changing your beliefs and words, trying to please everyone around you. But you were born to be lighthouses, not weather vanes.—Robert Cooper

As you continue *The Intent Course*, remember to begin and end from the correct premise of One Mind. Realize that you are already the qualities that you have chosen.

We are letting go of our collection of beliefs and perceptions that have driven our lives, mostly unconsciously.

As you do the *I am* part of your assignments, pay attention to the fact that the statement of *I am* is both an absolute being and an action statement.

It's the small things in life that bring us forward into Truth, and it is the small things that attempt to keep us locked in the prison of habitual thoughts of what isn't actually true at all.

This is why we concentrate on doing those small things! I often use the symbol of cleaning closets. When you take it all out, things look a mess. When you put it back in you throw away all that you no longer need, and a beautiful order remains. Don't be afraid of the mess if it comes. It is not who you are.

As you make this shift, some of it will feel easy, and some of it might feel difficult. There will be things that pop up into your awareness that have always been there, but you didn't notice before. Sometimes these are the things that will attempt to stop your escape into freedom.

The most important action you can take each day is doing your intent assignments.

Don't let the outside worldview and its intent override yours. When you find that you have, laugh it off, move on, and get back to it. No stories—just intent!

.....*nothing to matter whatsoever. Everything out there is an illusion. The only thing going on out there, is what is going on in here.*—Bill Bryson, *A Short History of Nearly Everything*.

As you continue to clarify your intent, it becomes clear why focusing on quality words and then putting them in order is important. As you do these assignments, it may be surprising how many hidden habits and patterns crop up to interfere with your dissolving of what isn't true about you so that your entire life can be in line with your pure intent.

The assignments in this course are not for teachers, as they were in school. They are entirely for you. They are designed to reach into every nook and cranny of your thinking and shift it. The quality word assignments will saturate your thinking with what is True. Isn't that a wonderful idea?

Sometimes, past habits and thoughts don't want to be shifted. Actually, most of the time they don't. It means that the end is near for them. However, for you, this is a time for rejoicing, because those habits and thoughts are not you!

If you feel like running and hiding, this is normal. Hang in there. It will pass, and you will feel lighter and freer than ever before.

As you shift your perception and begin all of your thinking and actions from Truth, then what isn't True stands out clearly.

I call this discovering *the monster under the bed.*

It's been hiding there all along. We've been careful not to live our life completely, just in case there is a monster that we don't want to "get us."

Stating the Truth is in effect calling out the monster and saying, "Show yourself, I am tired of being afraid of something and not knowing what you are."

Here's the tricky part. When it shows itself, and it will, it now knows that you have seen it and that it is facing the end of itself.

So what does it do?

It moves to the second stage of attack and attaches itself to you. It does this by telling you all the things you have done to create it. It tells you that it is your fault that it exists.

If you agree to this, you have done two things. First, you have stepped out of the One Mind and into the duality of the worldview. Your premise, your point of view, has become that there can be something other than omnipotent Love.

The second thing you have done is agreed to suffer for something you have never done. I am not telling you to ignore the problem. I am telling you to call it out and then throw it out because in One Mind there is no monster.

The *Bible* tells the story of Daniel in the lion's den. When he was thrown into the cage with the lions, he could have started telling that second story to himself. Perhaps he could have thought he should have kept his mouth shut, should have given up the premise of One God—lots of "should of's." But he didn't.

He declared his innocence and knew why it was true. The result—he was unharmed.

Del tells the story of one of his teachers, Twyla Nitsch. While visiting her home, they started talking about the sweat lodges that

456

he was leading. She told him that she would be willing to come to one, but if it got too hot, she was leaving.

She no longer felt the need to suffer.

This completely shifted Del's thinking about everything he was doing, including how hot he made sweat lodges. She was right. We are not made to, or need to, suffer to learn.

When we find ourselves in situations where the worldview is that suffering is required, we simply don't agree with that point of view.

I know that we have been taught that we learn best by suffering. But do you think this is something that Divine Love would do to itself?

Learn from what you have suffered, but don't make it an action of Love or a requirement for Grace. We only suffer while in our false perceptions. When we let them go, the suffering goes, too.

Here's a brief story of not accepting the second stage of the monster and the result of not agreeing to suffer.

Once, Del was delivering firewood to one of his clients when it started to snow heavily. His client's house was located far outside of town on a hill. By the time he arrived, the snow had covered the entrance to the little driveway to the home.

Wanting to deliver the load, Del backed the truck into what he thought was the driveway and ended up with a wheel in the ditch.

That monster under the bed, the voice in our head, the monkey mind, was immediately present, trying to convince him that there would be no help coming for a while. It was going to be a long cold wait, and he should have known better.

Instead, Del chose to know that help is always present. This was long before cell phones, so there was no way to call for help. However, he told his son, who was riding with him, to wait in the truck because someone would come around shortly.

He stepped outside and leaned against the truck. Within a few minutes, a large tow truck appeared out of nowhere and pulled them out.

Another thing that happens when we study Truth is that we often find ways to hide from doing the work. It's not really us hiding, it's what claims to be us hiding. We can find ourselves extra busy and not realize that is the same as running away.

Of course, we know this is a lot of work! But, hey—either choose this point of view, or try to make things happen on the outside. Try for years. Get discouraged. Or do this homework and eliminate years of doing things the hard way.

Do this and dissolve the past—which is only your perception of it, not what actually happened. Instead, begin to live as Light.

Looked at it that way, this is easy, and certainly more fun! Joy filled is who you are!

Dirt Time Assignments

As you work into these next assignments, notice where you appear to be stuck. During the day, are you doing the practice of Pause, Observe, Listen?

Before you begin your second week, take the time to answer these few questions. It will help you take part with an awareness, which adds to the power of this course.

If you are working within a mastermind group, share what happened with your intent and your homework. If you are working alone, still share, but with yourself.

What did you learn this week?

What was most confusing?

What happened in the "outside" world as a result of your intent this week?

Did you put off doing the assignments because you thought you didn't know how?

Did you do the assignments as given, or did you rearrange them to suit you?

Is this how you "do" life?

If so, are you willing to change it?

77

— · —

WEEK TWO ASSIGNMENT

T his week we are doing the Quality Word lists for *mental* and *life*. Remember to start from the standpoint and premise of perfection! Think of the word mental as if you have a perfect mental state of mind.

DIRT TIME ASSIGNMENTS

1. Do Quality Word lists for *mental* and *life*. You will find the worksheets after this assignment.

2. After completing the lists, find a partner to put each of your quality words into order.

Remember, you can't do this yourself. Someone else has to ask you the questions. Reread the chapter *How To Do Quality Word Lists*. Then complete the worksheets, putting the words in order on the lines provided.

3. Combine the two top words from your Quality Word lists into an *I am* statement. You would say this: *I am*_____ completing this phrase with the top two quality words from your list. For example, *I am Lovingly Calm.*

Repeat this sentence to yourself multiple times during the day. Feel what it means.

4. Use all your quality words to help write the story of your life as if you were living fully from your intents.

5. Do one thing every day that you don't want to do. Don't think too hard about this.

Don't make it something profound. Don't get caught up in the details of it. Don't worry about what has to happen next. Just do something that you have been putting off doing and do it now!

6. Practice: Calm Stability Countdowns from Ten to One.

7. Practice: Pause, Observe, Listen. Do often during the day.

8. Begin a new habit of 360 Soft Vision to replace automatic vision or tunnel vision.

9. Take thirty minutes a day to sit quietly and practice these tools.

10. Take action from that calm, still, inside, insightful state of mind.

Notes:

78

— · —

MENTAL QUALITY WORDS

I desire to be conscious of: *a perfect state of mind*

These are the qualities of how it would feel:

1. _____
2. _____
3. _____
4. _____
5. _____
6. _____
7. _____
8. _____
9. _____
10. _____

With your partner and put this Quality Word list into order.
These are the feel qualities of *mental* in order

1. _____
2. _____
3. _____
4. _____
5. _____
6. _____
7. _____

8. _____
9. _____
10. _____

DIRT TIME ASSIGNMENTS

My top quality word for mental is:

Is this currently my intent for my Mental State?

Take your top quality word and write a sentence using this word stating your intent.

Take the second quality word and write a sentence using this word stating your intent.

What are three action steps that you can take for your intent for Mental?
1.
2.
3.
Take one of these action steps and write Three to do's for it.
1.
2.
3.
What is stopping you from living from and as your intent?
Write a story about your life as if you were living fully from this intent.

79

— • —

LIFE QUALITY WORDS

I desire to be conscious of: *a perfect life*

These are the qualities of how it would feel:

1. _____
2. _____
3. _____
4. _____
5. _____
6. _____
7. _____
8. _____
9. _____
10. _____

Get together with your partner and put this Quality Word list into order.

These are the feel qualities of *life* in order

1. _____
2. _____
3. _____
4. _____

5. _____
6. _____
7. _____
8. _____
9. _____
10. _____

DIRT TIME ASSIGNMENTS

My top quality word for life is:

Is this currently my intent for life?

Take your top quality word and write a sentence using this word stating your intent.

Take the second quality word and write a sentence using this word stating your intent.

What are three action steps that you can take for your intent for Life?
1.
2.
3.
Take one of these action steps and write three to do's for it.
1.
2.
3.
What is stopping you from living from and as your intent?
Write a story about your life as if you were living fully from this intent.

80

— • —

WEEK TWO FOLLOW UP

There is no point in living our lives behind a facade of untruths. It takes a tremendous amount of work and effort to hide. Each of us has the Spiritual authority to choose to live our lives as the action of Truth and the quality words that we are discovering.

There is no longer any reason to be afraid of living as we really are, the action and expression of the Infinite One.

We can tell the Truth at all times, knowing that this will shift our lives to good, and never to an outcome that doesn't bless everyone involved. This decision takes faith, but not a blind faith in something we don't understand. It is a faith that the Principles found in Divine Love never fail.

It takes commitment and dedication to make the shift to spiritual perception, and I honor you for your willingness to do what it takes, despite the noise of the worldview.

Remember to always go back to the Truth of One Mind, which is infinite Love. Habit will kick in to fix what isn't working in a not-divine way. Permanent relief comes from Truth.

It's so important to remember that you already are the qualities that you are choosing. If you have my book *Living in Grace: The Shift to Spiritual Perception*, read the *God First* chapter about what to do with your lists. Otherwise, refer to the chapter in this book on *How To Do Quality Word Lists*.

Pay attention to the *I am* part of the homework. Make this in an important part of your day. Notice that the statement *I am* is both an absolute being and an action statement. Hold to these statements, say them often to yourself, and they will bring you both comfort and courage.

A very important part of this shift is calming our state of mind. The Calm, Stability, Countdown is one tool we can use any time of the day or night, no matter what we are doing.

Sometimes it is useful to take the time to do a deeper countdown. Never use a formula or make it a ritual. However, here is one way to do a countdown from fifty-to-one.

Start at fifty, and with each exhale, softly say the number to yourself. Keep starting over until you can count down to one without drifting to thinking, or get distracted and forget where you are.

Once you are at one, and in a completely calm state of mind, take a journey down a path to a stairway. What the path and the stairway look like is entirely up to you, don't try to figure it out, just let it be as it appears to you.

Go down the stairway and through an arch into a secret or sacred space that belongs only to you. Again, what it looks like is up to you.

As you reside in your secret space, take one of your quality words and feel what it would feel like to be completely filled with and surrounded by this quality. This is the process of Felt-Imagining. Stay as long as you wish, focusing on as many qualities as you wish.

Allow the qualities to become all there is, both within and without. When you are finished, walk back out. Go through the arch, back up the stairs and up the path.

This a process of going deep into Divine Feminine, the intuition, the still small voice, and really listening to what it is, and what it is telling you and how it feels to be it.

It is important to walk back out for many reasons, but one very important one is it takes you to action and the true male of *manhood*.

This is why I keep stressing taking action on what you hear within.

Most of us rarely access our true manhood. Most of us act from the counterfeit male which doesn't listen to the feminine and instead tries to control and suppress it.

We are all clear about the disastrous results of the ego, counterfeit male, in action.

It is true manhood that protects, and nurtures based on the divine feminine's directions.

DIRT TIME ASSIGNMENTS

If you are working within a mastermind group, share what happened with your intent and your homework. If you are working alone, still share, but with yourself.

Where are you stuck?

What have you learned so far and then put into action?

What is most confusing?

What happened in the "outside" world as a result of your intent this week?

what did you discover about yourself?

Is what you discovered True or a lie about you?

Are you willing to let go?

81

— • —

WEEK THREE ASSIGNMENTS

This week we begin studying the concept I call, *What I can't stop myself from doing.* This concept is covered in more depth in our other programs, but this overview will be helpful for you.

This is the "thing" that you do no matter how many times it "gets you in trouble." It is what you do even when others, or even yourself, have asked you to stop doing it.

When we first start talking about this concept most people think about things they can't stop doing that are negative habits. This is not what is meant by this. We are not talking about the habits that you want to stop like smoking, or eating, or drinking too much.

I am referring to your USB, your *Unique Spiritual Blessing.* This is what you are, and do, and can't stop yourself from doing no matter how hard you might try, just as a rose can never stop behaving like a rose.

Yes, it often does show up in negative actions because either we don't understand who we are, or we wish we weren't what we see.

However, in its real state our USB is never a negative concept. Once we understand and begin to live our USB, the negative goes away revealing what has always been True. It is a blessing to share.

The fundamental delusion of humanity is to suppose that I am here and you are out there.—Yasutani Roshi, Zen master

This quote really expands an intent behind what we are doing in The Intent Course. We are discovering our own perceived reality by listening and understanding others, because the others are us.

Following that line of thought, please review how you are dealing with your partner if you are working with one in this course, or with another partner in your life. Ask yourself, "Is this how I deal with partners in life, from business to personal?"

Did you act and respond from your quality list? How did you feel about how your partner dealt with you?

If you are not sure how you acted with your partner, go ahead and ask. Please be willing to respond and listen in kindness, knowing that we are all staying in the knowledge that each of us is the unique action of the One Mind and that anything else will dissolve away as it is uncovered.

Everything we do in life involves a partner. Sometimes it is just a quick partnership with the check out clerk at the grocery store, and others are lifetime companion partners. Working with partners in *The Intent Course* reveals our point of view, our habits and patterns about partnerships, and that will shift every partnership in our lives.

As you review your work for the past two weeks, ask yourself, "Where am I stuck?" Everyone is stuck somewhere, where are you stuck?

How did your countdown from ten-to-one, or fifty-to-one go, or did you not even get to doing it. How are you doing with your worksheets? Bring all of this "stuck-ness out" so you can let it all go.

Notice that when you are stuck, the world seems stuck. Actually, often we look out in the world and see that other people are stuck, but don't notice that we are the ones that are stuck in a point of view or state of mind perception.

If we want to un-stick the world, we must begin within, and with an awareness of who we are and what is True.

What is True is that there are not two universes, one material and one spiritual.

There is just one, and it is spiritual. In this course we are in the process of training ourselves to look through what appears to be material and see the One, which is spiritual.

In the material, or physical point of view of the universe, we are always cycling between good and bad. You know this. How many times have you said to yourself, "Things have been going so good, it will get bad soon," or visa versa, "It's been so bad that the only way is up"?

There are no answers in the material universe although we look for them all the time. In that state of mind, or point of view perception there are only questions that lead to more questions and chaos, perhaps ordered chaos, but always chaos.

In the Spiritual One Universe there is neither here nor there, a ping-pong, or a cycle. There are no shadows where light shines directly, which is exactly what Love does. It shines directly.

As the *Bible* says, *Every good gift and every perfect gift is from above, and cometh down from the Father of lights, with whom is no variableness, neither shadow of turning.* —James 1:17

Paying attention to these questions helps you know what has been going on for you.

By this week in *The Intent Course* many people are feeling that they have reached a week of upheaval, and change. Of course, in a way that is absolutely true. You are shifting. Yes! That is what it is all about, shifting, the good, the bad, and the ugly of it.

However, the results are always beautiful and perfect because that is what you are, and have always been. What we have been doing is extinguishing the stirring mind and polishing the shining mind as discussed in the book *Taoist Classics*.

Let's choose to walk in Truth, and give up the story about our life, which is only that, a story that we tell, and often cherish.

Are you ready? Here we go with the homework for this third week. Don't stop now, you are on the home stretch for living as you intend to live.

This week we are doing the Quality Word lists for Health and Relationships. Remember to start from the standpoint and premise of perfection!

Answer these questions, as the first part of this week's assignments.

My intent for working with my Mastermind group and/or myself this week is:

Last week, did I fulfill my intent?

what Am I Observing?

DIRT TIME ASSIGNMENTS

1. Do Quality Word lists for Health and Relationships.

2. After completing the list, find a partner to put each of your quality words into order.

3. Combine the two top words from your Quality Word lists into an *I am* statement.

You would say this: "I am _____" completing this phrase with the top two quality words from your list. For example, *I am Joyfully Ordered*. Don't forget to actually use these sentences throughout the day!

4. Use all your quality words to help write the story of your life as if you were living fully from your intents.

5. Do one thing every day that you don't want to do. You will find lots of ideas as you do your homework sheets. This week, write down what you did.

Remember, the size of what you did doesn't matter. It's the fact that you did it! Remove one twig at a time and let the river flow! You can list what you do each day here, or a piece of paper, tablet, or in your workbook.

It's easy to forget what has been good in your life, let's reverse that habit!

Day 1

Day 2

Day 3

Day 4

Day 5

Day 6

Day 7

6. Practice: Calm Stability Countdowns from ten to one, or fifty to one.

7. Practice: Pause, Observe, Listen. Do often during the day.

8. Begin a new habit of 360 Soft Vision to replace automatic vision or tunnel vision.

9. Take thirty minutes a day to sit quietly and practice these tools.

10. Take action from that calm, still, inside, insightful, state of mind.

Notes:

82

— • —

HEALTH QUALITY WORDS

I desire to be conscious of: *perfect health*

    These are the qualities of how it would *feel:*

1. _____
2. _____
3. _____
4. _____
5. _____
6. _____
7. _____
8. _____
9. _____
10. _____

Get together with your partner and put this Quality Word list into order.

These are the feel qualities of *health* in order

1. _____
2. _____
3. _____
4. _____

5. _____
6. _____
7. _____
8. _____
9. _____
10. _____

DIRT TIME ASSIGNMENTS

My top quality word for Health is:

Is this currently my intent for health?

Take your top quality word and write a sentence using this word stating your intent.

Take the second quality word and write a sentence using this word stating your intent.

What are three action steps that you can take for your intent for Health?
1.
2.
3.
Take one of these action steps and write three to do's for it.
1.
2.
3.
What is stopping you from living from and as your intent?
Write a story about your life as if you were living fully from this intent.

83

—·—

RELATIONSHIP QUALITY WORDS

I desire to be conscious of: *perfect relationships*

These are the qualities of how it would feel:

1. _____
2. _____
3. _____
4. _____
5. _____
6._____
7. _____
8. _____
9. _____
10. _____

With your partner put this Quality Word list into order.

These are the feel qualities of relationship in order

1._____
2._____
3. _____
4. _____
5. _____

6. _____
7. _____
8. _____
9. _____
10. _____

DIRT TIME ASSIGNMENTS

My top quality word for Relationship is:

Is this currently my intent for Relationship?

Take your top quality word and write a sentence using this word stating your intent.

Take the second quality word and write a sentence using this word stating your intent.

What are three action steps that you can take for your intent for Relationship?
1.
2.
3.
Take one of these action steps and write three to do's for it.
1.
2.
3.
What is stopping you from living from and as your intent?
Write a story about your life as if you were living fully from this intent.

84

— · —

WEEK THREE FOLLOW UP

A s soon as you trust yourself, you will know how to live. —Goethe

As we finish up this third week of *The Intent Course,* we discover that much of what we are doing is letting go of old beliefs. As we let them go, life becomes easier, although sometimes a bit more messy then usual. (Remember the closet cleaning?)

Whenever the internal dialog stops, the world collapses and extraordinary facets of ourselves surface, as though they had been kept heavily guarded by our words. You are like you are, because you tell yourself that you are that way. —Carlos Castaneda, *Tales Of Power*

Are you also observing your behaviors? Remember that found within what you always do is your USB, your Unique Spiritual Blessing, your unique expression of the One Mind.

In the beginning of this uncovering your USB it may appear to you as the "thing" that is bugging you, or causing discomfort.

Of course, it is never negative, but when we don't recognize ourselves and see the truth behind what is happening, we may think it is a bad thing or we may force it on others rather than living it ourselves. Whatever you see and experience is always a symbol, and symbols are either the Truth or the inversion of Truth.

Once we really know ourselves what will happen? Years ago my youngest daughter asked me that question. She asked what would happen if we finally "got" all Truth completely. Out of my mouth popped the words, "I guess we would just go poof!" Well, that is probably not what would happen, but in one sense it is true.

The worldview is entirely our own perception.

When we are completely shifted back to where there is only One Perception—One Mind, and we have let go of our personality and become completely the individual expression and action of Divine Love—what we perceive will look completely different.

There are not two worlds. Just one. It is Spiritual.

What we perceive as material is really spiritual.

The quality words that we continually work with bring us back to that awareness! We are turning things back into thoughts from which they sprang.

We are not trying to put two universes together, or prepare for a future heaven.

We are shifting perceptions to see that what appears as a material, human universe is in Reality spiritual.

The quality words that we are doing are spiritual. They cannot be measured. They are not energy (which can be). They are the ground of our being, "the force," the words that describe the one Mind, Spirit, God.

As the *Bible* says: *For now we see through a glass, darkly; but then face to face: now I know in part; but then shall I know even as also I am known.*—Cor. 13:12

You are already these qualities. Claim them. Live them. Don't let habit rob you of them.

They demand action, which is sometimes a conscious non-action. They are not passive. It is not sitting around saying, "I am love and therefore everything must be good." It is living Love.

Always starting from within.

Turn around and face the enemy that suggests otherwise. If that suggestion has gotten tired of trying to convince you that matter is real in one way, it may try another approach. Shut the door on its face. Laugh at it.

Never associate this lie with a person, place, or thing. However, if it appears in your life in that form, don't give in to it because you love the person, place, or thing that is suggesting it to you.

Pause, Observe, Listen. The truth of Life is always present, and always the Reality. No matter how loudly unreality screams or how subtle its suggestion, it is still not true.

All that it takes is that shift of perception to see what has always been and always will be present for you. *What you perceive to be reality magnifies!* Magnify what is True!

You are always faced with a situation that is the same as the one that you never resolved —Carlos Castaneda, *The Active Side of Infinity*

It's time to move on to your assignments for week four. I know these assignments can sometimes feel like hard things to do, but the reward is infinite.

If you are having trouble doing them because you are feeling too busy, remind yourself that this is for you to be free. Not busy work. Free work.

Find a way to complete them in your own way. It is all for you! You have completely set yourself outside of "how it was" and that result will shift your entire life.

Keep practicing. Don't go back to that old prison thinking. You have the keys to keep yourself free!

If you do not permit the outward to become the inward, the inward will take care of the outward.—Mary Baker Eddy

As you work into these next assignments notice where you appear to be stuck. During the day are you doing the practice of Pause, Observe, Listen?

If you are working within a mastermind group, share what happened with your intent and your homework. If you are working alone, still share, but with yourself.

Dirt Time Assignments

What did you learn this week?

What was most confusing?

What happened in the "outside" world as a result of your intent this week?

What have you learned so far?

85

— · —

WEEK FOUR ASSIGNMENTS

T hree weeks of intensive shifting done! Just one more week to go!

Do you see the light at the end of this? You are almost done, and the difference this will make in your life will be staggeringly evident for years and years to come.

Take some time before beginning this week's assignment to review your first assignment. Have you fulfilled your intent for this course? What, if anything, would you do differently?

One question to ask yourself is if you were totally engaged in the process—and if not, why not?

How do you see yourself today? How do others see you now?

As always, don't attach to what you observe. Remember, observation only, because in Truth you are the presence of One Mind, always perfect.

Also, if you haven't completed all your assignments, finish them up this week. It will be worth it!

Continue to be present with your assignments. You are doing this for yourself, remember? This week we are doing the Quality Word lists for Spiritual and Wealth.

Remember to start from the standpoint and premise of perfection!

DIRT TIME ASSIGNMENTS

1. Do Quality Word lists for Spiritual and Wealth.

2. After completing the list, find a partner to put each of your quality words into order. Remember, you can't do this yourself. Someone else has to ask you the questions.

3. Combine the two top words from your quality lists into an I am statement. You would say this: "I am_____" completing this phrase with the top two quality words from your list.
For example, *I am Lovingly Calm.*
Use these sentences as affirmations. Imagine what it would feel like to fully understand that they are stating the Truth about you.

4. Use all your quality words to help write the story of your life as if you were living fully from your intents.

5. Do one thing every day that you don't want to do.
Aren't you finding that doing this unlocks many things in your life? You won't experience this result if you don't do that work.

6. Practice: Calm Stability Countdowns.

7. Practice: Pause, Observe, Listen. Do often.

8. Begin a new habit of 360 Soft Vision to replace automatic vision or tunnel vision.

9. Take thirty minutes a day to sit quietly and practice these tools.

10. Take action from that calm, still, inside, insightful state of mind.

Notes:

86

— . —

SPIRITUAL QUALITY WORDS

I desire to be conscious of: *the essence of spirit*

These are the qualities of how it would *feel:*

1. _____
2. _____
3. _____
4. _____
5. _____
6. _____
7. _____
8. _____
9. _____
10. _____

Get together with your partner and put this Quality Word list into order.

These are the *feel* qualities of *spiritual* in order

1. _____
2. _____
3. _____
4. _____

5. _____
6. _____
7. _____
8. _____
9. _____
10. _____

Dirt Time Assignments

My top quality word for spiritual is:

Is this currently my intent for Spiritual?

Take your top quality word and write a sentence using this word stating your intent.

Take the second quality word and write a sentence using this word stating your intent.

What are three action steps that you can take for your intent for Spiritual?
1.
2.
3.
Take one of these action steps and write three to do's for it.
1.
2.
3.
What is stopping you from living from, and as, your intent?
Write a story about your life as if you were living fully from this intent.

87

—•—

WEALTH QUALITY WORDS

I desire to be conscious of: *the essence of wealth*

These are the qualities of how it would *feel*:

1. _____
2. _____
3. _____
4. _____
5. _____
6. _____
7. _____
8. _____
9. _____
10. _____

Get together with your partner and put this Quality Word list into order.

These are the *feel* qualities of wealth in order

1. _____
2. _____
3. _____
4. _____

5. _____
6. _____
7. _____
8. _____
9. _____
10. _____

Dirt Time Assignments

My top quality word for wealth is:

Is this currently my intent for wealth?

Take your top quality word and write a sentence using this word stating your intent.

Take the second quality word and write a sentence using this word stating your intent.

What are three action steps that you can take for your intent for Wealth?
1.
2.
3.
Take one of these action steps and write Three to do's for it.
1.
2.
3.
What is stopping you from living from and as your intent?
Write a story about your life as if you were living fully from this intent.

88

---·---

WEEK FOUR FOLLOW UP

F our weeks! You did it! However, this is just the beginning. Continue with what you have started. Continue to dissolve what isn't True and live as what is!

Remember, don't let fear, or confusion, or secrets pull you away from dancing the dance of your life. I am calling you out to dance on the streets of life with me.

Let the world see the beauty of who you are!

I do have one last assignment for you to wrap all of this work into one quality word that you can carry with you as your own personal guiding star.

In this last assignment, you will take the **top eight words** from the **eight quality lists** that you have done in the past four weeks, and then put those eight words into order.

This will be your *Master Intent List*.

Can you see how valuable this would be? When you write your sentence after doing the list, you will have a statement that describes the current baseline intent for your entire life.

Using your *Master Intent,* you will be able to make quick decisions, and take action knowing that you are remaining on the path you what to take.

Take the time to do this last list, and cap off all your work with this simple way of reminding yourself who you are and what is important to you.

89

— • —

My Master Intent

These are my eight top Quality Words from the previously prepared Quality Word lists.

1. _____
2. _____
3. _____
4. _____
5. _____
6. _____
7. _____
8. _____

Get together with your partner and put this Quality Word list into order.

These are the qualities in order

1. _____
2. _____
3. _____
4. _____
5. _____
6. _____
7. _____

8. _____

DIRT TIME ASSIGNMENTS

Take the top word from this Master Quality List and enter it here as the baseline intent of your life and as the I am statement.

My Baseline Word of Intent For My Life Is:

Take your top quality word and write a sentence using this word stating your intent.

Take the next quality word and write a sentence using this word stating your intent.

Take the top word and the second word on your Master Quality List and combine the two. For example: *I am the Awareness of Light.*

Or, take the top word on two of your lists and combine them—the combinations are endless!
I am:

What are three action steps that you can take for your intent for your life?
1.
2.
3.
Take one of these action steps and write three to do's for it.
1.
2.
3.
What is stopping you from living from, and as, your intent?

Write a story about your life as if you were living this intent fully.

Keep up your POL assignments and live your quality words in your sacred space.

Take some time to review with your mastermind partners, or with yourself, where you are today.

What has changed?

What has stayed the same?

Write a sentence using all of your eight quality words. Read this sentence every day. This is your Master Intent.

You have set the course of your life based on your own consciously chosen clear values and priorities, and now they can become the intents that direct your life.

When you know your intent based on these pure values, you cannot be manipulated, swayed, or distracted.

Instead, you will feel the strong, steady support of the universe working in harmony and accord to the greatest outcome for you and your loved ones.

Mastering the skill of how to set intents can be applied to every aspect of your life, from deciding what is for dinner to your life purpose.

You choose and the universe answers in kind.

THE DAILY SHIFT

90

— · —

ABOUT THE BOOK

O ur lives are a projection of our thoughts and beliefs. These thoughts and beliefs build our perceptions, and it is our perceptions that determine what we experience.

The good news is that perceptions create nothing, they only hide from view what is already present; the abundance of the Infinite, which is so much better than what we think.

It is what I call the big R Reality.

We experience this Reality of Infinite Good more and more in our daily lives as we let go of limited thinking and perceptions, and shift to seeing Life as the I AM knows it to be.

To help you make that shift, I set this book up in *7–Day Shift Sessions.*

I wrote it so that the reader could read one day at a time, ponder its message, and then come back the next day for more on the same theme.

However, read the book the way that works best for you.

Read it all the way through, and then come back and just read a session a day, or pick a theme that you want to work on and start there.

It doesn't matter, it works best the way you want it to work!

If you would like to explore in more depth some of the concepts that mentioned throughout this book, you might like my other books in *The Shift Series.* You will find them listed at the end of this book.

My intent for this book is to provide a tool that can be returned to, repeatedly that will help bring all of your life's experiences into Infinite Good and meet your daily needs.

91

— · —

WEALTH

WEALTH—DAY ONE

For our first *7–Day Shift Session* we are going to immerse ourselves in the Truth about Wealth!

Understand that Wealth is something you already possess. Yes I know, it often doesn't feel that way, especially as the worldview is set up to encourage all of us to fear that there is not enough.

Most people succumb to this fear at one time or another, and become obsessed with finding ways to get more—usually money—because that is the currency we think is Wealth.

Have you ever noticed that when you are living in the fear of not enough and working hard to have enough, there is never enough?

We are going to start from the premise that the "not enough" is a lie. Why? Because, *What you perceive to be reality magnifies.*

If you and I agree with the worldview that there is not enough: There won't be—for you, for me, for anyone.

To release yourself and others to Wealth we all need to Wake Up! Wake up—Wake up—the W in Wealth.

To see and experience your Wealth and prosperity, the key is to decide to focus on the Wealth already present in your life. Not money. Wealth.

Money will follow when you decide to eliminate any thought about what you and others don't have.

Instead, focus entirely on what you do have.

Change your idea of Wealth to the qualities of Wealth evident in your life. Look for beauty, love, courage, grace, happiness, joy, etc.

Take time today to make a list of quality words that for you are Wealth, and then look for them in every person, place, or thing that crosses your path.

Enjoy the day fully awake and aware of the Wealth and prosperity that is evident when you decide to look for it.

Wealth is yours now!

WEALTH—DAY TWO

The E in Wealth stands for Enthusiasm. It is an essential ingredient to seeing and experiencing your Wealth and prosperity.

The original meaning of the word *Enthusiasm is divine inspiration, or a god within.*

If you used your quality list from yesterday at least a few times during the day, then probably you have already started to feel divine inspiration.

Today let's practice the invisible to feel and experience even more Enthusiasm.

The key to always seeing and experiencing your Wealth and prosperity is to have a variety of ways to corral your wandering thoughts that have drifted off to the worldview of lack, limitation, and fear, and bring them back to what you want to experience in your life.

Focus entirely on your qualities of Wealth.

Practice the invisible. Take your quality list—which will probably grow daily—and choose a quality or two from it to practice today.

For example: if you choose the quality of love as a quality of Wealth, today not only practice **seeing** it everywhere, but practice **being** it everywhere.

Ask yourself throughout the day, "Are my thoughts loving towards others? Are my thoughts loving towards myself?"

As you do this, expect to feel the divine inspiration of this practice.

In fact, practicing the invisible is the most fun you can experience once you get the hang of it and get in the habit. It can be done anywhere, anytime.

Enthusiasm is you! It's a brilliant day today.

WEALTH—DAY THREE

The A in Wealth stands for Angel Ideas, those marvelous ideas that seem to pop out of nowhere, bringing light to any situation.

These Angel Ideas are always immediately available. In fact, they are ready for you even before you ask for them. They wait for you to listen for them.

When you do, they bring you the solution to a problem, an idea for something new, a way to see something differently, and joy to the moment.

Angel Ideas are different than thoughts.

Thoughts keep us in the worldview by repeating back to us only what appears to be true, and then making it appear even more real by explaining why it must be true. Nothing about thoughts releases us from our current point of view.

Angel Ideas lift us above and out of the worldview.

For those people who don't honor Angel Ideas, they may appear to be the impossible, silly, never-been-done, how-will-that-work, can-I-really-do-that, kind of ideas. But, when we accept, honor, and love Angel Ideas, they are pure Wealth.

So today, listen and expect to hear and be moved by innumerable Angel Ideas, and revel in the delightful, brilliant light that they bring to every corner of your life, dissolving all limitations in the process.

Remember the phrase we all learned before crossing the street when we were kids: Stop, Look, and Listen. What a perfect reminder.

Before doing anything today, Stop, Look, and Listen for Angel Ideas. They are always there for you!

WEALTH—DAY FOUR

Love is the L in my interpretation of the word Wealth.

It seems obvious, doesn't it? If we have Love we are wealthy. However, we often do have Love and still don't feel wealthy or prosperous. There is something you can do to increase both Love and your experience of Wealth.

You can Love.

You can refuse to do anything but Love. No matter what the person, place or situation looks like, you can find something good to Love about it.

You can refuse to be tempted to discuss, think about, or be afraid of anything that does not appear to be good.

Why not try it for today?

You can think of it as a thought diet, instead of a food diet. Today you will avoid all those thoughts that are bad for you. Like magic, it will also affect anyone else within the radiance and radius of your thought.

Imagine that! Others will have the benefit of your diet.

Don't worry about how this thought diet will bring you Wealth and prosperity. In fact that worry is something that you are dieting from today. In this Love diet you can Love every second of the day. Don't hold back.

Stuff yourself with Love.

Feels good to be full of Love doesn't it?

The cool thing is, when you are filled up full with Love—well wait—I'll let you discover what happens!

WEALTH—DAY FIVE

Yes, you guessed it. Thanks is the T in my interpretation of the word Wealth.

What a privilege to be able to say Thanks. But how often do you do it? Very seldom! I know this to be true, because there are so many things for which all of us forget to be thankful.

I'll prove it.

Stop right now and look around you. Really look. No matter where you are, there are countless things that have been provided for you.

For example, you are reading this book! Think of that. Think of the millions of events that have taken place that have made it possible for you to be able to read this book wherever you are! Imagine what has been provided for you in each tiny part of the production of this book, the electricity, the software, etc.

Think of the dedication, energy, love, and care that so many people have given to create each element of what you so casually use.

You could spend hours giving Thanks just for the things you are aware of within the circle of your arms.

I know another thing that you are not thankful enough for: the talents that have been given to you.

No matter how good you are at giving Thanks for them, I know you have missed a few. Most of us have missed almost all of them. To rediscover your talents, start small.

Once again, start where you are sitting. What are you doing?

Think of the gifts and talents you have been given that allow you to do that. Expand out into your day, then your community.

Notice how you express unlimited talents and gifts each second of the day.

Give Thanks today. Give Thanks out loud when an Angel Idea moves you to speak. Give Thanks inside for everything.

Remember, we are seeing what has been given, and today we give Thanks.

Giving Thanks for you and your unique gifts and talents.

Wealth—Day Six

When I first heard the Angel Idea of using the word Wealth, I thought the H was Help Others. When I listened again, I realized that the Help means, "Help yourself first."

Before you can effectively help others, you must help yourself.

You are now. You are taking the time to redirect your thinking, to shift your perceptions, to know the truth about Wealth—because if you understand Wealth, you will have it and be able to share it.

But, what about other times? Have you ever found that you are distracting yourself from your true wishes and passion by helping others before you helped yourself?

Isn't this action one of the most draining, stifling and ultimately Wealth-stealing things you can do?

Yes it is; and in the end you have nothing left to help others with—no desires, no motivation, no resources. Sometimes we use this lack as a weapon against others. (Example: "I gave up all my dreams for you.")

Helping yourself first may take just a moment of thought-shifting, or many days, weeks, or months.

However, when you start with yourself, you will find that you will naturally move out into the world and ask, "How can I help you?"

You will be so filled with Wealth that sharing it, and using it, will become your nature. Your desire to help will expand into a dream bigger than yourself that will become the motive of your days and will outlive your personal time on earth.

So no matter how much you Help now, stop and **Help yourself first**, and then let that flow out of you into whatever action the Angel Ideas lead you to do.

Wealth—Day Seven

Together we have arrived at the 7th day of our shift to Wealth. This week you have learned how to use the word *Wealth* as your guide.

W—Wake Up, E—Enthusiasm, A—Angel Ideas, L—Love, T—Thanks, H—Help

During these last 7 days you have increased your understanding of True Wealth.

You have done this because you know that when you understand **this** Wealth, you will never worry about lack again.

Now that you have started this process, don't stop! Continue to practice the Truth about Wealth, just as you practice any other skill. Some days will feel easier than others, but the results will far outweigh any discomfort along the way.

What this practice will reveal to you is the treasure that can never be taken from you. It is one that you can spend with the assurance that it will never be depleted.

Never worry about the outcome of what you are guided to do. That is not your job.

You can't control what other people say, think, or do. Your job is to start with the correct premise in your own thinking and to constantly pay attention to your motives for all the actions you take, or don't take.

If you discover that you don't always walk in True Wealth, (none of us do yet) be thankful for that awareness, and then let it go.

Never hold on to those things you discover about yourself that are not beautiful and loving.

Don't say to yourself, "This is who I am" unless it is completely loving. Don't beat yourself up for your mistakes, big or small. Let them go.

Set yourself free to be and experience True Wealth.

I know that you are walking now in the light of the Truth about Wealth—and I am privileged to have been able to spend this time with you!

Wealth is you!

92

— • —

LOVE

Let's talk about Love for the next *7–Day Shift Session*! It's the perfect choice because Love is a key component of understanding wealth.

We begin the same way as we did with wealth, understanding that it is something that you already possess. Once again, the worldview tries to make us believe there is not enough, and of course this distorted view applies to Love, too.

We are afraid that there is not enough Love to go around, or that we will do something that will cause us to be unlovable.

Since the worldview is in charge of manipulating what we see, until we take that control back, we will constantly be swamped with lies about Love.

People do despicable things under the guise of Love, but that is not Love at all, is it?

One of the most perfect descriptions of Love can be found in the Bible, I Corinthians 13, so let's use it as our premise of Love for these next 7 days.

Love is patient, love is kind.
It does not envy, it does not boast, it is not proud.

It is not rude,
It is not self-seeking,
It is not easily angered, it keeps no record of wrongs.
Love does not delight in evil but rejoices with the truth.
It always protects, always trusts, always hopes, always perseveres.
Love never fails.

This is the Truth about Love—imagine that!

Love—Day Two

Yesterday we discovered some of the qualities of Love. We learned that it is kind, patient, forgiving, protective, hopeful, trusting, good, and ongoing.

We also discovered what Love is not. It is not rude, self-seeking, easily angered, or revengeful.

The question for today is: Do you believe this to be True about Love? This is an important question to ponder. Don't just answer it off the top of your head. Think about it. Feel about it.

Throughout the day as you work, play, take care of home, family, and yourself ask yourself, "Do I believe that Love is kind, patient, forgiving, protective, hopeful, trusting, good, and ongoing—and that Love is not rude, self-seeking, easily angered, or revengeful?"

Pay attention to the answer. It may not be what you expect. Don't try to make up the answer; just listen.

Once you discover what you believe about Love it will so much easier to shift it to something even better. But if you lie to yourself and try to cover it up with positive thinking, nothing will ever permanently change for the better.

Don't get attached to what you discover. Just observe and keep notes.

Love—Day Three

What did you discover yesterday that you believe about Love?

Did it match our list? Do you believe that Love is kind, patient, forgiving, protective, hopeful, trusting, good, and ongoing—and not rude, self-seeking, easily angered, or revengeful?"

Whether you believed all of it, none of it, or some of it, there is one more step to take.

That is the step of asking yourself, **do you want this to be True?** Are you willing to give up any story that you have about Love that doesn't match these qualities?

This is a harder question to answer than what might appear on the surface. We all get something out of our "unloved and unlovable" stories.

But, is what we get worth holding onto these beliefs and stories? What if by giving them up we could experience perfect Love?

The question for today is one that carries with it great significance.

For today, ask yourself, "Am I willing to give up all the beliefs I have, and the stories I tell, that do not match the Truth about Love?"

You may find you are not willing to give these up yet, but that's okay.

If you tell the truth, it is the beginning of the end of their grip on you.

Once again, if you cover up these beliefs with positive thinking and don't completely face what is running your life, it will continue to be the unseen dictator that locks you away in a room by yourself, far from True Love.

Are you willing to Love and be Loved?

Love—Day Four

BECA LEWIS

At the beginning of this section on Love, we talked about the qualities of Love.

Yesterday I asked you if you were ready and willing to be loved and to Love, and to give up stories that keep this from happening.

So what if you did find a teeny tiny part of you that isn't willing to be loved or to Love, or even a big part of you that isn't willing to be loved or to Love because—get ready—there is good news here, because you have discovered one of those "monsters under the bed" that has been scaring you all these years.

Now that it has been seen, you can dissolve it with awareness and Truth.

Today will be fun because you are going to list all the reasons you are afraid of loving or being loved, otherwise known as "monsters under the bed."

Now, you may say that you have no resistance at all to Love, so if you really think that is true, skip this part.

But, if you are like the rest of us, there is a residual in there somewhere. Let me give you some possible ideas:

You might be secretly thinking, "Love is a responsibility. Do I want it?

Love means I have to give up part of myself. Love demands more than I have to give. Anybody that loves me must be crazy, so why would I Love them back?"

Do these prime the pump for you? So now you get to write down these kinds of thoughts. Don't worry, it won't create anything bad.

Your thoughts aren't creating anything they are only hiding what is. So writing them down will just bring them out in the open.

Have fun, no judgment, just observation.

LOVE—DAY FIVE

In this section we are practicing the qualities of Love found in the Bible, I Corinthians 13. We have agreed that Love is kind, patient, forgiving, protective, hopeful, trusting, good, and ongoing.

Did you have fun yesterday uncovering what we used to be afraid of, those "monsters under the bed"?

In reality these are only little "dust bunnies" of thoughts that have been clouding your Love view of these qualities in your life.

Let's sweep some of them away today with the broom of the Truth about Love.

Let me give you an example. Let's take the thought that you might have uncovered: that Love is a responsibility that is too much to handle.

Here's the thought:

"I can't handle the responsibility of Love."

Here's the broom:

"Since Love is gentle and Love is kind, the responsibility of Love must be to be gentle and kind. I find it easy to be gentle and kind to myself and others."

You can substitute any of the quality words you want to in your broom, or add them all. There are even more quality words you can add to your broom.

So if you think of them, write them down. In the meantime, start sweeping away those dust bunnies.

To make sure they don't return, you could pretend they are dust bunnies made of darkness and your broom is made of light. When the two meet, you know that the light will dissolve the darkness.

Love—Day Six

Yesterday we swept away the dust bunnies of thought that were clouding our ability to see the present availability of Love.

We used the broom of light with its strands of the qualities of Love to sweep those dark thoughts away, dissolving them into their native nothingness.

Now that our home, our consciousness, has been cleared out, we are prepared to be the qualities of Love ourselves.

It's easy to wish that others were more kind, patient, forgiving, protective, hopeful, trusting, good, and ongoing, but much harder to take responsibility to be those qualities ourselves.

But, it is here that we must begin and end, within ourselves.

Of course our desire is to be more kind, patient, forgiving, protective, hopeful, trusting, good, and ongoing to others; but really, we have to be all these qualities **to ourselves first.**

When we try it the other way around, sooner or later, something will throw us off balance and we will bounce back to what Love is not.

Or we may keep everything together on the surface, covering up a deep unhappiness.

When we begin by treating ourselves with Love first, we will have plenty of all the qualities of Love, like kindness, left over to spread to everyone we meet.

Happiness will begin within, blooming into an ongoing feeling that is consistently present, just like Love! So today is the day we pay attention to how we treat ourselves.

As yourself, "Am I being, kind, patient, forgiving, protective, hopeful, trusting, good, and ongoing to myself"? If yes, celebrate and do more. If not, well, you know the answer—since you are Love Loving Itself!

LOVE—DAY SEVEN

Hasn't this been a wonderful 7–Day Shift Session about Love?

We have rung the bell of Love this week, calling out to ourselves to see and be the qualities of Love.

We have stopped asking others to be something we are not practicing on ourselves. We have swept away the "monsters under the bed."

We have declared that Love Is Always Loving Itself, and that of course means us!

As we continue on this Daily Shift together, there are two things you can do.

First, you can celebrate with gratitude! You can fill up your heart with the gratitude that no matter it may seem in your life at this moment, Love is all there is. Love is filling all the spaces in your life.

Celebrate this as fact, knowing that nothing will ever change this Truth, and that you are awake and aware of the omnipresence of Love.

The second thing to do is to continue **to practice what you have started.**

Remember, the habit of a lifetime takes a discipline of habit to dissolve. Don't be discouraged by this. The dissolving of what is not true is a wonderful unfolding, just as a garden growing is a beautiful sight.

Let's end, as we began, with the description of Love found in the Bible, I Corinthians 13.

Love is patient, love is kind.
It does not envy, it does not boast, it is not proud.
It is not rude,
It is not self-seeking,
It is not easily angered, it keeps no record of wrongs.
Love does not delight in evil but rejoices with the truth.
It always protects, always trusts, always hopes, always perseveres.

Love never fails.

This is the Truth about Love—live it!

93

— · —

HOME

In the first *7–Day Shift Session* we talked about wealth. In the second we focused on love. For the next 7–day session we are going to visit the concept of Home.

Everyone wants to feel wealthy, everyone wants to be loved, and everyone wants to have a Home. No matter how different our homes are, we all want a place where we feel we belong.

Home is not where you live, but where they understand you.—Christian Morgenstern

If we look at the concept of Home on the surface, it is just the place where we live. Some of us rent our homes; some of us own our homes. Some of us feel as if we have never had a "real" Home, and some of us are afraid of losing the Home we have.

Some of us are happy at Home; some of us feel trapped at Home.

There appears to be a wide gulf between those who have no Home to those who build huge and elaborate Homes, often to house just one or two people.

We have a multitude of TV programs and "make- money gurus" showing us how to build, decorate, flip, buy, sell, and make money from our homes.

There are huge industries built around the fear of not having a Home, or the greed of making money from our homes.

We need to ask this question: Is this what we mean by Home?

That is the focus of the next 7 days. What and where is Home?

When visiting sites on the web, we click the word Home as the place to return to.

We may also think of our personal Homes the same way. As T.S. Elliot said, *Home is where one starts from.*

Let's start there. To make this more personal, let's begin by exploring this question, "Where do you live?"

Richard Bach said, *The simplest questions are the most profound. Where were you born? Where is your home? Where are you going? What are you doing? Think about these once in a while and watch your answers change.*

Of course, you do remember that Home is not just a place, but also a *point of view,* and a *state of mind.*

HOME—DAY TWO

Yesterday we asked, "Where do you live?"—understanding that Home is not just a place, but also a point of view, and a state of mind.

What you want in a Home may not be what I want in a Home. Beginning with your own personal idea of the qualities of Home will ensure the process of living within the space, time, mindset, and actual structure that means Home to you.

Some qualities can change over time.

I have lived in the middle of a large city and in the middle of nowhere. Both homes brought me joy because for that time the qualities they offered exactly what I wanted. However, there are qualities that are important to me that have never changed, no matter where I lived.

What are those qualities of Home that have never changed for you? What kind of living experience are you looking for to call Home?

Are you looking for hustle and bustle, or silence? Do you want a view outside, or does the inside mean the most? Do you need outside space or inside space? Do you want privacy or lots of community interaction?

Choosing another person's idea of what Home means will never make us happy.

Imagine a turtle thinking what an elephant calls Home would work for him. Sounds ridiculous, but really that is what the worldview tries to sell us, that a Home is the same for everyone.

The Shift® always begins within, which means we start within ourselves to find the answers to what will then appear on the outside, including our homes.

It's true what Pliny the Elder said, *Home is where the heart is.*
Your heart: Where is it?

HOME—DAY THREE

Love begins at home, and it is not how much we do, but how much love we put in that action.—Mother Teresa

Can a Home that begins with Love in action ever be devalued? Can this Home ever be taken from us? Of course not!

It also wouldn't matter if we actually owned a Home, or rented a Home, or lived in our car, if we began with, and stayed within, the Home of *Love in action.*

Beginning with Love in action, our homes are built on the solid rock of Truth. Then no matter how hard the wolf tries to blow it down, it will stand.

I had a friend who taught me the value of living the qualities of Home before, during, and after shopping for a Home.

She had a nice place to live, but her family was growing, and they wanted to move out of town to a quieter area and a bigger Home.

She began to study the qualities of what Home was to her and her family. She studied the promise of Divine Love: that the outcome of understanding and acting from Divine Love always provides for and meets every human need.

On the surface they didn't have enough money to buy the Home that was forming within her heart, but she never worried about it. She just kept learning more about the qualities of Home.

In the meantime she demonstrated Love in action in all that she did. For me, for two weeks she took my 3 very young children into her small Home where she already had 5 small children of her own, so I could attend a very important class.

This was typical of what she did. She didn't just speak Love, she acted Love.

Not long after that she easily moved her family into an even better home than they had originally desired. Those watching on the outside might have said it was "magic" that brought all the events that came into play to provide the Home.

But, it wasn't magic, it was a natural result of what my friend was doing. She knew where her heart was, and she demonstrated that knowing, through the living action of Love.

Isn't this a wonderful idea to practice, living the action of Love to discover Home!

Home—Day Four

I used to search for Home all the time.

Wherever I would go I would ask myself, "Could I live here, in this place, or in this Home?" I have asked myself that question in almost every state in the United States plus even in a few other countries.

What most confused me was that the answer was always "yes" and "no." Yes, I could see the beauty of each place and find joy in what it had to offer, and "no" because no place fulfilled something within me that was always searching for somewhere else.

Now I am learning that the human idea of myself will always search, but it always searches within the idea of human; and the answer will never be found there. The human point of view is the lack of understanding of Oneness, so no matter how long we search within that point of view for anything, we will never find it.

I realized that I could have a house in every location I have ever loved, and still I would not feel at Home—until I understood completely that Home is not a physical place or dwelling, it is a spiritual fact.

Home is where the heart is, but not the human heart. Home is in the heart of Love.

It doesn't matter whether we are in a car, the woods, a hotel, a train, a resort, a castle, or a store. It doesn't matter if the view is ocean, woods, field, rocks, desert, or the city; if we remain present in the awareness of Where I Am is Home, then Home is where we are.

Beginning with the correct premise of Home, then it doesn't matter what the worldview says about where we live.

As we stay within our own awareness of the qualities that make up the idea of the Home, this awareness automatically translates to what appears as a physical Home, which matches more and more those qualities that we already live within, in the Heart of Love.

If that doesn't appear true to you, look again; but look through the lens of the qualities of Home, not the physical measurements of size, cost, and location.

Everything has already been provided, including Home. We must just learn to look differently to see it.

HOME—DAY FIVE

My home has always been show business. —Sammy Davis, Jr.

This is another way to look at Home. Home as the way we express ourselves.

Have you ever experienced doing something so completely that everything vanished except you and what you were doing?

Did it matter where you were at the time? Did you feel content, safe, secure, inspired, happy and content?

Aren't these all qualities that we want to feel when we are Home?

As a writer, a place that I feel most at Home is when I am writing. Sometimes I write better in cafes, other times I love the stillness of someplace I have never been before. Most of the time it is at my desk, but it isn't the place that gives me peace, it is the doing.

Home is where we are thinking and doing what we love; Home is much more than where our physical body lives.

Of course, as we become aware of the qualities of Home, honor them, rejoice in them, and realize that they are ever-present in every area of our lives, this internal shift will express itself into a better and better picture of Home that matches our own idea of the qualities of Home, not another's idea of Home.

This is an important key. Home does not look the same to everyone, just as the way we spend our day and express ourselves is not the same. We do not need, require, or want the same type of Home as another.

There is no value in feeling less than another because our Home is not as grand as theirs. In fact the feeling of "less than" begins within.

It begins with thinking that we are not as important or grand as another; and it is within our thinking that we must dissolve it.

We are each unique expressions of the One Mind. Comparing ourselves to another is ludicrous since there is no "other." There is only One Mind expressing itself.

Wanting what we don't have, wanting what others have, throws us out the door of our ever permanent Home within the One Mind, into the wilderness of human thinking.

Once we stop that comparison, we can pick ourselves back up and enter again into the true idea of Home.

Ask yourself, "When do I feel the most at Home?" Listen quietly and patiently for the answer, and it will reveal itself to you.

HOME—DAY SIX

Welcome to the silence, Feel your heart's alliance, Close your eyes, Breathe in the empty space, Welcome home to the sweet state of grace.—Johnny Elkins, from the musical Leap.

The dictionary defines grace as the unmerited divine assistance given to humans. Reading this definition, most of us feel a sense of disquiet. This is not what we know grace to be. It is much more than that.

The problem with this definition is that it is within the worldview and about the worldview.

It implies that grace pops into our lives periodically without warning and gives us some assistance even though we didn't do anything to deserve it. It breaks human laws and gives us some respite from the limitation and lack within the worldview.

But this isn't Divine Grace, is it? Grace is a living state of being; it is the spiritual presence of Divine Love, felt, lived, enjoyed, and acknowledged. Not because we are humans and deserve it, but because we are the action of the spiritual presence of Grace.

The best way to find our Home in grace is to live it. Grace is not a dead idea. We can't just sit on the couch and say "grace will take care of it." We have to live the qualities and ideas of grace to actually feel its presence.

As we see, acknowledge and then live the beauty of grace, the joy of grace, the safety of grace, and the love of grace, we find ourselves at Home in the state of living in grace.

At peace in this awareness, and trusting in its truth, we can rest in the knowledge that wherever we are, grace is always present.

Grace does not break human laws—it supersedes them. It overrides the worldview illusion and brings us into the safety of the spiritual law of Divine Love.

Daily we can say to ourselves, "Welcome Home, dear one, to the sweet state of grace, the perfect and only real Home."

HOME—DAY SEVEN

Pilgrim on earth, home and heaven are within thee. —Walford Davies

We have traveled far these last few days in our search for Home. We have moved from thinking Home is a building to understanding that Home is a point of view and a state of mind.

We have dismissed the belief that Home is something we own, or must acquire.

We have sighed in relief over the awareness that grace is where we live, not something we have to earn, but only to acknowledge and understand.

Since *what we perceive to be reality magnifies* we can trust that as we continue this awareness, while dropping our baggage containing our preconceived notions, fears, regrets, and sorrows, we will no longer live with clipped wings within a human concept of Home.

Instead, we continue to discover that we are free to live wherever we are, whatever Home may look like.

We celebrate that we are always living within the many mansions of Divine Love.

Someday we will all learn to speak and live from the Truth at all times, but in the meantime, we can begin by acknowledging it within our hearts.

Because we know this is not a material world, we can fully acknowledge the Truth in this promise, and trust its provision: *In my Father's house are many mansions: If it were not so, I would have told you. I go to prepare a place for you.*—John 14:2

Our Home has been prepared long in advance of our needing it. Let's let grace carry us over its threshold to live there as intended, "happily ever after."

94

— • —

Purpose

Purpose—Day One

The next *7-Day Shift Session* will be very exciting because we are going to talk about Purpose. Once again I am going to use the letters in a word—this time the word Purpose—as our starting point.

For such a glorious subject, the idea of living from Purpose can feel like a burden rather than a blessing when we think we don't understand our own Personal Purpose.

Personal—that is the P in Purpose.

Personal, meaning your unique expression of Infinite Mind; not personal, as in personality. This is an important distinction.

If our Purpose is defined in terms of personality, then it would revolve around a limited human sense, with both positive and negative aspects. That would imply that those with charm and presence would seem to have a higher Purpose than those who have different ways of expressing themselves.

In society, we make the mistake of following personality instead of substance. In fact we are taught that if we follow the personality of others, we may actually be able to look like them, or be like them, t oo.

The Personal that I am referring to is becoming aware of yourself as the unique idea and action of Infinite Mind. To make this easier to talk about, I call this your USB, or Unique Spiritual Blessing. This is something that radiates as you, without effort.

It will produce the same response as looking at a flower and feeling what it has to offer without any effort on its part. Each flower's Purpose is Personal to it. It couldn't stop doing what it is even if it tried.

This is the same for you.

No matter how hidden from view it may be, you have a Personal Purpose —Unique Spiritual Blessing—that you radiate without effort. To discover your USB can often take time to uncover until it becomes the cornerstone, or Purpose, of our lives, but it can and must be done. Tomorrow we'll talk about ways to begin to uncover your Personal USB.

Purpose—Day Two

Today we are going to Uncover—the U in Purpose—your Unique Spiritual Blessing.

Your USB is something that you can't stop yourself from doing, no matter how hard you may try. However, for most of us this is an elusive idea.

In fact, when I first teach this concept, almost everyone first comes up with something negative about themselves.

It's a start, but not the end. Your USB is a positive, like the perfume from a rose, that affects everyone equally who is willing to "stop and smell" it.

Our USB is often the easiest thing in the world for us to do, so we are inclined to think it is useless, or not very important. It is often the thing we did as a child that we were told to stop. Usually this is because we didn't know how to present it with finesse.

The negative that you may first think is your Purpose does contain clues that will guide you to your real USB, but the negative is never your Purpose or who you are.

I'll use myself as an example. Examining my life, I realized that I couldn't stop myself from shifting people's perception.

As a child I would often say (to adults too), "If you look at this differently then you could do what you want to do; or you wouldn't be stuck; or things would be better."

Since this rarely produced a good result for me, I came to view this behavior as a negative, and told myself to shut up. But no matter how hard I tried to make myself stop talking about shifting perceptions, I did it all the time anyway.

As a choreographer I would say to a dancer who couldn't do a step, "Show me how you can't do it." The result was a shifted perception on the other dancer's part, and an ability to do what she thought she couldn't do.

You can see that as an adult I had begun to temper how I shifted perceptions, and it is still a skill I am learning.

But, I couldn't, and still can't, stop myself from doing this no matter what profession or job I am doing.

As a child I wasn't graceful or discerning about my purpose, so I tried to stop it. Actually, everyone tried to stop me from doing it, because I was very annoying.

I can still be annoying, but at least I now know and accept my USB, and I practice being more graceful and mindful in its execution.

Look back at your own life; do you see your USB hiding within the folds of your life?

Tomorrow we will discuss the revealing of your Purpose to yourself.

PURPOSE—DAY THREE

The word Reveal is our R in Purpose. It is not the words resist, replace, or even renewal. It is Reveal.

Why? Because your unique Purpose is not something that has to be renewed, nor replaced with something else, nor resisted. It only needs to be Revealed.

As you looked back through your life, did you find a common thread?

If you look at your daily activities, do they all stem from one common desire? Are there things that you do that bring you more joy than others? What part of them?

One place to get these answers is to ask people who know you. Just as it is often easier to see another's faults than it is to see our own, it is often easier to see the basic essence of another than it is to see our own.

Why go to the trouble of Revealing your Purpose?

Imagine living each moment in the now, enjoying what you are doing, finding reason for your being that can never be taken away.

And, it is even more than that.

Each of us is an integral idea in Infinite Mind.

This means that it takes all of us expressing our Unique Spiritual Blessing to be the full completeness of the I AM.

No matter how hard we may try to hide from the Truth about ourselves, it is always present.

The word "hard" gives us a clue; because it is much harder to hide from the Truth than it is to release ourselves to living as a unique action of Truth.

Let your uniqueness be Revealed to you, and release yourself to the relief and joy that this awareness will reveal.

PURPOSE—DAY FOUR

Does your Purpose Provide? Is it your Provision? Yes it does, and yes it is. These two words are our next P in the word Purpose.

Provide and Provision.

Let's start by looking at the definitions of these two words that are linked together in meaning.

Provide: "To make preparation to meet a need."

Provision: "A measure taken beforehand to deal with a need."

Wouldn't it be wonderful if we understood both through our heartfelt awareness and our logical thinking sense—that our Unique Spiritual Blessing is our Provision?

Wouldn't it be a relief to fully realize that our Purpose is our Provision, the pre-planned, prepared, taken beforehand measure, that Provides for us?

The Truth is, who we are is Mind knowing itself.

If we fully understood this, wouldn't we be more willing to undercover and live our Purpose, instead of busying ourselves with things to do, so we could buy more things, own more things, and control more things?

Wouldn't we be more willing to step out of the Dilbert Cube of the worldview and live as our USB? Take a moment and think it through. Would Divine Love that is Infinite Intelligence always take care of Itself? Of course!

Therefore, since we are the Ideas and Action of Divine Love, Loving Itself, it makes perfect sense that who we are is Provision Itself.

Of course, it doesn't make sense, if we are determined to hold on to our own personal personality ego, and the point of view that we are the ones in control and that we are personal creators.

Since this personal sense does not really Provide, nor contain our true Purpose, at some point we all must become willing to give it up.

When we give up personal sense, we arrive at the Provision of Purpose. This makes the exploration of the Revealing of Purpose a task worth doing.

Purpose—Day Five

When I was writing this, I had a bird feeder that hung just outside of my second-floor window. At different times of the day and different times of the year I had a multitude of different kinds of birds that visited the feeder.

After watching them for two years, something become very obvious to me.

I could see that each bird is entirely Original, even within the same species.

Original is our O in Purpose.

Each of us is an Original and unique action and idea of the Divine Intelligence called God. It takes concentrated observation to be able to tell the birds at the feeder apart, the same way it takes dedicated observation to see your Original expression of your Purpose.

To be accurate, all of us have just one Purpose: to be what we are, which is God in action.

However, the infinity and originality of what appears to us as the universe makes it clear to us that every idea of God has an Original way that Purpose is fulfilled.

Uncovering and revealing your USB, your Unique Spiritual Blessing, is the Purpose of these 7 days.

Depending on your state of mind and point of view, this is either an exciting treasure hunt, with the pot of gold being the discovery of your own Original expression, or it's an exercise in futility.

Think of it: we are each the Original idea of Infinite Intelligence. What an amazing Love this Divine Mind must have for each of Its Original Ideas —one of which appears as you.

Let's choose the point of view that reveals the treasure chest of joy that is the inevitable outcome of living your Purpose as an Original idea of Divine Mind!

PURPOSE—DAY SIX

Let's look at one more definition, the definition of Purpose, which is: "Something to set up as an object or end to be attained."

It is interesting that the word Purpose comes from the word meaning "intend" or "by intent; intentionally."

Now let's look at that definition of Spiritually, our S in the word Purpose, and see how it applies to each of us.

By Spiritually I mean "seen without the material overlay, or the human personality ego, or the worldview training."

As best as we can imagine, let's look at it as God would. Would you do a little mental adventure exercise with me? Here we go!

Since we know that what we call human is really the compound idea of God, then couldn't we say that we are God's Purpose?

Let me give you an example, using the sun as a symbol. The result of the sun, being itself, is light.

The beams of light that appear to come from the sun is a misperception. We see the light broken up into beams because of the dust, or impurities, in the air.

If the dust particles or impurities in the air weren't present, then we would see the light from the sun as it is, unbroken, undivided, and everywhere.

The sun is seen because of its action, or expression, or idea, we call light. That is the sun's intent and Purpose: light.

God, by being All, is "seen" because of Its action, or expression, or ideas we call individual humans, only because we are looking through an imperfect lens of perception.

A clear awareness, without the imperfection of our mist-perception, would reveal only the I AM or the Us that is the I AM. That would mean we are God's Purpose, or God's Intent.

Think on that, my friends. If nothing else, it will expand your awareness of the infinity of the Purpose of God that we call "me" and what we call our own personal Purpose.

Purpose—Day Seven

Now that we have reached the seventh day in our exploration of looking at Purpose differently, I hope that I have given you an idea of the Expansion of Purpose. Yes, the E in Purpose is Expansion.

When we think of our Purpose as a badge of personal honor or obligation, we are within the human realm of personality and ego, and not in the freedom of knowing that Purpose is the outcome of Love Knowing Itself.

Too often, we get stuck in doing something, or being something, because we think it is linked to a "calling" we have to answer. The Expansion of our Purpose may appear as something to do, but this is not where we start.

We start with Truth and listening within, to the sweet Original song that is you. As you listen within you will know what action to take that will lead you to a Purpose-filled life by singing your clearest song.

It will be the one that you knew all along.

Your clearest song, your Purpose, is the one that you have been observing these last 7 days, and you have been translating it back to its spiritual origin.

As you continue Uncovering and Revealing, the Expansion of your Purpose is the natural outcome.

The only obligation that you have is to come away from the human prison of personal Purpose, and into the freedom of Divine Mind's Purpose, seen as you.

95

―――― ● ――――

HAPPINESS

HAPPINESS—DAY ONE

Abraham Lincoln said, *Most folks are as happy as they make up their minds to be.* This is a perception-shifting statement isn't it? Of course this is true, but the problem is, how do we make up our minds to be happy?

The United States' Constitution says we have the right to pursue Happiness. It doesn't actually say we have the right to be happy.

So why not go to a higher power than the Constitution, and claim our right to be happy?

It's the words "right to be" that are the key to the puzzle of how to make up our minds to be happy.

If we have been trained to feel as if we don't have a right to happy, then being happy may feel wrong.

For the next 7 days, let's shift that "taught to us perception" of not having a right to be happy, to knowing absolutely that not only do we have a right to Happiness, but that Happiness is a quality that is innate in each one of us, and we can and will find it and live it.

There are many causes and reasons for unhappiness, but in the end there is only one way to be happy.

This is the good news, isn't it; because when we learn how to choose and accept Happiness, we will eliminate all those reasons and causes of unhappiness.

There's no time like the present to be happy, so let's get started!

Each day for the next 7 days I will give you a short and simple exercise to eliminate unhappiness and reveal Happiness.

Here's your exercise for the day. It's just one question.

Who do you think is happier than you?

HAPPINESS—DAY TWO

Today is an observation day. As we have talked about in the past shift series, in order to shift our perceptions, and not just cover them up, we need to know our current point of view.

We have to discover the hidden beliefs and perceptions, and even the not-so-hidden beliefs and perceptions, in order—in this case—to be utterly happy for apparently no good reason.

Think of this as your big cleaning out the closet day.

You know, the day you take all your clothes out and decide which ones you want to keep, and which ones don't fit or don't make you look good. It may produce a messy room for a bit, but in the end, it feels great.

Ready? Your exercise today is a series of questions.

Here we go:

- Did you make a list of who you think is happier than you?

- Was it hard or easy to do?

- Is it okay with you that some people are happier than you?

- Would you rather that I had asked who is sadder than you?

- What do those people, who are happier than you, have —that you don't have—that allows them to be so happy?

- If you had the exact thing they do, would you allow yourself to be happy?

- If you were really happy all the time, what would your best friend, spouse, parents, and children say?

Happiness—Day Three

When I was a teenager I alternated between Happiness and depression. When I was depressed, I wrote poems about depression and left them around where I was sure my mom would see them, since I believed that a large portion of my unhappiness was my parents' fault.

Perhaps all teenagers think it's their parents' fault that they are unhappy; but we are adults now and able to take full responsibility for our own Happiness.

To shift our past perception that is affecting our current Happiness, we can "revisit" scenes from the past, and see them through different eyes.

Instead of the person we were then, we can be the awareness that we are now.

Don't worry about which scene from the past is the most important; just take the one that occurs to you now and re-see it.

Visit it now as an aware adult who understands that Divine Love has always been present.

See it with the Truth that you have never been abandoned or betrayed or damaged.

Yes, I know that the memory is often these very things. However, if we want to be happy, we need to rewrite the script.

It is not changing Truth; it is re-seeing what happened as a lie about the Truth.

You'll get better at this as you let go of the idea that what happened was real, and therefore must be suffered for or paid for. It's not, and it doesn't.

What can you lose? Try out a scene and see what happens.

Move on to the next one. Would you rather be right about the past, or happy in the present? You choose.

Here are your two questions for the day.

- Whose fault is it when you are unhappy?

- Why?

In order to be utterly happy the only thing necessary is to refrain from comparing this moment with other moments in the past, which I often did not fully enjoy because I was comparing them with other moments of the future. —Andre Gide

HAPPINESS—DAY FOUR

Yesterday we asked, "Whose fault is it that you are unhappy, and why?" Of course, we often feel as if someone or something else has done something that has caused us to be unhappy.

We can be unhappy due to jobs, income, parents, spouses, children, living conditions, health issues, too much or too little money, governments, terrorists, mosquitoes, too hot or too cold—okay, you and I know that I could go on with this list forever.

Nevertheless, doesn't everyone face all these issues at one time or another, and yet some people are always happy anyway?

So if we have to assign fault to anyone, it really must come back to us.

This is actually good news, because it makes it easier to be happy, since we don't have to fix anyone or anything else.

All we have to do is shift our own perception to an awareness and acceptance of Happiness.

However, we can sometimes feel so unhappy, we can't remember what makes us happy.

This is where a Happiness list of why and what makes us happy comes in handy. I made a list like this once. I was sitting in a café, and realized that I was happy for the first time in weeks.

I grabbed a piece of paper and a pen and started writing down what made me happy, so if I forgot I could get out the list and remember.

There were simple things on that list, starting with sitting in a good café, and then I added reading a good book, going to the movies, getting a child to smile at me, etc.

None of what was on the list was "profound," they were all simple activities. I kept that list, and every time I found myself feeling unhappy I did something on the list. It always worked.

As I expanded my awareness of the quality of Happiness, I rarely needed to look at the list anymore, but it was a great place to start.

This your assignment for the day.

- See yourself as happy.

- What are you doing?

- What are you thinking?

- Start a list!

The smallest fact is a window through which the infinite may be seen.—Aldous Huxley

HAPPINESS—DAY FIVE

Sometimes we are happy, but we act unhappy and don't realize it.

I had a vivacious grandmother who was a lover of life. However, she constantly complained under her breath. I am sure she had no idea at all that she was doing it.

I have a clear memory of her looking under the sink trying to get something out and the running commentary of her complaining while she was doing it. I do that same thing sometimes. When I am observing myself, I am amazed that it is happening.

Family habit! It can be dissolved!

She was happy, I am happy. However, if you heard that complaining, would you know?

When we complain, either consciously or unconsciously, we are reinforcing the human computer program that produces what we perceive as our life.

This program doesn't know that we are happy; it doesn't know we don't mean what we are complaining about.

It "hears" unhappiness and assumes that is what we want more and so it shrinks our perception down to what it thinks we believe, actually reducing the possibilities of our lives.

Or, said more simply, *What we perceive to be reality magnifies.*

It's up to us to choose a different reality.

If you are reading this, you either want to, or have already chosen, the point of view of the Reality of Infinite Mind. The next step, which is imperative, is to actually live in Reality, to consciously choose the state of mind that reinforces this point of view.

Consciously choose Happiness, consciously stay in the state of mind of Happiness, and it will reveal what is already true: that

Happiness is, because divine Love is. To help us get to, and stay in, this state of mind, our new habit will be to observe Happiness. What does it look like?

So here is your question for the day.

- Who is the happiest person you know?

Happiness is not a matter of intensity, but of balance, order, rhythm, and harmony.—Thomas Merton

HAPPINESS—DAY SIX

It's spring as I write this. Although I grew up in Pennsylvania, I lived in California as an adult.

Every spring I would say to my family in the East, "Yes it is spring here too," and they would smile and say, "Hum."

And now that I am back in the East I know what they meant. The spring here is even more intense.

We wait for spring with a passion.

In February I look in vain for signs of spring. A little green shoot—anything.

When spring does come, it sweeps in like the wind. One day it is dark and dreary, and the next the trees are wearing gorgeous halos of red and yellow buds.

The daffodils are not visible one day, and nodding their golden heads in the breeze the next. You have to carefully watch each day not to miss spring as it bursts forth from winter.

The harbingers and celebrators of spring are the birds. They sing with every fiber of their being. I watched a tiny goldfinch belt out a song that could be heard around the block. Sitting on the tree limb it glowed with Happiness.

Yes, this is all about Happiness.

Buried beneath what may appear as a winter of unhappiness are the seeds of Happiness—just waiting for the warmth of love to burst forth.

I can see each of you on your tree of life, singing of joy with every fiber of your being.

Before the sun comes up, the bird begin their dawn chorus of song. You can begin now too, knowing that nothing can stop the sun, or your Happiness from rising.

Your assignment today:

- Wherever you live, get up early enough to listen to the morning chorus of birds. Imagine how it must feel to be filled with as much joy and love of life.

HAPPINESS—DAY SEVEN

We began this *7-Day Shift Session* with the realization that we have a right to be happy, and an awareness of why we might have unconsciously chosen to not be happy.

We followed up with some tools we can use to let go of those reasons, and to live as Happiness itself.

There is no reason to stop at a sort of happy place.

As we understand the true nature of Love as the only presence, the only activity, the only cause and creator, then the mist of false perceptions of what claim to be situations and circumstances that produce unhappiness will dissolve.

This allows us to see Happiness as a basic element and quality of life.

With this understanding of Happiness, all the reasons for unhappiness are eliminated in one fell swoop, because they all begin and end from the false premise of duality and separation.

Now that you have cleaned out your mental closet, don't go putting those old beliefs and perceptions back in.

Be careful about what you choose to perceive.

- Don't buy all that stuff that claims that suffering is necessary and that we must be unhappy to be good.

- Check your closet often to make sure unhappiness has not slipped back in without your noticing.

- Daily give yourself full permission to be utterly and unreasonably happy.

- Pull out your list of what makes you happy once in awhile and do something on it. Sing with the birds at least once a season, and experience what they know.

- Continue with this Happiness shift so that when you ask the question, "Who is the happiest person I know?" you will be able to answer without hesitation, "It is me!"

Celebrating Happiness!

96

— • —

INTENT

INTENT—DAY ONE

Is there something you want?

Of course there is!

We are all filled with wants and desires, and depending on what point of view we are in when we want something, and what point of view we are in when we take action to receive what we want, we are either frustrated or fulfilled.

It's interesting how on the outside the same action can convey many different points of view. An aware observer can tell the difference through the fruits of those actions and the methods employed.

If we are in the worldview—the dualistic, lack, fight-to-survive point of view—it will easy be to witness the fearful, competition-to-win, me-first methods, which people employ to get what they want.

When we are in the One Mind, only one cause and creator, and we are living Divine Love Loving Itself, well—it's easy to see that we will be much more likely to operate with kindness, joy, courage, and sharing.

A wonderful example of this happened with a high school girl's softball team.

The girl at bat hit her first home run ever, but as she reached first base her knee gave out. Her own team was not allowed to help her, so the opposing team carried her around the bases knowing full well that the run she hit was the winning run.

What do you think that team's Intent was?

It's easy to see that they were coming from Love Loving Itself. The results of this action will carry the fruits of their action far past that one game, into inspiring others to think differently.

This was different from setting a goal to win, isn't it? It is clear in this action that Intent and goals need to be placed in the proper order.

We are taught goals first, Intent last—if ever.

For the next 7 days, let's put Intent first, and let goals be the outcome, not the cause. To do this, we need to understand the difference, which will be one of the results of these 7 days.

- In the meantime, why not make a list of things you want?

It's not bad to want something, so go for it. By the end of the week you will be much clearer about what that list means.

Intent Day Two

Whoever has the clearest Intent wins.

Oh gosh I know, this doesn't sound very spiritual given that someone "wins," but it is true.

Let me give you a few scenarios to clarify what I mean.

You go to the grocery store with the Intent of buying just a few items. On the way through the aisles you pick up many more items, and maybe even a few more as you check out.

Who had the clearer Intent, you or the grocery store?

You have a perfectly clear Intent not to eat dessert at the family gathering. However, once there, everyone teases you about it and you feel guilty for not eating, so you join them. Who has the clearer Intent. You or the rest of the family?

You decide to spend the day doing something you really want to do, but a friend calls and asks you to go with her to do an errand. Who has the clearest Intent: you or your friend?

You see, I am not saying one is right and one is wrong; it's just that when we are not clear about our Intent, or the reasons for our Intent, we are very often swayed to another person's plans.

However, it is actually very easy to end up with two clear Intents and both parties being happy with the outcome.

As I began the writing of this day, my husband asked me if I wanted to go to the movies with him and a few other members of our family.

Yes, I did want to go to the movies, and I was tempted to drop everything and go.

However, I had a very clear Intent, and reasons for my Intent, so I was happy to say "no" and neither of us felt badly about my decision to stay at work, or about his decision to go to the movies.

For your assignment today, choose one thing off of your list of what you want, which you made yesterday, and listen within for the reasons you want it.

Add those reasons to your list.

Enjoy yourself. This is a fun week!

INTENT—DAY THREE

Did you come up with reasons for why you want something on your list?

Whether it was hard or easy, do you see how these reasons are the foundation for Intent? Once you know them, it will be much easier to keep your Intent—which really means keeping your word to yourself.

To illustrate the next step in our clarifying Intent process, let me give you some of the reasons behind my Intent to get my work done yesterday and not to go to the movies.

My reasoning went something like this: "I have a commitment to others to have this piece of writing done. If I finish my writing and my business obligations, I will be able to take a week off to see my daughter and grandchildren without taking my work with me.

"Also, since we are moving in a few weeks, I know that I will want to spend time designing our new home environment. If I don't complete these tasks before I leave I will not have the freedom to do this."

Notice that I had clear reasons, and that they were also attached to a feeling.

I compared the brief feeling of taking time off to go to the movies, and the deeper longer-lasting feeling of having freedom to visit with loved ones and to design some spaces, something I find joy in doing. After doing that, it was easy to know what my Intent was, I honored it, and so did my husband.

I once stopped eating something that I didn't want to be eating, because I compared how I felt when I didn't eat it, to how I felt when I did.

Reasons attached to feelings will help you clarify any Intent.

Notice I did not say emotions. Emotions are based in the dualistic human worldview; when we act from emotion, we will most often get the exact opposite of our true Intent.

- Let's go back to your list. You picked something you want, and you gave reasons for why you want it.

- Now take some quiet time, and feel why you want it. What feelings does it give you?

You may discover in this process that you don't want it at all, or you may also find that you already have it, hidden in plain sight.

Intent—Day Four

Most of us equate being busy with living fully. However, if we are not clear about our own Intents, being busy is just a way to run and hide from our true desires.

This makes it even more important to to get clear about Intent.

Clear Intents are the way to become much less busy, happier, calmer, and more abundant than ever.

Now that we've added reasons and feelings to our list of what we want, let's talk about the difference between Intents and goals, so that we don't get confused by the two.

They are entirely different.

We live in a goal-orientated world. We are encouraged to write our goals down each year, otherwise known as New Year's resolutions.

Then later we get to face up to what we did or didn't do with our goals or resolutions.

Even when we actually do accomplish our goals, it rarely produces a feeling of satisfaction, unless we started the goal process with Intent first.

Goals fade away, or we forget that we made them, while our Intent remains long afterwords, because we have reasons and feelings about i t.

Goals can only be stated from what we already know about, while Intent begins with "imagine what if."

Goals begin from the outside and are imposed on our thinking and feelings, which often rebel.

Intent begins internally, which is actually where all that appears to be external begins.

Goals can breed fear of failure and fear of success, while Intent reveals what has already been perfectly created—so there is no place for fear.

Goals require continual effort and out-putting of energy. **Intent allows effortless action.**

- Let's go back to your list. Now that you have a clear Intent about at least one item on your list, let's do one more thing.

- No, not make a goal list; make a what do I think I have to do to get this list.

- Write everything down. All of it, even the parts you don't like. I'll tell you what to do with them tomorrow.

Intent—Day Five

The word *Intent* carries with it an unspoken agreement, and that agreement is that you are willing to do what it takes; any of it and all of it.

Sometimes we wonder why nothing happens after we have stated our Intent.

Often it is because we have an unconscious—and sometimes not-so-unconscious—aversion to doing a part of what it would take to accomplish or even allow the Intent to take place.

Somewhere hidden within our choices, we have that feeling, "that would mean I might have to," and whatever that "might have to" is, we feel we could not handle it, or we are not willing to do what would be required.

Here's an example of what this looked like once to me many years ago.

I was thinking about returning to the financial planning field to support myself as I was writing. It was a field I knew well, and I knew I would be successful once again at it, but I delayed and delayed and delayed, while the bills got farther and farther behind.

Until one day, the suffering from not having enough money to take care of my family was great enough that I was finally willing to see that a huge "I don't want to do that" was holding me back.

I knew that I would be required to go to New York for a month of training. It wasn't that I didn't want to go; I was afraid that my husband would leave me if I did. Yes, there was a story behind that, but the story doesn't matter. It was the fear of it that made me unwilling.

Once the reason was uncovered, I consciously chose to do what had to be done to fulfill my Intent of caring for those I loved. I joined the firm; I went to New York and had a wonderful month that was full of blessings for everyone, and of course that feared scenario did not take place.

So go back to your "what I want" list, and your intention for the items on it, and take another look at your willing list. What aren't you willing to do? Are you willing now to let the resistance go?

One last thing to know: Often, in fact almost always, you don't really end up having to do all those things; you just have to be willing. **Be willing!**

INTENT—DAY SIX

While I was writing this, we moved to a new home. That meant I had to call utilities, canceling some and getting others.

Since we were getting a fresh start, I decided to get a new DSL provider. I had a list of providers who service our area, so I went to each of their websites to get information on their services and phone numbers to call them.

One of those providers—a big name provider that I won't name but you all know it—had a nice Website with lots of information. However, I could not find the phone number to call them directly anywhere on their Website; the only option was to order online without help.

I am an Internet person but I was still not going to order that kind of service without speaking directly to someone to make sure it was what I wanted.

No phone number anywhere. It is a business that is in the business of connection; yet, there was no way for me to connect to them personally. Imagine that!

There is an Intent point to this story.

It is a useful way to examine our own Intents.

Go back to the list you have been working on of what you want—which of course now you can see is actually a list of Intents.

May I assume that one of those Intents is to be more abundant in some form in your life? It could be money, relationships, or health, it doesn't matter which one. Look at that Intent carefully.

Is there any way you are making it impossible for it to occur because there is no way to connect it to you? Or perhaps there is a small connection but not enough for it to fully succeed.

Yes, this is part of the "be willing" concept.

- Look at the practical way it is being carried out, or how you are not letting it happen.

- Take some time today to check your list once or twice.

- Tomorrow we wrap up all that we have learned about Intent and how to apply it to your life.

INTENT—DAY SEVEN

Intents reveal. Intents expand. Intents bring clarity.

Intents, combined with reasons and feelings that begin from within, don't require stress or effort to accomplish.

It is our willingness to do the things that need to be done that allows them to unfold without the strain of thinking we must make it happen.

We can set goals now based on our Intent.

I watched a movie where an injured man made his way down a mountainside by crawling, falling, and dragging himself to safety step by step. His Intent sprang from within. He was willing to do whatever it took to survive, and that meant getting down the mountain.

His goals were tiny. Get to that rock just a foot away, now the next one, then the next one.

Intents are long-range. Goals are step-by-step, day-by-day.

Have you ever biked or run up a hill?

Your Intent is to get up the hill. The goals are to the next tree, to the purple flower, to the twig on the road.

When the going gets difficult, sometimes it is best not to look up and judge the distance. Sometimes it is best to see the short-term goals ticked off one at a time. The Intent carries us forward to completion.

A goal doesn't carry with it the real reason for its accomplishment, does it? It is a means to fulfill the Intent.

Imagine the power and ease of an Intent that begins from the correct premise —that everything is already present, and all we are doing is revealing it, step-by-step.

Perhaps the mountain climber saw himself already down the mountain. Perhaps the biker saw herself at the top of the hill. You are one step ahead. You know yourself as an expression of the qualities of the climber, the biker, and the hill.

Beginning with the premise of One Mind's perfection eliminates any unwillingness, and completes the connections.

Start with Intent, and live in the Grace that is Life Itself.

97

— · —

LISTENING

LISTENING—DAY ONE

For the next *7–Day Shift Session* we are going to focus on Listening.

Maybe we should have started with this idea, since nothing will ever change until we learn how to listen within—to the still small voice that is always guiding us.

On the other hand, perhaps now we can see the importance of this quality, and it is perfect timing!

As we practice Listening, we gain insights, small and large, that help us live our lives more gracefully, and see or recall what we have missed or forgotten.

Once I had to go to the bank, which is about a 20-minute drive away. I got there at the time that I thought it opened, but found I had a 30-minute wait. It was too far to go home and come back, so instead of pacing around being upset, I decided to simply use that 30 minutes to listen.

I parked the car, opened the window, and listened. I listened to the birds, the quiet, and the traffic, all of it without really trying to "do" something with it. In the middle of all that, I heard a voice in my head. It was my dad saying, "Hi, George."

In that moment I recalled a very precious memory that I had forgotten. It had started a few days earlier when I told my sister about a turtle that came to visit me. She wrote and asked me if we could call him George.

I had no idea why she wanted me to call the turtle George, and I filed it away for another time.

As I heard my dad say, "Hi George," I remembered him coming up the stairs when we were children, and the little turtle in the fish bowl splashing around with excitement knowing that it meant he was going to be fed. Of course it was that turtle that my dad was saying "Hi" to.

Yes, a small incident, a tiny memory, but a completely forgotten picture of something very special and caring that was demonstrated by my dad, which revealed a deeper picture of who he is to me.

Listening within, I remembered what had never been lost.

Wouldn't that be just one really good reason to take a few minutes a day to simply listen?

Listening—Day Two

When I pack for a trip, I take all my trip stuff out, and then pick what I need for that particular trip.

As I finished packing for my last trip, I was getting ready to put away the little bag in my hand when I heard a voice say, "Keep it, you might need it."

I responded, "Whatever for? It is just one more thing to pack." But, I heard the "Keep it, you might need it" voice again and decided what could I lose, as it was an easily foldable bag; so I tucked it away in my carry-on luggage.

Later, as I was boarding the plane with my water bottle, and book in my hand, trying to balance that while holding my boarding pass and dragging my luggage, I remembered that little bag, pulled it out and hung in on the handle.

I tucked the water bottle, the book, and my boarding pass into it, and suddenly life was a lot easier.

Yes, such a small incident. However, that is what our days are made up of, small incidents that we either blow up into big ones, or miss altogether. Then we wonder why, after a time, we feel stressed, tired, frustrated, or depressed—all those emotions that build up over time because we are not Listening to that still, small voice that guides us, with often very practical suggestions.

We are geared to thinking that we need big miracles to prove that there is an infinite intelligence called God. We pray for signs, for help, for the flash of light that changes everything. But, that is a false teaching which hides the every-moment guidance and provision of that Infinite Intelligence for Itself, and we are Itself expressed.

Pausing, observing, and Listening, we find that the awareness of the Infinite Intelligence of Love, or God, becomes an easily understandable and present awareness.

We can feel that divine guidance is as close to us as our thoughts.

Listen, you can hear it now; trust in Love's guidance and provision. It then becomes an awareness that goes beyond faith; it becomes knowing.

LISTENING—DAY THREE

Now that we have begun to practice Listening, we may discover that there appear to be two voices in our head.

It may feel like that old picture of an angel on one shoulder and the devil on the other.

Which is which? How can we tell if the voice we are Listening to is the still, small voice guiding us to the perfection and good of divine

Mind, or the voice that only pretends to be us, distracting us from Truth?

Obviously, this is an extremely important distinction to make. How do we know?

Often it is an easy distinction to make.

If the voice in your head is telling you that you are not good enough, not capable, or it is angry, or disparaging, or in any way makes you feel less than loved, it is not God guiding you or speaking to you. Not! Not! Not!

So who is it? It's not you either.

Most of us think that when we hear a voice talking to us, it is ourselves talking to ourselves. Which is clearly crazy if we think about it, because why would we be so mean to ourselves? Why would we say those things? Why would we treat ourselves with such cruelty?

We wouldn't. The voice in your head is not you. I know it sounds like you. I know it speaks in your voice and uses your inflections and your own arguments, but it is not you. It disguises itself as you so you will listen.

If I popped into your head and started saying all those things to you it would be very unlikely that you would continue to listen, and hopefully you would throw me out your mental door.

And this is exactly what you need to do with that voice. Throw it out your mental door. It doesn't matter what you name it, just throw it out.

It is not Love speaking to you this way.

Love does guide, but It is not cruel. It leads the way with Its arm around you, and by walking beside you. It doesn't push you forward to walk alone, and It doesn't hold out a carrot promising you a future that isn't already yours.

Listen, yes; but be discerning.

What voice are you hearing? Pay attention to the one that gives you hope, the one that is loving and kind; and throw the other one out, locking the door behind it!

Listening—Day Four

What about the art of Listening to each other? Do we? Do we really just sit and listen when someone speaks? Most of the time we are multitasking, aren't we?

We are thinking things like, "What shall I cook for dinner, when can I do the report that is due, maybe a new curtain would look nice here, wonder what's on TV," all of these thoughts that go on and on and occupy a portion of our thinking when others are talking.

Even if we do listen, our next impulse is often to fix or comment upon or judge what has been said.

How often do we deeply listen without multitasking or fixing or judging?

If we are Listening with spiritual ears, we hear something completely different from what we hear when we if we listen with a material, dualistic, gotta-take-action state of Listening.

When we listen with spiritual perception we can accomplish two things at once, the perfect multitasking.

In order to use spiritual perception as we listen, we have to actually listen. Not just to the words, but to the meaning behind them. As we listen, we get a deeper sense of what is being said. We get into the heart of the matter.

The word matter leads perfectly into the second part of spiritual-perception Listening. As we listen, we learn to translate what we are hearing away from matter, the material sense of what is being said, and into the Truth of what is really going on.

For example: We hear a story of discouragement at work or home, and as we deeply listen without distraction, we replace the heart of the matter with the heart of the Truth.

We can understand and have compassion for the human dilemma, while at the same time knowing that there is no discouragement in the Life that is Living Itself.

The right idea will come into our thinking, as we listen both within, to the still, small voice that is guiding us, and without, to the person who is sharing with us.

This is the gift that gives in many ways.

It is the gift to others of Listening, and the gift of knowing what is actually True for the other person.

This also gives us the even greater gift of being aware of the presence of the guidance of Love that is always present within each of us, if we would but listen.

LISTENING—DAY FIVE

Can we get to spiritual awareness by Listening to material claims? No and yes. If we listen to what the material world tells us, and accept it as true, then the essence and grace of spiritual awareness eludes us.

If we observe—a different form of Listening—what the material world is telling us, and use it to point the way to Truth, then, yes, it can be helpful.

Here's an example that I imagine everyone has experienced: paying bills and balancing check books. Whether we do it by hand, or use a computer program, there is usually one of two outcomes, when we are Listening to material sense.

There is either more money in our account than we thought, producing a temporary sense of euphoria or security, or less money in our account, which produces a more lasting sense of fear and discouragement.

If we switch the activity around, from finding out what material sense is telling us about our state of wealth, to observing the activity of the qualities of order and balance and awareness (to name just a few that can be attached to this activity), we begin in the arena of spiritual Truth.

Starting with this right premise, then whatever the result may be, it produces neither euphoria nor fear, but only guidance to stating the Truth about our wealth. Our Wealth is permanent, has nothing to do with numbers, and is always present and available.

But first we must listen.

We must listen to what we are being guided to do by the still, small voice.

We must listen to the spiritual facts before we take action, and we must listen to the spiritual sense of what may appear as a material reality.

Listening first, every activity, every thought, every idea, springs from the Truth of our being. When we begin within from this pure state of Listening, we can trust that what may appear as an outward picture will match our highest understanding of the qualities of God.

It doesn't take time to do this; it just takes practice.

Listening—Day Six

Have you ever thought about the difference between Listening and hearing?

Hearing is something we do with our ears; Listening is something that happens within the quiet of our intention.

As I sat on my deck yesterday I heard many animals and birds. It was quite a variety. To distinguish between them, and to understand the meaning behind their sounds, I had to listen.

As I have been practicing Listening to the animals, I knew that the squirrel was telling me that a predator (in this case a cat) was sneaking up the side of our hill.

Of course, a cat wasn't a scary event for me, but the skills of Listening translate easily to everyday life.

Listening within we are aware of what is going on around us, and we can immediately take internal action, as well as external practical action as needed.

As we listen, we become more present in the moment.

We discover that there is no past or future to listen to, or to fear, or even to be elated about.

As we practice the art of Listening, we become more aware of the gift that is contained within each moment.

Hearing tends to be noisy. Listening is a quiet affair.

Take just a few minutes today to sit someplace familiar, and instead of hearing what is happening, listen to what is happening.

Notice the difference.

LISTENING—DAY SEVEN

Listen with the ear that is in the center of your chest. Hear what's behind what I say. —Rumi

As we finish up this week of Listening we are really just beginning. As we practice Listening we will see the practical effects in our life.

For example to get ready for a party at our house, I cleaned off my desk and put away some curtain rings for later. A few days later, curtain in hand, I went looking for the rings. Not only couldn't I find them, I had absolutely no memory of what I had done with them.

Obviously I **wasn't** Listening when I put them away, I was multitasking without awareness. I looked for a few minutes, and then chased away the voice in my head that told me how, once again, I wasn't paying attention, and I went back to work.

Later I got up from my desk, walked to my sewing box, opened it, and found the rings. There was no conscious thought that they were there. I just followed an inward guidance without outward expectations.

Here is one last story that is an example of the power of Listening.

I have a very powerful tiny magnet that I use to hold up recipes when I am cooking. When I am not using it, I keep it on the metal container on my counter.

During that same party, I forgot that it was there and passed a metal cooking sheet pan by it and it got stuck on the magnet.

As I said, this is a very powerful magnet, and it took quite a bit of pulling to release my sheet pan. It would have been so much easier if I could have demagnetized the pan.

What has this got to do with Listening?

We are always being guided. However, every day, all day, there are magnets that pull us to them. They disguise themselves as thoughts—people, events, places, and things—all claiming to have a power that can keep us attached to the material world and its distractions and lies.

It is easier to avoid those magnets when you remember that they are there. However, if one of those magnets pulls you in, there is a simple way to free yourself.

Return to Listening within. This will demagnetize you, and you will be immediately released. No suffering, pain, or time required.

As we said in our first day of Listening, when we pause, observe, and listen, we find that the awareness of the Infinite Intelligence of Love, or God, becomes an easily understandable and present awareness.

We begin to feel that divine guidance is as close to us as our thoughts.

As we listen, we learn to trust in Love's guidance and provision.

98

— • —

SILENCE

In our last *7–Day Shift Session*, we practiced listening. Practicing Silence is the perfect next step. We often think they are the same thing, and they are not.

When we are listening, we hear sounds. When we are in Silence we are in perfect stillness, with no sound, or noise at all.

When we are in Silence, we are like a clear, calm, and perfectly still lake that reflects its surroundings like a mirror.

In Silence, we understand that we are the perfect reflection of God.

Mother Teresa said, *We need to find God, and he cannot be found in noise and restlessness. God is the friend of silence. See how nature—trees, flowers, grass—grows in silence; see the stars, the moon and the sun, how they move in silence.*

We need silence to be able to touch souls."

Silence calls us all, amidst the noise and motion of our everyday lives.

We want to be silent.

We want to understand that stillness; but how do we get there?

Let's begin by noticing when it isn't silent.

- Notice the noise.

- Notice the distraction.

- Notice the uneasiness.

- Notice the constant doing.

- Notice, but don't judge.

Stay still in your thinking as you listen and observe.
Shhh....

SILENCE—DAY TWO

Did you notice the noise when you practiced listening?

That's the beginning. Now we are going to practice listening for the Silence.

Elisabeth Kubler-Ross said, *There is no need to go to India or anywhere else to find peace.*

You will find that deep place of Silence right in your room, your garden, or even your bathtub."

This makes perfect sense, doesn't it, when we realize that Silence comes from within. It is the opposite of the trance state—of addiction to the outside world and its focus on objects one at a time.

But, for most of us, listening to the Silence is a foreign concept. We may ask, "What good will it do?" or "How do I even do that?"

Have you ever felt disconnected, frustrated, out of control, sad, lonely, or stuck?

If so, then learning to listen to the Silence, and then learning to live your life from that Silence, will dissolve the feelings of disconnection, frustration, helplessness, sadness, loneliness or being stuck.

In that deep place of Silence, you will find the unending well of peace from which life blooms—without a hint of discontent.

So today, give it a try.

Take some time, even if it is only five minutes, and stop and listen for the Silence.

Silence—Day Three

The world is awash with consistent noise.

As I was writing this, I had heard the distant rumble of cars, and the closer sound of a neighbor with some kind of big machine in his yard, and the occasional plane overhead.

In between all of those kinds of noises there were a number of bird calls, a squirrel hopping from tree to tree, and then, as the morning turned to afternoon, I could hear the loud drone of the newly emerged cicadas.

That was the hearing noise.

But there was also visual noise, and smell noise, and touch noise, and even taste noise. Most of all there was the mental noise: the mental noise of tasks, and wants, and do-this, and get-that, noise.

Where was the Silence?

Even in my silent time on a rock overlooking the creek, there was still all that noise. However, there was that moment when Silence emerged, through the noise.

It was the attitude of Silence as described by Mahatma Gandhi: "In the attitude of Silence the soul finds the path in a clearer light, and what is elusive and deceptive resolves itself into crystal clearness."

We can begin there, in the attitude of Silence.

We can learn to sift through what appears as noise, and hear the clarity of Silence.

SILENCE—DAY FOUR

Jon Young tells the story of Gilbert Walking Bull, who talked about the training of their children around nature and Silence. He recalls that their parents would always say, "Sh... Sh... Listen."

And although they didn't know what they were listening for, soon it became a habit to hear not only previously unheard sounds, but also the sacred Silence.

When their parents gave them tasks, like finding herbs on the mountainside, they would travel as a group, in Silence. What a difference from our modern world, where our children travel loudly.

In our drive to be always connected, we are becoming increasingly unconnected to the essence of the Infinite.

Unconnected, we work hard to be and do. The noise of materiality makes us feel stuck, lost and alone.

Within the shift of perception, to seeing that all things are present as God only, we can let go of the fear of being alone, and find all that we need within the silent communication with Spirit.

Within that connection and communication there is no effort. Instead, we feel the harmony of One.

As we practice listening to the Silence, we will find ourselves eliminating the noise in our lives—all forms of noise. We will relax into the peace found within the Silence of the Infinite.

SILENCE—DAY FIVE

It's almost impossible for the modern mind to be still enough to be in Silence. It is so easily distracted.

We are busy planning, and worrying, and wishing. Re-learning how to be still is an art that takes consecrated practice.

Is the benefit of listening to the Silence worth the time it takes to learn to be still? If you have experienced it, you know there are no words to describe the experience, no matter how fleeting it might have been. If you haven't, you can feel your heart's yearning towards it.

It isn't that we no longer hear the noise when we have learned to hear the Silence. It's that what we hear instead is the essence of it, not the material overlay.

In this Silence, we become better able to see through everything that appears material, and see its true substance as the ideas of Infinite Mind.

In the Silence, we learn how to direct our thinking away from the experiences we don't want, and into the ones we do.

In the Silence, we let go of trying to make things happen, and follow instead the direction of the still, small voice, the feminine Principle of Love.

In the Silence, we find the peace that defies the material sense of the world, overrides all distractions, stills troubled minds, and reveals the spiritual essence of all life.

Taking the time to listen to and be Silence results in an overflowing of immeasurable, yet completely tangible, blessings.

So no matter how hard our modern minds may find it to do this practice, let's do it anyway.

SILENCE—DAY SIX

As I write this, the morning chorus of birds has begun. It is a celebration of life. They don't need a cup of coffee to wake up. They call in joy to the morning. They announce the dawn of a new day before it is visible to the eye.

There is a morning chorus every place in the world. Although a different bird begins the morning chorus, depending on the location, it is the same bird that begins it in each place. Where we live, it is the cardinal.

At this time of the year around 5:15 a.m. he sends out one call. To me it sounds like "Hello, Hello, Pretty, Pretty."

Then Silence.

About 25 minutes later, the rest of the calls begin, one bird at a time saying, "I am here, are you? Let's celebrate."

If we listen, we find that within these joyful calls, we find the Silence.

As we study a flower, observe a grain of sand, really look at another person through the spiritual lens of love, we find the Silence.

Within this Silence we can not only imagine divine Mind Knowing Itself, Love Loving Itself, Life Living Itself, but we can feel it.

In the Silence, this feeling overpowers the intellectual process of the worldview and material perception, and reveals to us personally, without anyone else needing to tell us, the Oneness of It all.

SILENCE—DAY SEVEn

What are we doing when we listen to Silence?

We are altering our point of view and state of mind. We are consciously choosing to be free.

Listening to the Silence can be done all the time. It doesn't require that we sit still for hours, or become mute, or ask for absolutely no noise.

It means we listen to the Silence found within what we are saying and hearing. In quiet times and in busy times, Silence can still be found.

As we practice this skill, we are expanding into a greater awareness of the consciousness of Mind. We are allowing the harmony and grace of divine Love to be revealed to us.

As we unite with the Silence, we are effectively dissolving perceptions that blind us to big R Reality.

We are freed from the confining binds of the worldview. Our imagination leaps into what was the unknowable, and gives us a glimpse of the Infinite Intelligence that underlies, contains, and is what we call the universe.

No wonder listening to the Silence feels so good.

Within the Silence, we let go of will-power, and instead become aware of the qualities of everything we perceive.

We stop trying to make things happen, in essence admitting that we are not the creators and the controllers of our lives, and instead we feel the power of the Infinite One as the only cause and creator.

We experience perfection in the Silence, and that perfection becomes our experience; all of this because we have taken the time to practice listening to the Silence, a doorway to the awareness of One.

99

— • —

SELF LOVE

SELF-LOVE—DAY ONE

For our next *7–Day Shift Session* we are going to explore the concept of Self-love. It's a tricky subject.

Most of us know that we would be happier if we did have Self-love, but we aren't really sure how to get to that state of mind.

Plus, we wonder if it is right to love ourselves, because we have been told that Self-love is selfish.

Obviously it is important to understand the difference between the Self-love we want, and the Self-love we don't want, since it turns out the word Self-love can mean the exact opposite, depending on who is saying it and how it is used.

Mary Baker Eddy said, "Self-love is more opaque than a solid body."

When I first heard this quote I thought it couldn't pertain to me, because I was so often "down on myself."

Now I see that "being down" on oneself is the negative version of Self-love, the kind we don't want.

For the next 7 days, let's observe the difference between negative Self-love and spiritual Self-love, and see what a difference it makes in the quality of our lives.

Self-Love—Day Two

Do we need Self-love? Absolutely. Without it we cannot be happy. **But which kind do we need, and how can we easily tell the difference?**

When we are attempting to fill something we need by giving to others so that we can have what we think we lack, we act from the place where, "it's all about me."

That is what negative Self-love looks like. It rests in the human personality and ego of self, and, not surprisingly, it does not ever bring permanent happiness.

We rarely mean to make life "all about me."

However, when we don't understand that Self-love is not about loving the human-personality self, but instead loving the qualities of God, present as ourselves, we are always in some form of need, which means that without realizing it, our life is often "all about me."

Jesus' admonition to "love thy neighbor as thyself" states clearly that we better love ourselves well if we are going to treat our neighbors well too.

This is tricky I know. **Same phrase, entirely different meanings and entirely different results.**

Perhaps the first step to seeing the difference between the two kinds of self-love is to begin with the question, "What premise is our Self-love based upon?"

Observe your actions today.

Do most of them stem from personal Self-love or from spiritual Self-love? For heaven's sake, don't judge what you see, that would most definitely not be Self-love. Just observe and while you do, be kind to yourself.

Self-Love—Day Three

The Self-love beginning with the premise of a human personality and needs means that we take care of ourselves through will-power, positive thinking, control, destructive behavior (which is actually inverted control and will-power), and hard work.

The Self-love beginning with the premise that we are the presence of Infinite Intelligent Love eliminates need.

In this Self-love, we love ourselves because we are the reflection and expression of God. We care for ourselves within the context of caring for the gift that we are to each other.

What did you observe yesterday?

Were you able to remain kind to yourself?

Did you find that you are often in some form of struggle?

Isn't it odd that struggle is really a form of "it's all about me"?

We all are tired of this struggle, and willing and ready to understand and live true Self-love. Let's give up negative Self-love, and begin to really focus on the qualities of God that we uniquely express. Let's cherish their presence as us.

Take a moment and write down everything that you like about yourself.

It's not hard; no one will see the list but you.

This is the beginning of letting go of being stuck in struggle, so take the time; it will be worth it.

Self-Love—Day Four

As knowledge of ourselves as the qualities of divine Love increases, so does our Self-love. This is an easy love to have.

This Self-love removes ego. It eliminates fear. It dissolves being stuck in negative descriptions of ourselves.

We learn to love and treasure the qualities we express. We give thanks for who we are. We find life flows from this kind of love, and we no longer need to use any form of human control.

Practicing this kind of Self-love is immediately effective and extremely practical.

Here's an example.

Washing the dishes, mowing the lawn, and running the sweeper are all examples of those tasks that we find we have to do over and over again.

It's easy to get into the mode of "why can't someone help me, I'm tired of always having to do this, why am I always the one who gets this done?" and on and on in this same vein.

We all have moments during the day when this kind of thought creeps in and brings unhappiness with it.

If we stayed with material Self-love, then we would feel very righteous with these thoughts; but rarely does this way of thinking produce any kind of positive result.

Switching to spiritual Self-love, we love the qualities we are expressing while doing these tasks.

We love how diligent we are, how orderly, how detailed, and consistent. We love that we honor beauty and clarity. Oh gosh, we could go on for hours with this kind of Self-love.

What are we doing? We are loving the qualities of God, the qualities that we are expressing and reflecting. This is true Self-love.

For the next 24 hours give this kind of Self-love a try.

There are plenty of ways to practice it. Feel the difference between material Self-love and spiritual Self-love, and witness the outcome.

SELF-LOVE—DAY FIVE

Isn't it easy to tell which Self-love we are practicing? In the human version of the Self-love experience, "we need."

We have all experienced this need. It is a need for anything we feel we don't have—like love, money, health, or time. Needing is not a good experience or feeling.

However, within divine Self-love, there is no need; there is only the experience in each moment of the qualities of who we are, present and being, lived as us.

In divine Self-love we find plenty of everything, and our love for ourselves flows to our neighbors equally, without effort.

In human Self-love we ask, "Notice me, help me, give to me, and take care of me."

In divine Self-love, the I AM is present.

Within this Self-love our personality, and ego step aside so that we can be seen as we are: the reflection and expression of God.

Spiritual leader Eknath Easwaran said, "The spiritual life is a call to action. But it is a call to action without any selfish attachment to the results."

Action and lack of attachment are the natural outcome of practicing spiritual Self-love. We automatically no longer worry about results, because our attention is on loving the qualities of God that we are expressing in action.

Self-love within a spiritual context is a marvelous way to live.

Did you practice spiritual Self-love yesterday? Did you notice the difference?

Let's continue this practice. Each day we will become more and more skilled, until one day all we will know is true Self-love.

Self-Love—Day Six

Let's go back to that quote from Mary Baker Eddy, "Self-love is more opaque than a solid body."

I knew that the word opaque means not being able to see through something, but with further study, I realized it also means not letting the light shine through.

Where there is no light, there is only darkness. When we realize that negative Self-love is actually darkness, it makes it even more of an unwanted state of mind. Through the darkened lens of human Self-love, we are unable to see the light of Truth in any situation.

However, as we are willing to know ourselves as the qualities of God, the opaqueness dissolves, and in the resulting clarity we find our freedom from need.

We experience instead the joy of divine Self-love, which is always overflowing, filling our lives full of blessings without measure.

It may seem at first that there is only a subtle distinction between the opaque Self-love that blinds us to Truth and the light of Self-love that is the Truth; but with practice we become aware of the immense gap between them. In fact, they are so opposite they can never be in the same place at the same time.

By observing our actions, we can begin to unearth our hidden, and not so hidden, perceptions.

When we realize that the world is the subjective state of our personal point of view, then noticing when we act from negative Self-love becomes a learning and shifting experience.

With this awareness, we can choose to immediately shift to loving ourselves as the qualities of God, and experience without any limitation the Self-love that is Light Itself.

Self-Love—Day Seven

Now that we know how to love ourselves in the proper context, Jesus' saying, love thy neighbor as thyself, makes much more sense. Of course, we will love our neighbor as ourselves, because we see that t hey **are ourselves.**

Seen as the subjective point of view that we entertain, we know them as we know ourselves. Seen through the eyes of God, where the subjective state is God in action, we know them as God knows them, One as ourselves. Within spiritual Self-love the phrase "thou

shalt not" found within the 10 commandments makes more sense t
oo.

Shalt not—not meaning "don't or else," but meaning, "you can't."

**Remember negative Self-love and divine or spiritual
Self-love cannot exist at the same place and time.**

Therefore, there is no way for us to do anything that isn't based in
perfect Self-love of the Love of Loving Itself, when we understand
and live in true divine Self-love.

Each moment spent in true Self-love erases more of the illusionary
boundary lines between each other. Instead we see each other as a
unique expression of the One that we are.

Within this awareness there is no jealously or competition. We step
completely outside the game of the worldview and see the Truth: We
are all One.

This is true divine Self-love.

100

— · —

KINDNESS

KINDNESS—DAY ONE

I was emailing one of my granddaughters and said, "I know that it is not always easy, but if you stick to being true to yourself and kind to others, you will always be happy, and what is better than that?"

Really, what is better than that?

In the last *7–Day Shift Session* we talked about self-love, which is certainly being true to oneself, so we have that covered, right?

Now we are ready in this *7–Day Shift Session* to discover Kindness.

In a study of 37 cultures around the world, 16,000 subjects were asked about their most desired traits in a mate.

For both sexes, the first preference was Kindness, the second was intelligence.

In the early 80's a phrase swept the country: Practice random acts of kindness and senseless acts of beauty.*

This phrase grew into a book, websites, and many current phenomena such as the book and movie "Pay it Forward."

At the end of the movie, "Evan Almighty," God tells Evan that the way to change the world is by doing one Act of Random Kindness at a time(ARK).

So we know Kindness is important. We want it more than anything. We love the idea of it.

But what is it? What does it mean to be kind? Are random acts of Kindness enough?

If God practiced **random** acts of Kindness, would we even be here? Or is Kindness one of those underlying necessities and Principles of the infinite universe upon which all the rest is based?

Let's think on those questions, and I'll meet you here tomorrow for the discovery of Kindness.

*Peace activist Anne Herbert says she wrote this phrase on a placemat at a Sausalito restaurant in 1982 or 1983.

KINDNESS—DAY TWO

Isn't it the strangest thing that in the quest for enlightenment the understanding and acting out of Kindness often vanishes?

When we turn within for our own self-enlightenment and forget the needs of others, could that be enlightenment?

Can it be Kindness if we choose the path of renouncing the world, and let others take up the slack we have left behind?

Coach John Wooden said, *You can't live a perfect day without doing something for someone who will never be able to repay you.*

Lao Tzu listed Kindness as the first of three great treasures, and the Buddha taught that generosity is a primary quality of an awakened mind.

All spiritual teachings have strong roots in the ethics of the daily interactions of each of us.

Remember the story in the Bible of the injured man by the side of the road who was ignored by many before being noticed and taken care of by a passing stranger.

Isn't this a lesson on Kindness?

Living the idea of Kindness in a practical-day-to day manner is essential to a happy personal life, and necessary for every person in our world to flourish.

Before going any further, let's take a day and think through what we perceive as Kindness.

Look around. Pay attention.

What Kindness do you see and what Kindness are you doing? What are the qualities of Kindness?

When I was young, I used to admire intelligent people; as I grow older, I admire kind people.—Abraham Joshua Heschel

KINDNESS—DAY THREE

We have asked ourselves what it means to be kind, and we have looked for the qualities of Kindness in action.

Confucius urged his followers to "recompense kindness with kindness." And Albert Schweitzer said, "Constant kindness can accomplish much. As the sun makes ice melt, kindness causes misunderstanding, mistrust, and hostility to evaporate."

Wouldn't it be wonderful if the media and their commentaries were spoken with Kindness?

Imagine how world-shifting that would be!

Instead of telling lies, and stretching the truth in order to be on top, what if we were only concerned with being kind?

Of course, we can not make others act from Kindness; to do that, we would probably have to resort to being unkind. However, we can do it for ourselves.

We can choose not to participate in any activity that is unkind.

We can refuse to listen to, watch, or support in any way any conscious act of unkindness.

We can take action and say "No" when we see unkindness in action.

We can choose to live kindly.

We can monitor what we say about others.

We can act from the intent of Kindness, and not from the need to be right.

We can choose the awareness that it is possible to remain kind and still be wise.

This of course means that we must be aware of what it means to be kind, and not allow unkind things to be said or done to ourselves—even that which we do to ourselves by ourselves.

Yesterday, as you noticed the qualities of Kindness, did you see that some of its qualities are patience, wisdom, understanding, gentleness, strength, awareness, loving, and grace?

There are many people living these qualities on a moment-to-moment basis, and yet it is rarely noticed, because unkindness makes so much noise.

However, we can notice.

Charles Kuralt said, "The everyday kindness of the back roads more than makes up for the acts of greed in the headlines."

This is who we are; let's act that way—not randomly—but consistently.

KINDNESS—DAY FOUR

Let's take a day away from this *7–Day Shift Session* to be kind to others, and instead focus what it means to be kind to ourself.

Why? Because it is so often not done, and it is so imperative that we learn to do so.

The standard of behavior is actually to be unkind to ourselves. In fact, we could appear to be the kindest person anyone has ever met, and still be a bully and cruel to ourself.

We speak internally to ourselves in the most unkind ways, and accept it as if it were natural, even beyond natural: required.

We allow the voice inside ourselves to tell us that we are not good enough, not capable, not allowed, and not worthy.

We have thousands and thousands of unkind thoughts about ourselves on a daily basis, and yet rarely do anything about it. Perhaps halfheartedly we say, "Yes I know I should be more kind to myself, but."

And in that but, the unkind, cruel, mean, bullying, authoritarian, dictator, voice begins again, with its mantra that we are not capable, allowed or worthy.

Just because we know that God is Love doesn't send that voice away. In fact, that can make it worse.

"Yes, God is Love for everyone else, but not for me," we say to ourselves.

Isn't this crazy? It gives us a clue why there is so much unkindness being done in the world. We haven't stopped it within first.

What that bully says to us are those simple phrases that seem to be so correct. "You eat too much; you are wrong about that; you didn't do the right thing; you will never be well; you are required to suffer; they deserve it more than you." Yes, I could go on for pages and pages.

All of these suggestions are unkind. If you heard them outside of yourself spoken to another you would recognize the lie.

Because it speaks within, and in your own voice and inflection, it is accepted.

Tell it no! Begin now to be kind to yourself at all times. Be wise, be strong, push that bully out the door—and never let it in again.

There is no duality—with some people over there and you alone over here.

There is only God Loving Itself, and that is you.

Honor this awareness by not succumbing to unkindness. Instead take action in true Kindness: beginning within. Don't listen to the bully but only to the still, small voice that is God.

We are the leaves of one branch, the drops of one sea, the flowers of one garden. —Jean Baptiste Henry Lacordaire

Kindness—Day Five

I was sitting outside thinking about Kindness, and nature arranged a wonderful symbol for me to share with you.

What I was thinking about was the question, "What do we do when we see that others are not being treated kindly? Do we look away? Do we think, 'I am so glad that's not me?' Or perhaps we remain apathetic, thinking that there is nothing we can do."

It was the blue jays who answered my question for me.

As I walked into the house to begin to write, I heard them squawking. Anyone who has ever listened to birds knows they have a variety of ways of speaking, depending on what is happening; and in this case I recognized that they were upset about something.

It was so loud I stepped back outside to see what it was they were so alarmed about.

There they were, the three blue jays that live in our woods, surrounding our resident hawk and screaming at him. They circled, and switched sides, and kept him boxed in with the noise.

He tried going higher, and they went with him. In a few minutes two more neighboring blue jays joined them, and for a time those five jays kept up their screaming, until the hawk must have agreed to fly away, because the jays left and then so did the hawk.

What was happening? Kindness in action.

Those blue jays saw a potential danger for a member of their community, and they protected it. I couldn't see what they were protecting, but it was obvious they were. Blue jays are much smaller than a hawk, and the hawk is a mighty predator, but they were not afraid to face him down when it was necessary.

We could do at least as much for those in our community—whether it be local or family or universal.

Like the blue jays, we can take action within the context of Kindness. This is different from talking about the value of Kindness; this is living its power, and expecting to be the victor over unkindness in whatever form it presents itself and wherever it is found, from within families to governments.

We can be just like those blue jays. Be the first to start, or join those that have already begun; just do what you can do. Blue jays had a voice, and they used it. Let's use ours too.

Silent gratitude isn't much use to anyone.—Gladys Browyn Stern

Kindness—Day Six

In the Talmud, we read that "deeds of kindness are equal in weight to all the commandments."

At first glance this seems like an impossible statement. However, when we examine the depths and breadth of Kindness, we can see that this is entirely true.

If we acted out of Kindness, we would not be able to steal, cheat, lie, or harm anyone in any way.

If we acted from Kindness, we would be putting the Principle of Love first, which means we would be following the commandment of not putting any other gods before God, Love.

It would be easy to know what to do in all situations if we asked ourselves whether what we were contemplating was kind to ourselves first, and then as a direct correlation, kind to another.

Amelia Earhart said, "No kind action ever stops with itself. One kind action leads to another. Good example is followed. A single act of Kindness throws out roots in all directions, and the roots spring up and make new trees. The greatest work that Kindness does to others is that it makes them kind themselves."

When we become too self-absorbed to notice that we are not being kind, we are selfish. When we are selfish, we miss the wholeness of creation.

This is sad for everyone.

It will be sad for us because we will miss the glory of Life, and sad for others because we will most likely not be acting out of generosity, since that is difficult for both the selfish miser and the glutton.

Have you ever proved a mathematical problem by reversing what you did to make sure the answer works both ways? In grade school my math teacher made us do that all the time, and I still find myself doing it in the rare times I don't use my calculator.

In the same way, we can prove to ourselves whether we are being kind by seeing the mirror of life, which reverses back to us what we perceive and believe to be reality. If we find despair, sadness, frustration, unhappiness within, it is very possible that we not acting from our intent of Kindness.

Nature in its beauty is awash in Kindness.

As we are Kindness Itself, we are awash in beauty.

KINDNESS—DAY SEVEN

Fredrich Nietzche said, *Kindness and love, the most curative herbs and agents in human intercourse are such precious finds that one would hope these balsamlike remedies would be used as economically as possible; but this is impossible. Only the boldest Utopians would dream of the economy of kindness.*

Within this context, I am proud that he would call me a bold Utopian, because I do believe that it is not only possible, but absolutely imperative for every individual not to only dream of the economy of Kindness but to implement it.

In fact, let's go a step further and say that since there is only one Life force, and Its Principle is the Principle of Love, then Kindness composes the DNA of each of us.

Kindness is hard-wired into our system because we are the action and expression and reflection of Divine Love.

It is only logical and scientific that we contain exactly what God contains, and this is Kindness in all its forms.

So when we appear to act unkindly or see unkindness in others, we realize that we are not trying to change ingrained situations or lives.

Instead we are shifting our perception to Truth, and staying there, and as we do so, we see things as they really are, as Love in action.

Within this spiritual perception, all that is unkind vanishes into the nothingness of the missed perception from whence it came. Yes, it takes awareness and practice to cultivate and maintain the spiritual perception that reveals only Love in action.

Seeing and living the qualities of Kindness is a spiritual practice that will reveal the Truth to us and transform our lives, which in turn transforms the world.

One kind thought and action at time. We can do it. We can be bold in our declaration of Kindness.

After all, Kindness is the ground of our being.

Three things in human life are important. The first is to be kind. The second is to be kind. The third is to be kind.—Henry James

101

RIGHT ACTION

RIGHT ACTION—DAY ONE

In the world of sales training there was a very graphic sales technique on how to get more business. It was, "Throw enough sh** up against the wall and some of it will stick."

Whenever I heard this, all I could think of was, "Yuck, what a mess."

Recently I heard a very successful businessman declare that this was the technique he used, and it worked extremely well for him. Instead of thinking things through, he simply gets up and does something, and he worries about the consequences later.

As I heard him describe this technique, I inwardly shook my head in amazement. I wondered how he could continue to live in that state of mind and point of view.

I would not want to be like this businessman no matter how successful he is, because someday he will have to ask, "Is this what my life is about?" Then he will have to start cleaning up the mess, and learn how every action appears with spiritual awareness.

On the other side of the sliding scale we have those who have been lulled into non-action; perhaps because they are afraid of doing the wrong thing, or perhaps because they think God will take care of it. In the meantime they live in state of poverty of one kind or another.

The problem lies in a missed perception on both sides.

Does waiting for another person to fulfill our needs seem like what is meant by constant provision and abundance? Is there really freedom in doing nothing?

On the other hand, is it really spiritual awareness to throw things up against the wall to see if they will stick? Do we need to prove that God will take care of the messes we make?

These two points of view, the throwing and the waiting, are ingrained in many of us, and they run the show silently and deeply. **Neither one of them is based on Truth.**

Wouldn't omnipresent order move things precisely, at the right time, in the right place, as the omniaction of the Infinite Principle of Love?

So if Right Action is neither "the throw stuff at it" nor "the wait for God to take care of it," what is it?

That's what we'll talk about for the next 7 days. In the meantime, take some time today and become aware of the "throw" and the "wait" actions in your life.

The perfection of a clock is not to go fast, but to be accurate. —Luc de Clapiers

RIGHT ACTION—DAY TWO

What did you discover yesterday about Right Action in your life? Do you lean more to the "throw" or the "wait"?

Sometimes we are both. Without taking the time to pause and listen, I have often blindly rushed ahead thinking that no matter what happened I would be able to handle it. No matter how big the mess, I was capable of cleaning it up.

On the other hand, I have paused in poverty more than once, laboring under a false perception.

I had once read an account of monks who trusted in God to provide them with everything, so they had nothing, expecting that when they needed it, somehow it would be provided.

I perceived that as a trust or faith that was a wonderful asset and I wanted to have that trust too.

It took me years to figure out that because of that desire I had been living just like those monks, while thinking that I was striving towards understanding abundance.

Because of the underlying missed perception—that trust and faith are proved by having nothing—I had nothing, and if by chance I gained something I quickly lost it. Just like those monks I was living hand to mouth.

So on one hand I was declaring abundance, and on the other I was denying it.

In order to have Right Action we must use all the knowledge we have gained about listening, silence, self-love, awareness, kindness, and intent.

As in all things, understanding, and consciously choosing our point of view, and actively bringing our state of mind into that point of view are all the key to Right Action.

Today, take the time to consciously choose the point of view from which you want to live.

Then actively bring your state of mind into that point of view, so that your emotions and feelings reside in the same place as your intent.

Then and only then will the actions you take be consistent with the choice of how you want to live your life.

Right Action—Day Three

Now that you are ready to take Right Action, you may have discovered that you are not taking any action at all.

That's because there is a hidden stumbling block that we all trip over. Let's dissolve that one today and get on with our lives.

Within every action there is buried within it the moment of decision. It is the moment we decide to take action or not to take action.

Many people dread that moment, and actively take action not to take action.

One of the reasons for this choice of non-action we discussed yesterday. We know that when we are not sure what our point of view is, and our state of mind is not in line with it, confusion ensues, and it then often feels easier to stand still rather than move anywhere at all.

Today, let's talk about another reason for taking no action.

It is the stumbling block of thinking too broadly and with too much detail. Because of this, we are too confused or afraid to make a decision.

To take Right Action, we must divide our decisions into smaller decisions.

Here's an example of making a decision.

Let's pretend that we want to move somewhere. How would we go about deciding and taking action and actually moving? Break the decisions into small decisions.

It may go like this: The first decision would be willing to consider moving. The next decision is to be willing to decide to move. If everything feels right, then the next decision is the decision to move.

This is the stumbling block for most of us.

We can see that any decision carries with it details and consequences. So in making the first decision, we think that it impacts all the logics of carrying it out, and it doesn't.

Just because you decide to move doesn't mean that you have to actually move. In fact, at this point you may realize that it doesn't feel right to move, and you can change your mind and stay where you are.

Assuming it still feels okay to move, go to the next decision.

Decide that you are willing to find the perfect place. Then divide that decision down into smaller pieces, like area, people, climate, etc.

Take the logistics of every decision as a separate decision, and life becomes much simpler.

It also becomes easier as you remember that making conscious choices means you must be aware of your point of view and state of mind. Then, you are able to, allowed to, and must, change your mind about what you are doing to fit how you want to live your life.

Try this out today. Finally, decide about something you have been tabling for another day.

See how it clears out your thinking and leaves you free to take the next action in your life.

RIGHT ACTION—DAY FOUR

Now that we have decided to decide to break our decisions down into smaller decisions, we are free to take action. But what action? How do we know if the action we are taking is the Right Action?

First, what do we mean by Right Action? In this case we are referring to action taken from within, and not imposed from without.

Most action is not action, it is a reaction.

Something happens, we react. We see it every day within ourselves and in the world. The stock market moves down and panic moves up. We react to news whether it is good or bad. We are happy when good, sad when bad.

Right Action is a response based on the impulsion of Love. We respond with ideas.

These ideas that flow to us are like a direct line to the Infinite. We call this type of idea Angel Ideas. They are those ideas that are nurtured in dreams, and brought forth into action based on the Principles of Love.

It's not hard to know if we are in Right Action or not. If we have to justify the means to the end then we are not in Right Action. Is it unkind to ourselves or others? Not Right Action.

To know if we are in Right Action, we have to be listening within. We have to be still enough long enough to hear those Angel Ideas, or to hear the disquiet within when we are tempted to make a decision not based on the impulsion of divine Love.

We are all tempted to take wrong action or to react to the machinations of the worldview. Its goal is to keep us distracted and in reaction.

Our intent must be to step away from that worldview and delve deeply into the awareness of the unerring direction of Divine Love.

Take some quiet time all through your day today and deeply listen. Pause before acting, either mentally or physically. Deny reaction its power.

Choose to make Right Action the imperative direction of your life.

Dharma is not what you do, not what you should do, not even what you want to do, but what you were born to do. —Aadil Palkhivala

RIGHT ACTION—DAY FIVE

Have you ever experienced the *what-if monster*?

Here's what usually happens. You have figured out what you want to do, you know how to do it, and it feels right to do it—all of which are components of Right Action.

However, as you start to move forward, you encounter the *what-if monster.*

I bet it says the same thing to you that it does to me, perhaps with a few minor variations (all worldview monsters are not very creative—subtle, but not creative).

It says, "What if you are wrong? What if you don't really know how to do it? What if you hurt someone? What if it makes someone mad? What if you start and can't finish? What if you really don't want to do it? What if you get stuck in what you are doing but can't get out?"

I could go on with these for pages, but all of these what if's stem from this one: "What if you make a mistake that can never be changed or corrected?"

Of course we will make mistakes. We will offend people, we will hurt the ones we love, we will go down the wrong path, we will make someone mad, we will say the wrong thing at the wrong time, we will buy the wrong investment, and we will start something we don't want to finish.

There is no what if about it at all, because all of these things will happen, sometime.

Does that mean we do nothing? Should we just narrow down our choices and our lives to the safest path we can think of? Even then we are in trouble. There is no safety anywhere if we are afraid of the what if.

Instead, let's agree with it when it says that we will make a mistake.

However, there is one thing that the monster says that is completely untrue. And we knowing what it is, dispels its power to make us afraid.

We can never make a mistake that can't be corrected or changed.

The reason for this is simple. It never happened. It only happens within the illusion of humanness.

In the spiritual awareness that is Truth, it didn't happen—ever.

No matter how badly we appear to mess it up, we never actually changed anything at all in the Infinite Divine Mind of Love.

Our fears, guilt, and dramas exist only within our own thinking. Right Action begins and ends with the right motive and intent of uncovering who and what we really are: Love Loving Itself.

In this place, we have been and always will be innocent.

Right Action begins and ends within the context of the Truth of Love.

Armed with that knowledge, we can be aware of the *what-if monster* and still take action without fear.

Only those who will risk going too far can possibly find out how far you can go.—T.S. Eliot

RIGHT ACTION—DAY SIX

Right Action of course involves doing something, but what and when? Actually we are always doing something, even when we think we are not.

Vegging in front of the TV is doing something. The question is: "Is it the right something at the right time?"

Often in the middle of what I think is something I have to get done, I also have to get up from my desk and go make dinner.

There is a clue about Right Action in what I just said. I really don't have to do either. I could choose not to write, I could choose not to make dinner. But, the days that I make a conscious decision, which is the beginning of Right Action, they may appear to be in conflict.

If I get up to make dinner and wish I were still in my office, or feel upset or angry because I have to make dinner, or the kitchen is a mess, or there is nothing in the fridge I want to eat, or I think how come it is always me?—you know those thoughts—then I am surely not in Right Action.

However, it only takes a moment to shift that point of view and state of mind, to something like this: "I am grateful to have someone to make dinner for. Won't it feel good for him to come home to this food? I get to be creative with what I am doing. I have food to eat. I know how to do this."

All of those types of thoughts begin with a different intent. It is an intent with a bigger purpose than just me.

With an intent and awareness that every action is the expression of Love Loving Itself, then it makes no difference what we are doing,

No matter the task, we can see that we are doing it as God in Action. This is always Right Action.

Household chores are just as important, if done with the commitment to do them as Right Action, as any other seemingly important-to-the-world action we could take.

I often think of the quote by Dag Hammarskjold, "It is more noble to give yourself completely to one individual than to labor diligently for the salvation of the masses."

The next time we "have to" do a task that seems pedestrian and routine and "below ourselves," we could either stay in the "why me?" point of view that produces all those upsetting states of mind, or we could choose to see every task, no matter how big or small, as a chance to be aware of, and present with, the harmonious care and attention of the Infinite Mind of Love.

If you have ever switched your perception from one of irritation to one of gratitude, you know in that instant, everything that appeared to be going wrong suddenly internally dissolves.

Give it a try once or twice this week, and experience the shift for yourself. It can and will change everything.

How do we keep our inner fire alive? Two things, at minimum, are needed: an ability to appreciate the positives in our life—and a commitment to action. Every day, it's important to ask and answer these questions: 'What's good in my life?' and 'What needs to be done?—Nathaniel Branden

Right Action—Day Seven

In the 70's people would often say, "Everything is copacetic."

This saying made me cringe because I felt that it was mostly used it as a cover-up to not really communicate, and to not become aware of what needed to be done.

In the big R Reality, yes everything is copacetic.

However, that is not the reality from which people were making that statement. It was clear to me that there was something to be done, there was communication to be made, and there were commitments to make and keep.

All of these practical actions can be done within the context of the big R Reality of the Infinite Principle of Love with the practical outcome of more and more of the world experiencing the freedom of being released from the prison of the worldview.

As we have discussed these last 7 days, everything that we do can be done with Right Action.

In Truth we are always in Right Action, because we are the action of that Principle of the Infinite.

To really experience what that means is the basis of all the joy in our lives.

You have heard me say countless times *what you perceive to be reality magnifies.* However, you have also heard it phrased in other ways by many people wiser than I am.

The Apostle Paul said, *Finally, brethren, whatsoever things are true, whatsoever things are honest, whatsoever things are just, whatsoever things are pure, whatsoever things are lovely, whatsoever things are of good report; if there be any virtue, and if there be any praise, think on these things.* —Philippians 4:8."

Mary Baker Eddy said, *Hold thought steadfastly to the enduring, the good, and the true, and you will bring these into your experience proportionately to their occupancy of your thoughts.* —Science and Health: 261:65

This is Right Action. Holding thought steadfastly to the enduring, the good, and the true.

Be grateful for the awareness that we are not the creators, but instead the beloved idea of Love and therefore always living in the perfection of grace.

We can choose the state of mind of being overjoyed with the knowledge that all it takes is a simple shift of perception to once again be aware of the unconditional light of that Love which shines continuously, and without qualification, on every aspect of every life.

This is Right Action, and in Truth there is no other kind.

102

— • —

RELATIONSHIPS

RELATIONSHIPS—DAY ONE

Life is all about relationships, isn't it? Everything we do involves a relationship—from the clothes we wear, to the food we eat, and the money we spend.

For our next *7–Day Shift Session* we will turn our attention to the Relationships we have, or want to have, with the people we love, or want to love.

Most of us want to jump from not being able to get along with people we hardly know, like the other drivers on the road, to the big relationship we so often call *soulmates*. We think that we will feel differently about being with these special people because after all, they will be "like us."

Plus, we will love them, and they will love us; and love solves everything

Can you hear me saying it? "Not!"

Of course you know that, too. Yes, Love as Divine Love is all there is, but what we call love has been built within the worldview. In order to experience Love as It is, we first must begin by shifting our personal perception about it.

As always and with everything, it all begins within.

This can be a hard idea to face and embrace. After all, those outside Relationships seem to be behaving as if they have nothing to do with us.

Even if we know and accept that Relationships actually are within ourselves, how helpful and practical is that awareness? Especially when we find ourselves in Relationships that are so extremely unhappy or frightening that we can see no way out of them.

In these times, to hear the statement, start within can seem both impossible and futile.

Yet, it's not only true that all Relationships begin within, it is also good news, and a relief. Because, once we begin from within and from the correct premise, the release from Relationships that are unhappy or frightening becomes an after-the-fact occurrence.

What about the other side of this equation—the wanting to be in a relationship, and not understanding why we don't have one?

If we begin on the outside to fix this lack, we end up in Relationships that make us unhappy, or frighten us.

So since sooner or later we have to begin within, why not now?

What might not seem obvious is that even good and great Relationships can become even more wonderful, as we begin within.

Therefore, if you want to give yourself and those you love a gift of a *relation-shift*—it all begins with you, and it all begins within.

Shall we shift together into a more complete awareness and understanding of Love?

The first step in this shift is noticing what you believe about love. We talked about Love at the beginning of this book, and now we are going to expand on those ideas.

What you think you know about love is what you have been telling yourself—and is not what is actually the driving perception, or belief, about love in your life.

How can you discover what you believe about love? By observing your life.

I have always loved mystery stories. I love the process of seeing things differently to discover clues that lead to solving the mystery. Think of your life as a mystery story, and you are the detective.

Your job is to look for clues, unearth evidence, and remain neutral about what you find. If you get caught up in your discovery, you are no longer the detective.

Get in the habit of finding a way to make notes about what you observe during the day. A notebook, pieces of paper in your pocket, or a document on your computer will work.

Observe how others treat you. Observe how you treat and feel about others. Look around you. How do the people you see treat each other?

As you do this, please remember not to judge either yourself or others. You are on a mission quest.

As you go through the day, have a little *statement of Truth* running through your thoughts to hold onto. Try something like, "Love Is Always Loving Itself" which we have been stating throughout this book. Holding to this fact will help unearth those clues.

I hope you are excited, because what could be more joyful then wonderful Relationships.

The fundamental delusion of humanity is to suppose that I am here and you are out there.—Yasutani Roshi

RELATIONSHIPS—DAY TWO

Yesterday, we began the process of shifting to a more complete awareness and understanding of Relationships.

Our first step in this shift was to become aware about what we believe about love in Relationships. We did this because we know that what we *perceive to be reality magnifies*.

This means if we are not clear what we believe about Relationships, we will continue to magnify *our small version* of an Infinite idea.

We began by observing our life, by looking for clues, by unearthing evidence, and remaining neutral about what we found.

We started the habit of finding a way to make notes about what we observed about how others treat us; about how we treat and feel about others; and about how other people treat each other.

The statement we used went something like this: "Love Is Always Loving Itself."

Why did we have a statement of Truth, while looking for what is essentially not true? This idea is an essential part of *The Shift System* process.

Instead of beginning with the idea that something is wrong, and therefore it needs to be fixed, we begin with the idea that there is nothing wrong at all. It is just us living within a misperception of Truth that begs to be dissolved.

The first time I really went on a discovery mission about what I felt about love, I discovered I believed that love could at the same time love me and abandon me. Because of this underlying belief in love, that is exactly what I experienced in all areas of my life.

I could have whined and complained about this discovery. There was a solid reason why I believed it to be true. People would have agreed with me, given my life story. I could have said I had a right to have that perception.

But, I didn't want to live out that perception anymore.

And this is the next step.

Are you willing to give up your life story about what you believe about love? Are you willing to stop getting the secret rewards that we all receive by staying in our human drama?

Most of all, are you willing to be loved and to love?

Even if you are not sure about the willingness part, let's keep going, because, sooner or later, you will be.

What's next, then?

Here's what I did. I started a new True statement. I said to myself, "Love has never abandoned me."

Did I believe this? No. Remember, I had good reason to believe in love's abandonment. But, I chose instead the point of view that Infinite Love is always present, never mean, never unkind, and always loving.

It didn't matter if I experienced it or not: it was True, and I was simply blind to the fact's fulfillment. I said it all the time to myself.

One day while driving around a big cloverleaf on a downtown Los Angeles freeway, I understood exactly how it was True!

I wasn't just saying it anymore to myself, I felt and understood it! Most amazing of all, I saw that it was humanly true too. I saw my whole life completely differently.

What happened? I started laughing, right there in my car on the freeway, all the way home and for hours afterward. I was truly released from that misperception.

I knew absolutely that Love does not abandon. That was the beginning of the end of that cycle of love and abandonment in my life.

So, what did *you* discover?

Be honest.

Now make up a True statement about this discovery to say to yourself.

Don't worry if it feels silly, or if you don't believe it. Imagine what would feel like if it were true, and keep doing it anyway.

RELATIONSHIPS—DAY THREE

So far, we have worked on discovering what we believe about love. Then we decided to give up those beliefs in exchange for being completely willing to be loved and to love.

We agreed to begin and end with the idea that Infinite Love is always Loving Itself, which includes everyone, including you and me.

We started a new True statement that we said to ourselves all the time, even if we didn't believe it.

Did you do it? What happened? Keep going! Be willing to let the Truth about Love reveal Love to you.

This brings us to the next step in this relation-shift.

You are going to discover what you want love to look like for you.

To do this, we are going to put our detective hat back on and search out the clues to what kind of love we want in our Relationships. It's almost like picking a style of a house to live in, but much more important.

It took me awhile to figure out what I wanted love to look like, because I was living my perception based on how I saw my parents' love, on love in the movies, on friends, and of course those love songs.

So I started again, just as you are going to do. I put my love in a Relationship picture, piece by piece.

Once I saw a couple I knew and admired at a picnic who had been married for many years. They were standing at opposite ends of the field. When they saw each other they started running towards each other. She jumped into his arms and they spun around in happiness. "Okay," I thought, "I want that! I want that joy and spontaneous response to love."

I watched another couple negotiate with respect and love everything in their lives together. They were so different, and yet so together, because it was important to each of them that both of them got what they needed to be happy.

Another couple often disagreed with each other, but it didn't change anything about their relationship. They never blamed or whined or complained. They disagreed, figured out how to make it work for both of them, and laughed, and moved on.

Some things I learned because people told me. They told me that love was kind and always available when you need it.

This was a major revelation to me. I had always attempted to be kind and available when I was needed, but I didn't expect others who claimed to love me to reciprocate. I was happy with once-in-awhile: but one day, once-in-awhile was not enough.

These examples should get you started.

Don't forget to write down all this information you are discovering! Your Relationships filled with love should be motivation enough to keep your discovery ongoing and exciting.

RELATIONSHIPS—DAY FOUR

We are discovering what we want our Relationships to be like. We are playing detective by looking for clues, observing love everywhere, and keeping notes about what we've seen, and what we want for ourselves.

We have been studying the love in Relationships!

What did you find? Were you willing to take the time to really observe love? Are you seeing love in a new light?

Remember, everything begins within. Our worldview training is the opposite. It tells us to fix everything outside, and then we will feel better inside. Not only is this bad training, it is a lie.

Trying to fix what started inside by working on the outside picture is as silly and useless as hitting the movie screen when it gets fuzzy. We have to ask the person running the projector to focus the projector, and in this case, we are the person running the projector.

Our agreement with false ideas makes the outside screen of our life fuzzy, or goofy, or sad, or lonely.

What we are doing now is stopping the agreement with what we see, and checking what we believe. We are doing this because there is a law that absolutely cannot be broken within the framework of the world we believe we live in. You know that law as what we perceive to be reality magnifies.™

We are uncovering what we perceive now to be reality, and then shifting it to something much, much, better. All the things you discovered have already begun to shift your life, because it has shifted your perception. You may or may not notice it, but it has!

To have it become more visible you are going to put on your scientist hat. You are going to be a scientist like Albert Einstein who said, "Imagination is more important than knowledge."

Isn't this the same as saying, what we perceive to be reality magnifies?

Perhaps it doesn't feel that way to you yet. However, it will, because next you are going to imagine what it feels like to be loved.

Practice becoming childlike, and imagine what it feels like to be completely, unlimitedly, unconditionally loved. All thinking in the world will never focus the projector of your perception like imagination will, so have at it!

By the way, I did not say, "visualize love." This would be remaining in the worldview of how you *think* love would be. I said *imagine* it! Feel the absolute Truth of it for yourself.

This is going to be fun. It's a time for absolute imagination outside of this world! Enjoy it!

RELATIONSHIPS—DAY FIVE

We have been practicing being aware of what we believe about love, and then decided to be completely willing to be loved and to love.

Next, we discovered what we wanted love to look like for ourselves, and imagined what it would feel like to be perfectly loved!

It's quite a trip, isn't it? It's a journey into our own thinking.

It takes us into the past, where we decided, consciously or unconsciously, to believe things that aren't necessarily true. It shows us the history of the worldview, and its determination to keep us locked into duality and lack.

Understanding that our viewpoint is the view, or our perception is our life—and that there is no difference between the two—we know that we must begin within, to shift our perception to the Truth of One, called Divine Love.

This is the shift that facilitates what appears to us as the outside world to resolve into a brighter picture.

It's good to remember at this point that we are not trying to create love. We are not making up a picture in our heads of how love should look. We are shifting our perception to Truth, because that is what we want to know: the Truth about Love.

It is both a relief and a joy to know that Love will also bring practical evidence of Itself into our lives. This is simply like a wake following a boat. The purpose of the boat is not to produce a wake; the wake is a natural result.

Staying with Truth also naturally results in a never-ending supply of whatever is needed, including love.

However, if we get distracted by the goodies this awareness of Truth reveals, it can be like turning the motor off on the boat. The good news is we can always restart the engine of Truth.

This is the main point to think about today.

You are not the creator of your love life, or of any part of your life. You, haven't messed it up, or stopped it, or done anything at all to Relationships in your life, nor has anyone else! Love has always been present for you, and for everyone equally.

All that has happened is that your beliefs and perceptions have covered it up, so you can't see or experience its fullness.

Since you have been imagining what it feels like to be perfectly loved, it's time to choose this as the Truth for yourself.

It doesn't matter if the world isn't showing that to you right now. What does matter is that you begin with this Truth in your thinking.

When we use the phrase I AM we want it to be from the standpoint of Divine Love.

This means we will have to pay attention to anything we say to ourselves that begins with "I am" that is not coming from the qualities of Love.

Instead of having old perceptions be the habit of our thinking, let's choose to make this new shift of perception be a habitual way of thinking, and acting.

This week let's say: "I Am Love Loving Itself." Go ahead, say it, and keep saying it.

Watch what happens!

All perfection and every divine virtue are hidden within you. Reveal them to the world.—Babaji

RELATIONSHIPS—DAY SIX

Is it working? Wait, don't answer that yet.

First, let's look back at our love in Relationships journey.

We have become aware of our belief systems about love.

We decided to be willing to love and be loved.

We discovered what we want love to look like in our lives.

We imagined ourselves perfectly loved.

We realized that we are not the creator of Love, we are Love Itself.

We chose to state that point of view as our personal point of view, by stating "I Am Love Loving Itself."

So, I know you can answer the question, "Is it working?"

The answer absolutely is yes, because if you are doing any shifting at all, then your life is shifting too. There is no way for it not to be, and there is no way to stop it.

So the more accurate question is, "Have you noticed it?"

The shift may be occurring in a way that you want it to. You may be experiencing more love in your Relationships. Or, it may be occurring in a way that you wish it weren't.

You may be noticing that what you thought was love, is not. Or, you may be unwilling to see love in its present package, because you want it to look a certain way. In most cases, all three of these events are occurring.

You are experiencing more love. Look closely and see the qualities of love that make up your daily life. Don't look for it to be in a perfectly wrapped present, just look for the qualities of Love and let it reveal Itself to you.

You are also noticing that some things you called love, are not. This is appropriate and wonderful. They had been here all along and you had accepted them as love. Now, continue to hold to the Truth about Love. Don't get distracted. Plant yourself in love and stay there.

The next step is obvious, isn't it? If we are going to say that Love is all around, and that Love is present for everyone, we must all act from Love ourselves.

If we are noticing that others are not acting from the qualities of Love we must also turn that searchlight on ourselves and ask ourselves, in all that we do, "Is this loving to others?"

I almost hesitate to go to this idea; because some people will think I am saying that to love we must lie down and take it, as if Love is a doormat.

That is not Love. That is not Love Loving Itself.

No. Letting others, or situations, mistreat us, is not love. However, when we notice how we are not loving to others, and begin to actually be Love Loving Itself, then those who are not loving to us will either begin to shift themselves (on their own, by the way) or they will be moved in someway out of our lives (without our making it happen).

So today, be Love Loving Itself. Be the qualities of Love that you have discovered.

When you find that you haven't been loving, forgive yourself, and move on.

Remember, this work that you are doing for yourself will bless everyone around you. It doesn't matter if they notice or not. It doesn't matter if you never get acknowledged. What matters is that your shift to Love, shifts all Relationships to Love.

That's it! You are Love Loving Itself in action.

RELATIONSHIPS—DAY SEVEN

It's time to be grateful for what we have. This is such a simple thing to do, but something we all have an amazingly large resistance to doing.

Instead of giving thanks, we compare.

Sometimes we judge our own lives, resulting in our thinking that another time was, or will be, better than it is at this moment.

We compare what someone acted like before to what they act like now, even if it was just a moment ago. For example, we may think, "They loved me more yesterday than today. What have I done wrong?"

We compare our love lives with another person's love life, even though we actually have no idea what is really true about any other person's life.

We may believe that others have a better love life than we do because they have—or do not have—a significant other.

We are often in judgement and rarely in gratitude.

I once asked a client to find something to be grateful for, and this person honestly answered, "I don't want to." This is true for all of us. We all hide from gratitude some of the time.

Why is this? Because we know that being grateful immediately shifts our perception to good, and if that happens, it would ruin what we get out of our comparison habit.

However, we can get over the comparison habit. I believe that it is true that we all want to experience the omnipresence of Love—all its qualities in all Its forms, in all Its various and subtle ways—from the tiny to the large, from the seemingly important to the trivial.

We all, more than anything else, want to experience first-hand that the omnipresence of Love is present as our life.

Let's do it, then! Let's choose to be grateful. Let's make now the time to stop hiding from Love.

Take this moment to breathe in and breathe out while feeling that omnipresence of Love. Take this moment to fully and completely give thanks.

Let Love be the essence of your life, without any kind of comparison at all. Let yourself, and your life, be grounded in gratitude.

Love Is. And nothing will ever change that.

Live in thanks now, and experience this Reality.

103

— • —

MONEY

MONEY—DAY ONE

There is no other symbol in the world today that affects anyone more that Money. There is no one who is not touched by the reach of Money.

It's as pervasive as the basic life-sustaining elements of our world, from the sun to the air we breathe. Even if we claim we have no use for it and run from it, it still is driving our decisions. In this case to run.

For those who say they love Money, they may run a different way; they run towards it and sometimes away from everything else.

This is a complex subject, but in this 7–Day Shift Session we are going to narrow it down to a few key points, as we move ourselves to an understanding that Money is neither good nor evil. It depends on how we perceive it.

Of course, Money has not always been paper or metal. In fact, today Money is no longer just paper and metal, it is has become in many ways just numbers, almost as intangible as air.

As with all worldview symbols we must look past what we see, and understand what it is within its true spiritual state.

It's interesting that our Money system used to be based upon a solid, measurable system. It acted like an underlying principle that everyone could see. It was the gold system.

Today there is no underlying tangible system upon which the Money we spend and lend is based. We have come to a place where Money is an agreed perception that has no real basis.

To operate a human system of Money on this premise may be folly; so to try to understand the Truth about Money as a spiritual fact, we must establish a solid principle upon which to build. We must build on our spiritual gold system.

Let's set our gold system then, as we always must, on the strong foundation that there is only One Mind, Intelligent Love, supplying and governing Itself, because that is what It does.

Unlike the human point of view about Money that slides between greed ("I must have more, no matter what the cost") and fear ("what if there is not enough for me?"), the Principle of our system stands firm on Its awareness that all that exists is Itself.

There is no instability, no cycles, no economic swings, no greed, and no fear.

As always, we begin with the awareness that *what we perceive to be reality magnifies.*

In the case of Money, there are very few of us with a purely spiritual perception about Money. We are almost always governed, in some degree, by greed or fear about Money in our lives.

For these next 7 days, we get to practice shifting ourselves to that stable and strong foundation of the Truth about Money. We get to stand on the Principle of One Mind supplying Itself.

Let's begin by becoming aware of what people, including us, say and believe about Money in the worldview.

Get out a pen and paper and start taking notes.

Don't take the easy route and write what you think you think about Money. Instead, pay attention and really notice.

If I told you that you had 7 days to practice for a game show, where you could win big bucks by being aware of the lies and Truths about Money, you would spend the time doing this practice.

So imagine that is what is happening here.

During this 7 days you could shift your perception to a point where big bucks—whatever that means to you—would be in your life without it being either a burden or a savior. It would just be What Is.

Have at it! See you tomorrow!

Let your capital be simplicity and contentment.—Henry David Thoreau

Money—Day Two

Yesterday, we practiced becoming aware of what people, including us, say and believe about Money within the worldview. Did you notice one key point about Money?

Did you notice that Money is about 2% logic and 98% emotion?

It is our emotion about Money, or our state of mind about Money, that not only drives our actions about Money, but also blinds us to the Truth about Money in our lives.

This means that it remains very important to be continually aware of the emotions we are feeling about Money as we deal with it on a daily basis, and continue through this series.

For example, do you shop to fill a want, a need, or an emotional hole?

Do you feel better before, during, or after spending Money? Are you willing to spend Money now because you feel you want or need something, and are you less concerned about the consequences to your future self?

As we stay aware, the next step is to see what Money actually does in the world.

Once we notice what is done with Money, we can begin to understand the basic qualities that make up what we call Money, and find its true nature. This quest will lead us to examine if it is possible to have something, without getting it with Money.

Let's start with what we now believe we need Money to acquire. Here's an example of this: Most of us feel that in order to have a home we need to have Money. In this scenario Money would get us what? In other words, what are the qualities of home?

Home will represent different qualities for each of us, but for the purpose of this exercise let's agree that some of the qualities of home are security, safety, peace, and beauty. This would mean that Money, which bought us a home, would also be buying us security, safety, peace, and beauty.

Is this true? I leave you with that thought for the day. Spend some time breaking down into qualities the things that you feel Money alone can obtain for you.

Then ask yourself, "Does Money also buy me the qualities that make up these things?"

Don't judge the answers; just observe them. We have only begun the path down the road to the Truth about Money.

We've been conditioned to believe that the external world is more real than the internal world. Quantum physics says just the opposite. It says what's happening within us will create what's happening outside of us. —Dr. Joseph Dispenza

MONEY—DAY THREE

We talked about the fact that Money is 2% logic and 98% emotion, and of course that the worldview believes that we must have Money to acquire what we need and want.

Beginning with the idea of home, we asked ourselves if Money will buy us the qualities of home, such as security, safety, peace, and beauty.

We can play with this idea with anything that we may want or need. Does Money buy the qualities of that thing? Or are the qualities innate within it, which actually make up the wholeness of it?

Many years ago my sister and I decided to visit our grandmother, who lived a few hours from New Orleans. I flew in a day early to explore a garden I had heard about within the city.

As I walked the garden I took notes on the many beautiful flowers and trees, thinking that someday I might want them in my own garden.

The garden was so beautiful it took my breath away, so I wanted to be able to reproduce it for myself.

However, as I took notes I realized I was moving away from feeling relaxed and happy, to the empty feeling of wanting and lack. I could not see how I would ever be able to have such a garden for myself.

It was in that moment that I realized I actually had that garden. Right then, and always, because it existed, not because I had to own it.

If I could actually buy all those flowers and plants, it would mean I would be responsible for the personal care of them.

I knew that was not really what I wanted to do with my days. Instead, I rejoiced in the sudden awareness that the garden was mine—without labor and responsibility.

Understanding that the qualities of what we want are always present, and not something that has to be bought, and knowing that owning something does not necessarily involve personal ownership, is another step towards becoming aware of the Truth about Money.

Money—Day Four

Many a man thinks he is buying pleasure, when he is really selling himself to it.—Benjamin Franklin

In his book Geography of Bliss, author Eric Weiner researches what makes people happy. Do you think it's Money? How much?

Here is what he discovered: A little extra Money brings happiness, a lot more does not.

However, we too easily fall into the drug and addiction of chasing Money.

In this state of mind, we are not thinking about what qualities Money represents. Instead, we are willing to give away our time to its pursuit, sacrificing the time with our family, our friends and the joys of living.

As with all addictions, this one does not bring happiness—just more toys. We become the janitors of our possessions.

Working for years as a Certified Financial Planner, I was very aware of this fact. It didn't matter how much— or how little—Money people had, they were not happy until, and if, they learned how to translate Money into something actually much more tangible: the quality of their life. They had to escape the pull of Money as a drug.

There is another side of this picture. Yes, if we work for the sake of acquiring Money, we become its slave. Not only that, if we are afraid to have Money, we are just as much its slave; but in this case, sometimes we can be without even enough Money to at least feel comfortable.

Many of us have been taught, mostly without our conscious consent, that if we are truly spiritual, we don't need or want Money; that if we are successful, we have done something wrong.

This is an outrageously cruel worldview lie that has caused enough suffering.

Declare yourself free.

Choose instead to see Money as it really is. Money is not energy, which can be measured and therefore material.

Money expresses qualities that are the essence of God, Divine Love Itself.

Imagine if all the people who have allowed themselves to be starved of the wealth of God, chose instead to be overflowing with the wealth of God.

Imagine what would happen if we all accepted into our lives the most obvious symbol of God's ever- present Love: Money.

Think of the outreach possible. Money can travel where we cannot, making it a symbol of omnipresence.

Money can be anonymous, changing every life it touches, without need for a personal ego being attached. It can provide items representing beauty, safety, comfort, and security.

However, Money can do none of these things when only seen as a material form that must be acquired. It can and will do all these things as soon as we choose to see it only as the qualities of God in Action, and allow ourselves to receive it wholeheartedly.

Then we will see this promise fulfilled: Bring ye all the tithes into the storehouse, that there may be meat in mine house, and prove me now herewith, saith the Lord of hosts, if I will not open you the windows of heaven, and pour you out a blessing, that there shall not be room enough to receive it.—Malachi 3:10

MONEY—DAY FIVE

Today, let's cover the subject of debt. Debt often begins with the perception that we need more than what we currently have in order to be happy, and we need it now.

This point of view often propels us into too much Money debt, where we spend more Money than we have on hand. It's a disease perpetuated by the worldview as it continues its massive lie—that there is not enough, so we better get our fair share now!

But there is a second part of that lie that we rarely talk about, and it is even more dangerous.

To uncover it, let's begin with Matthew's version of The Lord's Prayer, "And forgive us our debts, as we forgive our debtors."

What does this mean?

Does it mean that an anthropomorphic god will take away our human debts, if we forgive those who owe us? Or is there a deeper meaning embedded in this message?

Our first task might be to discover what is meant by debt. Can it just be about Money? It's not likely that this is what Jesus meant by this prayer.

The answer may be found in the second part of the lie of the dualistic worldview, which teaches us that pleasure and happiness can be found only through material means—and here is the really dangerous part of that lie—that the material world owes it to us.

We ask for everything materially, and believe we have a right to it—from Money to love. We feel entitled and privileged—materially.

If we begin from the point of view that we are owed something, then we are already in debt, whether we have borrowed from someone officially or not. We are in debt to that point of view, because debt is a two-sided equation.

Now the phrase, "And forgive us our debts, as we forgive our debtors," makes more sense. We must give up the sense that the material world owes us, and this will release us from our debt to it.

Doing this, we begin to unravel ourselves from the material worldview's prison, and we will find ourselves free from the debt of needing what we already have.

We will know that what we see, in actuality, is already something we already possess. We will know that the qualities of what we see are already part of who we are as the activity and expression of Divine Mind, or God.

Sometimes we do need to borrow Money to purchase a car, a home, or a business. When we do, it's the intention behind our request and the intention of the lender that count.

Take the time to examine both.

It is possible both to borrow and to lend Money—not from a sense of entitlement and obligation—but from the awareness that Love provides for Itself, and as a result, meets every human need.

Beginning and ending with this point of view, Mary Baker Eddy's interpretation of the passage, "And forgive us our debts, as we forgive our debtors," makes perfect sense. She says, "And Love is reflected in love."

The price we pay for money is paid in liberty.—Robert Louis Stevenson

Money—Day Six

When we think about whether we have Money, or don't have Money, we are usually referring to a place that we have it or don't have it—like our purse or wallet, or our bank account.

However, since we have agreed that God is omnipresent, omnipotent, omniscient, or simply All, then there is no room left for a material thing to be localized or personal.

Which means that when we think of Money being in a pinpoint locality, like our bank account, we have made it both personal, and localized. So, what we have really done is take an illusion, and made it a solid point within our thinking.

Can you hear the doors of perception slamming?

The more fear, worry, and disquiet we allow to enter into our thinking, the smaller the pinpoint of our perception. Than we become more and more limited in our awareness of the Infinite.

It's a vicious cycle. Why do we allow this to happen?

It's a habit, an agreement, and the acceptance of the blatant, aggressive lie that what we are seeing is material, controllable, ownable, and limited.

It is all perception—all of it.

What we perceive to be reality is reality. What we think is true, is true. What we perceive about something is the thing itself.

This is the truth about Money, too. Money is one of the deepest symbols of the omnipresence and substance of God, but instead we hold it within a perception of limited, controllable, personal, localized assets.

We can sidestep this worldview by becoming aware that it is only our agreement with the perception that there is something else controlling our assets, our future, our presence, and our abilities that gives money its power.

If we stop agreeing with it the whole story vanishes. Let's let it go for God's sake. Literally.

Since what we call God is the non-localized, non-personal, substance of Love Loving Itself, then it is absolute complete insanity to drill down to a localized bank account, and call it substance and real.

Let's make it a constant habit to pause and feel the doors of perception opening. Let's see things as they really are: infinite One as all, and all as the infinitely abundant One.

I had a friend who threw himself out of a poverty-diseased state of mind perception by making a habit of saying about everything he saw that he loved, "This is mine."

What was he doing? He was seeing everything as it is. He was practicing awareness of the Truth of infinite provision, so he could see the non-personal, non-localized supply shining through the mist-perception of human sense.

He was acknowledging that the substance of all, including Money, is everywhere, and for everyone, at all times, because it is the ground of our being.

The ability to do this is available to us all. Let's break the poverty habit by knowing the Truth about Money, and by not agreeing with the worldview perception of limitation.

If the doors of perception were cleansed everything would appear to man as it is, infinite. For man has closed himself up, till he sees all things through narrow chinks of his cavern. —William Blake

MONEY—DAY SEVEN

My shuttle driver was a talker.

Within our forty minute ride to the airport I learned about his children, his life as a marine, why he drives a shuttle, his desire for a companion, his political views, and, most of all I learned his life view.

He said that he had learned that life was not about acquiring things, or being greedy, but about living each day in happiness. He lamented he hadn't seen this earlier in his life, and that it had taken so many life lessons to figure it out.

We don't have to wait until we are a certain age to live this life view, nor do we have to have many lessons to figure it out.

We can simply choose to walk away from the general worldview of need and greed.

For the past 6 days we have looked at Money differently. We have realized that Money is not a material thing, or even energy; it is a symbol of the omnipresence and substance of Divine Love. It is not localized or personal.

We know that we can be fully abundant without what the world calls Money, as we spend and receive the currency of Infinite Love loving Itself.

We are also willing to have an overflowing supply of what the world calls Money, without the guilt, responsibility, or fear that accompanies Money when it is seen as a limited commodity.

Most of us spend much of our time doing what the worldview calls working for Money.

Even those with lots of Money still work for their Money; it just looks different. However, all of us know in our hearts, even as we spend our days working for Money, that this couldn't possibly be what Spirit had in mind for Its beloved.

Witness the following passage from the Bible.

Consider the lilies of the field, how they grow; they toil not, neither do they spin: And yet I say unto you, That even Solomon in all his glory was not arrayed like one of these. Wherefore, if God so clothes the grass of the field, which to-day is, and to-morrow is cast into the oven, shall he not much more clothe you, O ye of little faith? Therefore take no thought, saying, What shall we eat? or, What shall we drink? or, Wherewithal shall we be clothed? (For after all these things do the Gentiles seek:) for your heavenly Father knoweth that ye have need of all these things. But seek ye first the kingdom of God, and his righteousness; and all these things shall be added unto you. Matthew 6:28–33

From this passage we learn that our daily work is to seek first Love (God) and Truth (righteousness), and then all things, including what we call Money, will be present in our lives as needed.

Since our perception of something is actually the thing itself, let's shift our perception of money from an object we must earn, to its rightful place—as a symbol and the substance of God's Love, Loving Itself, called us.

The real measure of our wealth is how much we'd be worth if we lost all our money.—John Henry Jowett

104

RENEWAL

RENEWAL—DAY ONE

Biologists claim that 98% of the molecules that make up the human body replace themselves about once a year.

Some aspects of the human body are even faster than that, the liver and skeleton every few months, the skin about once a month and the stomach lining about every 5 days.

If this is true, and there is no reason to think it's not, then why is it that what appears as the body seems to deteriorate?

Even on a human level, we are symbolically shown that all ideas continually renew themselves; and yet what we experience is at best status quo, and, at the worst, decline, in most areas of our lives.

Doesn't this simple observation prove the error of believing in the intelligence of matter? If we believe the body to be real, made of molecules that renew themselves, and yet we do not see that result, we can easily see that there is an error in the premise.

How can the very building blocks of the structure be renewed and get worse at the same time?

The very things we rely on for intelligence and health—like the brain, heart, and vital organs—are made up of atoms, which have been proven to have no intelligence whatsoever.

When we go a little deeper in understanding, we can see that the body is not constructed of molecules of matter, but it is constructed of systems of beliefs. It is a reflection of our education, conditioning, and training.

We see exactly what we believe, or perceive.

This is true not only for what we call the body, but for everything that constitutes what appears as matter. It is what we call a Frozen Focus.

Using the word Renewal with its definition of "bringing back to an original or unimpaired condition," let's take the next 7 days and renew our focus by replacing false belief systems with Truth.

It's the spiritual version of Replacement Therapy. There is nothing we need to buy, nothing to give power to; it's just a simple replacement of thought and identity from false to True.

It's Renewal time!

RENEWAL—DAY TWO

Yesterday, we discussed the fact that everything that constitutes matter is the thought of the thing itself. We know that what we are experiencing as *signs following* is a result of what we believe to be true, and what we focus upon. We called it a Frozen Focus of attention. In short, we can tell what we think is reality as we observe what is happening in our life.

We can get stuck on a specific point of view, and live it out, without any awareness of why the stories of our life continue to happen again and again.

We often find it easier to see someone else's story.

It would be interesting to observe the conversations we participate in and notice how many times we fall for trying to change someone else's point of view. While we are doing this, we are not realizing that it is our own point of view that we must change, not another's.

For Renewal to take place in our lives, our intention must be to dissolve our own Frozen Focus by replacing false belief systems with Truth.

This is an awareness exercise that takes practice. Dr. Albert Ellis, an early advocate of cognitive therapy, said we walk around with about 5,000 distorted ideas about ourselves. This means we may have about 50,000 negative thoughts a day, all of which must be replaced with Truth.

We have the habit of seeing what does not work, which is the absence of Truth, and as we continue to support that focus, we validate the result.

We are not *creating* what we see, as in making it happen; we are seeing what is really happening inaccurately—through the lens of our own belief systems.

This puts our responsibility in the correct place, since we are not responsible for something bad or good happening; we are only responsible for our point of view and state of mind. Although this may not seem like an important distinction, it is the crux of the issue.

This Renewal is not about rebuilding, or recreating, or even building and creating; it is about shifting our perception. This is a much easier task, since the end result has already been created by the Infinite to perfection.

Instead of trying to bring back health, or wealth, or love, we only have to take off the glasses of a misperception that have distorted the Truth. As we shift our internal focus to this new point of view, fully immersing ourselves in the Truth and the Spirit of it, what will come into focus is what appears as an outside world, with the perfect provision of health, wealth, and love, to meet our current need.

It's Renewal from the inside out!

RENEWAL—DAY THREE

There is a new medical science called regeneration, in which scientists are working on telling cells, muscles, and tissue to grow to make new body parts. Scientists have discovered that cells are programmed to grow and make new tissue. The trick is to figure out how to tell them to do so.

Don't we already know this? Don't we already know that it is Life's Intent to grow?

Yes, these are marvelous breakthroughs in science, but let's look at them in the correct context.

Instead of seeing them as the leading edge of science, let's see them for what they actually are: signs following the dawning awareness of Reality.

The science of regeneration is full of signs and symbols from which we can correctly interpret what is happening.

For example, it's interesting that these regeneration processes take place in a sterile environment where no germs can enter. Isn't this the same as a mental environment—where negative, material-based thinking, otherwise know as germs, are not allowed to enter into our thought and perception?

We often find it easier to believe that it is possible for people to have a change of heart and completely rearrange their point of view with the signs following, then it is to believe that it is possible for regeneration or Renewal to take place within what appears as a material body or material object.

And yet this is the same process.

In fact, it is the shifting of perception, or change of heart, that brings about what appears as a material demonstration of signs following, whether it be an improved life style, or a change in bodily or material conditions.

The science of regeneration is not actually creating the new world; it is the signs following of the shift of perception to what is possible, based on the understanding God as Life Itself. These marvelous breakthroughs are just that: breakthroughs from material perception into spiritual perception, much like the sun breaking through the mist.

We will witness even more of these breakthroughs as more and more people stand in the Truth of Life. Instead of seeing them as a future promise, we can see it as the effect of Truth being revealed.

Embraced from this altitude of thought, we are no longer the effect of what happens to a material body and life, but instead we are the outcome of Life's Intent to constantly renew Itself.

Renewal—Day Four

Renewal. What a blessed word, filled with promise.

We can have Renewal of hearts, neighborhoods, families, lives, homes, governments, forests, gardens, friendships, and even bodies.

One of the definitions of Renewal is the act of renewing, which makes it a verb, or action, rather than a static statement. Another definition of renewing is the reestablish on a new, usually improved, basis, or make new, or like new.

Oh! Re–New–Ing!

Beginning, as we know all things do, from within, from our thinking, from our perception, we could be re-new-ing every second of the day. But, we don't. It's a habit to not renew.

Don't believe me? Just for one hour today notice your thoughts and perceptions. Or if it is too hard to see your own, put yourself someplace where you can observe others as they talk about their lives. Are they expressing Renewal thoughts and perceptions?

Our lives, for the most part, are like an old script. We simply keep repeating a version of a habitual script over and over again. Scripts, which we have accepted as truth, begin with the objective of having us believe we are powerless, individual humans, trying to return to, or get back to, One.

Depending on our point of view, this can either be accomplished here, or only by getting to heaven.

Both of these points of view begin with the wrong premise.

Remember it is the intent of dualism, The One Lie of two equal powers—that we will not remember our divine nature. This lie can't change who we are, but it can hide it from us, if we are not constantly practicing a Renewal of our thought and perception.

Begin with the correct premise: that you are the reflection and idea of Infinity. The word Infinity contains the obvious fact that it is constantly renewing. To return to the Truth of ourselves we have to discard the old habitual scripts, one word at a time if necessary.

Watch your words; choose them based on the correct premise.

Watch your thinking; replace limitation with the awareness of Infinity.

With these simple actions, each moment of your life becomes one of Re-New-Ing with signs following, as they must and will.

Just notice! How glorious is that!

Renewal—Day Five

We live in a world where we have been trained to want everything now, and we want it to be easy!

We want a magic pill, or machine, or idea, that will transform our lives, our bodies, and perhaps even our thinking, with a minimum of effort and commitment.

In the human realm there is always a flip side to everything, and the flip side of wanting everything now are the feelings of despair, discouragement, and doubt. In this state of mind we don't want to do anything at all because we think, "What's the point?"

Whether we are in the want or the why bother mode, we have let ourselves be dumbed down, until we take no responsibility for the outcome of our perception called our lives.

We think that it is easier to pay money for something that might transform and renew us than it is let go of either version of the garbage thinking that blinds us to the renewing power of Truth.

Every Thursday night, well actually on Friday mornings, our garbage gets collected, and we never see it again. One morning I woke up to hear the roar of the truck as it came through our street. In my mind's eye I saw them picking up the garbage.

But, I didn't envision them picking up the garbage in the cans; they were picking up the garbage thoughts and actions in the lives of everyone on our block. I imagined how wonderful it would be if we dumped the garbage thoughts and actions in our lives as easily as we put out the garbage every week.

It really is that easy. It takes a commitment from us every Thursday night to put the garbage cans out. In the same way, it takes a commitment to throw away every useless idea, thought, and perception.

We can tell it is a garbage thought when it keeps us either in the *want* or the *why*, it begins with the premise of human duality, and it is not celebrating the constant Renewal that is Life.

Today, take the time to collect garbage thoughts and actions, and put them out to be picked up and dissolved forever. Imagine the Renewal that will take place with that simple action. It is actually the magic that everyone is looking for. It is immediate, and it is free!

By the way, garbage thoughts are not recyclable. Once dumped, leave them dumped. Don't take them back no matter what new form they try to tempt you with.

And for heavens sake, don't go dumpster diving, hoping to find them again!

Renewal—Day Six

The word Renewal doesn't mean fixing something that is broken, or making something whole that has become less in some way. This would be beginning with the incorrect premise—that there is something wrong that must be righted.

Instead, we see Renewal as the constantly ever-expanding awareness of the Infinite Divine Mind, otherwise known as God.

When we forget what we mean by Renewal, it is very easy to fall back into the fix or make whole habit, which sends us back to the prison of the material sense of everything.

The question we want to continually ask of ourselves is, "Where have I placed my focus?"

When we are focused on fix or make whole, then we are stuck in a now that is the product of the past, and in a now that is the fear of the future.

If we are focused on the correct premise of All as One, with no past or future, or Life Living Itself, then we are never stuck.

Being stuck looks different for different people. For example being stuck may mean we feel scared, frustrated, bored, depressed, or angry. What these emotions have in common is that they are all based on the idea that something or someone has to changed, be fixed, or made whole, in order for us to be free.

None of these emotions have the feeling of the joy that permeates Renewal.

We can expect that with the focus of Renewal, what appears as daily life will shift from stuck to freedom.

This is not the fake freedom of running away, which is really just stuck, in motion; this is the real freedom that comes by staying within the correct premise and not being swayed off that stance, no matter what the five senses may tell us is true.

Within the freedom of Renewal, there is a lightness of being.

For almost a year, my husband, Del, and I traveled around the country. Some friends gave us a song to listen to as we drove away from a visit to their home.

We played it many times after that, bouncing in our seats with the joy of the freedom of Renewal. You don't have to travel around the country to get this sense of freedom.

Just take the quick trip from the land of fix-it to the constant of Renewal.

Listen to *Beyond The Blue Horizon*, written by Harlan Howard, and Hank Cochran. Sung by: Lou Christie

Here's the first line: *Beyond the blue horizon Waits a beautiful day*

RENEWAL—DAY SEVEN

We started our shift to Renewal with the biologists' claim that 98% of the molecules that make up the human body replace themselves about once a year, with some aspects of the human body even faster than that.

Yet, our primary experience is of decline and decay. Since even within the human point of view we have the ability to undergo constant Renewal, why we don't experience it?

It's our perception, or thinking, or point of view that it is not possible for us that determines our experience. Instead of trying to understand human Renewal, let's go straight to the big R Reality Renewal, where it is never about fixing or repairing but simply the continuous unfolding of the perfection of Infinite Intelligence.

In Reality, what appears to decline or decay is only the illusion of the absence of Truth.

This shifting of perception, or change of heart, brings about what appears as a material demonstration, or signs following. These signs and symbols will appear in the most practical manner, whether it is an improved life style or a change in bodily or material conditions.

However, it is not that God heard us; it is we heard God, and this awareness cleared the mist that hide our current perfection.

With the new habit of watching our words and thinking, we are grounding our perception in the unlimited possibilities of Infinity. We expect Renewal in all areas of our lives.

As in all things, it is a dedication to the Principle of what we are doing that actually does the "work?" Taking one step at a time, and not worrying about the outcome, is always part of the process.

Choosing to not be discouraged at what might sometimes appear as lack of progress is easier to do when we remember that we are not creating something, or fixing it; we are only letting go of false beliefs and perceptions.

Much like the artist Michelangelo when he sculpted, we are taking away what does not belong to the finished product. This is so much easier than trying to figure out how to grow something that is gone, or fix something that is broken; all we have to do is to be willing to see what is already present.

Renewal is not a renewal of material objects; it is a renewal of perception.

Let's keep our mind's eye on the perfection of Infinite Love, and let the rest go.

105

— · —

Manhood

Manhood—Day One

This *7–Day Shift Session* to Manhood will not be complete until we finish the next *7–Day Shift Session*, which will be about Womanhood. This means for the next 14 days, we will explore what is true Manhood and Womanhood, and also what often masquerades as their qualities.

It is important to understand both, because the male and female aspect of each of us must be completely present, aware, and balanced; and in Truth, it is. However, in the worldview, it is extremely unbalanced, and we can see the results of this imbalance in all of our l ives.

We have been trained so long in the worldview of the counterfeit male and female, that the true essence of Manhood and Womanhood is rarely seen and celebrated for what it is: the essential power and ingredient of the Principle of Love that is the foundation of what we call the One Mind, or God.

In the worldview of duality thinking, Manhood and womanhood appear to belong to men and women respectively. However, in the point of view of One Mind, we can see the equality and harmony of true Manhood and Womanhood in each of us.

Although we may see men and women as separate entities in the awareness that we live in now, in the big R Reality they are One within; and therefore, eventually we will see this unity externally.

This means we can't blame men for the mess that the world appears to be in at the moment, no matter how much we might wish to. It is the counterfeit male, disguising itself as Manhood, that is the basis of the conflict and discord—whether that counterfeit male is found in a man or a woman.

It is also never a person that is the source of the problem; it is always the counterfeit quality, appearing real.

The purpose of this shift session to Manhood is to reveal the qualities of true Manhood, to unmask the tyranny of the counterfeit male, and to shift our point of view, our state of mind, and our actions, to correspond to true Manhood found within each of us.

During this session I will also refer to true Womanhood, but we will discuss it in more detail in the next session.

As always, we must begin at the beginning, which means the first step is to discover what we currently think is Manhood. The best way to find that out is to observe the men in our lives, including yourself, if you are a male. We know of course that what we see is what we believe.

In order to shift to true Manhood we have to first find out what we think it is, and then translate all that back to the Truth.

Don't hide from these questions. This is important.

How would you describe the actions of the men in your life? Don't think just about the men in your family, or work; expand into the community and into the world.

How are the men behaving? What are they exhibiting? Remember, this is not judgment; it is an observation of what is claiming to be Manhood—the good, the bad, and yes, the ugly.

We are cleaning the closets of our minds again. What's in there, hiding out, running our perceptions without our conscious consent or agreement?

Let's pull those beliefs out, and then choose the point of view we wish to keep. Don't worry about the mess this makes, it will be cleaned up, and you will love the new look to your world.

Manhood—Day Two

Today let's begin with the Truth that male and female are not separate, but One. In Genesis (1:27) we read: "So God created man in his own image, in the image of God created he him; male and female created he them."

There is no division here. There is male and female as One, at one time. This is not a dualist statement, where we are divided up into men and women, one from Mars and the other from Venus.

This Truth means that each of us includes every male and female, Manhood and Womanhood, fatherhood and motherhood, quality equally and at the same time—no matter what our outward appearance may be.

Starting with this correct premise, we will begin to clearly see what has been masquerading as Manhood and Womanhood. This clarity begins the counterfeit's demise by uprooting the premise of its existence.

Of course you know we are focusing on the qualities of Manhood in this 7 day shift. This is a wonderful place to begin, because Manhood represents the Principle of divine Love. Our intention is to see and live from that Principle, and not from the counterfeit idea.

We are observing the actions of the men in our lives. How are they behaving? What are they exhibiting?

I know we each saw some of the wonderful qualities of Manhood in action in our lives; but all of us living in the earth state of mind also see each day the counterfeit qualities of Manhood in action.

Instead of using the quality of strength that belongs to Manhood to support and care for others, that quality is often reversed—to using strength to own, conquer, and suppress.

Today, let's observe the quality of strength in ourselves, in relationship to others and as well as ourselves.

Is the strength of Manhood supporting you, or suppressing you? Begin within, while seeing the outside world as your mirror showing you what you perceive to be real.

As you spend time observing Manhood, stay with Truth by continuing to acknowledge that all that exists is the Manhood of the Principle of divine Love in action.

Keep a statement like this in mind this week: "I know that the strength of Love always supports me."

Notice the shift in your life from this simple statement of Truth.

MANHOOD—DAY THREE

Have you noticed the strength of Manhood supporting you in your life? Perhaps you saw it in the actions of others or in your own actions towards yourself and others.

Did you see it in the leafing out of a tree, the flight of a bird, a door opening, a safe mode of transportation, a computer to work on, a store full of needed supplies?—you see I could go on and on forever with these questions.

Manhood is easy to see; it is present everywhere. There could be no life as we know it without the quality of support that is Manhood. Our habit of perception is to see more often how strength suppresses or controls. However, when we stop and observe the whole of life, we can see that much more prevalent is strength that is upholding, supporting, providing, and caring through its actions.

The counterfeit male has a drive to suppress the feminine, from which springs True action.

Counterfeit male believes that listening to and following Womanhood, or the feminine, will take away its power, which actually is true for the counterfeit male, so it acts from self-preservation.

When action does not stem from the awareness of One, the only way it can survive is by control and suppression.

This fear within the counterfeit male begins with the point of view of duality and the ping-pong slide of humanness, from greed to fear.

In order to survive, the counterfeit male must try to keep Truth in its place, by attempting to achieve power and control over everyone.

This doesn't mean that this counterfeit male is found only in men. Manhood and Womanhood are in Reality wedded as One.

In the same way, the counterfeit male and the counterfeit female can be found in all of us. Found, and dissolved—not tolerated, not feared, not ignored, not fought with, but dissolved.

To dissolve what isn't true; we begin with Truth.

So let's look at another quality of Manhood and how in Truth it behaves. Let's observe the Manhood quality of life found in vitality and vigor.

Where are these qualities found in your life? Where are they not?

Are there ways that you are unconsciously suppressing your vitality and vigor? Observe, don't judge, and claim yourself as True Manhood in action.

MANHOOD—DAY FOUR

When you observed the men in your life, what did you see? Perhaps you saw both the qualities of true Manhood and the counterfeit male.

As I observe myself, and others, I notice that the Manhood qualities of vitality and vigor are often suppressed within us.

As humans, we are sometimes shamed or forced into controlling the outpouring of this vitality, the joy that is an innate quality in all mankind. We are shushed, seated, and shut in far too much.

The counterfeit male does this because it finds the exuberance of vigor and vitality dangerous. True Manhood, on the other hand, finds a way to utilize these qualities as it expands into expressing a higher and higher awareness of the activity of Infinite Mind.

While writing this, I watched a male finch dance around a female finch. He is expressing Manhood. He is in the unashamed action of vitality, vigor, and life. He is literally dancing the dance of life. Nature does not know about suppression. The Manhood qualities of life are expressed everywhere in nature, channeled appropriately, but not drugged, suppressed, or destroyed.

Expressing life is what we do. We are Life Living Itself.

Why doesn't it always appear this way?

Remember the curse found in the second chapter of Genesis in the Bible? It states that man must work and work and work and never gain pleasure. This is true in the dualistic material world.

But, we are not material; we are spiritual.

We do not need to live the rules of suppression found in the dualistic worldview. We are the expression of God, so there is no need to accept any curse, because it does not reside in spiritual Reality. In Truth, there is no knowing about or acting from curses of any kind.

There is no fate; there is only Life Living Itself.

Beginning with the Truth that there is only One as our premise and our big R Reality, we see that in each of us is the quality of Life Living Itself, as the expression of our Manhood.

Let it be! Let Life Live within you and as you.

ᴍᴀɴʜᴏᴏᴅ—Dᴀʏ Fɪᴠᴇ

Spiritual Understanding—would you think this is a quality of Manhood? Probably not, but it is! It is interesting how the counterfeit man gives us so many clues into true Manhood.

It's a popular joke that men don't ask for directions. Isn't that the counterfeit of understanding or knowing? This is the opposite of Manhood, which listens for guidance from the feminine.

Of course, let's remember that this isn't about male and female. It's about the counterfeit male claiming to have power. The only power it has is within the human realm.

As we claim and act from spiritual understanding, which is Manhood, we have stepped outside of the human realm completely, so what appeared as real just a second before has vanished.

In their right desire to be free from tyranny, and to be seen as equal, many a woman has attached herself to the counterfeit male, within and without, and taken action from that premise.

In doing so women often become more abusive to themselves, and sometimes even to others, than a man acting from the counterfeit male position might do. They develop counterfeit male strategies, instead of strengthening first their spiritual understanding of Manhood, so that True male qualities can emerge.

When I was young, I often stood up to my dad as he tried to tell me that I couldn't do what my brother was allowed to do. I couldn't stay out as late, go where he went, or do what he did. I would argue with my dad, "man to man". Did either of us win? No. Instead, both of us, standing in our counterfeit male positions, grew apart, and I became an often unhappy teenager.

Now that I have learned how to allow True Manhood to be present in and as me in my actions, I am seen for who I am. Not a girl, or a woman, but complete as One; and my dad and I have grown closer.

The authority, right place, and freedom that women seek is found not by listening to and acting from the counterfeit male, but by listening within and allowing the feminine principle of Womanhood to guide outward action.

This is true for both men and women, as these qualities reside equally in both. As men recognize this equality within, they will find greater and greater freedom from the tyranny that claims to be a man. This tyranny suggests that we must resist the direction of the inner feminine principle.

Recognizing that the feminine principle also resides within themselves, men may also find freedom from the excessive desire to outwardly connect to women physically.

As both sexes identify themselves correctly, they will find that the connections they make on the outside are far more fulfilling and complete.

Manhood—Day Six

Control: a well-known and well-used counterfeit male quality—prevalent not only in men but in women. It's easy to say, "Let go and let God," but how often do we do it?

Male or female, much of our day is spent thinking that we can do it better than someone else; or that if we don't do it ourselves it will never get done; or if we don't supervise it the outcome will be less than expected; or if we don't step in something will go wrong; or of course that we are the only ones who know how to do it right.

There is no point in heaping coals of fire upon ourselves for being this way, because actually that is how it probably happened in the first place.

Feeling as if there were no control, we took control, some measure of it, wherever we could find it. Some of us take more than others, but except for the very few who thrive in "evil," the rest of us would prefer to give it up if we could just trust that it is safe to do so, and we could find a way to let it happen.

As sit on my deck in the morning, there are trees blowing in the wind, birds singing, squirrels playing, flowers blooming, grass growing, and infinitely more happening than I can see. All of this is going on without my control. It goes on in perfect order, working in perfect timing and in perfect harmony. It is a beautiful orchestration of Infinite Intelligence.

If we make it a habit to notice the constant evidence of being cared for by Infinite Intelligence, and our obvious lack of ability to actually make anything happen (beyond the smallest, in proportion to the rest of what is going on, action), perhaps we would be willing to let go of the struggle to hold it together within the prison of human perception, and let God take the reins.

This evidence of perfect Principle is the quality of Manhood that gives us the peace of mind that all is well, has always been well, and will continue into eternity as well, without any control necessary on our part. This guarantee of continuous safety and security is a natural result of activity and provision of true Manhood.

The awareness of these qualities of Manhood brings with it a glorious freedom from personal control, knowing that control rests only within the only cause and creator: the Principle, the Manhood, of Love.

Manhood—Day Seven

We've reached the end of our 7–Day Shift Session. Before we move onto Womanhood, let's review what we have learned.

First we agreed that there is no division between Womanhood and Manhood, and that it is equally balanced in both what appears as male and female.

We rejoiced in the awareness that Manhood is the essential power and ingredient of the Principle of Love, which is the foundation of what we call the One Mind, or God. In the big R Reality, they are One within, and therefore eventually we will see this in our experience.

Let's also review the qualities of Manhood that we discovered, uncovered, and put into practice over the last 7 days.

We started with the Manhood quality of strength that is used not to own, conquer, and suppress, but to support and care for others. We learned that it is okay to be delighted with the outpouring and exuberance of vigor and vitality, and with the joy that is an innate quality in all Manhood.

Next we realized that Manhood expresses spiritual understanding. As we learn to claim and act from spiritual understanding, Manhood, we step outside of the human realm completely. Then what appeared as real just a second before vanishes into a more complete awareness of the presence of God.

We have learned how to allow true Manhood to be present in and as ourselves in action. We found authority, right place, and freedom by listening within and allowing the feminine principle to guide our outward actions.

We have given up control in favor of the Manhood qualities found in perfect order, perfect timing, and perfect harmony, in the beautiful orchestration of Infinite Intelligence.

In this giving up of control, we found the qualities of Manhood—the strength, life, consciousness, spiritual understanding, vitality, and vigor—present as a clear awareness of the peace that comes from resting within the arms of the Principle of Love.

106

— · —

WOMANHOOD

WOMANHOOD—DAY ONE

This week we begin our exploration of true Womanhood. Not the Womanhood that the dictionary defines as a woman who is no longer a girl, but the Womanhood that is the essence of Love found within each of us, no matter what age, and no matter if we appear to be a male or a female.

It is the quality of tenderness that underlies all of creation. The Manhood quality of Principle upholds this tenderness, keeps the law of it in place, but it is the tenderness of Love that each of us yearns to feel, experience, give, and receive.

One of the most beautiful aspects of discovering true Womanhood and true Manhood is that it releases each of us to be free to be who we really are, and not what the material world dictates within different societal structures.

Instead, we reach into the depths of being and know that Womanhood is the power that heals, because it begins and ends with Love. It leaves no space for error or materiality to enter into our thinking and our lives.

Womanhood has infinite patience, as it allows creation to appear without the effort of making it happen. It relaxes into the awareness of the strength of the singular power of the infinite intelligence of Love.

Womanhood is the quality of motherhood that protects, nurtures, and releases all into the awareness of the Infinite.

Womanhood represents the highest ideal of love. What a glorious 7 days we will share together as we embrace our Womanhood and Manhood in perfect balance.

Once again, let's begin at the beginning, with our first step of discovering what we currently think is Womanhood.

Observe the women in your lives, including yourself, if you are a female. Of course we will bring this all back to the spiritual truth; but discovering what we perceive to be true is the beginning of the end for counterfeit womanhood.

How would you describe the actions of the women in your life?

Don't think just about the women in your family, or work; expand into the community and into the world. How are the women behaving? What are they exhibiting? Remember, this is not judgment, it is observation.

What an exciting time this is. You are restoring the power of Womanhood for yourself and your life.

Let the blessings multiply!

WOMANHOOD—DAY TWO

As we continue down this path of exploring Womanhood, let's remember the Truth—that male and female are not separate, but One. Manhood and Womanhood exist in perfect balance within and as each of us.

Beginning with this true premise, each of us is able to rest securely in the awareness that we are never without the perfect qualities of Manhood or Womanhood, whichever is needed in the moment.

As we always do, when we begin a new focus, we take the time to observe what we perceive to be reality. This is easy to do since the outside world is the picture of our internal beliefs, habits, and perceptions. So by observing women, what did you notice?

Did you notice that the qualities of Womanhood are ever-present? Did you notice that although ever-present, they are often hidden, mistreated, rejected, not respected, and in some cases even hated and killed?

I know this sounds harsh, but in order to dissolve a lie, it must be exposed. The power of Womanhood, the feminine, is often feared. Why? Because, it is powerful and brings change. Not through violence and the counterfeit male, but by standing in the principle of Love, and by not allowing anything that isn't good to be present in anyone's life.

Notice the result of being less than powerful in Love, or silencing Womanhood, or allowing mistreatment of ourselves or others. Now is the time, for each of us to step into our Womanhood. It doesn't matter if we are male or female. This is about qualities of God being present, as and in our lives.

Allowing the tenderness, love, and beauty of Womanhood to guide the strength of the outreach of manhood will uncover what has been hidden, in order for it to be dissolved in the light of Truth.

There is no effort in this action, because we are not the creator or the cause. What we are is the effect of Love.

We are the Womanhood and Manhood of God demonstrated.

Take time this day to savor this fact, and let anything that wants to imprison your Womanhood to be swept away by the mighty wind of Truth.

WOMANHOOD—DAY THREE

This week let's explore a part of the third chapter of Genesis in the Bible and decide if we want to abide by that story, or shift it for ourselves. It is a story of a curse imposed on men and women by the Lord God.

Before we explore the curse, let's see if the Lord God is the same God that we have been talking about in this series. Is the Lord God the God of Infinite Divine Love?

Beginning in the second chapter of Genesis we meet the Lord God who appears to have very human actions and ideas. He rules, judges, condemns, punishes, and sometimes grants miracles.

In the first chapter of Genesis we met God. This God is the Divine Infinite Principle of Love. This God made man and woman like this: "So God created man in his own image, in the image of God created he him; male and female created he them."—Genesis 1:27

In this first record of creation, God created men and women easily and in the image of Itself, Divine Infinite Love.

However, in the second chapter, men and women are tempted by a serpent to know both good and evil. With that decision, to know both good and evil, began the material reality, which causes it own punishment.

That knowing of good and evil cursed men and women, after dividing them into two separate, and not equal, entities. Having a Lord God cause and administer the curse perhaps made it easier to accept, not being willing to accept that we cursed ourselves by accepting duality.

In any case, here is the curse on men and women: "Unto the woman he said, I will greatly multiply thy sorrow and thy conception; in sorrow thou shalt bring forth children; and thy desire shall be to thy husband, and he shall rule over thee.

And unto Adam he said, Because thou hast hearkened unto the voice of thy wife, and hast eaten of the tree, of which I commanded thee, saying, Thou shalt not eat of it: cursed is the ground for thy sake; in sorrow shalt thou eat of it all the days of thy life; Thorns also and thistles shall it bring forth to thee; and thou shalt eat the herb of the field; In the sweat of thy face shalt thou eat bread, till thou return unto the ground; for out of it wast thou taken: for dust thou art, and unto dust shalt thou return."—Genesis 3:16–19

In simple terms, women have been cursed to suffer from just being a woman, and all of the functions of being a woman will be difficult; and of course, women will be ruled over by the counterfeit male. For men, the curse is to work hard with no satisfaction, until life is over.

This is cause for celebration, because we do not have to accept a curse given to us by a dualistic Lord God who knows good and evil. God who is entirely the Principle of Infinite Good is unaware of anything but good. This means that we can step outside of this illusionary state and return to knowing good, God.

Here is another cause for celebration. Right in that curse it tells us what will happen. That curse—the illusion—came from nothing (dust) and it will return to nothing.

There is no time frame here. Let's step outside of duality, return to One, and dissolve the curse for everyone right now.

WOMANHOOD—DAY FOUR

My daughter sent me a copy of a real article found in the July 1943 issue of *Transportation* magazine entitled, *1943 Guide To Hiring Women.* It included the subhead of: *Eleven Tips on Getting More Efficiency Out of Women.*

Here are a few samples of what is in that article:

"Give the female employee a definite day-long schedule of duties so that they'll keep busy without bothering the management for instructions every few minutes."

"Numerous properties say that women make excellent workers when they have their jobs cut out for them, but they lack initiative in finding work themselves."

There are many more statements that are just as outrageous as these.

Even when that article was written, there were many women changing lives, earning a living, running businesses and families (often on their own), and doing everything this article says could not be expected of a woman.

Is it different today? Yes and no. In some places in the world, an article like this would never be accepted. In others, it is the same or worse.

However, no matter where we live, the point of view that says women are inferior remains hidden beneath the surface.

Dissolving this belief forever means that each of us must fully embrace and live the true power of Womanhood, with the respect and admiration and kindness that it deserves. This begins within.

Are we listening to our own Womanhood? Do we respect, admire, and care for the sweetness, loveliness, and purity that are the power of Womanhood?

Or do we adopt the counterfeit male point of view in order to get ahead and survive in the world? Let's not forget that when we let go of the counterfeit male, and embrace true Manhood, there is no longer any need to push, strive, gut it out, put down, hide, or control.

In order to fully leave both the counterfeit male and the counterfeit female in the dust, we must step out of the human, material point of view of lack and duality.

When we choose the point of view that we are all One, and that we are the action and awareness of Love Loving Itself, we will leave the dualistic point of view that created the counterfeits of control and greed.

As we consciously choose One, we will find our true Womanhood, which is the spiritual bliss of the awareness of Infinite Love.

WOMANHOOD—DAY FIVE

There is a quality of Womanhood that is often both misunderstood and missed altogether: that is the quality of innocence. The quality of innocence supersedes and dissolves the constant worldview suggestions of guilt and not enough.

In order to experience the quality of innocence, not only do we have to stop blaming ourselves, we also have to stop blaming others. Instead of finding fault, we find innocence. Instead of stupidity, we find innocence. Instead of jealously, we find innocence.

It's a quality easy to miss, because the opposite of innocent is the prevailing message that is broadcast everywhere—from the media to our own personal mindset.

Daniel's statement of innocency within the lion's den seems a fable impossible to bring into everyday life. But, he was innocent. He disobeyed a law that was designed to trap him; it had no legitimate power, or basis of truth.

Even though he was aware that a trap had been set for him, he didn't succumb to the next part of the trap, which was to go into blame and revenge.

He blamed no one at all. He found no guilt within himself as he remained with his prayer of acknowledging the "living God."

We spend much of our time reliving all the mistakes we have made. We may think of our huge life mistakes, or our tiny everyday mistakes like bringing home the wrong kind of bread from the store. Within that focus of fault, we are led to believe that we are not innocent. Therefore, neither is anyone else.

However, we are critical thinkers. We question what appears as reality. We question if what others tell us is true. We question the internal voice that brings disharmony.

We ask ourselves, "Is this true?" "What if this isn't true? "Is this the Truth?"

Within that context, we expand from the narrow worldview of never good enough, to the unlimited viewpoint of original perfection. From that unlimitedness, it is easy to see that what the worldview says we are is not the Truth of our being.

We have never left the state of being innocent.

We have never eaten of the tree of good and evil. We remain as we have always been: the qualities of the infinite idea of Love expressed.

Womanhood embraces this Truth. Womanhood holds to the innocent nature of each of Its loved ones, beginning with self. This means that like Daniel, who did not obey the material point of view because he knew only the Principle of Love, we can say, "I am innocent."

Womanhood — Day Six

When we bought our home, I was the first name on the loan and on the title. We did this on purpose for a number of reasons. However, neither of us was expecting what would happen as a result.

If you have ever bought a home, you know that for the next couple of months you receive lots and lots of snail mail from people like Welcome Wagon, to stores with all kinds of coupons, and ads for a variety of other things to buy.

The interesting part of it was that it was all addressed to my husband, and not to me. I wasn't even present on the information. This means that real people actually looked at the information they found on the loan and the title, and decided to not address it to the primary homeowner, who was a woman, but to the man of the house.

What does this tell us? It tells us that in spite of the fact that even in the material picture of the world, where women control over 70 percent of the wealth, and make over 90 percent of the decisions involving spending money, there is still a real resistance to putting, or allowing, Womanhood first.

Using that as a barometer of the worldview's hold on our perception, we realize we have more work to do as we relearn how to honor the power and insight of Womanhood.

Instead of giving it lip service and talking about how wonderful Womanhood is, we need to put it into its proper place—first—in every area of our lives.

Let's review together our actions and make sure that in all that we do, we begin with the Womanhood within. Let's make sure that we don't reassign the priority of first place to the counterfeit male—back to the habit of making things happen instead of the universes quiet habit of natural unfolding action.

Let's revisit our commitment to the habit of pause, observe, and listen. Let's stand firm in our understanding of the union of true Womanhood and Manhood as One, within and as each of us.

Then we can never be unconsciously forced to choose the false power found in the worldview of control and domination. Instead, we will rest in the consistent, gentle, permanent, strength of the tenderness of Divine Love as represented by Womanhood.

WOMANHOOD—DAY SEVEN

We have reached the end of our two 7–Day Shift Sessions exploring the "hoods," Manhood and Womanhood.

We have exposed the counterfeit male's desire to control, manipulate, and dominate. Within true manhood we have found strength, life, pure consciousness, spiritual understanding, vitality, and vigor.

We have learned that action is the directive of manhood, and that its direction comes from the feminine principle of true Womanhood found within each of us.

Instead of shame and shyness, we have stepped into the tenderness, love, beauty, loveliness, sweetness, spiritual bliss, purity, and innocence of Womanhood.

Instead of separating male and female qualities and thinking of them as at odds with each other, we know them as dancing together in perfect unity. We understand that one does not exist without the other.

As we discard our misperceptions of manhood and Womanhood, we see the perfect harmony and order of the Principle of Love in action.

Instead of searching outside of ourselves to find unity with another, we look inward and discover that we have always been the reflection of perfect manhood and Womanhood.

Many of us may have found that the counterfeit male has often ruled our lives both within and without.

Perhaps we discovered that for much of our lives we have acted like a counterfeit male. Because this has been our training within the worldview, it would be a common experience for both men and women. So being kind to oneself in this discovery is a wise and Womanhood choice.

As we shift our perceptions to Truth, our past false perceptions, knowing their end is near, may attempt to make us feel guilty in a last-ditch effort to survive.

Seeing false perceptions is the first step to freedom. Recognizing their lack of power is the next.

Embracing the innocence of Womanhood, we can take another step to freedom by releasing it from both our memories and our current experiences.

Step fully into the true Manhood and Womanhood that is the truth of you.

Experience the relief of stepping into your natural environment of the divine Principle of Love—Manhood and Womanhood fully wedded as One.

107

—·—

RIPE TOMATOES

RIPE TOMATOES—ONE

Did I get your attention? Tomatoes? We are going to spend our next *7–Day Shift Session* on growing tomatoes?

Yes and No.

On the day I was deciding on the next topic for this session, we were harvesting the Tomatoes that I had planted in the spring. My husband said, "Isn't growing Tomatoes a perfect metaphor for life?"

Well it certainly is. So that is what we are going to talk about: the metaphor of growing Tomatoes and life.

What do we start with when growing a tomato? Of course we begin with a seed. Not just any seed, but a good seed. And we often plant more than one seed to make sure that at least one of them will grow into a sturdy plant.

A seed is really an idea, isn't it? Enclosed within a tomato seed is the entire plant. Enclosed within an idea is the fulfillment of that idea.

However, just as we can't see that tomato plant within the seed, we can't see the outcome of our idea.

This means that we often don't trust that the idea is worth anything—since, unlike a tomato, we don't know what it will look like. And so we often never bother to plant the seed of our ideas.

But first, where do we get idea seeds? Yes it's back to that skill of listening within. Listening within, we are open and willing to hear the multitude of Angel Ideas, constantly present, from which to choose.

Since there are millions of ideas always available (yes there are), sometimes we are not sure which one to plant. Just like choosing a good seed to plant for Tomatoes, we want to choose a good idea to plant into our life. How do we do that?

Tomatoes come in a variety of options, and depending on what kind you love, that's the kind you plant. You also plant seeds that have a chance of sprouting. Hybrid tomato seeds don't sprout.

What kind of idea would you love to grow? What works for your life? Is it an idea that has a chance of sprouting? Will you tend it after it grows?

And while we are at it, choosing more than one kind of idea is good plan. Like tomato plants, ideas grow at different speeds and produce fruit at different times.

Why not get a continual year-around harvest?

Pause often in your life to observe and listen, and then pick a few good ideas to plant.

We'll do the next step tomorrow.

Ripe Tomatoes—Day Two

Yesterday we talked about choosing the seed, or idea, that you would like to grow. Years ago, I was given some very special seeds from someone's garden.

I have saved them all these years, waiting for the perfect time to plant them.

Ideas are like that, too. We have lots of ideas saved up, ready to plant when the time is right. Of course, we have to remember where we put them; so be sure to look in all those places in your thought where you might have stored something wonderful.

Shall we go back to the metaphor of planting Tomatoes? Once we have chosen a variety of Tomato seeds what do we need next?

Here's a hint:

"And when he sowed, some seeds fell by the way side, and the fowls came and devoured them up: Some fell upon stony places, where they had not much earth: and forthwith they sprung up, because they had no deepness of earth: And when the sun was up, they were scorched; and because they had no root, they withered away. And some fell among thorns; and the thorns sprung up, and choked them: But other fell into good ground, and brought forth fruit, some an hundredfold, some sixtyfold, some thirtyfold."—Matthew 13: 4 –8

Yes, good ground—or dirt! In today's world we can obtain any kind of dirt we want to use for planting our seeds. Paying attention to the kind of soil each seed prefers insures a greater harvest.

Planting our idea seeds in good ground is also imperative. Good ground in this case means beginning with the right premise or point of view, which is the ground of your being.

What is the ground of your being? Is your premise that you are the creator and cause and therefore responsible for all that occurs in life, making you way too busy to allow a seed to germinate in good dirt?

Or, have you chosen to live from the point of view that divine Intelligence is the creator and cause, leaving you free to receive and support ideas?

Do you have a barren soil point of view—that no matter what you do, your ideas will not sprout?

Or do you have the fertile point of view—that within the idea is all that is necessary for it to bear fruit?

Let the ground of your being be good ground, ready to accept good idea seeds and nurture them.

Ripe Tomatoes—Day Three

We have our good seed, we have good dirt; what do we need now? We need something to put them in. Of course the container could be as large as a garden, but it could also be a pot on the porch. Does it matter?

It does.

The year I first planted Tomatoes I knew that we were going to move to a new home after the Tomatoes were planted, so I planted them in containers. Once I ran out of big containers, I planted a few Tomatoes in smaller pots.

They all received equal care, but the Tomatoes in the smaller pots didn't bear as much fruit or last as long.

This concept applies to our idea seeds. Do we give them room enough to grow? Or do we contain them within the bounds of what we know?

Planting them within the small container of our current knowledge stunts their growth and keeps them from bearing the fruit that they were meant to grow.

Have you ever had a wonderful idea, got excited, started working on it, and then your energy and delight with it simply fizzled away?

Perhaps this happened because instead of planting it in the large garden of life, and letting its roots spread out, it was planted in too small of a container.

Today think back on ideas you have had that didn't work out. Perhaps they just need to be repotted in a larger possibility. The Infinite has plenty of room for Its ideas to grow. Let's plant them safely in that container.

Ripe Tomatoes—Day Four

"Where do you like to grow?" Don't we ask our plants that question? "Do you like full sun, partial sun, shade, or partial shade?"

If we choose to plant our Tomatoes in shade, when they prefer full sun, we will certainly notice the difference. No amount of extra care will make up for the fact that Tomatoes like full sun to fully reach their potential and bear fruit.

Some of my container plants on our deck were easy to move about. The ones that I kept moving as the sun shifted in the horizon did better than the ones that I left in their original location. Finally, I put them all on wheels to make their moving easier.

What about you? Where do you grow best? Do you grow best in groups, partial groups, solitude, or partial solitude? Like plants, no amount of extra care will make up for the fact that to reach your full potential and produce the fruit of your life you must plant yourself in your preferred location.

Of course, for each of us, that preferred location begins within, as our mental state, or state of mind. However, our mental state is affected by where and with whom we plant ourselves. If we are being drained by too much of one kind of location, or too little of another, we will feel the difference.

Do you know your preferred location?

Once again the answer is found in personal observation and awareness. But remember, you have a choice. We are mobile—like my Tomatoes on wheels.

You can consistently move yourself where you will grow best for the time.

We had a coaching client speak to us about a job he was thinking of taking. It would involve a few years of work and sacrifice. That wasn't what worried him the most. He knew himself well enough to know that if he took that job it would lock him into an idea of himself that would last for his whole working life.

He chose not to take the job, but to remain mobile and continue to plant himself in the perfect location for the time of his life. How about you? Take the time to test out locations. And since you have a choice, plant yourself there.

Ripe Tomatoes—Day Five

We have chosen our good Tomato seeds, planted them in the best soil possible in the perfect container, and placed them in their preferred sunny location.

How about you? Have you found your good ideas, planted them in the soil of Mind's Perfection, planted them in the largest space you could find—the Infinite—and then placed them in the sunshine of Love?

On Mother's day, I received a pot designed to hold an indoor garden of herbs. I waited to plant it until fall, so that my new herb garden would be ready when my summer herb garden rested for the winter.

I placed the pot in the perfect location, and forgot about it, thinking it would take many days before the seeds sprouted. I was wrong.

A few days later, I happened to glance at the pot and there were little seedlings everywhere. I had forgotten about them! After doing all that work of the first four steps, I almost forgot to care for their growth by watering and feeding them!

Tomatoes love a regularly scheduled deep watering. In fact, a gardening book says it helps them avoid stress, which in a tomato shows up as that mushy, black or brown discoloration on the bottom of Tomatoes, called blossom end rot.

They also like to be fed or fertilized regularly.

This is just like our ideas, which need to be attended to regularly—not tucked away somewhere out of sight and left to fend for themselves.

Some ideas sprout quickly, like my herb seeds. Have you noticed? Or are you too busy worrying about other things to take care of what you have planted?

To avoid stress—water and feed yourself and your ideas frequently—with Truth.

Since you are Love Loving Itself, this will be simple to do, if you remember who you are.

Ripe Tomatoes—Day Six

Now that you have planted, fed, and watered your ideas, you must be seeing some of those tender shoots beginning to grow.

In fact, by now, they might have gotten big enough that they seem to have a life of their own.

As Tomato plants grow bigger, they start leaning and falling; and if not staked in some way they lose much of their fruit to bugs and rot.

Ideas, not staked or cared for by propping them up in some way, will also lose some of their fruit.

This is also the time you may want to look at your Tomato plants and pinch off some of the extra growth, so that more nutrients can be directed to the coming fruit.

Ideas are the same. They need to be tended to and those extra sprouting ideas pinched back, to allow your time and resources to be directed to what is closest to bearing fruit.

Before you begin pinching you will want to know whether your Tomato plant is determinate or indeterminate.

Determinate Tomato plants are compact, or somewhat bushy.

"This type of Tomato plant is full-grown before bearing Tomatoes, and has a predetermined number of stems, leaves, and flowers hardwired into their genetic structure," says Frank Ferrandino in Kitchen Gardener. "The development of these plants follows a well-defined pattern."

Of course, with this type of Tomato there is no pruning necessary; and if you did, you would have no Tomatoes.

There are some ideas that are the same way.

They have a predetermined life and structure. No pruning necessary. Pay attention, and it will be obvious which is which.

For those Tomatoes that do need to be pruned or pinched, you could actually root some of the shoots that you have pinched off and grow a new plant.

Again, in the same way, when you pinch back one of your current ideas, those smaller ideas can be re-rooted to grow into another stand-alone idea for later.

This way you have a continuing source of fruit- bearing Tomatoes, and ideas, to feed you and your loved ones for a long time.

Though they appear to be separate tasks, pruning and staking truly go together.

If you prune your plants, and wonderful Tomatoes appear, but the plants are not staked, you have wasted your time.

Of course, you could choose not to prune or stake your ideas, or Tomatoes—if you are willing to settle for less than the best possible outcome.

But, with all the care you have taken so far, why stop now?

RIPE TOMATOES—DAY SEVEN

For the past 7 days, we have found the perfect seeds for our Tomatoes—and our ideas. We provided them with the best soil, found wonderful containers, located them in the sunlight of love, watered them, fed them, cared for them by staking and pruning, and now we are ready.

Okay, actually it takes longer than 7 days to take a Tomato from seed to fruit; and of course ideas can take many weeks, months, and years to grow from an idea to fruition.

But the concept is clear. Pick what you have grown, or it will rot.

This sounds like one of those duh statements, but it happens so often that it is more like a geez statement.

We are so busy just doing tasks that we often forget to check our Tomatoes and ideas—to see if they are bearing or have borne fruit.

We are so caught up in the details of life that we are blind to the joys of life.

We are so programmed to think that the time for our reward is sometime in the future, we forget that in every moment there is a harvest.

Jesus said, "Say not ye, There are yet four months, and then cometh harvest, behold, I say unto you, Lift up your eyes, and look on the fields; for they are white already to harvest."—John 4: 35

Yes, in every moment the fields are ripe already for the harvest. There is joy, love, patience, and happiness to be found in each breath. Ideas do bear fruit. The acorn does grow into a tree. We are always supplied; there is always a harvest.

Look now. Get quiet for a moment, breath in, breath out, and experience what is present now for you to savor.

Our role is to take action as led by the still, small voice and to enjoy, but not to create.

That's been done for us. We just have to pause, observe, and listen more often to be aware of it.

Do that now, and feel the harvest that is waiting for you!

108

— · —

RIGHT THINKING

RIGHT THINKING—DAY ONE

Let's spend our last 7 days together doing the most important thing we can do, shift our normal everyday thinking to Right Thinking. There are *7 Steps to Right Thinking*, which is perfect for our 7 days together.

After all these shifts together we are most certainly ready for this subject! Our spiritual muscles have been built up and made strong, and we are now ready to leave a habitual material perception for a constant spiritual perception.

We can stop living as if there were two worlds, and choose to live in big R Reality.

The disciples had a Pentecostal experience as they were all in one accord in one place. They were filled with the Holy Ghost, or the spirit of awareness of God. They were one in the recognition of the Divine Reality.

We can experience this too, as we gather in one accord in one place (Right Thinking). We can be filled with the awareness of God. We can live in the recognition of Divine Reality.

We begin with the first step of Right Intent. We covered this briefly at the beginning of the book. Let's look more deeply at it today.

We know that we have to begin with Right Intent in order for everything else to be grounded in the correct principle.

Do you know your Intent in each thought and action? Is it grounded in the first commandment of "Thou shalt have no other Gods before me"?

Years ago, I discovered a prayer that helps me establish my Intent in every action, but especially in the ones I am afraid to do, or don't want to do, which, not surprisingly, are often the same thing.

It is part of a poem written by Mary Baker Eddy and it goes like this, "...my prayer, some daily good to do for Thine, for Thee; and offering pure of Love whereto God leadeth me."

This kind of prayer is about desiring an Intent that is in line with spiritual perception.

We are not asking for something from a human-like god, we are starting with the Intent to act as God's expression.

What a great place to start!

So today, let's be sure we are thinking and acting from pure Right Intent. Of course, to do this, we'll need to pull in all our perception skills.

Pause often. Observe without judgment. Listen deeply.

Right Thinking—Day Two

Yesterday, we began by practicing Right Intent. Without stopping that practice, let's continue to the next R in the *7 Steps To Right Thinking:* Right Premise.

In The Shift® we always refer to the two modes of perception: point of view and state of mind. With Right Premise, we are choosing the point of view of One as our Premise.

It's easy to say we are all One, but what does that mean? All One what? Or said another way, One with what? Do we mean we are one with each other, or One with the One?

It important to be clear what Premise we are beginning with as our point of view, isn't it?

Since everything flows from our Intent and Premise, we must know what we believe to be the ground of our being, the force or intelligence of what we see as life.

It doesn't matter what we call this Divine Intelligence, but God is the name that many people know.

I like using this word for the Divine Intelligence since the word God comes from the word good.

I made up an acronym for the word God, *Guarantee of Delivery.*

An omnipresent, omnipotent, omniscient, omniaction God always delivers. It also goes along with the law that *what you perceive to be reality magnifies.* It is a guarantee of delivery.

Since God is All-Good, then there is a guarantee of the delivery of all-good.

However, if we begin with a premise other than God as Infinite Good, our life won't always deliver good.

Instead, it will deliver garbage—the amount and quality of which will be in direct correlation to our missed perception of God.

Therefore, it is imperative to think and act from the Right Premise as God and as our Right Intent.

Mary Baker Eddy's definition of God is: "The great I AM, the all-knowing, all-seeing, all-acting, all-wise, all-loving, and eternal; Principle; Mind; Soul; Spirit; Live; Truth; Love; all substance; intelligence."

Applying these 7 Synonyms for God to our thinking gives us a good litmus test to discover if we are acting from the Right Premise.

It will also make clear how we are One.

RIGHT THINKING—DAY THREE

We have covered the first two steps of Right Thinking—Right Intent and Right Premise—which leads us logically to the next step: Right Identity.

When I have an idea about doing something expansive, I sometimes hear a worldview voice that says, "Just who do you think you are?"

I am sure that you have heard it, too.

As we attempt something new in thought, or action, that voice pops up and attempts to stop us in our tracks.

If we are not awake and aware, it freezes us in place for many more moments than are necessary. Sometimes years or even lifetimes pass before we gain the wisdom and courage to answer correctly.

You are at the point now where you have the wisdom and courage to answer, "I am the active expression and reflection of the Infinite Intelligence of the Divine Mind of Love."

Man (as in mankind) is the reflection, or manifestation, of God.

Each of us reflects, in consciousness, all the qualities of God, individualized as our true selfhood.

This is the Christ-consciousness, yours and mine, which we declare as Truth. And from that Principle of Truth we find our Right Identity.

We are not our personality. We are not our history. We are not the stories that we have told about ourselves, no matter how many times we have told them, or how many people believe them.

Looking past what appears to be material, we see the spiritual nature of man and the universe—including us!

So when that voice says, "Just who do you think you are?" we answer without reservation or hesitation, "I am the presence of that I AM."

No man has a prosperity so high or firm, but that two or three words can dishearten it; and there is no calamity which right words will not begin to redress.—Ralph Waldo Emerson

RIGHT THINKING—DAY FOUR

Today is an important day. Today we learn about Right Resistance.

It sounds strange doesn't it? We spend so much time learning not to resist; why spend time learning how to resist? The key to understanding this is to know what, and when, to resist.

Of course, we don't want to resist the infinite divine impulsion of Love at any time.

We always want to yield to the One guiding Principle in every aspect of our lives.

However, our worldview training is exactly the opposite. We have been taught to resist good and let evil alone.

Now that we have begun to learn how not to resist good, it is time to learn how not to let evil alone, but to discern what it is, resist its compulsion in our lives, and forever dissolve its power to destroy lives.

Before proceeding, let's define what we are calling evil. I am using this definition from Ann Beals: A universal incorporeal mental force in human existence claiming to be a hypnotic power opposed to God.

Note the word human and the word claiming. As we stand completely with the Truth—that we are spiritual beings—we have already stepped outside of the agreement, and the assumed power, of evil.

However, until we are completely aware of Truth, and living It all of the time, we must pay attention to what this hypnotic power is attempting to do. Why? Because it is compulsively aggressive, and uses fear as control. It applies the devil's favorite tool of doubt at every opportunity.

Right Resistance is about resisting any form of this lie, and dissolving it with Truth.

We say, "No" to its various forms—like hypnotic states, depression, sickness, lack, discord, irritation, resentment, grief, sensualism, loneliness, and human personality traits.

We do this by adhering to and living within the Principles of the Infinite Intelligence of the Mind of Love.

This decisive resistance, which is not running away from, but standing in Truth, will dissolve all that is unlike Good, or God.

The lie of evil is one lie. It is the lie that there are two powers, good and evil. Both cannot be in the same place at the same time.

In Right Resistance we stand in good, and thus dissolve the dualistic lie of evil in whatever form in which it attempts to masquerade.

In Tom Brown's book, Vision, he quotes the man he calls Grandfather, as saying, "Grandson, a true warrior is the last one to pick up the lance or go to battle. His battles are fought with the lance of love and understanding. His enemies are prejudice, greed and bad medicine, and the biggest battles are always fought within himself. So do not go out upon the earth to battle unseen demons of the physical world, for your hatred will be like theirs. Instead, go out as a true warrior, with love and understanding."

Start to notice how often you decide to not resist evil.

Decide instead to be a true warrior for Truth.

Take up the sword of Love and understanding, which is Right Resistance.

I am not only a pacifist but a militant pacifist. I am willing to fight for peace.—Albert Einstein

Right Thinking—Day Five

Now that we have applied Right Resistance, we can move to the next step in Right Thinking, the R of Right Reasoning.

The hard part is behind us. Now we can stand in the actual Truth of our being. This awareness of Truth is what heals, appearing as healing. In reality, it is simply the uncovering of what is already True, the perfectness of the Infinite. We are never healing or fixing; we are discovering the perfection of God.

This is the step where we apply logic. Not the logic of trying to make old habits and beliefs fit into what we want them to mean within the Infinite.

Instead we are applying the logic that says because the Infinite is omnipresent, omniscient, omniaction, and omnipotent, there is absolutely no room for two powers.

Only one can exist. Which one? Infinite Good, or infinite evil?

Let's assume we cannot figure out the answer to this question yet. We are not sure. We have doubt.

This is where Right Reasoning comes in handy.

If we begin with what we know to be true—that *what we perceive to be reality magnifies*—we know that whichever power we pick is what we will live with.

If we decide that there are two powers, then we are not agreeing that there is an Infinite One; we have stated instead that there is duality.

Then, that's exactly what we'll get; duality. Life will be sometimes good, sometimes bad, never safe, and always confusing.

As we make the decision to choose the point of view that there is an infinite One, which one shall we pick? Good or evil?

Perhaps we need to discover which one will win, and take that side.

Once again, exercise your Right Reasoning. Look around. Evil makes a lot of noise. It is promoted at every opportunity. But which one wins in the end? Good or evil?

I know which one I choose. I know which one wins, because I have reasoned it through.

Take some time and see which one you think wins. And then, ask yourself if you have thoroughly chosen that side, or if you have been walking the dualistic line.

We all do sometimes. We all must stop sometime. Why not now?

RIGHT THINKING—DAY SIX

If you have ever taken any kind of lesson—like music, dance, sports, or art—you have been taught Right Practice, the next R in t he *7 Steps of Right Thinking*.

You were taught that practice makes perfect. You learned that you have to practice the basic principles over and over again in order to be a master at what you are doing.

In every discipline there is a basic core that must be repeated, no matter how many years we have been doing it. Piano players play scales, ballet dancers do a daily barre, golfers practice their swing and their puts.

No matter how good we get at what we are doing, we are always a student of it, if we want to keep gathering every last drop of the essence of what the discipline has to offer.

So even though we may be doing the same movement that we did yesterday, the same scales, or the same swing, if we are paying attention, we notice that it is always different. We are in a different state of mind each day. If we have been practicing, we are also living with a different skill set. Practicing makes us present in what we are doing.

If you have practiced something over and over again, you have also probably experienced that moment when something "clicked" and everything shifted into place, and then a new view of what you had heard before became clear.

This clarity shifts everything, not just what you have been practicing, but everything.

It's as if you stepped into a brand new world; and in essence that is exactly what happened.

It seems obvious, doesn't it? The worldview, or that which does not want us to remember who we are and does not want us to figure out that it is putting forth an illusion (because then it will simply dissolve into its nothingness) will do anything at all to distract us from practicing Truth.

Right Practice is the Repetition of what we have heard or known before. It is reading it again, listening again, and studying again. Being a student of Truth, like all disciplines, is Repetition and practice.

When I lived in Santa Monica, California, I knew a woman who ran three miles every day down to the beach and back. She told me that many people said to her, "Oh, I could do that."

She would invite them to join her—and some did for a day or two–but then they would not come back. Soon she would answer those who said, "I could do that" by asking, "But could you do it every day?"

That's the true sign of a student who desires to know the subject. Not going for the quick high from doing something once, but for the love of the learning and doing—for the pleasure in the knowledge that repetition and practice build a basis that can never be undone.

The student of Truth receives even more pleasure, because every day brings clarity and peace and strength—built on the Principle of Love.

The result is stated perfectly in the Bible passage, *For now we see through a glass, darkly; but then face to face: now I know in part; but then shall I know even as also I am known.*—I Corinthians 13:12

To know as we are known by the Divine. I can't think of anything more wonderful than that, can you?

RIGHT THINKING—DAY SEVEN

As we finish up our *7 Steps To Right Thinking,* it is appropriate to end with Right Action.

We have everything in place in order to take Right Action. Perhaps this is the most important step: taking action. Otherwise, all that we have learned is simply theoretical and impractical.

American Indians are well known for their point of view: that all action takes place only after having a clear Intent on how it will affect 7 generations.

This Intent springs from a deep understanding of the interconnection of everything, and the knowledge that every action we take sends concentric rings outward that continue, and continue, and continue.

When we take action from Right Intent, this is good news, because it means we don't have to look for the result of what we do to know whether or not we have done the right thing. Sometimes results are not immediately seen. Instead, we can rest in the awareness that the effect will remain forever, and we can turn our attention to continuing to do the right thing.

Martin Luther King, Jr. said, *Cowardice asks the question, 'Is it safe?' Expediency asks the question, 'Is it politic?' Vanity asks the question, 'Is it popular?' But, conscience asks the question, 'Is it right?' And there comes a time when one must take a position that is neither safe, nor politic, nor popular, but one must take it because one's conscience tells one that it is right.*

Before taking action of any kind, pause. Ask yourself, "Have I tried it this way before? Did I have the same point of view before? Am I in the same state of mind that I was in before?"

If you have answered "yes" to any of these questions, it is best to not take action yet. Reset your point of view to your current highest understanding of the divine Infinite Mind of Love. Then reset your state of mind to calmness and awareness of the power of that point of view.

Listen deeply to hear direction from the feminine voice within, the power of true Womanhood; then, and only then, take action using the power of true Manhood that exists within.

Albert Einstein defined insanity as "doing the same thing over and over again and expecting different results." He also said, "The only real valuable thing is intuition," and "The true sign of intelligence is not knowledge, but imagination."

Put these three ideas together, and we have Right Action.

And as we gather together all that we have learned through these 7–Day Shift Sessions, we have all the tools necessary to move forward into each day, grounded in the Truth of the Principle of Divine Love in action.

We are the awareness of that Principle called God. We are God in action.

We can let everything else go, and just be that.

Then we can clearly see the evidence that we are living in and as Grace—now and forever.

Be in the Right Mind, everything else is insanity.

ACKNOWLEDGEMENTS

I could never write a book without the help of my friends and my book community. Thank you, Jet Tucker, Jamie Lewis, Barbara Budan, and Diana Cormier for taking the time to do the final reader proof. You are a loyal and much-loved reader team. You can't imagine how much I appreciate it.

A huge thank you to Laura Moliter for her fantastic book editing.

Thank you to every other member of my Book Community who helps me make so many decisions that help the book be the best book possible.

Thank you to all the people who tell me they love to read these stories. Those random comments from friends and strangers are more valuable than gold.

And as always, thank you to my beloved husband, Del, for being my daily sounding board, for putting up with all my questions, my constant need to want to make things better, and for being the love of my life, in more than just this one lifetime.

Connect with me online:

Facebook: https://www.facebook.com/becalewiscreative

BECA LEWIS

Instagram: https://instagram.com/becalewis
TikTok: https://tiktok.com/@becalewis
Twitter: http://twitter.com/becalewis
LinkedIn: https://linkedin.com/in/becalewis
Youtube: https://www.youtube.com/c/becalewis

OTHER PLACES TO FIND BECA

- Facebook: facebook.com/becalewiscreative

- Instagram: instagram.com/becalewis

- Twitter: twitter.com/becalewis

- LinkedIn: linkedin.com/in/becalewis

- Youtube: www.youtube.com/c/becalewis

About Beca

Beca writes books she hopes will change people's perceptions of themselves and the world, and open possibilities to things and ideas that are waiting to be seen and experienced.

At sixteen, Beca founded her own dance studio. Later, she received a Master's Degree in Dance in Choreography from UCLA and founded the Harbinger Dance Theatre, a multimedia dance company, while continuing to run her dance school.

After graduating—to better support her three children—Beca switched to the sales field, where she worked as an employee and independent contractor to many industries, excelling in each while perfecting and teaching her Shift System® and writing books.

She joined the financial industry in 1983 and became an Associate Vice President of Investments at a major stock brokerage firm, and was a licensed Certified Financial Planner for over twenty years.

This diversity, along with a variety of life challenges, helped fuel the desire to share what she's learned by writing and speaking, hoping it will make a difference in other people's lives.

Beca grew up in State College, PA, with the dream of becoming a dancer and then a writer. She carried that dream forward as she fulfilled a childhood wish by moving to Southern California in 1968. Beca told her family she would never move back to the cold.

After living there for thirty-one years, she met her husband Delbert Lee Piper, Sr., at a retreat in Virginia, and everything changed. They decided to find a place they could call their own, which sent them off traveling around the United States. They lived and worked in a few different places before returning to live in the cold once again near Del's family in a small town in Northeast Ohio, not too far from State College.

When not working and teaching together, they love to visit and play with their combined family of eight children and five grandchildren, read, study, do yoga or taiji, feed birds, and work in their garden.